THE BEST AMERICAN MAGAZINE WRITING

2020

THE BEST AMERICAN MAGAZINE WRITING 2020

Edited by
Sid Holt for the
American Society
of Magazine
Editors

Columbia University Press New York

publication supported by a grant from
The Community Foundation *for* Greater New Haven
as part of the Urban Haven Project

Columbia University Press
Publishers Since 1893
New York Chichester, West Sussex
cup.columbia.edu

Library of Congress Cataloging-in-Publication Data
ISSN 1541-0978
ISBN 978-0-231-19801-1 (pbk.)

Columbia University Press books are printed on permanent and durable
acid-free paper.
Printed in the United States of America

Cover design: Julia Kushnirsky

Contents

Jonathan Dorn

Introduction

Greetings from the Before Time. It's spring 2020, and the specter of 7 million virus-plagued Americans remains distant and incomprehensible. The West Coast isn't burning, RGB is hanging in there, and there's little worry about a peaceful transition of presidential power. The days are getting warmer, and hope is growing that a few weeks of mask wearing will bring the economy roaring back. And somewhere in Minneapolis, there's a forty-six-year-old guy shooting hoops on a cracked blacktop court, unknown to the world, and still breathing.

From our vantage point in these early days of May, we couldn't possibly predict the calamities that will make this year unlike any we've experienced. Not the Second Surge, not 50 million unemployed, not the murder of a young EMT in Louisville, not the hellfire that will permanently eliminate any reasonable doubt about global warming. And certainly not the shaky street-corner video that is going to ignite antiracism protests from coast to coast.

Or maybe, sitting here in May, we could predict it all. George Floyd. Breonna Taylor. An economy in shambles. Thousands upon thousands of lonely deaths cutting short robust lives without respect to age or station.

After all, we've had ample warning in the stories featured in this compilation of 2019's best magazine writing. No matter that they'll be a year old by the time this book reaches you, or that their lighter moments will seem a bit quaint (in-person interviews, how precious! mask-free socializing—was that a thing?). No matter that they lack the underlying bewilderment so pervasive in the journalism we'll read months from now. The writing in this collection is shockingly prescient for a Before Time collection.

Take Nikole Hannah-Jones's tour-de-force essay from "The 1619 Project," a special issue of the *New York Times Magazine*. A previous National Magazine Award winner, Hannah-Jones incisively crystallizes the modern-day relevance of a 400-year legacy of racial injustice in her introduction to this issue. Like the rest of the issue, a towering work of journalism that spurred (and advanced) national debate, she's looking back while looking forward. It's impossible to read her words and not recognize that a national reckoning on race is right around the corner.

Similarly, three stories reporting on deep inequities in America's prison system are threaded with meaningful insights about the pernicious impact of a bent judicial process on marginalized communities. Piper Kerman and Keri Blakinger in separate articles in the *Washington Post Magazine* and Pamela in a *ProPublica / New York Times* joint investigation, each in their own way call our attention to the daily effects of institutional racism on incarcerated people of color.

And don't forget Erika Fry's timely telling of *another* virus story in "Epidemic of Fear." This *Fortune* feature and National Magazine Award finalist is a disconcerting tale of vaccine blunders and misinformation that should serve as a pressing reminder of how complex your challenge will be this fall in trusting the word of pharmaceutical companies racing for a cure in a heated political environment.

Together, these powerful stories and the others in this collection remind us why magazine journalism matters so much. The medium is uniquely equipped to synthesize current events and historical realities into thoughtful outlooks on the road ahead. It enables writers to make the past present and to warn us, directly or indirectly, of the challenges we will face as individuals and as a nation. And magazines provide an important and nuanced counterbalance to the attention-deprived blurb economy of Twitter and Facebook.

Read these stories, relish their insights and relevance, and let's hope that next year's volume of *Best American Magazine Writing* is all about the After Time.

Sid Holt

Acknowledgments

This edition of *Best American Magazine Writing* is unique—it was compiled and edited in the shadow of the coronavirus pandemic—but in every other way, *BAMW 2020* does what every other entry in the series has done since it began in 2000: reflect the concerns and sometimes fears of the present moment in ways that will endure long after newspaper headlines and cable-news chyrons have faded from memory. Here are stories on mass incarceration at home; illiberal governments abroad; questions of gender, ethnicity, and difference; little-known manifestations of popular culture; tragic failures; spirit-lifting triumphs; and, of course, golf.

Each story in *BAMW 2020* speaks both to the past and to the future, but two of the articles included here seem especially pertinent as 2020 gives way to 2021. In "Epidemic of Fear," Erika Fry describes the consequences for public health—and rational self-governance—when a distrustful people are asked to embrace a new vaccine, and in "Our Democracy's Founding Ideals Were False When They Were Written. Black Americans Have Fought to Make Them True"—the introduction to "The 1619 Project"—Nikole Hannah-Jones shows how Black Americans' continuing struggle for real freedom fulfills the promise of America for all its people.

Many of the writers here will be familiar to readers of past installments of *Best American Magazine Writing*: stories by Pamela Colloff, Hannah-Jones, T. Christian Miller, and Rebecca Traister have appeared in recent editions. So, too, magazines and websites like *New York*, the *New Yorker*, the *New York Times Magazine*, the *Paris Review*, *Poetry*, and *ProPublica*. But others are new to these pages—*Catapult*, the *Georgia Review*, the *Washington Post Magazine*, John Lee Clark, Jordan Kisner, s.e. smith, Sarah A. Topol—and all the more exciting for it. And many of the writes here are young: Jonathan Escoffery and Jia Tolentino are little more than thirty.

Each of the stories in BAMW 2020 was published in 2019 and was either nominated for a National Magazine Award or received an Ellie—the copper statuette modeled on Alexander Calder's 1942 stabile *Elephant Walking* that is given to the winners. The only exception is Ecoffery's "Under the Ackee Tree," which was one of three stories that earned the *Paris Review* the ASME Award for Fiction, a special honor established in 2018 to recognize the historic link between literary fiction and magazine journalism. There were, of course, dozens of other finalists and winners; a complete list with links can be found at https://www.asme.media.

First presented in 1966—the sole winner that year was *Look* "for its skillful editing, imagination and editorial integrity, all of which were reflected particularly in its treatment of the racial issue during 1965"—the National Magazine Awards honor print and digital publications that consistently demonstrate superior execution of editorial objectives, innovative techniques, noteworthy enterprise, and imaginative design. Originally limited to print magazines, the awards now recognize magazine-quality journalism published in any medium. Since their founding, the awards have been sponsored and administered by the American Society of Magazine Editors and the Columbia Journalism School.

The Ellie Awards also provide support for the Osborn Elliott Scholarship at the Columbia Journalism School. Named in honor of the former editor in chief of *Newsweek,* who also served as president of ASME and dean of the Columbia Journalism School, the Osborn Elliott Scholarship is awarded to students who intend to pursue careers in magazine journalism.

This year the editors of more than 250 publications submitted nearly 1,300 entries to the National Magazine Awards. Many were large-circulation publications whose names are familiar to every reader. Others were city or regional magazines or publications inspired by the passionate interests of their readers—fishing, bicycling, cooking, gardening, literature, music, photography—but each demonstrated a dedication to the craft of magazine making, though of course magazine journalism today takes forms unimaginable to the founders of the awards a half century ago: not only the printed word but also websites, podcasts, and videos.

More than 300 writers, editors, art directors, and photo editors participated in the judging of the awards this year. The judges received preliminary reading in mid-December then met at Columbia University in mid-January to choose five finalists in each of the twenty-two categories (seven in the most popular category, Feature Writing). The judges then chose the winner in each category. After the judges finished their work, the National Magazine Awards Board, composed of current and former ASME officers, veteran judges, and representatives of the Columbia Journalism School, reviewed and sanctioned the results.

Sixty-two media organizations received Ellie Award nominations in 2020, led by the *New York Times Magazine* with ten. The *Times Magazine* also won five awards, including three—in General Excellence, Podcasting, and Public Interest—that in some way honored "The 1619 Project." The other top finalists were *New York,* with nine nominations; *National Geographic* with eight; *Bon Appétit* and the *New Yorker*, both with six; and *Self* and *Texas Monthly* with four.

Twenty publications were nominated for the most prestigious honor, General Excellence. Nominees included large-circulation titles such as *Cosmopolitan* (which also received its seventh-consecutive nomination in Personal Service), regional titles like *Atlanta*, special-interest magazines like *National Parks*, literary journals like *Oxford American*, and digital-first publications like *The Trace*. The General Excellence winners were the *New York Times Magazine*, *Bon Appétit*, the *Hollywood Reporter*, and *Quanta*.

Originally scheduled for early March, the presentation of the awards was delayed by the outbreak of COVID-19. As a result, the awards were presented virtually in late May. The Ellies show is now posted on the ASME YouTube channel. Watch if only for the presentation of the Magazine Editors' Hall of Fame Award to David Granger, the longtime editor in chief of *Esquire*.

Hundreds of magazine journalists make the Ellies possible. Among them are the editors in chief who choose to enter the awards; the many editorial staff members who organize the submissions; and the judges, who receive dozens of stories to read the week before the year-end holidays begin then gather in New York in the dead of winter to spend two days reading, debating, and voting in usually cramped, sometimes overheated classrooms. All of them deserve our thanks.

The ASME board of directors is responsible for overseeing the administration of the Ellies, which include not only the National Magazine Awards and the ASME Award for Fiction but also the ASME Next Awards for Journalists Under 30. The sixteen members of the 2019–2020 board—all of whom are journalism educators or the editors in chief of well-known publications—are listed, along with the judges, at https://www.asme.media/. The success of the 2019 Ellies was especially attributable to the work of the president of ASME, Jonathan Dorn, who also hosted the virtual presentation of the awards and wrote the introduction for this book.

As director of operations at ASME, Nina Fortuna is largely responsible for the day-to-day management of the Ellies. Her constant cheerfulness and easy efficiency come as a surprise only to first-time award entrants. Also deserving of gratitude are Overland Entertainment's Leane Romeo and Michael Scarna, the longtime producers of the Ellie Awards show.

On behalf of ASME, I want to thank Steve Coll, the Pulitzer Prize–winning reporter who now serves as the dean and Henry R. Luce Professor of Journalism at the Columbia Journalism School, and Abi Wright, the executive director of professional prizes at Columbia, for their continuing support of the National Magazine Awards.

Thanks are also owed to David McCormick for his tenacious representation of ASME's interests and the editors of *Best American Magazine Writing* at the Columbia University Press, Philip Leventhal and Michael Haskell. Their enthusiasm for the BAMW series—and their patience during the prolonged preparation of this edition of the series—is truly appreciated.

But most deserving of thanks are the writers who graciously consented to the publication of their work in the 2020 edition of *Best American Magazine Writing*. Their continuing dedication to their craft, even as traditional forms of support for magazine journalism grow ever more uncertain, is always cause for celebration.

THE BEST AMERICAN MAGAZINE WRITING 2020

New York Times Magazine* in partnership with *ProPublica

WINNER—REPORTING

This is how the ASME judges explained their decision to give "False Witness" the 2020 National Magazine Award for Reporting: "Pamela Colloff tracked one jailhouse informant through the criminal system to shine a light on a devastating national problem—the widespread use of unreliable jailhouse informants to send innocent defendants to prison and sometimes Death Row. Reporting for nearly a year, Colloff reconstructed the 43-year journey of Paul Skalnik, a known liar, con man and sexual predator, who may be the most prolific jailhouse informant on record." Colloff is one of the most recognized writers in the more-than-fifty-year history of the National Magazine Awards. The nomination of "False Witness" was her seventh; the award, her second (her story "The Innocent Man"—which depicted the ordeal of a Texan wrongfully convicted for the murder of his wife—won the award for Feature Writing for Texas Monthly *in 2013).*

Pamela Colloff

False Witness

When detective John Halliday paid a visit to the Pinellas County Jail on December 4, 1986, his highest-profile murder case was in trouble. Halliday, who was thirty-five and investigated homicides for the local sheriff's office, had spent more than a decade policing Pinellas County, a peninsula edged by white-sugar-sand beaches on Florida's Gulf Coast, west of Tampa. It is a place that outpaces virtually all other counties in the nation in the number of defendants it has sentenced to death. Prosecutors who pursued the biggest cases there in the 1980s relied on Halliday, who embodied the county's law-and-order ethos. Powerfully built and six-foot-four, with a mane of dirty blond hair and a tan mustache, he was skilled at marshaling the facts that prosecutors needed to win convictions.

He had worked the case for the past year and a half, ever since the body of a fourteen-year-old girl named Shelly Boggio was found, nude, floating in an inland waterway near the town of Indian Rocks Beach. Her murder was singular in its violence. Her body bore thirty-one stab wounds, many of them to her hands, as if she had tried to shield herself from the ferocity of the attack. She was most likely still alive, the medical examiner determined, when she was dragged into the water and left to drown. Her older sister identified her by the silver ring, eagle-shaped and inset with turquoise, that she wore on her left hand.

The crime scene yielded few clues. No murder weapon was left behind, and no fingerprints or other forensic evidence were recovered. If Boggio was sexually assaulted, the medical examiner found, any trace of sperm may have been washed away during her time in the water. "It was one of Pinellas County's cruelest murders," the *St. Petersburg Times* observed, "and there was little evidence."

Halliday's investigation quickly zeroed in on two men, Jack Pearcy and James Dailey, who lived together and were new to Pinellas County. The facts, what few there were, pointed overwhelmingly to Pearcy, a twenty-nine-year-old construction worker with a history of arrests for violence against women. Pearcy pursued the teenager before her death, and Pearcy picked her up on the last afternoon of her life, when she was thumbing a ride with her twin sister and a friend. The girls spent the afternoon and evening with Pearcy, Dailey, and other housemates, drinking wine coolers and smoking marijuana. After the other two girls went home, Pearcy took Boggio to a beachfront bar, where she was last seen, barefoot and disheveled, around midnight.

Pearcy acknowledged that he drove her to the lovers' lane along the Intracoastal Waterway where she was killed. But he tried to shift blame to Dailey, claiming that he picked up his housemate before he and Boggio headed down to the water. And while Pearcy admitted to the police that he stabbed Boggio at least once, and he provided details about the crime that were known only to investigators, he insisted that it was Dailey who was the actual killer.

This was all that connected Dailey, a thirty-eight-year-old itinerant Vietnam veteran, to the crime: the word of its prime suspect. No physical or forensic evidence linked him to the murder, nor did any discernible motive. He would later say he had been asleep in the early-morning hours when Pearcy was out alone with Boggio, only to be awaked by Pearcy, who said he needed to talk; Pearcy drove him to a nearby causeway, where they drank beer and smoked a few joints at the water's edge. Pearcy's girlfriend and a longtime friend of Pearcy's said they saw the two men come home together that morning, hours before Boggio's body was found, and that Dailey's jeans were wet.

The state attorney's office in Clearwater pressed forward with the most serious charge it could bring against the men, ensuring that they would be tried for first-degree murder—a crime punishable by death. Pearcy's trial came first and ended with a guilty verdict in November 1986. But at the penalty phase, the jury recommended that he be sentenced to life in prison. It was a blow to the state attorney's office, which would argue, in a forceful sentencing memo to the court, that "no evidence exists that Pearcy was not the main actor in this child's brutal murder." Pearcy had dodged the electric chair after participating in and most likely carrying out one of the county's most monstrous crimes. Prosecutors had only one more chance to secure a death sentence for Boggio's murder.

Ten days after the conclusion of Pearcy's trial, Halliday visited the Pinellas County Jail. At his direction, jailers began pulling inmates who were housed near Dailey out of their cells. One by one, the men were taken to a small, windowless room, where Halliday was waiting. He pressed each man for information. Had Dailey ever talked about his case? Ever admitted to anything?

Four men who were questioned that day testified at a 2018 evidentiary hearing to the same unsettling detail in the interview room. Newspaper articles about Boggio's murder were laid out conspicuously before them. "I got a very uneasy feeling looking at the newspaper articles," Michael Sorrentino, one of the four, testified at the hearing. "Had I wanted to say something, or fabricate something, all the tools were there to give them whatever they might be looking for."

Halliday testified at the hearing that there were no newspapers in the interview room. Either way, no one gave Halliday any useful information that day. In a slender, lined notebook, the detective recorded what each inmate told him. "Nothing," he jotted down after one interview. After others, he wrote:

> Said Dailey denies charge
> doesn't know a thing
> Nothing
> Knows nothing. Didn't even know Dailey.
> stays to himself. Knows nothing.
> Refused to come to be interviewed.
> "Wish I could have helped you but its a little outa my league."

Halliday's visit was a bust. But in the Pinellas County Jail, the word was out: The Boggio case needed a snitch.

• • •

In jail, it is widely understood that helping prosecutors and the police can earn extraordinary benefits, from reduced sentences to dismissed charges. By the time Dailey's trial began the following summer in Clearwater, in June 1987, no fewer than three inmates had come forward claiming to have heard Dailey confess to the killing. The first two worked in the jail's law library, where they professed to have heard Dailey say about the murder, "I'm the one that did it." They also told the jury of ferrying several handwritten notes between Dailey and Pearcy; in the letters shown to the jury, Dailey appeared eager to appease his codefendant, whom prosecutors planned to put on the stand. But the two jailhouse informants were eclipsed by a third inmate, who had contacted Halliday to say that he had some information. He told a much more damning story—one that placed Dailey at the scene of the crime and put the knife in his hand. It was exactly what prosecutors needed.

That witness was Paul Skalnik, a familiar figure around the Pinellas County Courthouse. He had appeared before the court numerous times as a jailhouse informant and was skilled at providing the sort of incendiary details that brought a defendant's guilt into sudden, terrible focus. Skalnik began working with Halliday in 1983, when the detective was investigating a triple homicide, and Skalnik helped send two men to death row, cementing his status as an invaluable resource. Because he was a known snitch, he was held in protective custody, in a single cell where he was shielded from inmates who might want to do him harm. Despite this considerable impediment, Skalnik claimed—just a few weeks before jury selection in Dailey's trial began—to have procured Dailey's confession.

Assistant State Attorney Beverly Andrews called Skalnik to the stand before resting her case on a Friday afternoon, ensuring that Skalnik's words would be left to linger in jurors' minds over the weekend. Pearcy—the only person to have offered an account of the murder—had by then refused to testify against Dailey, leaving a gaping hole at the center of the state's case. Skalnik, who was facing twenty years in prison on charges of grand theft, stepped into the void. Dark-haired and stocky, with olive skin that offset his gray-blue eyes, Skalnik had a wide, expressive face that was malleable like an actor's, registering emotions with almost vaudevillian embellishment. His words had a stagy yet captivating sincerity.

Andrews began by leading him through a series of questions that were designed to establish his trustworthiness. No, he had not been promised anything in return for his testimony, he assured the jury solemnly. And yes, he conceded, he had been convicted of some felonies—"five or six, if I am not mistaken"—but he was quick to tell the jury that he had not only assisted the state numerous times as a jailhouse informant; he had also once been a police officer. "I still do have law enforcement inside of me," he said.

The story he told the jury was simple but arresting. He was passing by Dailey's cell early one morning, he explained, when Dailey sought his counsel. Dailey was under the impression that Skalnik had worked as a private investigator, Skalnik said, and wanted his legal advice.

It was then, Skalnik testified, as they stood at the bars of Dailey's cell, that Dailey came clean, confiding that he had stabbed the girl and then thrown the knife away. What Dailey said "was so hard to comprehend and to accept," he told the jury earnestly. "I had seen this gentleman walking in the hallways, laughing and kidding with other inmates. And all of a sudden, to see a man's eyes, and to describe how he can stab a young girl—and she was screaming and staring at him and would not die. . . ."

"Were those Mr. Dailey's words as best you can remember?" Andrews asked.

"As best I can recall," Skalnik said gravely. "'She is screaming, staring at me, and would not die.'"

It didn't matter that Skalnik had few other details about the murder. Any questions as to his truthfulness were put to rest when Andrews called Halliday as her final witness. The detective vouched for Skalnik, testifying that the inmate had supplied him with reliable information in other cases, yielding "extremely positive results."

Dailey would not testify on the advice of his attorneys, but Skalnik offered a vivid, first-person account of a confession. In a trial that had been long on conjecture but short on hard evidence, his testimony became the linchpin of the state's case—so much so that Andrews would cite him more than a dozen times in her closing argument. She assured the jury that Skalnik was "honest" and "reliable."

It was with that imprimatur of credibility that jurors found Dailey guilty. They also recommended, by a rare unanimous vote, that he be executed. Judge Thomas Penick Jr. of the Circuit Court formally sentenced Dailey to death on August 7, 1987.

Five days later, Skalnik was released from jail. A Florida Parole and Probation Commission memo stated that his release was "due to his cooperation with the State Attorney's Office in the first-degree murder trial." It was a remarkable turn of events given that he had been identified as a flight risk just a year earlier, after violating the terms of his parole. "This man has been, is and always will be a danger to society," his parole officer had warned. Now he was released on his own recognizance and did not have to post bond. Skalnik was a free man.

By then, Skalnik had been in and out of jail half a dozen times. One of his earliest brushes with the law came nearly a decade earlier, in Texas, through an unusual series of events that began with a misbegotten Christmas present for his third wife, Rozelle Rogers. Their whirlwind romance started in 1977, when Rogers, a divorced mother of two, was leading a quiet life near her well-to-do parents in Friendswood, south of Houston. "He just came in out of nowhere and swept her off her feet," said Rogers's daughter, Lisa Rogers.

At twenty-eight, Skalnik already had two brief marriages behind him, but Rogers, who knew little about his past, saw the promise of a new future in the magnetic, seemingly worldly man who lavished her with rapturous flattery and told her he was a top executive at Southwest Airlines. He was less conventional than someone in the corporate world—he wore a gold necklace and a diamond-studded watch with his three-piece suit—but he seemed like a catch.

After getting married in Las Vegas, Skalnik moved into Rogers's condo, where he soon established a routine. On weekday mornings, he bounded out the door, briefcase in hand, telling Rogers he was headed to the airport to fly to Dallas, where Southwest is headquartered, and assuring her that he would be back home in time for dinner. He always carried a business-size checkbook with him, with which he was profligate, treating her to jewelry, stays at posh big-city hotels, and box seats at University of Texas football games, where he boasted of once having been a running back for the team. He tried to outdo himself with each ostentatious flourish, giving Rogers not just one but two brand-new vehicles: a baby-blue Lincoln Continental and a customized Dodge van with red velvet curtains and CB radios. Once he presented Lisa, then fourteen, with a gold-nugget Seiko watch that sparkled with diamonds. When the eighth grader asked him, point blank, if it was real, Skalnik grinned and replied, "Looks real to me."

Lisa had taken note of Skalnik's idiosyncrasies: how he filched the robes and towels from their luxury hotel rooms and squirreled away the purple velvet bags that his Crown Royal came in after he had drained the bottles. It didn't escape her attention, either, that he always kept his handgun within reach, even stashing it under the driver's seat when he was behind the wheel. In the months that followed, Skalnik's behavior became more unpredictable, and he began heading out of town "on business," he said. Eventually, his absences stretched into weeks and then months, until he disappeared altogether.

Unknown to Rogers—who would ultimately have to post notices in the newspaper announcing her intent to divorce him—Skalnik had, by the spring of 1978, landed in the Harris County Jail, in Houston, for passing a dozen bad checks, one of which he had used to buy Rogers a microwave for Christmas. Everything Skalnik had told her was a lie. He had financed their new vehicles, and nearly everything else, on the strength of her good credit, taking out loans he never paid back, opening credit cards in her name, and draining her checking account. Rogers, who died in 2005, was left reeling. "He wrecked my mom's credit, and he wrecked her life," Lisa said.

His arrest was the first time he found himself in serious trouble, though he had been grifting since at least the early 1970s, when he worked as a police officer. He had lasted just fourteen months with the Austin Police Department, stepping down in

1973 after he wrote a string of bad checks. After apologizing for any embarrassment he had brought upon the department, he was never charged. He got off easy again when he was arrested for grand larceny in Orange County, Florida, three years later, after he posed as a furniture salesman and pocketed $700 from an unwitting customer. Even though the police found evidence in his car that suggested he was running another scam—he had a stash of checks, IDs, and stationery bearing the seal of the Texas State House of Representatives—he received probation. Only his arrest in Houston in the spring of 1978, which violated the terms of his Florida probation, brought his lucky streak to an end. Suddenly he was behind bars and looking at jail time in another state.

It was here, at the Harris County Jail, that Skalnik's career as an informant began. As he sat contemplating his future, Thomas Hirschi, a defendant in a case that was all over the news, was booked into the jail and placed in a nearby cell. Hirschi was one of the "Moody Park Three," a trio of anti-police-brutality activists whom the DA's office had charged with inciting a riot at Moody Park, in Houston, that left fifteen people hospitalized. The uprising came a year after the death of a twenty-three-year-old laborer named José Campos Torres at the hands of Houston police officers. The officers who beat Torres and pushed him into a bayou to drown—"Let's see if the wetback can swim," one famously taunted—received only slaps on the wrist. City leaders blamed "outside agitators" like Hirschi, who had called for Torres's killers to be brought to justice, for the riot rather than acknowledging that years of police brutality pushed the Mexican American community to its breaking point. To the Moody Park Three's supporters, it was a frame-up. To prosecutors, it was a case they needed to win.

Skalnik would later place a call to the DA's office, claiming to have information on the case. Prosecutors put him on the stand when Hirschi and his codefendants, Travis Morales and Mara Youngdahl, were tried together in May 1979.

Skalnik's first time testifying as a jailhouse informant was less sure-footed than his later turns as a witness for the state, but he hewed closely to a story line that he would use again and again in the years to come. He told the jury that he was standing outside Hirschi's cell when the young activist decided to unburden himself and confess that Morales's plan all along had been "to incite the Mexican American youngsters," Skalnik said. As Skalnik spoke, Hirschi sat at the defense table in disbelief. "I'd never seen the guy before," Hirschi told me. "Never seen his face, didn't know his name."

Hirschi and his codefendants were looking at up to twenty years in prison if convicted. "We weren't naïve, but to actually see this unfold in front of us—to watch him lie when our lives were on the line—was pretty shocking," Hirschi said.

Skalnik's strategy paid off. Prosecutors prevailed in the end; the Moody Park Three were found guilty, though the jury declined to give them any prison time. After Skalnik spent two months in jail in Houston, he was sentenced that November to a year in the Orange County Jail, in Florida, for violating his probation. But four days before Christmas, a Florida Circuit Court judge abruptly reversed course, stating that he had "received a recommendation" that Skalnik be moved from the jail to a work-release program—a privilege normally forbidden to repeat offenders. The judge did not specify whether Texas prosecutors were behind that recommendation. But the lesson was unmistakable: The best way for a man behind bars to help himself was to help prosecutors.

Just two months later, in February 1980, Skalnik was not only out of jail but also married to a woman who believed that her clean-cut, churchgoing husband was a law student. It was this marriage—his fourth—that brought him to Pinellas County. While living with her in St. Petersburg, he got engaged to another woman in nearby Largo, telling her he was a Dallas attorney who wanted to move his law practice to Florida. He persuaded her to take out $3,500 in loans to help him set up his new law office—money he promised to pay back but never did. His wife learned of his engagement only when he was arrested for grand theft. Skalnik, who faced up to five years in prison, was left in the Pinellas County Jail to await his trial.

Skalnik had another plan. As he had done in Houston, he placed a call to prosecutors. So began a years-long working relationship between Skalnik and the state attorney's office in Clearwater, which would extend through much of the 1980s and involve at least eleven local prosecutors. "The state attorney's office has always characterized me as an honest, forthright witness," he later wrote to a judge, "and together, we never lost a case."

Ten days before his grand-theft case went to trial in August 1981, Skalnik provided the state attorney's office with information on three different defendants who were charged with murder but whose cases had not yet gone to trial. In return, prosecutors offered him a deal. If he pleaded guilty, they would recommend that he spend no more than three years in prison—two fewer than he was facing. They also left open the possibility that he could secure a sweeter deal if he cooperated further. ("Probation was discussed!" states a handwritten note in the state attorney's files.) Skalnik took the plea, and his sentencing was postponed while he quietly went to work as a jailhouse informant. Prosecutors would hold off on making a sentencing recommendation until they saw exactly how much Skalnik had to offer and how helpful he could be to them. In the meantime, he would remain in jail, a snitch.

Skalnik made himself busy that fall and winter and into the following June, testifying for the state in two drug-trafficking trials and providing a damaging deposition in a high-profile murder case. In each case, Skalnik could truthfully say under oath that he had not been promised anything in return for his testimony because no specific agreements had yet been struck. The narratives he told were strikingly similar, featuring inmates who not only freely admitted their guilt but also did so spontaneously in the same oddly stilted language. In a drug-trafficking case that ended in a guilty verdict, Skalnik testified that the defendant had struck up a conversation with him—midway through the accused's trial, no less—that began with the declaration, "We were loading the boat with 24,000 pounds of marijuana in Colombia."

Skalnik was rewarded on June 30, 1982, when, with the backing of the state attorney's office, he was sentenced to probation. For someone who had racked up five criminal charges in nearly as many years and left the state the last time he was on probation, it was an astonishing feat.

• • •

Buried deep in thousands of pages of court records spread across two states lies evidence to suggest that Skalnik was one of the most prolific, and most effective, jailhouse informants in American history. "I have placed 34 individuals in prison, including four on death row," he boasted in a 1984 letter to Senator Lawton Chiles of Florida, in a request for favorable treatment—a number that, while inflated at the time, would ultimately prove accurate. During a single six-year span, from 1981 to 1987, Skalnik testified or supplied information in at least thirty-seven cases in Pinellas County alone. Many were cases in which people faced the most serious possible charges and the most severe penalties. Eighteen defendants whose cases Skalnik provided information on were under indictment for murder. A vast majority of their cases ended in convictions or plea deals. Four were sentenced to death.

The state attorney's office in Clearwater, in an e-mailed statement, said Skalnik independently got fellow inmates to confide in him, then contacted prosecutors or the Pinellas County sheriff's office. "He at no time was an 'agent' of the sheriff's office or the state attorney's office," it said. "The state attorney's office never provided any leniency to Paul Skalnik in exchange for his testimony." All information provided by Skalnik, the statement said, was independently verified, and the office has never received any information to indicate that his testimony was "incorrect."

Still, Skalnik's journey through the criminal-justice system affords a rare opportunity to see exactly how prosecutors and jailhouse informants work together. These insights are possible because of a rare confluence of forces, including Skalnik's extensive history of informing and Florida's strong public-record laws, which enabled *ProPublica* and the *New York Times Magazine* to obtain thousands of pages of police reports, arrest records, jail logs, probation and parole records, pretrial interviews, and correspondence that document his activity in sometimes granular detail. This reporting follows decades of litigation waged by public defenders and pro bono attorneys representing death-row inmates in whose cases Skalnik played a role. The full record provides a vivid picture of how jailhouse informants are used, showing which benefits Skalnik was afforded, which crimes he eluded punishment for, and, most clearly, how the state attorney's office put this witness, who was dubbed "a con man extraordinaire," in the words of one warrant for his arrest, on the stand in cases where defendants' lives hung in the balance.

In response to detailed questions about the Dailey trial, Beverly Andrews (now Beverly Andringa), who prosecuted the case, said in an e-mail that she has "very little memory" of the more-than-thirty-year-old case, but she said that she "never willfully and intentionally provided false evidence or testimony to a court or jury on any case." Robert Heyman, a prosecutor who tried the case with her, pointed out that Skalnik had been vetted by law enforcement and called to testify by other prosecutors. "If we did not believe that his testimony was truthful, we wouldn't have had him testify," Heyman said.

Yet again and again, prosecutors have shown that they are willing to rely on the testimony of witnesses like Skalnik, even in cases in which the death penalty is in play. "Jailhouse informants are common in prosecutions of very serious crimes, including ones that carry life and even death sentences," said Michelle Feldman, the Innocence Project's state campaigns director, whose work focuses on legislative efforts to regulate the use of jailhouse informants. "Since the courts don't track them, it's hard to say which jurisdictions use them the most or how often they testify. But they remain an entrenched feature of criminal prosecutions, even though they are the most unreliable kind of witnesses."

What makes them so unreliable, she emphasized, is the widespread understanding in jail that prosecutors can offer substantial benefits in exchange for cooperation—rewards that may include not just reduced sentences or improved jail conditions but cash payments. "There is a very strong incentive to lie and very little disincentive not to," Feldman said.

• • •

The consequences of snitch testimony can be catastrophic. Of the 367 DNA exonerations in the United States to date, jailhouse informants played a role in nearly one in five of the underlying wrongful convictions. A seminal 2004 study conducted by Northwestern Law School's Center on Wrongful Convictions found that testimony from jailhouse snitches and other criminal informants was the leading cause of wrongful convictions in capital cases. Today nearly a quarter of death-row exonerations—22 percent—stem from cases in which prosecutors relied on a jailhouse informant.

Informants often end up on the stand when other evidence is weak; a case that is based on rigorous forensic work or witness testimony that can be independently corroborated does not need a snitch to paper over the gaps. The most unreliable witnesses, then, may testify in the least sound cases—and in cases in which the stakes are the highest.

Given how opaque and unchecked prosecutors' use of jailhouse informants is, it is impossible to quantify how often they factor into criminal cases. Usually the only glimpse of the government's reliance on them comes when a scandal erupts, as it did in Los Angeles in the late 1980s, after a serial snitch named Leslie Vernon White went public. In an interview for *60 Minutes*, he demonstrated how easy it was to manufacture a confession, procuring key details of a murder on camera in the course of just a few phone calls. His claims led to a grand-jury investigation into jailhouse informants that was the first of its kind. The inquiry exposed extensive prosecutorial misconduct and the widespread misuse of jailhouse informants, who had concocted persuasive-sounding confessions in a variety of ingenious ways. Some impersonated law-enforcement officers to make calls eliciting information; others sent friends and relatives to court hearings to suss out other defendants' cases. Many were fed information by law enforcement, who shared arrest reports, photos, and case files with inmates, even escorting them to crime scenes so they could better shape their testimony to fit the evidence. The grand jury identified upward of 150 cases, and perhaps as many as 250, that were affected.

In the wake of the scandal, the Los Angeles County district attorney's office instituted reforms to provide more oversight of prosecutors who put jailhouse informants on the stand, but beyond Los Angeles, little changed. The *Chicago Tribune* raised the alarm in 1999, when it highlighted prosecutors' overreliance on jailhouse informants in death-penalty cases in Illinois and found that such testimony had helped convict or condemn four of the state's twelve death-row exonerees. In the aftermath of the report, which identified numerous problems with the death penalty in Illinois, Gov. George Ryan declared a statewide moratorium on executions, but nationally, the harms of jailhouse informants went unaddressed.

In the 1990s and 2000s, the accrual of DNA exonerations—made possible by the advent of a then-new and revelatory technology—laid bare the fact that snitch testimony had contributed to wrongful convictions across the country. Nevertheless, the authors of the 2004 Northwestern Law study were fatalistic, writing, "The reality is that neither legislatures nor courts are about to ban snitch testimony in the prevailing tough-on-crime political climate."

In 2014, a quarter century after the Los Angeles snitch scandal began, another scandal broke in neighboring Orange County. A local public defender was able to show that for years, sheriff's deputies had engaged in a practice of strategically planting informants in the cells of defendants who were awaiting trial. Inmates who produced incriminating information—including "confessions" they elicited with threats of violence—were rewarded with money and sentence reductions.

Orange County's top prosecutors and law-enforcement officials were implicated, and according to a pending ACLU lawsuit against the county's district attorney's office and sheriff's department, at least 140 cases were tainted. Though no law-enforcement officials were fired or disciplined, the scandal contributed to voters' ouster of Orange County's longtime district attorney, Tony Rackauckas, and convictions in dozens of cases were subsequently challenged.

Alexandra Natapoff, a law professor at the University of California, Irvine, who is the nation's foremost legal scholar on criminal informants, said the parallels between the two California scandals show how little has changed in thirty years and how little we know about how often jailhouse informants continue to be used across the country. "In Orange County, a sophisticated jailhouse-informant system remained under the radar, not disclosed in court cases for decades," Natapoff said. "The accident is that we know about it, not that it happened."

The benefits jailhouse informants receive, she added, are rarely apparent to jurors, because prosecutors often bestow them on the back end, after a trial's conclusion. "Many jailhouse informants can truthfully state to the jury that they have not been promised any benefit, even though realistically they expect to be compensated for their testimony," Natapoff said. "Ironically, jurors will often be the only people in the courtroom who do not understand this arrangement."

• • •

Karen Parker was twelve when she crossed paths with Skalnik. "He appeared out of nowhere," she told me. "He befriended my mom and dad, and suddenly he was in our life." It was July 1982, the middle of a long and restive summer, and Parker usually passed the time at the beach or riding her bike around her working-class neighborhood in Seminole, south of Clearwater. Skalnik—who had found work with her next-door neighbor's brother, a private investigator—was often around, holding her father rapt with stories of his days as a police officer. He struck Parker as impossibly cool, a sharp dresser with a certain louche charm. "He was magnetic, out of the ordinary—not like other people I knew," she said. "And he was very attentive to me. He'd give me that extra look, and I had the sense that he was interested. I was drawn in." She was thirsty for male approval; at home, where her father was stern and critical, she received none. To Parker, Skalnik's attention was exhilarating.

One day that July, she went fishing with her next-door neighbors in Largo, and Skalnik joined them for the outing. It was dark when they returned to Seminole, and he summoned her to come sit beside him in the front seat of his silver Cadillac. By then, her neighbors had gone inside. Suddenly he was kissing Parker, his hands slipping under her T-shirt. Then his fingers were inside her.

"He took my hand and put it on his penis," she said. "He had me masturbate him until he ejaculated." Parker had just finished the seventh grade. Skalnik was thirty-two.

His voice turned cold afterward, she said, when he advised her, obliquely, to keep quiet. "One of these days you're going to open your mouth too many times," he said, suggesting that doing so could land her in "JDC"—juvenile detention. "The only one who is going to be in trouble is you."

Parker spoke to only one person about what had happened, a sixteen-year-old girl who lived next door and glimpsed Skalnik kissing her in the car. But the story eventually leaked out later that year, after Skalnik was arrested for grand theft. Upon learning of the assault, Parker's parents took her to the sheriff's office. Skalnik was charged in December 1982 with "lewd and lascivious conduct on a child under fourteen," a felony punishable by up to fifteen years in prison.

The case against him was a strong one. Parker's description of the assault was bolstered by the eyewitness account from the sixteen-year-old neighbor she confided in and another from the sixteen-year-old's boyfriend, who, as he approached the car, saw "movement in the suspect's lap (suspect's hand or victim's) of a masturbatory nature," according to the police report. And unlike some victims of child sexual abuse, Parker was old enough to clearly articulate what happened to her and was willing to testify. "I don't think it is right that he is calling me a liar and I am not," she told investigators. There were also the results of a polygraph examination that the sheriff's office administered to Parker. ("Have you ever heard of a twelve-year-old girl having to take a polygraph?" she asked me, still incredulous.) Polygraphs have since been shown to be unreliable and are not generally admissible in court, but they were central to many law-enforcement agencies' investigations in the 1980s; the fact that Parker passed, and that her account of the assault was found to be truthful, was meaningful at the time. All told, prosecutors had a case they could take to trial. Child sexual-assault cases are routinely prosecuted on far less.

But the state attorney's office would ultimately decline to try Skalnik. In a plea hearing that took place on March 10, 1983, prosecutors agreed to dismiss the molestation charge. In return, Skalnik pleaded no contest to new charges of grand theft, for which he had been arrested the previous November. (True to form, Skalnik had tricked a woman into giving him nearly $5,000 on the promise of starting a travel agency together and defrauded a couple out of more than $20,000 by assuring them that he could deliver discounted cars that were forfeited to the state in narcotics cases—all of which violated his probation in the previous grand-theft case involving his fiancée.) These charges carried much lighter punishments than child molestation. The state attorney's notice to the court dismissing the lewd-and-lascivious conduct charge said simply, "There is insufficient evidence available at this time."

Skalnik took the plea deal, for which he received concurrent five-year sentences. But instead of being sent to state prison to serve out his punishment, he would remain in the Pinellas County Jail, where he could continue to work as a jailhouse informant, gathering information on defendants who had not yet gone to trial. (Prosecutors argued that keeping him in the county jail was for his safety, given that his testimony had helped send men to prison.) And with the child-molestation charge out of the way, Skalnik came across to jurors as a far more innocuous figure than he actually was—that is, as a former police officer turned small-time scam artist, rather than as a child molester.

Parker belongs to a group of crime victims who remain forgotten in a criminal-justice system that allows jailhouse informants to be released and to continue committing crimes because prosecutors exchanged leniency for their testimony. Parker never knew about prosecutors' deal with Skalnik, only that he was never punished for what he did to her. "No one ever said, 'That's wrong,'" she told me. “The message I got was that what he did was OK—that it wasn’t serious, it wasn’t a crime.” In her father’s eyes, she said, it was she who was to blame for what happened. “Everyone liked Paul, and they believed Paul, and I was seen as the trouble-maker,” she said. After Skalnik’s arrest, her father’s harsh criticism of her escalated, until it became unbearable. Parker ran away the following year, when she was thirteen, and left home for good when she was fourteen, taking refuge at a runaway shelter. “I didn’t trust anyone for a long, long time,” she said.

• • •

Skalnik, meanwhile, continued to be valuable to the state attorney’s office after his molestation charge was dismissed in 1983. That year and the next, he testified in four high-profile murder trials, three of which ended with death sentences. All three of the men who were condemned to die—Richard Cooper, Kenneth Gardner and J. D. Walton—had, without question, been present at the scenes of the horrendous crimes they stood accused of. But because several people were charged in connection to each murder, the key question at Cooper’s, Gardner’s, and Walton’s trials was one of culpability: How much of a role did the accused play, and were his actions egregious enough to warrant the electric chair? Prosecutors used Skalnik to show that each man was not just guilty but also deserved death.

At the time, in the 1980s, appearing soft on crime was a surefire way to be voted out of office. “In Florida, prosecutors, judges, the attorney general, the governor—everyone wanted to prove how tough they were,” Stephen Bright told me. Bright, one of the nation’s preeminent capital defense attorneys and a visiting lecturer at Yale Law School, went to Clearwater in 1985 to challenge the conviction and death sentence of a man who was bound for the electric chair. Gov. Bob Graham of Florida, who earned the nickname Governor Jell-O because he was seen as weak and ineffective, reinvented himself by signing death warrants, increasing the number of warrants he signed when he ran for reelection in 1982, and again when he ran for Senate in 1986. "In Florida," Bright added, "it seemed like there couldn't be enough death sentences."

Even so, Pinellas County stood out. For a three-year period, from 1982 to 1984, it sent more people to death row than any other county in Florida. At the time, the state attorney's office was run by a hard-charging prosecutor named James T. Russell, who stood just five-foot-five but enjoyed a fearsome reputation. A perfectionist whose moral universe had no shades of gray, Russell pursued a law-and-order agenda that appealed to his constituents, who were disproportionately older and overwhelmingly white. "Put more criminals in prison, and there will be less crime on the streets," he told a local civic group in 1981, condemning what he perceived to be a system that placed too much emphasis on rehabilitating people who broke the law. (Russell died in 2006.) Few questioned the bare-knuckled tactics behind his office's conviction rate, which reached 92 percent in 1990. So fierce was the drive to rack up wins that prosecutors "sought the death penalty in nearly every first-degree murder case," according to a 1988 survey by a local public defender—a strategy that allowed them to leverage the threat of the electric chair to extract guilty pleas from defendants.

The demand for convictions and long, tough sentences made Skalnik's testimony invaluable. The confessions he recounted were lurid and dramatic, strewn with provocative details that prosecutors used not just to show the guilt of the defendants but also to establish that they were diabolically evil. Skalnik told of victims' begging for their lives and of remorseless killers who laughed after their slaughters, boasting that they had outsmarted prosecutors and the police. Gardner, who was convicted in a grisly stabbing death of a hardware-store owner, supposedly bragged to Skalnik, "I killed him, but they'll never prove it." Walton, who was found guilty of carrying out the execution of three men after a botched robbery, considered the whole thing "a funny joke," Skalnik told jurors. And Cooper, one of Walton's codefendants, supposedly introduced himself to Skalnik with the brash declaration, "I'm one of the men involved in the triple-murder slayings they thought was a mafia gangland killing."

Though Cooper might have earned the jury's mercy because he was a teenager, Skalnik turned that potentially mitigating fact on its head by sharing an offhand comment he attributed to Cooper. "He said no jury would ever sentence him to the death chair," Skalnik testified, "because he's nineteen years old and because he's got that little baby face." The jury recommended that Cooper be put to death. (Gardner and Cooper would eventually be resentenced to life in prison.)

The confessions he claimed these men volunteered to him—and that the state attorney's office had him repeat to juries—were all the more extraordinary given that he was held in protective custody and that his reputation as a snitch was well known to other men in the jail. "Beginning to encounter more and more inmates who recognize him," stated a note in his file from January 1983. Nevertheless, Skalnik was sometimes moved closer to, or even into the same cell as, a defendant in a newsworthy case. Cooper was assigned to a two-man cell with Skalnik; Gardner was later assigned to a cell that adjoined Skalnik's. It was during their brief time in proximity to him that each supposedly came clean. A third inmate, a codefendant of Cooper's named Terry Van Royal, protested when Skalnik was moved into his cell. "I told the guard I would not be in the same cell with him," Van Royal later wrote in an affidavit, "because I knew who he was and what he did."

If defense attorneys tried to suggest that Skalnik's preternatural ability to extract men's most closely held secrets was too good to be true, Skalnik would insist that he stood to gain nothing from his testimony, as he did during the 1983 murder trial of Freddie

Gaines. A twenty-four-year-old handyman, Gaines was charged with stabbing his girlfriend's ex-lover to death in a bar brawl—a chance encounter, Gaines told the jury, that turned violent. But Skalnik's testimony jettisoned any notion that Gaines acted spontaneously; to hear him tell it, Gaines had carried out a calculated, coldblooded murder. Skalnik said Gaines boasted of bringing a knife to the bar and seeking out the victim, telling Skalnik he should have been charged "with open-heart surgery." Skalnik's voice swelled with emotion as he spoke, so much that he once appeared to be on the brink of tears.

Gaines told me that he was floored when he heard Skalnik testify and that he leaned over and told his lawyer: "He's sitting right there telling a lie. Me and this man ain't never talked before." But Skalnik's testimony was effective, recasting a possible crime of passion into a premeditated execution—a distinction that would help earn Gaines a conviction for first-degree murder and a life sentence, rather than a lesser charge like manslaughter, which carried a penalty of up to fifteen years.

Skalnik assured the jury that he had come forward with no other motive than to preserve public safety. "I used to be a police officer," he said, adding that he became an informant after hearing other men in the jail brag that they were going to beat their charges. Assistant State Attorney Bruce Young bolstered the idea that Skalnik's intentions were selfless. "It's your understanding that nothing can be done for you as far as eliminating or reducing your sentence?" Young asked.

"That's correct," Skalnik replied.

Young continued, "Even if your lawyer wanted to go in front of a judge, the judge would have no jurisdiction to reduce the sentence, is that correct?"

"Yes, sir," Skalnik said with a note of resignation. "That's correct."

Just three months later, Young wrote to the Florida Department of Corrections to request leniency. "Mr. Skalnik has been a state witness in a number of very important cases, including several first-degree murder cases, and his testimony has been honest and truthful in all cases," Young said. Expressing concern for Skalnik's safety, he asked that his star witness not be sent to state prison but remain in the jail; better yet, Young proposed, the State of Florida could simply release him. "If Mr. Skalnik is eligible for parole," he wrote, "I would urge that Mr. Skalnik be considered for parole." (Young did not respond to detailed requests for comment.)

One of Skalnik's most loyal supporters would also go to bat for him. John Halliday—the detective who previously worked with Skalnik and would later receive key information from him in the Dailey case—called the parole board that fall on his behalf. "Mr. Halliday would like the commission to know the subject has been of great assistance to the sheriff's office," reads an interoffice memo documenting the call. Halliday wrote directly to a parole commissioner the next month, urging him to consider Skalnik for release. "I have never done this for an inmate during my ten years in law enforcement," Halliday added.

(Halliday declined to review a detailed request for comment, referring it to Keith Johnson, an investigator for the state attorney's office. Johnson referred the request to the state attorney's office, which declined to comment about Halliday, as did a spokeswoman for the Pinellas County sheriff's office, who noted that the cases in question took place long ago.)

On March 19, 1985, Skalnik was paroled. Having served about half of his five-year sentence for grand theft, he was free, despite assessments from the Department of Corrections that judged him to be a "con artist of the highest degree" who was at "high risk of further unlawful behavior." Sure enough, after Skalnik was released, he cheated an elderly woman out of tens of thousands of dollars for two Lincoln Town Cars he never delivered; conned another woman out of thousands more with a phony real estate deal; and duped a jewelry-store clerk into taking a check from what turned out to be a defunct bank account for a $6,100 gold Rolex. He also married and divorced his fifth wife.

By November 24, 1986, he was back in the Pinellas County Jail, where he would claim, the following summer, to have procured James Dailey's confession. "Mr. Skalnik's deceitful nature knows no bounds," an unknown person wrote in a handwritten letter to the state attorney's office, urging prosecutors to punish him as harshly as the law would allow. "How many chances will this man be given? How many more people will he hurt and victimize?"

• • •

As reform-minded prosecutors have swept into office over the past five years in cities like Chicago, St. Louis, Dallas, Philadelphia, and Boston, some district attorney's offices have begun to reevaluate the way they have always done business. "People in these communities have made very clear that a win-at-all-costs approach is not what they want anymore and does not make them safer," said Miriam Krinsky, a former federal prosecutor and executive director of Fair and Just Prosecution, a network for progressive prosecutors. In an effort to stem mass incarceration, reformers have focused their energy on trying to address the big, structural problems that most directly affect people's liberty, like changing the cash-bail system and diverting defendants to drug treatment instead of prison.

So far, the use of jailhouse informants has received relatively little consideration. "It's an issue that is just starting to gain attention," Krinsky said. "There is a new dialogue about whether prosecutors should institute safeguards that would allow them to continue using jailhouse informants but proceed with caution, or whether to steer clear of jailhouse informants completely."

In some state legislatures, the idea of bringing greater scrutiny to jailhouse informants has slowly begun to gain traction. In 2017, Texas lawmakers tried to strip away the secretive nature of snitch deals by compelling prosecutors to keep track of and disclose the sort of rudimentary information that defendants and their lawyers are often lacking. This includes a full accounting of the benefits that jailhouse informants have received for their testimony, their criminal records and the previous cases in which they testified. Last year, Illinois passed legislation that requires judges to hold pretrial "reliability hearings" to evaluate whether informants, in light of the benefits they have been promised and their histories as informants, should be allowed to testify. In July, Connecticut became the first state to enact a statewide tracking system for jailhouse informants that documents where and when such witnesses have previously testified and what benefits they received in return.

Florida took action after a staggering number of its death-row inmates were exonerated; to date, twenty-nine condemned men have been cleared of their convictions, more than in any other state. A commission appointed by the Florida Supreme Court to study wrongful convictions recommended that prosecutors disclose the deals they make with jailhouse informants, and in response, the court changed the rules of criminal procedure in 2014 to require the disclosure of such deals as well as other details related to the informant. The new requirement was intended to introduce transparency—but in practice, it does not address the common problem that prosecutors may not need to make explicit promises at all, because the potential for leniency is implicit and well understood.

Reformers hope that new legislation, though imperfect, could still deter prosecutors from relying on jailhouse informants. "When you put reforms in place that require tracking and disclosing information about these witnesses, what often comes to light is a good deal of information that could discourage prosecutors from wanting to move forward," says Rebecca Brown, director of policy for the Innocence Project. "Once they have a fuller understanding of all the factors that would underlie that informant's testimony, they have to confront questions like: Is this reliable enough to move forward with?"

But in a vast majority of states, no reforms have been passed at all. Perjury charges for jailhouse snitches are very rare, even when their testimony is later proved to have been demonstratively false. So, too, are any meaningful consequences for prosecutors who fail to disclose agreements made with a jailhouse informant at the time of trial or who mislead juries into thinking that an informant will not receive rewards after testifying or who conceal facts about a jailhouse informant's criminal history that might undermine his credibility. No legislation has yet addressed the outsize but largely invisible role that jailhouse informants play in plea deals, in which prosecutors may use the mere specter of an informant's future testimony to intimidate defendants into not taking their cases to trial. And more radical ideas—like an outright ban on jailhouse informants in capital cases—have stalled, allowing prosecutors to continue using snitch testimony to secure the starkest, most irrevocable punishment.

• • •

On August 7, 1987, five weeks after James Dailey's trial ended in a guilty verdict, the forty-one-year-old Vietnam veteran came to court to be formally sentenced to death. He had remained mute throughout his trial, but that day, he finally rose to speak. Tall and angular, with dark hair and a long, mournful face, he began by recognizing the "terrible kind of pain" Shelly Boggio's murder had caused her twin sister, and the anguish felt by her family members, who sat in the courtroom, weeping. "I say these things as a caring human being and as a person wrongfully convicted of this heinous crime," he declared. He had been condemned by Pinellas County's "win at all costs" system of justice, he said, in which "truth is allowed to be manipulated and paid liars are allowed to testify." His trial, he added before he was led away in shackles, had been a "mockery of justice."

Skalnik, who was released five days later, was supposed to be back in court that October for his trial on charges of grand theft. But by the time his trial date rolled around, he had skipped town, having absconded with a rented Lincoln Town Car shortly before he was due to marry a woman who believed he worked undercover for the FBI. Prosecutors were left in the lurch; their star witness, who was slated to testify in three coming murder trials, was suddenly a fugitive from justice.

Skalnik, meanwhile, was hiding out in Austin, Texas, where he was busy practicing a sort of absurdist performance art. Passing himself off as "J. Paul Bourne," a high roller who was flush with oil money, he managed to buy $27,000 worth of jewelry with forged checks while also running "a new unknown type scam," according to documents from the Travis County district attorney's office—a con that involved opening bank accounts on the promise that millions of dollars would be wired in. He also married, and soon divorced, his sixth wife.

Following his arrest on a forgery charge in February 1988, he tried to reprise his role as a snitch, but an assistant district attorney in Austin saw what should have been clear to any prosecutor. Skalnik, she warned in an interoffice memo, "is a BIG con artist." Skalnik was soon extradited back to Florida, where he was booked, once again, into the Pinellas County Jail.

By then, his relationship with the state attorney's office had soured, his decision to bolt to Texas having made a farce of the trust it had put in him. But if prosecutors thought they could distance themselves from Skalnik, they had failed to discern the game he was playing. When they balked at his demands for a lenient plea deal in the summer of 1988, he turned on them.

With the help of his public defender, Skalnik filed a motion with the trial court in which he claimed a history of extensive prosecutorial misconduct. In the motion, he asserted that prosecutors had coached him on how to testify in numerous cases so as to give jurors the false impression that he "had actually heard all these 'confessions,' and had no agreement with the state for a reward for his testimony." Prosecutors "knew of the potential questionability of said confessions," the motion charged. Skalnik provided the names of eleven prosecutors whom he accused of misconduct but provided few specifics. He claimed to have given information or testimony in more than fifty cases and suggested that much of that evidence was tainted.

Just as the men whom Skalnik leveled outrageous claims against over the years had faced accusations that were maddeningly difficult to disprove, prosecutors found themselves on the defensive, scrambling to discredit what Skalnik claimed was the honest truth. In formal responses submitted to the court, the state attorney's office categorically denied his assertions, dismissing them as "falsehoods, ranging in degree from gross exaggeration to preposterous fabrication"—a richly paradoxical about-face for an office that had asked scores of jurors to take him at his word. Trying to preserve the integrity of the cases Skalnik had participated in, prosecutors simultaneously argued that his earlier testimony as a state witness "was credible, was often independently substantiated and withstood extensive cross-examination."

In fact, behind the scenes, an investigator with the state attorney's office had difficulty verifying that Skalnik had provided information that could be independently corroborated. Of the two examples Detective Halliday provided—he said Skalnik's tips led law enforcement to a ski mask worn during the committing of a murder and to a gun used in another killing—only the claim about the ski mask checked out; of the other, the investigator wrote: "This information is incorrect. The information from Skalnik was accurate; however it came months after the gun was retrieved."

Skalnik brought forth his grievances, the state attorney's office told the court, only after he failed to blackmail prosecutors into cutting him a favorable deal. Yet in the end, Skalnik got exactly what he wanted. After Skalnik withdrew his motion claiming that they had engaged in misconduct, he and prosecutors arrived at what appeared to be a mutually beneficial arrangement—one that would both appease Skalnik and send him far from Pinellas County. For a total of six felonies—four counts of grand theft and two counts of failure to appear in court—he would receive a five-year sentence. He entered his plea on the condition that his sentence be served in Texas, where he had time left on a bail-jumping charge.

Skalnik ended up evading even that relatively meager punishment. In November 1989, after completing seven months in prison in Huntsville, Texas, on the bail-jumping charge, the State of Texas—which never agreed to allow him to serve his Florida sentence there—released him. Ultimately Florida abandoned its efforts to extradite him. "The commission has received information which has caused it to conclude that return of said person is not warranted," read one notably oblique 1991 Florida Parole Commission memo.

Skalnik had been let loose on the world again.

• • •

In 1991, Misty Anderson was living with her mother and two younger sisters in Friendswood, Texas—the same town where Skalnik passed himself off as an airline executive in the late 1970s. Her mother, who declined to be interviewed for this article and whose name is being withheld to protect her privacy, wed Skalnik after a short courtship; she did not know that he was already married, much less that she was his eighth wife. (Skalnik married his seventh wife shortly after his release from prison.) Masquerading as a prosperous real estate developer, Skalnik lavished

Anderson's mother with gifts: big bouquets of roses, jewelry, even a used Jaguar. He also began sowing division between her and her eldest daughter.

In his campaign to undermine the fifteen-year-old, who disliked him from the start, Skalnik accused her of stealing the engagement ring he had given her mother—a ring whose glittering gemstone, he said, was a seven-carat diamond. Anderson, whose most fervent wish was for her parents to get back together, saw Skalnik as an interloper, and a calculating and tacky one at that. She was stunned when he accused her of stealing the ring, which she suspected was actually set with a cubic zirconium. "He said I'd taken it," she told me. "He set me up."

As punishment, Skalnik grounded Anderson, insisting that she could be reformed only through a punishing regimen that he ordered her to carry out over her summer vacation, when temperatures soared into the nineties. "Every day I had to dig holes in the ground along our fence line, under the hot sun, with no water," Anderson told me. "I was not allowed to shower, not allowed to brush my teeth. I was only allowed to eat once a day. I would get so faint that I would see stars." When Skalnik permitted her to come inside, she had to stay in her room, shut off from the rest of the world. Only after a month of isolation, when she was at her most desperate and vulnerable, did Skalnik offer her a way out. "He came in my bedroom and said, 'I have an idea that's going to make things better between us,'" she said.

Anderson did not speak a word about the sexual abuse that followed—"I didn't think anyone would believe me," she explained—until late that summer, when she summoned the courage to confide in a family friend. "She told me that she had to report the abuse, and that's how it all started," Anderson said. The spell Skalnik seemed to have cast over her mother was, in an instant, broken. "As soon as my mother heard what he'd been doing, she called the police," Anderson said. Skalnik was arrested and charged with sexual assault of a child.

In the eyes of the law, Skalnik was a first-time sex offender. "With a prior conviction for sexual assault of a child, he would have been looking at 25 years to life," said Margaret Hindman, the former assistant district attorney in Galveston County who prosecuted him. Instead, he faced two to twenty years. Still, Hindman pursued him with a vigor that Pinellas County prosecutors had not. She was astonished when I told her of Skalnik's long run as a state witness. "This guy clearly was grandiose, delusional, and had narcissistic-personality disorder," she said. "He boasted that he was with the FBI, that he was with the CIA, and none of it checked out. It's hard to believe prosecutors relied on him."

Skalnik professed his innocence, but he pleaded no contest in exchange for a ten-year prison sentence—a deal that was not as harsh as Anderson would have liked, though it spared her from having to endure a trial. She was in college when Skalnik first came up for parole, and she wrote to the parole board's members, urging them not to grant him early release, and they abided by her wishes.

In 2002, he was released after serving a decade in prison. Rather than register as a sex offender, as he was required to do by law, he simply disappeared. He was arrested the following year in Middlesex County, Massachusetts, just west of Boston, for larceny and forgery after he stole thousands of dollars from unsuspecting clients who had hired him under the false belief that he was an attorney. He pleaded guilty and served time in state prison, then fled the state around 2009 after repeatedly violating the terms of his probation.

He managed to live under the radar for the next six years in East Texas, where he went by the name E. Paul Smith. Claiming to be an attorney, an undercover Homeland Security agent, an ex-fighter pilot who had been shot down over Vietnam, and a terminally ill cancer patient, he worked a variety of small-time scams. "He was writing up people's wills, and doing legal work for them, and investing their money, though no one ever saw any returns," said Shirley Saathoff, a retired U.S. Marshals senior inspector who began investigating Skalnik in the summer of 2015 after the daughter of one of his love interests figured out his real name and looked up his criminal record. "He hurt and used a lot of women," Saathoff added. Everything, even his wedding to a woman named Judy Smith, who would have been his ninth wife, turned out to be a sham, down to the phony marriage license he had her date and sign. (She is now Judy Beaty.) "Paul put just enough truth into a lie to make you believe it," she told me.

When law enforcement finally caught up with him that October and arrested him for failing to register as a sex offender, he had over thirty fake IDs in his possession—as well as a framed law-school diploma, a legal dictionary embossed with the words E. PAUL SMITH, ESQ., ATTORNEY AT LAW, and a handgun. After he was arrested, he asked to speak to law enforcement. "He wanted to cut a deal," James Ferris, an investigator with the Panola County Sheriff's Department, told me one morning in his tidy office in Carthage, Texas. "He started telling me that he could be useful inside the jail, and I told him I was not interested in speaking with him further." Ferris was emphatic about why he wouldn't want to work with Skalnik. "I would never be able to say on the stand that I believed the information he gave me was true and credible."

• • •

As James Dailey's appeals slowly advanced through the courts, his attorneys at the Capital Collateral Regional Counsel—a state agency that represents indigent death-row inmates—argued that the state had, by putting Skalnik on the stand, used false testimony to convict him. To prove it, they pointed to the claims Skalnik himself made in 1988, when he accused prosecutors of knowing that the confessions he recounted were highly suspect and of concealing from juries the rewards he was given for his testimony. But the courts were indifferent. In a 2007 opinion, the Florida Supreme Court noted that Skalnik's claims of prosecutorial misconduct had never been substantiated. "Skalnik disavowed the accusations," read the opinion, and "unequivocally stated that they were false." The court also accepted the government's assurances that prosecutors had not engaged in wrongdoing. "The prosecutor in Dailey's case also testified that she believed Skalnik's testimony to be truthful at the time of trial," its justices wrote in their opinion. And with that, any hope of challenging the veracity of Skalnik's testimony effectively came to an end.

Eight years later, in 2015, the Florida Commission on Offender Review declined to recommend Dailey's case for a clemency hearing. By then, Dailey and another man, J. D. Walton, were the only people Skalnik testified against who remained on death row. Dailey's prospects looked grim; after several rounds of appeals, the inexorable fact of his execution loomed.

The following year, a new attorney at the CCRC, Chelsea Shirley, started digging into his case. Shirley, who was less than three years out of law school, brought fresh eyes and indefatigable energy to the decades-long case file and the effort to win Dailey a new trial. At twenty-seven, she was younger than the case itself.

As Shirley read the numerous accounts that Dailey's codefendant, Jack Pearcy, had given about the night of the crime, she saw nothing to suggest that her client had actually taken part in the murder. "Through the years, Pearcy suggested—but never explicitly said—that he committed this crime by himself," Shirley told me. She was particularly struck by a sworn statement he made to Dailey's attorneys in 1993. In it, Pearcy divulged that he had been alone with Boggio in the early-morning hours of May 6, 1985, making him the last known person to see her alive; he did not say what happened to Boggio, only that he returned home alone. "I went in, got Jim up," Pearcy said of Dailey. "I told him, 'Come on, let's go smoke a couple joints, drink a beer or something.'" He and Dailey then drove to a nearby causeway, he said, and began tossing a Frisbee around. "He ended up going out in the water," Pearcy said, "while we was playing Frisbee. We drank beer, we smoked a couple of joints." His account provided an explanation for why Dailey's jeans were wet when the two men returned home. It was the same story Dailey had told his attorneys before his own trial—a story they warned him sounded too far-fetched to repeat to a jury.

On April 20, 2017, Shirley drove to Sumter Correctional Institution in Bushnell, Florida, an hour north of Tampa, to see Pearcy. She was still in the early stages of her investigation; she did not yet know that she would interview two men who had been incarcerated with Pearcy at different times, who would tell her that Pearcy told them Dailey had nothing to do with the murder. Shirley went to see Pearcy only with the hope that he might be ready, after thirty years, to talk.

Pearcy, a compact, muscular man with penetrating blue eyes, did not seem surprised that she had come to visit him, and he agreed to meet with her. She began by reviewing several previous accounts he had given of the hours surrounding Boggio's murder, in which he suggested that Dailey was at home when he and the teenager headed out into the night. Pearcy listened and nodded along. Finally he asked if he could look at a document she had placed on the table between them; it was an affidavit she had prepared that summarized his previous statements, but it concluded with a declaration that went one step further. "James Dailey was not present when Shelly Boggio was killed," it read. "I alone am responsible for Shelly Boggio's death."

Pearcy read the affidavit line by line, and when he finally spoke, his voice was devoid of emotion. "If you can give me a pen, I'll sign it," he told Shirley. He said that he would be willing to testify in court to attest to the accuracy of the affidavit; he just wanted to tell his mother first, he said, to prepare her. It was an astounding admission—and it was enough, Shirley hoped, to win her client a new trial.

Pearcy's affidavit helped persuade a judge to grant an evidentiary hearing, which was held on January 3, 2018. Shirley brought some additional legal firepower. Laura Fernandez, a clinical lecturer and research scholar at Yale Law School, had recently joined Dailey's legal team. She—along with her colleague Cyd Oppenheimer, also a Yale-trained lawyer—would become a driving force in the effort to overturn Dailey's conviction. But when Pearcy was called to the stand, he had a change of heart. He explained that he had spoken to someone with the state—he did not specify whom—and was worried about how his testimony could affect his chances for parole. "I spoke with all my family, and they told me I needed to do what I thought was right, but that I needed to not make a rash decision, since my parole just got denied for seven years," he said. His family had advised him, he said, to "think about what I was doing." When questioned about the truthfulness of his affidavit, he invoked his Fifth Amendment right against self-incrimination. The judge denied Dailey's bid for a new trial.

Dailey's lawyers appealed the decision to the Florida Supreme Court, citing information they had uncovered that, they argued, warranted a new trial. This included revelations about the other two jailhouse informants, Pablo DeJesus and James Leitner, who testified against Dailey in 1987. Travis Smith, who was incarcerated at the Pinellas County Jail at the same time as the two informants, testified at the evidentiary hearing that he heard them concoct a fictitious story about Dailey, which they planned to take to prosecutors so they could win reduced sentences. (Pablo DeJesus died in 2012; Leitner has never publicly recanted his testimony.) The state attorney's office's records reflect that DeJesus and Leitner—who told jurors they would receive no reward for their testimony—haggled with prosecutors for reduced sentences in the months leading up to Dailey's trial, a benefit they were each granted after his conviction.

But Florida's highest criminal court was unmoved, finding that Smith's account, and other evidence Dailey's lawyers presented, including proof that Skalnik misrepresented his criminal record at Dailey's trial, had come to light too late. "Dailey neglects to explain why this information could not have been discovered earlier," the court stated in an opinion on October 3—in essence blaming Dailey's lawyers for not uncovering facts that prosecutors had spent years obfuscating.

It was the end of the road for Dailey. A week earlier, Gov. Ron DeSantis had signed his death warrant. "This was one of the most gruesome crimes in the history of Pinellas County," DeSantis, a native of the county who grew up just north of Clearwater, later told reporters. "This has been litigated over and over and over, and so at some point you need to do justice." The day and time of Dailey's death was set: His execution was to be carried out on November 7 at six p.m.

• • •

Earlier this fall, I went to see Skalnik in a nursing home in the East Texas town of Corsicana. I found him alone in a drab, cluttered room where the blinds were drawn and a television was on low. He had been released from prison in June, after having romanced the mother of another inmate, persuading her to fill his commissary account each week. He lay in bed, shirtless, his thinning gray hair uncombed. Even flat on his back, he cut a shockingly large, Falstaffian figure. He was bedridden and ill—though with what, he did not say. Every so often, nurses turned him so that he did not develop bedsores, and he sometimes grimaced in pain as he spoke. "I think I'm going to die," he whispered.

During the afternoon I spent with him, and on a subsequent visit, it became clear that the last person who could provide a deeper understanding of Paul Skalnik was Skalnik himself. He was a master of misdirection, sidestepping hard questions while portraying himself as the unfairly maligned hero of a story that featured a supporting cast of cunning and vindictive women who were after his riches. Of both charges of child molestation, he insisted that he had been wrongly accused, a victim of girls who lied to the authorities.

As we talked, I eyed his tattoos. His right shoulder was emblazoned with United States Marines iconography and his left shoulder bore the words "From Texas to Vietnam." Skalnik told me that the scar on his right knee was a result of being shot down over Laos when he fought in the Vietnam War. In fact, his available military records show that he was never on combat duty and never served overseas.

He insisted that his testimony in Dailey's trial, and in the many other cases he played a role in, had been truthful. "I never lied on the stand," he told me. "At least to the best of my knowledge." When I told him of Dailey's impending execution, he was unmoved. But he seemed surprised when I mentioned that Freddie Gaines—the twenty-four-year-old who stabbed his girlfriend's ex-lover in a bar brawl—was still in prison, thirty-six years later. "I think that was a crime of passion," Skalnik said. "He doesn't need life," he added, of Gaines's sentence. "I'd give him ten and let him go home."

When I reminded Skalnik that he was the witness whose testimony established premeditation at Gaines's trial, he appeared shocked. "This was your testimony, that he had planned this," I reminded him. "Does that ring true to you? Do you think he told you that?"

"No!" Skalnik cried. "No." He shook his head resolutely. But when I later tried to return to his apparent recantation, his tone shifted. There is no statute of limitations on perjury in Florida in capital felony cases, and Skalnik was reluctant to reverse himself. "I won't retract what I said," he told me. "Whatever I testified to was fact."

Proudly, he told me more than once, "I never lost a case."

A week later, I went to Florida State Prison in Raiford, west of Jacksonville, to interview Dailey. He had recently caught an unexpected break. On October 23, a Federal District Court judge granted him a limited stay of execution, to provide his newly appointed federal attorneys more time to research and present their appeals.

Florida State Prison is a monolithic, 1960s-era penitentiary hemmed in on all sides by level farmland and coils of razor wire. It is also home to the so-called death house, where inmates with active death warrants are held in the weeks leading up to their executions. For our meeting, Dailey was led into the tiny, fluorescent-lit room where final interviews with the condemned are conducted. His hands were manacled to a chain belt at his waist, and his feet were bound by leg irons. At seventy-three, he moved slowly. Behind his thick-framed, prison-issued glasses, he had heavy circles under his eyes.

Though Dailey had been granted a stay, it was clear that what lay ahead weighed heavily upon him. He had been convicted in the era of Old Sparky, the straight-backed oak chair in which 240 prisoners went to their deaths before 2000, when the Florida Legislature made lethal injection the preferred method of execution. As Dailey passed days and then weeks in the death house, he experienced another, different kind of torment: the anticipation of waiting. His cell was just thirty feet from the execution chamber. At the time of our interview, he had already been measured for his state-issued burial suit.

After more than three decades in prison, Dailey seemed even-tempered, agreeable, even acquiescent. A lieutenant at the prison would later take me aside to tell me that Dailey's disciplinary record was almost nonexistent—a feat for anyone who has been incarcerated for so long.

I asked Dailey about an observation his mother made when she testified during the penalty phase of his trial, hoping to persuade the jury to show him mercy. "I sent two lovely young men to the air force and marines," she said of Dailey and one of his brothers, "and they came back, and they were different boys."

Dailey closed his eyes at the memory. "I was messed up," he said. He explained that he was sent to Bien Hoa, an air base northeast of Saigon, in 1968 during the Tet Offensive; after rocket attacks hit the base, he and other soldiers assisted the injured—men whose limbs had been blown off, their faces ravaged, who drifted between life and death. "I wasn't built for that," he told me. "I started drinking real bad." To sleep, he had to finish as much as a fifth of alcohol. After three tours in Vietnam, he found no relief when he returned home. He sank into addiction and became, he told me, "a vagabond."

His relationship with Pearcy, whom he met in a bar in Kansas, was elemental. "We smoked dope together," Dailey said simply. He insisted that he had nothing to do with Boggio's murder and that he believed Pearcy was driving Boggio home when Pearcy left the house with the teenager, and he went to sleep.

Dailey understood that any chance of proving his innocence was lost when Skalnik took the stand. "I never talked to Paul Skalnik in my life," he told me, his voice rising. "We all knew he was an infamous snitch and an ex-police officer. We knew everything about him. We knew how many guys he had snitched on. There wasn't any hiding the fact. The officers would tell us! The officers that worked in the dang jail, they'd say, 'Don't talk to him.'

"It was impossible for him to get my confession the way he said he got it," he continued. Even if Skalnik—under protective custody, and a stranger to Dailey, no less—had somehow managed to strike up a conversation, the distance between the two men would have prohibited any sort of meaningful or intimate discussion. "He would've had to holler at me," Dailey said. "And I would have had to speak loudly to confess to him."

Dailey told me something that he'd thought back to many times over the years: He had been moved from one cell to another shortly before his trial was slated to begin. Jail logs, in which inmates' cell assignments are recorded, confirm that on May 1, 1987—just eighteen days before Dailey's scheduled trial—Dailey was moved from the lower G wing of the jail to the upper G wing, where Skalnik was held. "Right away, I told the sergeant, I said, 'Get me out of here,'" Dailey told me. "'This is a damn setup.'" Skalnik claimed to have elicited Dailey's confession just two days later. Five days after that, he was talking to the state attorney's office. It was one of many troubling facts that the jury in Dailey's trial never heard.

Dailey's stay of execution will remain in place through December 30. After that, Governor DeSantis can set a new execution date for as soon as January. When that day comes, Dailey will be asked to walk from his cell to the execution chamber, where he will lie down on the gurney. Leather restraining straps will be fastened across his body, and an IV line will be inserted into his arm. Finally, the signal will be given to the executioner to begin the flow of lethal drugs. At that moment, the State of Florida will be asking its citizens to trust that Dailey killed Shelly Boggio that night beside the dark water and that he received a fair trial and that justice has finally been served. It will be asking them, as it has time and time again, to believe the word of Paul Skalnik.

Washington Post Magazine

WINNER—SINGLE-TOPIC ISSUE

"A nation that locks up so many people and creates an expansive apparatus that relies on violence and confinement is a nation in which democracy, over the long term, cannot thrive," writes Piper Kerman in this short article, which served as the introduction to a special issue of the Washington Post Magazine *simply titled "Prison." Kerman is, of course, the author of* Orange Is the New Black, *and like every other writer, illustrator and photographer who contributed to this issue, she has seen prison from the inside—in her case, thirteen months in a federal penitentiary for money laundering and drug trafficking (the artist who illustrated Kerman's story, Thomas Bartlett Whitaker, was minutes away from being executed for the murder of his mother and brother when his sentence was commuted; he is now serving life without parole). "Prison" earned the* Washington Post Magazine *the 2020 National Magazine Award for Single-Topic Issue—the magazine's first nomination and first award in any category.*

Piper Kerman

We've Normalized Prison

When I was twenty-two, in the early 1990s, I committed a crime. More than a decade later, I was sent to federal prison for thirteen months for that crime—a first-time drug offense. In 2010, I published a book about my experience, *Orange Is the New Black: My Year in a Women's Prison*. The title is not only a sarcastic joke about orange jumpsuits but also a reference to the fact that the population of incarcerated or formerly incarcerated people in the United States has exploded: we lock up more of our own people than any other nation in history, and beyond the 2.3 million people confined on any given day, more than 73 million American adults have some sort of criminal record.

The reach of the American criminal punishment systems stretches to clutch far more people than many imagine. I know this not only from being incarcerated but also from teaching nonfiction writing classes in state prisons. My students' stories bravely reveal difficult personal truths and bring to light much wider realities in a way that only lived experience really can. What incarcerated writers' voices illustrate is that the American criminal justice system does not solve the problems—violence, mental illness, addiction—that it claims to address.

If prison curbed drug addiction or the ills that surround it, we would not be in the grip of an overdose crisis, having locked up unprecedented millions of people for drugs for more than four decades. If the threat of criminal punishment were effective against violence, then we would not see persistent and unequal rates of harm concentrated in some communities or against women or LGBTQ people. If we considered our failure to help children who witness or are targeted by violence alongside our unique willingness to sentence children to die in prison, perhaps more people would see our criminal punishment system for the vicious ouroboros that it is.

Indeed, far from solving our problems, the carceral state is *causing* a massive one: A nation that locks up so many people and creates an expansive apparatus that relies on violence and confinement is a nation in which democracy, over the long term, cannot thrive. For centuries, the U.S. political economy has relied on millions being sidelined from democratic participation, most notably African Americans and, before 1920, women. Violence, in the form of lynching, was always important to limit democracy in this country (and agents of law enforcement were often complicit). As we near 2020, civic exclusion is still a critical tool for those invested in preserving an inequitable status quo, and the policies surrounding mass incarceration are invaluable for continuing to deny participation to millions of Americans.

Last year, the citizens of Florida voted to amend the state constitution to allow people like me, with felony convictions, to regain the right to vote after returning home. Quickly and shamelessly, the Florida legislature and governor responded by passing a poll tax to prevent those voters—disproportionately people of color and poor people—from having a voice. Many other states also restrict voting rights of prisoners or ex-prisoners, especially states with large African American populations—not a coincidence, as they remain overly targeted and punished by the criminal justice system. As a result, we have not only normalized prison but normalized the exclusion of large groups of people from participating in our democracy.

It's important to remember that law is made and administered by those in power—and the less democratic we are, the less just the legal system will be. That's why police officers or Stanford athletes who rape get sentences of six months or probation while some of my students have served two decades for similar crimes and are still in prison. Prisons and jails do not serve feminist goals—few institutions are more hierarchical, more dominance-oriented, more patriarchal, and totally reliant on the threat and promise of violence. Being subject to violence does not make you less likely to enact it. We are at a moment in time when state violence—whether it's violence perpetrated by Immigration and Customs Enforcement agents against children and families, police violence documented on smartphones, or a woman paralyzed in a beating by prison workers—is coming into sharper relief for all Americans, even those who have not been targets of the state. If you're outraged by what you see the government doing with federal courts and detention facilities, look closely at what your local sheriff, prosecutors, and judges are doing, too.

Recent news stories about young children and families who are separated at the U.S.-Mexico border and held in desperate conditions in private prisons and public jails nationwide bewilder and disgust many Americans. But, in fact, the U.S. government has been separating families and punishing children throughout history, most notably African American and Native American families and children. Native American girls have the highest incarceration rate in our juvenile prisons, and that's not because they are perpetrating a crime wave. The most marginalized girls in the United States are often jailed for truancy, for homelessness due to abuse, for things that are not actually crimes, because as a community we have no substantive response to their lack of safety, other than a cage. Better approaches are well-understood but don't have political currency because the people who need them are considered expendable or even threatening by those in power.

At this watershed moment, it's critical for each of us to pause and ask: Why is all this happening? Am I okay with it? Whom am I listening to? What should I do? If the only people we listen to on questions of law and public safety are the people who hold the power to make or impose laws, ask yourself why, and whether they are actually trustworthy. We have to be especially wary of granting authority figures—many of whom have a deep stake in maintaining the status quo—exclusive control over what should count as "normal."

Freedom and safety are too often imagined as being in opposition, but nothing could be further from the truth. Americans who have the most freedom—freedom to learn, freedom from illness, freedom of movement, freedom from violence—are invariably the safest, and the whitest, and the richest. We did this to ourselves: mass incarceration is a result of policies that have grown out of a history of slavery, colonialism, and punishment of the poor. Until we reconcile with these hard truths, by listening to the people most affected by the loss of freedom, we will fall far short of equity. We have a choice: We can permit injustice to remain a growth industry or we can elect to have a more fair, restorative, and effective system. And this isn't an abstract choice—it is one you will make today, and tomorrow, and next week. Ending mass incarceration is imperative for democracy, safety, and freedom. Do you see what is happening in your own community? And are you ready to do your part?

Washington Post Magazine

WINNER—SINGLE-TOPIC ISSUE

In their prefatory note to "Prison," the editors of the Washington Post Magazine *said that "at a time when the subject of prison reform is receiving more attention than it has in decades, this special issue seeks to inform the conversation by focusing on American prisons and the lives of the people inside." It is this purpose—and a sense of shared experience—that suffuses Keri Blakinger's "Building a Better Women's Prison." Now a reporter for the Marshall Project, Blakinger still remembers the humiliation she experienced when she was a prisoner, as "male guards saunter[ed] around our dorms, sometimes peering into cells and cubicles as we changed clothes." The judges who awarded the* Washington Post Magazine *the National Magazine Award for Single-Topic Issue commended the editors not only for the comprehensiveness of the "Prison" issue but also for "overcoming the significant logistical barriers to commissioning and editing work by incarcerated writers and artists."*

Keri Blakinger

Can We Build a Better Women's Prison?

Lauren Johnson walked into the aging Travis County jail just outside Austin on a sunny Friday in July 2018 and steeled herself. Every time she passed through the door and the smell hit her, it all came rushing back: the humiliation of being shackled while nine months pregnant. The pang of seeing her children from behind a glass barrier. How she'd had to improvise with what little she had, crafting makeshift bras out of the disposable mesh underwear the jail provided. Between 2001 and 2010, she'd been in and out of the facility six times. Altogether, she'd spent about three and a half years of her life incarcerated.

Now she was returning to the jail, eight years after the last time she'd been released. But this time, it was to ask the incarcerated women questions that would've been unfathomable to her during her time there: What did they want? How could their experience be improved?

Johnson wore bold prints and her best jewelry that morning, and purposefully doused herself in perfume. She remembered how deprived she'd felt when she was inside; she wanted the women to see and smell the vibrancy of life beyond the razor wire. She sat in a dank jail classroom, surrounded by a dozen or so women wearing dingy uniforms. She told them about her past, then asked about their futures, and the future of the jail that housed them.

"Could we work for deodorant?" one woman asked. Like shampoo, conditioner, and other basic hygiene supplies, deodorant cost money at the commissary, and the women had no income. There were other problems: They weren't given bras or tampons (a possible security concern, according to the facility's medical director). They wanted access to education and to fresh vegetables. They wanted to see the sunlight more. "Basic f——ing needs," Johnson told me.

As a criminal justice outreach coordinator with the American Civil Liberties Union of Texas, Johnson is part of a committee of six women formed by the Travis County Sheriff's Office in early 2018 to plan a new building, one that aims to set a higher standard for a women's jail. The current structure is made up of twelve rundown housing units at the correctional complex in Del Valle, a suburb just over seven miles southeast of the pink capitol dome. The buildings on the suburban campus date to the 1980s and are starting to show signs of age, with peeling paint and recurring electrical and plumbing problems. Officials want better space for programs, and the facility isn't set up to house all the women together. Instead, they're spread out across five buildings, making it harder to foster a sense of community.

These were all problems Johnson remembered well, and she walked out the door feeling relieved that she *could* leave. But she was also brooding about what she'd heard, and how to incorporate the women's wishes into the sheriff's office's reform effort. What would a state-of-the-art women's jail—one focused on rehabilitation and second chances instead of punishment and retribution, with an eye to women's specific needs—look like?

• • •

The American prison system was built with men in mind. The uniforms are made to fit male bodies. About 70 percent of the guards are men. The rules are made to control male social structures and male violence. It's an outgrowth of necessity: even though the female prison population has grown twice as fast as the male prison population over the past thirty-five years, about 90 percent of incarcerated adults are men. Pop culture reflected this invisibility, too, until 2013, when the Netflix show *Orange Is the New Black* brought the struggles of women in prison to millions of viewers.

Men and women have similarly abysmal recidivism rates—five out of six prisoners released from state lockups are arrested again within nine years, according to the Bureau of Justice Statistics—but women are incarcerated for different reasons and bring with them different histories. They're more likely to commit nonviolent crimes, involving theft, fraud, and drugs. They have slightly higher rates of substance abuse than men, are more likely to be the primary caregiver of a young child, and typically earn less money than their male counterparts before getting locked up.

The system does little to account for such differences. Women tend to pose a lower risk of violence, but they're still subject to the same classifications as men—so they're often ranked at a higher security level than necessary, and, as a result, can be blocked from educational and treatment programs. And when violations do happen, they're often nonviolent offenses, like talking back to a guard. Whereas men might alter their clothes to show gang affiliation, women might do the same for style or fit, yet both could result in disciplinary action. On top of that, women often have fewer programming options, such as education, job training and twelve-step programs. This is, in part, a matter of economy of scale. Because there are fewer women in prison, there are fewer rehabilitative and training programs for them.

These are all things I've experienced firsthand. Before I became a reporter, I did time. After nearly a decade addicted to drugs, I got arrested in late 2010 with a Tupperware container full of heroin. When I set foot in a county jail in upstate New York for the first time, I noted the basic inequalities there. Women were offered one volunteer-led twelve-step class per week, while men had four. There wasn't a low-security housing area for women, while there were four for the men. Women couldn't be "trusties," meaning the inmates who served as porters and janitors and got extra privileges; men could.

The cellblock toilets were visible from the hallway, allowing passing male inmates and guards to see as you sat down to use the bathroom or change a pad. After I was transferred to a state prison, I watched male guards saunter around our dorms, sometimes peering into cells and cubicles as we changed clothes. It was a level of gender-specific shame and humiliation I did not know to expect, and at the time, I had no idea how widespread these sorts of problems were. Now, as a journalist focused on criminal justice, it's my job to know and to see the data and patterns behind what I lived. But nine years later, I can still feel a rising blush of embarrassment in my cheeks as I write this.

"The women who come in have different issues from men," Travis County sheriff Sally Hernandez told me. "They have abusive backgrounds; they're mothers; some are pregnant." When she took over the sheriff's office in 2017, Hernandez became responsible for the decaying county jail and found it ill-equipped to deal with women's needs, lacking in everything from on-site women's health services and supplies to vocational programs aligned with women's interests. The $97 million building she and her team are planning will be, she hopes, at the vanguard of a growing focus within criminal justice reform known as gender-responsive corrections: the idea that prisons and jails designed for women will net better outcomes, with more stories that end like Johnson's. "If we're really focused on reentry and on helping people not come back," Hernandez says, "we have to change what we're doing."

Although Travis County aims to set an example with a facility made for and run by women, a shift toward gender responsiveness is already playing out in jails and prisons nationwide. Sometimes the changes are small: supplying underwear and tampons or allowing small dignities like makeup and jewelry. Sometimes they're programmatic shifts, such as offering trauma-informed treatment or women-centered self-help programs. In New York state, a prison nursery program lets a small number of women who give birth while incarcerated keep their babies with them for up to eighteen months. In Connecticut, the state's only women's prison began a small pilot program aimed at reducing recidivism through a focus on dignity and autonomy. The Harris County jail in Houston opened vocational programs to female inmates for the first time this year. Last year, NPR reported on the newly built Iowa Correctional Institution for Women, where officers are being trained to write fewer tickets, allow the women more freedom, and listen to them, rather than barking orders.

California has already enshrined gender responsivity into law, and the state's prison system created a Female Offender Programs and Services Office. The legal shift affected only state lockups, but change has come to some county jails, too, including one now considered a gold standard for gender-responsive corrections: Las Colinas Detention and Reentry Facility, a women's jail in San Diego County.

Las Colinas was a full-scale rebuild, like what Hernandez envisions for the women's building of her jail on the outskirts of Austin. Jail officials in San Diego didn't want just a new building; they wanted something state-of-the-art. They called in Stephanie Covington, codirector of the Center for Gender and Justice, an organization that helps advise jails and prisons on how to address women's needs and treat them better. For two years, she and Barbara Bloom, who codirects the center, reviewed Las Colinas's policies and operations and advised officials on how to improve. They suggested policy tweaks, offered training for the staff, and monitored with regular visits to make sure it was implemented properly. "In a jail setting, you want women to experience what it would be like to live in a community in a healthy way," Covington says. "The majority of women are coming out and living in our communities, and we want people who are good community members."

That's the kind of outcome that Hernandez and her team aspire to. "As we did our research about what good stuff is going on in various places, Las Colinas was one that came to the fore," says Michele Deitch, a senior lecturer in criminal justice policy at the University of Texas at Austin and one of the nation's leading experts on women's prison issues, who's also on the planning committee for the Travis County facility. To see what the new Austin jail might become, I visited Las Colinas.

• • •

It's a warm May morning, and I've just made it through Las Colinas's security doors and stepped out into the Santee sun. "Welcome to Las Colinas!" chirps Jessica Barawed, the facility's reentry supervisor, while motioning across the grassy forty-five-acre campus. She's tall and blond, the spirit of a California postcard greeting me with a sincere warmth that seems out of place at a county jail.

There's a concrete amphitheater for movie nights to my left. Straight ahead, women are landscaping a palm-tree-lined walkway under the gaze of a plaid-shirted horticulture teacher. To my right are dorms with volleyball nets out front and scattered pieces of exercise equipment for the women who've earned their way to the prime housing assignments. And surrounding it all—the lime green palo verde trees, the pink-painted utility covers, and the 800 women who live here—is a brick wall. The five-year-old, $240 million facility is still a jail, but no razor wire is in sight.

More than 12,000 women pass through here every year. Although the facility can hold nearly 1,300, the average daily population typically hovers around two-thirds that, including inmates from maximum security all the way down to the "incentive-based housing" that's akin to an honors dorm. Most of the twenty-four housing units rely on a direct supervision model, meaning that the officers are stationed in the women's housing areas instead of separated behind a glass bubble. The idea is that keeping the guards closer will foster better communication with the women they watch and maybe help prevent conflicts.

Women who have good behavior and a low-enough security level can attend a book club run by a group of female judges; a six-week trauma class; anger-management programs; a handful of college courses; and vocational programs that offer certificates in culinary arts, sewing, landscaping and gardening. (The squash, tomatoes, cucumbers, and peppers they grow in the facility's garden are sold at a farmers market for officers.) There's job-readiness training and a worker on site to act as a liaison with the county's Child Welfare Services. There's yoga every Wednesday, theater programs, Thursday meditation classes, soda machines in the dorms, and a gourmet-coffee cart—which offers a vocational training certificate for incarcerated workers—available twice a week.

Capt. James Madsen has been with the sheriff's office for twenty-six years and is now Las Colinas's top administrator. He remembers when the jail did little more than warehouse people. It offered twelve-step programs, but some officials wanted something that felt more like a college campus and less like a jail. Years of tough reports from inspections helped grease the skids and push forward change. "There was some resistance initially," Madsen says. "But these folks are going to get out of jail. Do we want people who are still broken coming out into our communities, or do we want to get them better tools? Why can't we become part of the solution, instead of just keeping things status quo?" After the county built the new facility, assaults inside went down about 50 percent in the first year, he says, adding: "The inmates act differently because we treat them differently."

To Madsen, the changes have become the new way of life at Las Colinas, but to me, they were almost incomprehensible. I'd never seen a jail like it. As a reporter, I'd done my research and knew what to expect when I arrived on campus; as a former prisoner, I was stunned. If I'd been asked to design a jail, a coffee cart and a farmers market never would have occurred to me—they just weren't on my radar. But other features felt obvious, and I wondered why they couldn't be standard for prisons across the board. At Las Colinas, the women have access to unlimited feminine hygiene supplies, including tampons. Unlike at some facilities, they aren't routinely strip-searched when they walk in the door. The visiting area has a playroom for kids.

On a basic level, some of these shifts are just about treating inmates more humanely and could help usher in changes for inmates of all genders, Covington says. "Here's what those of us who have focused on women's services have said for years: If we can get it right for women, we can then turn and get it better for men," she says. "If you only focus on men, it never seems to get better for women."

This kind of programming isn't cheap: Housing a woman at Las Colinas costs about $240 per day, between $35 and $115 more than at any of the county's six jails for men. And it's not available to every inmate. Only one-quarter of the women there can access most of the privileges. For most inmates—those who aren't in the special dorms for intensive programs or inmate workers—life at Las Colinas is not that different than in a regular jail. The women in the general population units spend much of the day in their cells, typically venturing off the unit only to go to the mess hall, appointments, or visitation.

Tabatha Laumer remembers the old Las Colinas, the one before the coffee cart and gardening classes. Her first stay was almost twenty years ago, when she was seventeen. She was in and out in eight hours and vowed never to return. But a week later, she did. And then she was back again, and again. Sometimes it was just a few hours at a time, when she got picked up for being under the influence. Sometimes it was a couple of weeks for theft. One time, it was six months.

Now she's in jail for the twenty-ninth time, Laumer told me when we met. Twirling wisps of dusty blond hair poking out from behind her ears, she rattles off her litany of past charges like a laundry list of regret: stealing, possession, transporting across the border.

When Laumer was growing up in Oceanside, Calif., her mother worked multiple jobs, so Laumer spent a lot of time with other family members—including a cousin who introduced her to drugs at age eight or nine. "I didn't realize it was wrong," she says. She still did her homework and went to band practice, but she also started smoking pot and took part in crimes for which she never got caught. Over time, it all escalated: there were blurry nights, hard drugs, weeks she wishes she didn't remember, gangs, robberies, and rape.

In between trips to jail, Laumer had bouts of sobriety and held down a handful of jobs: deli manager, 7-Eleven clerk, door-to-door saleswoman. She had two sons, now fourteen and eighteen. She'd start to turn things around and eventually slip up again. At one point, she began running drugs across the Mexican border, not even sure what was in the cars she drove in exchange for a few hundred bucks or a small stash of drugs. When feds caught her at the border in May 2018, they found fourteen kilograms of methamphetamine in the trunk where the tire jack should have been. Once again, Laumer was on her way to Las Colinas.

The last time she was here, Las Colinas was a cluster of dark, decaying buildings with rotting floors. There were no college courses or Wednesday-night yoga sessions, and limited vocational programs. "This is a really nice facility compared to the old one," she says. "You've got this huge team of counselors, and they offer college, therapy, programs."

After she arrived last year, Laumer realized she wanted to change her life. It wasn't just because of the shift in thinking at Las Colinas, although that certainly helped. At the old Las Colinas, inmates had to keep their hands in their pockets while they walked and turn to the side if an officer passed. Those are no longer rules, she says: "Not having to put your head down every time someone walks by—it makes us feel like we're worthy. Not just another number."

This time around, Laumer earned a slew of certificates, got A's in college classes, and performed in a San Diego theater company's renditions of *A Midsummer Night's Dream* and *Romeo and Juliet*. Somewhere during it all, she realized she'd spent years letting her life tick away. "I'm too old for this," she says. "I'm thirty-seven and I got nothing. But I'm not dead yet."

• • •

Trauma is the common denominator underlying the life experience of the vast majority of female inmates, and trauma-informed care is a key piece of the gender-responsive approach. More than half of female prisoners are survivors of physical or sexual violence; 73 percent of female state inmates and 61 percent of female federal inmates have mental health problems. (Many men in prison have experienced trauma, too, but incarcerated women are more likely to have been through trauma than their male counterparts.) Corrections officials are starting to recognize this, but intensive programs that treat trauma are not nearly common enough.

Trauma-informed care often includes cognitive-behavioral therapy, a type of counseling that challenges negative thoughts and the behaviors they lead to. But the approach is more than just a programmatic shift, Deitch says. Trauma-informed care "is a mindset that infuses everything about how a jail or prison operates, as well as the programs offered in the facilities," she says. "It's about staff recognizing that the vast majority of women in custody have extensive histories of trauma, and that this history affects the women's behavior, thoughts and bodies. It's about training staff on communication methods and disciplinary approaches that are most effective with women, given this history. It's about helping women learn to self-regulate their emotional responses and defuse tense situations and helping them become more resilient."

In the hundred-page report that Deitch's committee created for the Travis County rebuild, trauma-informed treatment is mentioned more than three dozen times. "Women that are coming into the jail have been hurt and traumatized and don't see value in themselves, don't see value in others, and they stay in a vicious cycle," Hernandez told me. "You have to address their trauma so you can redirect them and help them get back into society effectively."

The gender-responsive approach is still gathering steam in the criminal justice world, so there's not much research to support its efficacy. A 2016 meta-analysis in the journal *Criminal Justice and Behavior* looked at a few dozen existing studies and cited research that gender-responsive programs are at least as successful as gender-neutral interventions and more successful for women whose past criminal behaviors were specifically linked to gendered issues. But even if gender-responsive interventions don't directly reduce recidivism, Deitch says, they're still a vital step toward a more humane corrections system. And lower recidivism rates are not the only marker of success. "The first goal is to do no harm," she says. "Hopefully, we end up with better results. But that doesn't have to be our first objective."

Hernandez and her team have advocated tirelessly for the new Austin facility, along with the budget to implement it, and it's wending its way through the approval process. If everything comes out as the committee hopes, the new jail won't have bolted-down furniture, clanging doors, metal bars or congregate showers.

"If a particular feature is not something that most people living outside a jail setting routinely experience in their daily lives," the report says, "it should raise serious questions about whether it is essential in this facility." They plan to prioritize privacy, with single rooms where possible (no bunk beds, reads the report, because "adults do not sleep in bunk beds"). The toilets should have lids, and the women should have access to laundry areas. They've planned for a breast-feeding room, natural light, no long-term segregation, and recreation areas with yoga mats and bicycles.

From the outset, the most outspoken opponents have not been tight-pursed elected officials, but rather criminal justice reform advocates and activist community members. A jail is a jail, and they didn't want any new ones. "Some of those buildings are old and need repair, and I get that piece," says Annette Price, interim codirector of GrassRoots Leadership in Austin, who served prison time in Illinois. "But to me, more jails and prisons is not the answer." She'd prefer to see more diversion programs to keep people out of jail, she says. Like Lauren Johnson, Price was part of the jail advisory committee; she knows incarcerated women often aren't able to receive the programming, medical care, and treatment they need. "But building a jail is not going to solve that."

Johnson understands those misgivings, even if the changes themselves are positive. As someone who spends her life fighting mass incarceration, she finds it hard to stomach the idea of supporting a new jail, no matter how bad the current one is. "Ultimately, I'd like to see us not incarcerating so many people," she says. "But [given] the amount of trauma most of these women have encountered in their lives, having something that is built to their needs is so important. People don't transform their lives when they're being dehumanized."

When you're stuck in the system, it can be hard to envision anything better—especially if you don't think you deserve it. A harsh system and a history of trauma can make it easy to believe you don't, just like the women Johnson talked to when she visited on that hot July day, who asked for the smallest of changes. I saw those same tensions playing out at Las Colinas, too. As I sat in the mess hall with the inmate workers during a lunch break, they griped a little about the bad conditions and shared their doubts about the good ones. So much freedom is "weird," said twenty-eight-year-old Isabel Mendoza. "It creeps me out."

If I hadn't done time, this probably would surprise me. But it's the sort of self-flagellating catchphrase of penitence my fellow inmates and I would repeat. "This isn't the Hilton," we'd say. "If you don't like the accommodations, don't make the reservations." We knew we shouldn't have to beg for tampons or offer sexual favors—as I saw women do when I was locked up—for more toilet paper. But many of us suffered from a kind of internalized oppression: No matter what we thought about self-worth and second chances, it seemed that, on some level, a lot of us didn't really believe we deserved to be treated decently. Being yelled at, degraded and told we'd lost the right to expect more from life was what so many of us thought jail had to be.

As I walked the grounds at Las Colinas, I wondered if its focus on women could make a lasting difference. There are so many other factors that keep people out of jail: privileges like stable housing, money, family support. But being surrounded by people invested in our futures—college teachers, counselors, mentors—could have helped some of us. The sheer number of times some of my friends bounced in and out of jails and prisons seemed testament enough to the fact that being treated as something less than a human certainly wasn't working. I shared these thoughts with Laumer. "As nice as it is, I don't *want* to come back," she said. "Maybe I've grown up a little bit."

The women in Laumer's dorm were sitting in front of the building, playing cards on a picnic table. Laumer was running the show, dealing out a hand of spades—the card game of choice in jails everywhere. It was barely eight a.m. and the cluster at the table was positively giddy, joking about making a Las Colinas–themed hip-hop album as Drake played on a radio in the background.

I knew I was seeing only a small slice of these women's lives, but Laumer and her friends didn't seem quite as miserable as the women I saw in so many other corrections facilities. "Don't count your days," they say, riffing on a quote usually attributed to Muhammad Ali. "Make your days count." No one said that when I did time. Maybe it was just a show or a fleeting, out-of-character moment. But as I watched them howl an out-of-key rendition of "We Are the Champions," I hoped so much that it was all real.

Fortune

FINALIST—REPORTING

The vaccine Dengvaxia had been expected to be a public health triumph and a financial bonanza for its manufacturer, the French pharmaceutical giant Sanofi—until the drug was blamed, perhaps mistakenly, for the deaths of 148 children in the Philippines. "What happened to Dengvaxia could happen to any imperfect medical innovation in the age of social media," writes Erika Fry in "Epidemic of Fear, "for here, in the emotional gyre of politics, anxiety, and misinformation, the rational questions and doubts of science can quickly be branded as crimes and conspiracies." Fry, said the judges, "deftly explains both complex science and social contagion, unpacking an issue—fear of vaccines—that is one of the most pressing of our day." A graduate of Dartmouth College and the Columbia School of Journalism, Fry worked as an investigative reporter at the Bangkok Post *before joining* Fortune *in 2012. She is now a senior writer at the magazine.*

Erika Fry

Epidemic of Fear

The scene is quiet, eerily so. A camera moves over a motionless child—dressed in church clothes, laid out on a metal table—and then pans over a huddle of grieving family members. There is another video just like it, and another, and another—an entire series that, collectively, offers a startling amount of footage showing children lying dead in a morgue in the Philippines.

Two stoic-looking women figure prominently in the videos. One of them, Annie Gabito, has a stern and commanding presence. The other, Persida Acosta, is typically at the center of the scene. Acosta, the chief public attorney of the Philippines, offers a word or hand to the grief-stricken family and, in one instance, with a look of serious inquiry prods the child's lifeless body.

Broadcast live on Facebook over the past two years, the videos have together been viewed millions of times. They were filmed after a forensic team assembled by the public attorney's office—rather than by the government's regular medical examiners—conducted autopsies of the children as part of its investigation into the deaths of 148 children.

Citing these autopsy results, Acosta and the family members all point to the same culprit for the children's deaths: Dengvaxia, made by French pharmaceutical giant Sanofi, the first and only vaccine approved to protect against the dengue virus, which infects an estimated 390 million people around the world each year.

I met the parents of eighteen of these children this July. They had come from all over the chaotic, gridlocked megacity of Manila one Saturday to the modest two-story home of Gabito, who works unpaid for a Filipino nonprofit called Volunteers Against Crime and Corruption and who now spends much of her time focusing on the families of the 148 dead children she calls the "Dengvaxia Victims."

While Gabito made lunch, I sat at a table in the upstairs kitchen as parents filed up, one by one, to share their stories. They each wore a T-shirt with a picture of their deceased child framed by name and the Dengvaxia Victim number assigned to them by Gabito's organization. Many of them came with their child's Dengvaxia card, documenting the dates of vaccination and a sleeve or two of photographs, before-and-after-inoculation pictures that showed their kids healthy (fourth-grade graduation, family photos, a selfie with a pet cat) and sick (swollen body parts or tethered to a hospital bed and an IV drip). A few volunteered photos from their child's autopsy, an image of a brain or internal organs, which they said showed the telltale signs of Dengvaxia's horrific effects.

Sumachen Dominguez, a lead organizer of the group, told me, "Nobody is listening to our anguish."

And there is some truth to that now. Last year, the story of the Dengvaxia Victims was the stuff of government hearings and wall-to-wall TV coverage—a made-for-the-movies narrative about dozens upon dozens of schoolkids dying, like sacrificial guinea pigs, as the Philippine government prematurely pushed its dengue immunization drive. There was even a fitting corporate villain—a foreign pharmaceutical giant, with $42 billion in annual revenue, that appeared to confess that its vaccine had a serious flaw.

But while the Philippine news media and most of the politicians involved have moved on, the Dengvaxia controversy continues to have a profound and lasting impact. A handful of Sanofi executives and employees have been charged with "reckless imprudence resulting in homicide," as have numerous Filipino government health officers and a couple of scientific researchers, for their alleged roles in the Dengvaxia immunization program. Those trials are planned for next year.

For Sanofi, it has been devastating financially as well. Right up through Dengvaxia's 2016 launch, the Paris-based company, one of the premier vaccine makers in the world, had projected booming sales and a major win in terms of global goodwill. It is struggling to sell Dengvaxia anywhere now—despite its regulatory approval in the United States, the EU, and an additional twenty countries—and the vaccine's inclusion on the World Health Organization's Essential Medicines List. (Sanofi took a $186 million write-down on Dengvaxia in 2017, but the total loss—counting everything the company spent on development and infrastructure, plus vanishing sales and damage to its reputation—is likely several times that.)

Much worse is the damage that has been done to public confidence in vaccines: In the Philippines, where immunization coverage was already dangerously low, the Dengvaxia scare caused vaccination rates to fall even further, opening the door to infectious diseases once believed to be on the wane. Over the past two years, there have been new outbreaks of measles and polio. When it comes to combating dengue itself—a scourge that can be bone-crushingly painful for some and deadly for others, and which in recent decades has emerged as the world's fastest-spreading and most common mosquito-borne illness—the opportunity cost has been grave as well.

Which brings up the first of this tale's tragic, even Shakespearean twists: the fact that the Dengvaxia controversy may well bury forever a vaccine that actually works—not for everyone but for huge swaths of populations in countries where dengue is an urgent and growing public health problem. Indeed, if the vaccine were an active part of global health campaigns, it would likely save many lives annually. That's plain to see, given that devastating dengue outbreaks have tested governments this year from Pakistan to Honduras to, yes, the Philippines.

Twist number two is this: there is a good chance that Dengvaxia didn't cause the tragic deaths of those 148 children in the Facebook videos.

A Fiasco Foretold

Innocuously titled "Sanofi updates information on dengue vaccine," the press release went out to the world, in both French and English, at 11:36 a.m. Eastern Time on November 29, 2017. In the Philippines, the country where the most doses of the world's first dengue vaccine, Dengvaxia, had been administered, it was just after midnight on November 30.

Twenty months earlier, the Philippines had proudly been the first country to launch a public immunization program involving Sanofi's vaccine, boldly taking aim at a disease that perennially caused agony for its citizens and taxed its overburdened health care system.

Dengvaxia, which the Filipino government gave to roughly 890,000 children, had been feted globally as a public health triumph. The development of Sanofi's vaccine was as complicated and technically challenging as they come. And it was the culmination of a broader effort that spanned decades and took billions of public and private dollars. Plus, in an admirably altruistic inversion of the Big Pharma playbook, the vaccine was being delivered first not to the rich Western countries that could pay the most but to a poorer one that needed it more. It was a story to celebrate.

But here in Sanofi's press release, buried in the middle of a dense paragraph of highly technical language, was a sentence that would surely give anyone in the Philippines pause:

"For those not previously infected by dengue virus, however, the analysis found that in the longer term, more cases of severe disease could occur following vaccination upon a subsequent dengue infection." In other words, there were some people who wouldn't be protected from dengue by Dengvaxia. In fact, the opposite: It put them at risk for getting sicker.

The statement, which Sanofi had sweated over and planned around for days, lacked context, local or otherwise. It didn't offer probabilities or degrees of risk; it didn't explain what "severe dengue" meant or give people in the Philippines or Brazil, where another mass immunization drive was underway, or in any of the other fifteen countries where Dengvaxia was licensed, any clue how worried they should be. It just recommended that people who had never previously had dengue not get the vaccine.

That was the moment the Dengvaxia fiasco began. It was also a fiasco foretold. While the vaccine had many boosters, a handful of scientists saw problems ahead. The most vocal of the critics was one of Sanofi's own consultants, who warned the world that the vaccine would work—but only with a critical asterisk that health officials and the public needed to understand. Which meant the news that jolted the Philippines into a spiraling calamity on November 30 was, among researchers, the subject of ongoing study and a much-discussed possibility.

"It seemed like a surprise, though it wasn't a surprise," says In-Kyu Yoon, a senior adviser for the International Vaccine Institute.

"The communication around this was difficult," says Gundo Weiler, a director with the World Health Organization (WHO) based in Manila. The intricacies of vaccine science and dengue, especially in an environment of fear, he adds, "are not so easy to understand—that was the problem of the whole situation."

Eric Domingo, who serves as undersecretary for the Department of Health of the Philippines, sums up the Dengvaxia tale best of all: "It just turned into this gigantic monster," he tells *Fortune*. But what's truly frightening is how quickly this monster formed and how easily. What happened to Dengvaxia could happen to any imperfect medical innovation in the age of social media—for here, in the emotional gyre of politics, anxiety, and misinformation, the rational questions and doubts of science can quickly be branded as crimes and conspiracies.

Nothing about the development or administration of Dengvaxia was intentionally reckless, it should be said—though its story does contain elements of hubris, blind optimism, and questionable haste.

That was clear from the start, when Chris Viehbacher became CEO of Sanofi in December 2008. Almost right away, he greenlit the building of a $398 million plant to produce Dengvaxia outside Lyon, France. The company was more than a decade into its dengue clinical development program, but this was a next-level, we're-in-it-to-win-it commitment. Or gamble, perhaps. At the time, the vaccine candidate was still in clinical trials and years from reaching the market. There was a decent chance it could fail outright—but then, the potential was enormous. On an earnings call in 2010, Viehbacher told analysts that the drug "promises to be potentially the biggest vaccine we've ever sold."

Preventing dengue, which epidemiologists call a "neglected tropical disease," was an enormous unmet need. There was no drug to prevent, treat, or cure the illness. And in the past half-century, as the virus swept from Southeast Asia to 128 countries, or roughly half the globe, cases had increased thirty-fold.

Dengue is carried by the female *Aedes aegypti* mosquito, a resilient, disease-spreading pest—it also efficiently transmits yellow fever, chikungunya, and Zika, among other viruses—that has thrived in the modern, globalized world. The flying menace moves around on cargo ships and breeds in water that collects in, say, plastic waste and used tires. "It's beautifully adapted to densely populated urban environments," says Jeremy Farrar, director of the Wellcome Trust, a UK-based charity focused on global health.

Sanofi executives expected that with a warming climate, the dengue-carrying mosquito's reach would expand, too, spreading the miserable disease.

Once commonly called breakbone fever, dengue is painful to endure. (The origin of the name "dengue" is not certain but is thought by some to come from the Swahili phrase *ka-dinga pepo*, meaning a cramplike seizure caused by an evil spirit.) Patients suffer debilitating spells of headaches, fever, and severe joint pain that can send them to the hospital with symptoms that can linger for two weeks. In the worst cases, patients experience "plasma leakage," a life-threatening process in which the protein-rich fluid of the blood seeps out of vessels and into surrounding tissues.

Most cases of dengue are not so severe (the majority are asymptomatic), but up to 5 percent of them are—resulting in patients who may in frighteningly abrupt fashion go into shock or suffer hemorrhagic fever that can lead to death.

Experts contend no one should die of dengue. There's a way to manage cases so that even the most severely ill recover, but that requires early detection and involves close monitoring and maintenance of a patient's fluid levels over a period of days. That's not easy for resource-strapped health systems, especially during outbreaks when dengue patients pile up in hospital wards. For that reason, dengue kills about 20,000 people a year.

Given all that, Sanofi expected governments, not to mention donors like the Gates Foundation and GAVI, an international vaccine alliance, to happily shell out dollars to prevent the disease. But the potential market was even bigger than that. Viehbacher envisioned that Dengvaxia could one day be a vaccine for everyone—not just for the people who live in dengue-endemic countries but also for those in rich, Western countries who travel to them.

That was exactly the sort of game-changing product Sanofi's new CEO needed in order to transform the storied but doddering French pharmaceutical firm. Three of Sanofi's top-selling drugs were soon to lose patent protection—and with them, a good chunk of the company's revenues.

Viehbacher himself symbolized change. The German-born Canadian was the first non-Frenchman to helm the company (which this year ranked number 288 on the Fortune Global 500), and many hoped he'd rev up Sanofi's slow-moving and rigidly hierarchical culture. (Viehbacher, who did not respond to requests for comment on this story, was ousted in 2014.)

Sanofi had grown into one of the world's largest pharmaceutical firms through acquisitions. But it traces its history back to the days of Louis Pasteur, the renowned French scientist who, among other things, invented the rabies and anthrax vaccines. He founded the Pasteur Institute, the respected biomedical research institute—part of which became Sanofi Pasteur, Sanofi's $6-billion-in-revenue Lyon-based vaccine business. Today Sanofi Pasteur produces much of the world's supply of inoculations against flu, polio, and meningitis. Viehbacher saw huge potential in the business.

Backed by Viehbacher, the dengue vaccine became a marquee project for the company, one that earned ink in Sanofi's annual reports and regular mentions on earnings calls as the sort of innovative, globally relevant product that could power the company's growth.

Sanofi had to move quickly though. A number of other organizations had their own dengue vaccines in the works.

Being first and fast to this potentially multibillion dollar market would be critical, and Sanofi tried to establish an edge by wringing excess time from the clinical and commercial development processes. Its trials ran on a compressed schedule, with

Dengvaxia's expensive Phase III studies beginning before Phase IIb had ended. The company also ramped up manufacturing years in advance so that it would have a ready supply when the vaccine was eventually approved.

Determined to do everything possible to ensure the vaccine would become a commercial success, Sanofi created a new internal structure, the Lyon-based Dengue Company, that was designed to be an agile and all-encompassing "team of teams." Every function—regulatory, marketing, distribution—was represented in the unit to more quickly coordinate work.

In May 2013, Viehbacher painted a rosy picture: "We've got ourselves a robust dengue vaccine," he told analysts. He predicted the company would be producing 100 million doses annually by 2015. "This is a major not only public health issue but I think a commercial opportunity," he said. "This affects half the world's population."

Sanofi's optimism, though, wasn't fully supported by the drug's test results: The company had already begun its two Phase III trials when the results from the Phase IIb trial came in. They were disappointing: Tested on 4,000 children in Thailand, the vaccine had reduced dengue infections in kids by just 30 percent in the two-year follow-up period. In short, the vaccine had fallen far short of expectations.

But the Phase III results—based on two studies of 31,000 children in ten countries—were more promising. Dengvaxia didn't work perfectly. But Sanofi and the scientific community believed they had a vaccine that could make a difference against dengue.

Tackling a Year-Round Killer

"Dengue is really, really difficult," says Stephen J. Thomas, a professor at SUNY Upstate Medical University who started studying the virus as a doctor with the U.S. Army a couple of decades ago. Questions that were raised about the virus in the early 1950s remain unanswered today. "Half of the world lives at daily risk of being infected with dengue," says Thomas, "but we don't know why some people get sick and some people don't. We don't know why some people get very sick and some don't. A lot of the questions that have plagued dengue researchers are the exact questions that have been so problematic to vaccine developers." There's not an animal model that comprehensively mimics the disease in humans, explains Thomas, who has been a paid adviser to numerous dengue vaccine developers, including Sanofi.

What we do know about dengue is that it's insidiously complicated. Its basic epidemiology reads like a Mensa logic problem.

Dengue virus comes in four similar but distinct varieties, known as Dengue serotypes 1 through 4. When individuals get a first dengue infection, they develop lifelong immunity from the infecting strain. For a brief period of time, they also enjoy protection from the other three. But that cross-protection wears off—after a period of anywhere from two months to two years—and the individual becomes vulnerable to getting more severely ill on a second infection.

That's why it's the second infection that health officials worry about. People tend to get only mildly sick or not sick at all after their first dengue infection, and for some reason, they hardly ever get sick on their third or fourth. The worst, life-threatening cases of dengue, the ones with plasma leakage that can lead to hemorrhagic fever or shock, almost always result from a second exposure.

To make matters more complicated, all four serotypes are constantly comingling in most dengue-endemic countries, meaning the chances are higher for a second infection to occur. (So is the likelihood of a genetic mutation, which could produce a more virulent virus.) That wasn't the case in most places even a couple of decades ago, and it helps explain why the number of dengue cases has risen so dramatically. Given these facts, virologists decided that the best strategy for beating dengue, along with mosquito control, was to develop a tetravalent vaccine—one that provided balanced protection, in the form of neutralizing antibodies, against all four serotypes.

That's what Sanofi was going for in Dengvaxia.

The global health and dengue research communities were, for all the right reasons, rooting for it. For decades, they had watched the virus creep around the world; they had seen old-school methods of mosquito control fail; they had seen the body count grow. The Dengue Vaccine Initiative (DVI), a collaboration of scientists, had worked to identify clinical trial sites and develop surveillance programs for viral outbreaks. Any vaccine, the DVI estimated, would require up to an eye-popping 3.5 billion doses in the first five years to meet demand. The WHO, meanwhile, wrote guidelines on how to design a dengue vaccine trial. And together the WHO and DVI hosted regulators from seven dengue-prone countries (the Philippines among them) for a technical consultation on the Dengvaxia data.

When Thomas Triomphe arrived as Sanofi Pasteur's new head of Asia-Pacific in January 2015, one of his top concerns about Dengvaxia was simple: Would there be enough? His territory was vast, nineteen countries from India to Australia, and just about every one of them was a potential market for the company's new dengue vaccine.

The Philippines was an obvious place to launch the vaccine. The virus had become a year-round killer there and was an estimated $345 million annual drag on the economy. That year, 2015, was an especially costly one, with 200,000 reported cases of the disease and 600 deaths. And Filipinos were frustrated that the government seemed to do little to stop it—with each epidemic "viewed by the public as a symbol of how the government is really taking care of its people," says Julius Lecciones, the executive director of the Philippine Children's Medical Center, which gets the country's most severe cases involving children. Beyond warning the public to stay vigilant, however, there wasn't a lot the government could do. Local officials could make a show of spraying against mosquitoes, but that was merely "political fogging," as some dengue experts call it.

As 2015 came to a close, the Filipino government saw its chance to act. There were unused funds in the budget that needed to be spent by year's end. Some $70 million was quickly allocated for Dengvaxia in December. That same month, the Philippines joined Brazil and Mexico in approving the drug.

The government moved fast to implement its mass vaccination program—a pilot targeting nine-year-olds in three regions of the Philippines. The nation's school-based dengue immunization effort began on April 4, 2016, the first day of summer break.

That struck some as odd timing. But the campaign's launch at a grade school in Manila drew a large crowd and some VIP attendees. The president of Sanofi Pasteur's Dengue Company, Guillaume LeRoy, was there as was Janette Garin, then the Philippine's health secretary and a trained physician, who jabbed one of the first little arms with an inaugural syringe. Later that day, Garin, who is now a congresswoman, showed up at another launch event in a province outside Manila, this time with then-president Benigno Aquino III. They wore yellow shirts, the color of the Liberal Party, and before a large, cheering crowd, Garin administered a shot, and Aquino gave a speech. The optics led some to other questions about timing: A general election was a month away. Aquino had served his maximum term and was not up for reelection, but some read the staging as a campaign event—the Liberal Party saving the nation from a miserable disease.

"You've got to monitor this closely"

• • •

Though Dengvaxia was now on the market in the Philippines, a debate continued among researchers about the effectiveness of the vaccine and how it should be administered.

In July 2015, a study had been published in the *New England Journal of Medicine* that caused dengue experts to reconsider the results of Dengvaxia's clinical trials. Drawing on three years of follow-up data from Phase IIb and III trials, the analysis validated much of Sanofi's optimism. But it also raised a red flag.

The banner headline: The vaccine worked—not for everyone, but for many. It appeared to work to some degree against all four strains of dengue (though more effectively against types 3 and 4), and it seemed to work both in children who had previously been infected with dengue and those who had not (though poorly in the latter).

Among children ages two to sixteen, there was a 60 percent reduction in dengue cases during the first twenty-five months following vaccination. That rate was higher—nearly 66 percent—for children age nine and above. Incidents of hospitalization and cases of severe dengue were significantly reduced in the vaccinated population, though the data did indicate a curious, if clear, trend—one, moreover, that only emerged in the third year of the study: very young kids who had been vaccinated and did get dengue were more likely to be hospitalized.

Children ages two to five who received Dengvaxia in the company's Phase III trial were, in fact, more than seven times as likely to be hospitalized for dengue as those who had not. The overall numbers were small: 19 children of the 3,598, or 0.6 percent of kids age two through eight who were vaccinated, were hospitalized owing to dengue versus 0.4% in the control population. The data did not show the same risk for vaccinated children ages nine and above, however.

The researchers didn't have definitive conclusions to explain the trend, but they posited a few theories that related to age (younger children were not as physically and immunologically robust) and serostatus—that is, whether or not the child had suffered a previous dengue infection. In the best-case scenario, Sanofi would have marketed the vaccine to kids as young as age two. The data analysis made that impossible. From now on, only children as old as nine would be given the drug.

When Scott Halstead read the *New England Journal* report in the summer of 2015, he says, he nearly fell off his chair. Halstead, now eighty-nine, is a towering figure in the dengue research community. He started studying the virus in 1957, when he was a young army doctor stationed in Asia. His career coincided with dengue's flourishing, and one way or another, he's had a hand in many of the foundational and pivotal findings in the field.

It was Halstead who opened Asia's first dengue laboratory. He was in Bangkok (in the 1960s) to help develop the standards of dengue diagnosis and case management. He was in a lab in New Haven (in the 1970s) to study the pathogenesis of dengue infections in monkeys. And he was in Cuba (in the 1980s) to help study the first-ever dengue hemorrhagic fever epidemic in the Americas, and in Geneva (in the 1990s) to help establish the WHO's dengue case classification system that Sanofi used in its Dengvaxia trials. Halstead founded the Pediatric Dengue Vaccine Initiative (later, DVI), an organization that received $55 million in Gates Foundation funding in 2003.

But perhaps Halstead's signature if controversial contribution is "antibody-dependent enhancement," the theory he developed in the 1970s—based in part from his study of dengue in monkeys—that aims to explain why people typically get more sick the second time they get dengue.

Halstead had been enlisted by Sanofi as a consultant on Dengvaxia. He says he flew to Paris for meetings a few times but found them pointless: "We never discussed anything!" Still, he says, he didn't anticipate problems with the vaccine. Halstead believed Dengvaxia had gotten around the problem of antibody-dependent enhancement by exposing people to all four strains at once. But as he pored over the new data in the *New England Journal* study about higher hospitalization rates of younger vaccinees, he had a sinking feeling. Halstead says he knew instantly that he had been wrong. He was sure this was his old theory in action: For those who hadn't been exposed to the virus, the vaccine acted like a first dengue infection, priming them for a potentially more severe infection when they later got dengue from a mosquito bite.

In February 2016, two months before the Philippines launched its school-based Dengvaxia program, Halstead and a former colleague published an article in the medical journal *Vaccine* warning that people not previously exposed to dengue would be at risk of a more severe case later if vaccinated. (He's since written more than a dozen papers outlining issues related to Dengvaxia.)

Halstead's argument didn't sway Sanofi, which challenged it in a published response. But it did get the attention of the Strategic Advisory Group of Experts (SAGE), the WHO-affiliated committee that makes recommendations to the international community on vaccine use.

SAGE's pronouncements carry weight. While governments make their own decisions about whether to approve a drug or implement it in a national scheme, many take their cues from SAGE, as does the all-important vaccine buyer, GAVI. Because Dengvaxia was geared toward lower-income countries, SAGE felt even greater responsibility to get this one right.

"When we first saw the [trial] results, we were all a bit disappointed," says Terry Nolan, who cochaired the SAGE Working Group (he is now a consultant for Sanofi). "It had definite effectiveness, but it was modest." Beyond that, though, was the question concerning the children who had gotten more severe infections. Was this age-related and limited to younger kids? Or did it have something to do with serostatus, as experts like Halstead vociferously argued, and so older children were also at risk?

In the end, the committee hedged its bets: SAGE's experts relied on models that assumed Dengvaxia was both less effective and more likely to cause severe disease in kids who'd never been exposed to a dengue infection. So SAGE recommended that the vaccine be used in places where infection rates of dengue in children were 70 percent or higher. But Dengvaxia should not be administered anyplace where less than half the population had been exposed to dengue. (The modeling projected vaccination of early adolescents would yield a 10 percent to 30 percent reduction in dengue hospitalizations over thirty years.) The goal was to apply the vaccine where its benefits would outweigh any possible risk involved—a challenge given the lack of quality data about infection rates.

Still, says Nolan, "we were very nervous about it, and we were very cautious in our initial recommendation and saying, 'Look, you've got to monitor this closely.'"

Cautious or not, though, the recommendation was interpreted as an endorsement of the Filipino government's Dengvaxia program. The vast majority of children in the Philippines have experienced at least one dengue infection by age nine, making them great candidates for the vaccine.

Halstead sniffs at the WHO committee's conclusion. ("They sort of gave Sanofi the green light," he says.) But he spreads some blame as well to the international dengue research community—the one he practically nursed from birth—and Sanofi especially for failing to acknowledge Dengvaxia's flaws sooner and for not doing enough to help the Philippines manage the vaccine scare and its aftermath. "It wasn't purposeful, it wasn't done with any malice," he says, "but we shouldn't just stand by and say, 'Gosh, isn't this too bad?'"

#DenGate Goes Viral

It was 1:20 a.m. when Antonio Dans, a professor at the University of the Philippines' College of Medicine, saw Sanofi's November 29, 2017, press release. He read the statement and promptly punched out a Facebook post, tagging twenty-five colleagues:

> Read this news alert from Sanofi. =(
>
> Our heart bleeds for more than 600,000 Filipino children who received dengue vaccine without assessment for prior infection.
>
> Sanofi, WHO, DOH—what happens to them now???

The post was soon shared more than a thousand times, and in the wee hours of November 30 it generated a number of comments and red-faced emojis. He and his wife, Leonila, who also teaches at UP, started a separate Facebook page, "Health Care Geeks," to handle Dengvaxia-related questions and commentary a few weeks later.

Many in the Filipino scientific community—including some of Sanofi's local leaders—point to the Danses' dramatic social media post as one of the Dengvaxia saga's igniting sparks. It pinged around the social media feeds of the Filipino medical community.

The couple were already highly visible and controversial critics of the country's Dengvaxia program and had been raising questions about the Sanofi vaccine even before the country's immunization drive began. A number of medical colleagues now refer to them as "antivaxxers."

The Danses, both of whom are clinical epidemiologists, physicians, and public health advocates, got concerned after reading about the soon-to-launch immunization program in the newspaper. They then turned to the analysis of the dengue vaccine trials in the *New England Journal of Medicine.* Worried the drug might cause harm to some children, the couple quickly dispatched a four-page letter, signed by eleven peers, to the Philippines' health secretary, Garin. In it, they also noted that the duration of the vaccine's protective benefit was unknown. And they argued that a three-dose vaccine would be hard to implement and that the supply of the vaccine for 1 million children—at a cost of $70 million, greater than the budget for all other vaccines in the public program combined—was very expensive.

The couple encouraged the government to put its vaccination program on hold, at least until the WHO weighed in. The Danses met with Garin and a roomful of experts the following morning. Garin assured them that the health department was well prepared for the launch and that the WHO had told her that its official recommendation was imminent.

The vaccination campaign began a week later.

The Danses decided they couldn't sit idly by. They found Halstead's paper and got in touch. They felt certain that the curious (if not statistically significant) "safety signals" in the trial data were due to the theoretical phenomenon that Halstead had outlined, and that Sanofi was willfully ignoring those signs.

They gave a handful of media interviews. Then, in October 2016, the couple posted a seven-minute video on Facebook, warning parents that Dengvaxia could be harmful to kids who hadn't had dengue before. Colleagues objected to the public way in which they were undermining a government health campaign.

Sanofi—which had twice sent scientists to review the clinical trial data with the couple—was frustrated as well, firing off a letter to the Danses to correct their "misleading communications." The couple wouldn't budge.

By then, the political atmosphere in the Philippines had changed as well. That summer, Aquino's party had lost the presidential election to the controversial populist Rodrigo Duterte. Garin was no longer health secretary, and her successor had taken a suspicious view of the Dengvaxia program. Congress and the senate, meanwhile, launched an inquiry into what some thought was the vaccination program's hasty implementation. But the trouble wouldn't really start until a year later, when Sanofi released its November 29, 2017, update on Dengvaxia.

Thomas Triomphe was at his office in Singapore on the morning of December 1 when that became absolutely clear. His attention was called to the television, which was showing a press conference underway in the Philippines—the government was suspending the vaccination program.

The news came as a shock to Triomphe. His team had been in touch with the Department of Health before and after Sanofi's November 29 press statement. "There were no red signals," says Triomphe. "Of course, when you present the data, it's complicated," he says. "It's not something you grasp in twenty seconds." The regulators wanted to understand what the finding meant for the Philippines, and Triomphe says the company invited an ongoing conversation.

But the story was no longer just a dialogue between Sanofi and government health officials. It had exploded with a raw emotional fury online.

Within days, senators were calling for investigations; #DenGate had popped up on Twitter; the word "genocide" had been invoked; political bloggers and distressed citizens alike expressed outrage that the former government had turned Filipino children into "lab rats" to test an "experimental drug." One widely followed pundit asked, "How many will Aquino's Dengvaxia kill before Christmas 2018?" President Duterte's spokesman, for his part, vowed to go after those "responsible for this shameless public health scam."

Physicians who offered levelheaded assessments of the vaccine, meanwhile, were mercilessly trolled. Edsel Salvana, an infectious disease specialist who has no ties to Sanofi and who had mixed feelings about the government's Dengvaxia campaign, went on CNN Philippines to offer a measured take on the very modest risk that children faced getting the vaccine, compared with the benefit they'd get. His Facebook page was promptly swarmed by angry posters, some of whom called for his kids to die. "It was terrible," he says. "I was just trying to call for sobriety." He still gets attacked online when Dengvaxia makes the news. "A lot of us were blindsided by the vitriol." He notes that many of the trolls had political agendas but not all of them—and it's those people's responses he found most disheartening and surprising: "People were willing to believe nondoctors and nonspecialists over doctors and specialist scientists."

On December 4, Sanofi executives held a press conference to try to calm the storm. It didn't work.

From Sanofi's vantage point, the growing outrage was all a big misunderstanding. The company felt the whole mess came down to one tiny mistake, really a single word in the November 29 press release: "severe." By saying that people without previous exposure to dengue were at higher risk of getting "severe dengue" if they were given Dengvaxia, Sanofi had caused unnecessary concern.

Sanofi had taken the word "severe" straight from the language of its clinical trial design. But out of that context, it took on a different meaning.

Ng Su Peing, Sanofi Pasteur's global medical head, had the job of fielding questions at the company's press conference. "The general public in the Philippines thinks of severe dengue as something that's devastating, that could lead to death," she says. "[The announcement] was conveyed in a way that really caused alarm."

"Severe dengue," by the study's definition, covered a broad category of symptoms—from fever and gum bleeding at one end of the spectrum to the sometimes fatal hemorrhaging and shock at the other. In the clinical trial, no participants died of dengue, and reported cases of "severe dengue" fell at the milder end of the spectrum. Four out of every 1,000 children vaccinated without a previous infection had a higher risk of developing such disease over a five-year period. That compared with 1.7 per every 1,000 children without a previous infection who weren't given the vaccine.

In the spirit of transparency and scientific accuracy, Sanofi had crafted its press release carefully to adhere to the trial's official terminology. But it had left out both the numbers and the nuance, leaving the public to interpret "severe dengue" as they would.

"If you were a lay person and you heard 'severe,' what else would you conclude?" says Anna Ong-Lim, a physician who is currently president of the Pediatric Disease Society in the Philippines.

Regulations prevented Sanofi from promoting Dengvaxia to the public directly, so the company stayed silent on social media. Instead, it continued to press its data-driven case with high-level stakeholders in the country. "Maybe it seemed overly scary, but actually it's not scary at all," says Triomphe, a former McKinsey consultant, recalling how frustrating it was to witness the public's panic build. "It's not changing at all the overall benefit/risk profile of the product." He says in hindsight, the situation was more politicized than he realized: "Probably our voice was not hearable or understandable," says Triomphe.

Nor was Sanofi the only one struggling to cut through the noise. So, too, was the Filipino health department. "Every day we were getting drowned out," says Eric Domingo, undersecretary of health. "It was exhausting."

In July 2019 I visited Domingo at his office at DOH's leafy campus in central Manila. He was dressed in shirtsleeves and running late. The department was one week into a dengue alert, months into a measles outbreak, and managing occasional reports of diphtheria.

The affable Domingo speaks like a man who is trying to piece together the past two years, or maybe like one trying to peel himself off the pavement after being run down by a truck for the sixth or seventh time. Worn down, beat up, but not unable to appreciate the occasional absurdity of all that has happened.

The Dengvaxia mess began, more or less, on his first day on the job. He started December 1, the morning the government suspended the vaccination program. The timing protected him from the accusations made against others in the department, and he became the agency's spokesperson and point man on the matter.

"It just snowballed into this gigantic thing," says Domingo. "We were thinking we have to communicate the risk—so sit down, now that we know this, what are the risks for these children, what are we going to do, how do we mitigate that risk, how do we take care of them and how do we tell them? I guess initially everybody just expected it to go smoothly."

What they didn't anticipate was the spark that would ignite the furor to come: the reports of "Dengvaxia deaths" that began bubbling up almost immediately. "It was all there on social media, and then quite a few TV stations were showing autopsies—death number one, death number two, like a countdown every day," says Domingo. Meanwhile, protests proliferated.

The country's health workers, typically beloved figures in their communities, were chased away as "child killers." Parents didn't want their vaccinations or even basic medicines like deworming pills.

The Health Department itself was struggling to get information on some of the death reports. Meanwhile, the public demanded answers.

It was during this particularly toxic period of confusion, fear, and outrage, with allegations, misinformation, and unsubstantiated reports of Dengvaxia deaths flying around the internet, that the Blue Ribbon Senate Committee in the Philippines conducted a series of hearings on the vaccine debacle in late 2017 and early 2018.

Ostensibly a fact-finding operation, the hearings—hours long and televised widely—served as something between popcorn-worthy political theater and a public flogging. At their center, as master of ceremonies, was Richard Gordon, a seventy-four-year-old senator with a special gift for grandstanding.

Gordon wasn't especially concerned with questions of risk and what, in real terms, Sanofi's announcement meant for the Philippines—it was a given that the country had bought a vaccine that put some children in harm's way—he was focused on how that had happened.

A news personality and litigator, Gordon presided over the hearings—and the large cast of summoned bureaucrats, politicians, scientists, and drug company representatives—with a gravitas that frequently gave way to fits of showy outrage. He grilled. He lambasted. He flashed righteous fury. When it came to discussion, he often wouldn't have it—barking at witnesses who tried to give more than a yes or no answer or flustered scientists who refused to reduce a complicated technical matter to one word. He admonished one trembling functionary for trying to read from a piece of paper.

He mocked everything from witnesses' accents (especially that of the Frenchman Triomphe, whom he referred to as "Mr. L'Arc de Triomphe") to their baldness. He made insinuations and reserved special ire for Garin, the former health secretary, despite the fact that she postponed an emergency appendectomy for four days in order to testify.

But Gordon had also come prepared, ready to connect some dots for a public that was hungry for someone to blame. While the previous government pleaded that it had pursued an urgent public health good with resourceful, red-tape-shredding efficiency, Gordon alleged it was a sneaky and corrupt conspiracy that recklessly endangered hundreds of thousands of Filipino school kids. The political agenda gave the hearings a through-the-looking-glass quality at times where even basic realities seemed in dispute—like whether dengue was that much of a public health concern at all.

He homed in on Garin and Aquino's meetings with Sanofi and raised questions about the timing—making hay of the fact that a few weeks before the Philippines approved Dengvaxia in December 2015, the president had received the drug company's executives in Paris. (Aquino had been in town for the Paris Climate

Agreement and met with many other French executives as well.) He hammered on the half-truth that the government was giving out Dengvaxia before its clinical trial had even ended. (Sanofi was conducting long-term follow-up of trial participants through 2017, but it had completed its study and registered the product in accordance with WHO guidelines.) Gordon went after Sanofi, too, pointing to the company's long history of settlements with pharmaceutical regulators around the world.

Over the course of the hearings, the media continued to report on suspected Dengvaxia deaths, cases in which children who had gotten the vaccine later died. Some outlets—but not all of them—were careful to report that the link between the vaccine and the deaths had yet to be substantiated. The parents of those children also participated in the hearings, at one point holding their photographs up to the audience in the room.

Gordon's committee ultimately produced a report on the Dengvaxia scandal calling for the prosecution of Aquino, Garin, and other officials, though some senators refused to sign it and wrote dissenting opinions. When I met Gordon in July, he was working late in his capacity as the chairman of the Red Cross in the Philippines. It was past seven p.m., and he and his staff were making arrangements to send medical tents to the regions most impacted by the ongoing dengue outbreak.

As for whether or not Dengvaxia caused the deaths of the children whose photos were displayed in his hearings, Gordon said, "I have no findings sufficient for a belief or a conclusion that it can kill. I just have the finding that [Sanofi] had been forewarned by everybody and his uncle" that Dengvaxia had problems.

The Gordon hearings were winding down when it became apparent that the Philippines had an even bigger but not totally unrelated health crisis on its hands: measles. The country recorded more than 21,800 cases in 2018, up from 4,585 the previous year. The year 2019 has been even worse: through October 19, the health department had tallied 42,612 reported cases and 566 deaths, many of them children under nine months of age.

The country's immunization coverage rates have lagged in recent years, and the Dengvaxia scare made things far worse: a survey from the UK-based Vaccine Confidence Project found just 32 percent of Filipinos thought vaccines were important in 2018, down from 93 percent in 2015.

Despite the sobering public health situation, the health department's Domingo says measles just opened up another round of finger-pointing over which side was more responsible. "When you have two completely polarized groups, it doesn't quiet down," he told me. "It just continues."

Indeed, the blame game was in full swing when I visited the Philippines over the summer. Few were spared, but one woman in particular came up over and over again.

A Dubious Assertion

Acosta, the chief public attorney, occupies a unique role in the Philippines. As part of the nation's Department of Justice, the Public Attorney's Office (PAO) has a charter to serve the indigent with free legal services. Acosta has led the office since being appointed to her post in 2001.

On the July day I visited the PAO, which occupies the top floor of a government building in Manila, the tiny foyer hummed with a semieffective air-conditioning unit and was crowded with members of the public. A large photographic portrait of Acosta hung on one wall. People looked busy all around, moving with a sense of purpose among stacks of paper that were piled high on tables, chairs, and every other surface.

For parents who believe their child died or fell ill because of Dengvaxia at the hands of the government's public immunization drive, Acosta's advocacy has earned their loyalty. She is the rare government official they trust, their lonely crusading champion for justice.

As I waited in a small plastic chair, a security guard showed me a video on his cell phone of a man being hacked to death, his way of explaining to me the types of cases they get there. I told him I was there about Dengvaxia, and he nodded. "Oh, many cases."

Acosta was not available to see me, but I was allowed time with two women attorneys (it was against their communications policy to give their names, they said) who had both worked for the PAO for roughly a decade. They had been leading the work on Dengvaxia cases, which at that point encompassed 144 investigations and 44 criminal cases. (PAO had filed 91 criminal and civil cases through early November.)

The two attorneys repeated to me a dubious and controversial assertion that their office had made in court filings—that it was Dengvaxia itself that had killed the children directly rather than a severe dengue infection of the kind that Sanofi had warned about.

They explained that PAO had autopsied all the bodies and in all cases found the underlying cause of death had been "viscero- and neurotropic-like disease" caused by Dengvaxia. They did not believe dengue, or vaccine-enhanced dengue, was related to the deaths (though among the deceased, one child's death certificate had listed dengue as the cause of death).

The attorneys dismissed criticism of the PAO's Dengvaxia work as "personal attacks" and defended the agency's methods and forensic findings, saying they were confident they would prevail in court. They argue they have seen evidence—the autopsied bodies—that PAO's many critics have not and rejected the idea that PAO was responsible for whipping up fear about vaccines in the country. That, they said, was caused by the launch of a drug, Dengvaxia, that hadn't been fully tested.

The stated causes of death the PAO attorneys have cited—viscerotropism and neurotropic-like disease—critics say, come not from credible autopsy findings but rather from Sanofi's boilerplate risk disclosures for Dengvaxia.

Many of the vaccines that protect us from terrible diseases present a small risk of adverse events. On very rare occasions, the shot for rotavirus, for example, causes a reversible tangling of the bowel called intussusception. Likewise, there's a one in 2.4 million chance one will contract polio from the live polio vaccine. And yellow fever vaccine very, very infrequently leads to viscerotropic disease, a deadly phenomenon involving organ failure.

Because Dengvaxia is constructed with the viral backbone of the yellow fever vaccine, Sanofi listed viscerotropism and neurotropism as possible risks for Dengvaxia, and studied the vaccine for this effect in trials. (None was observed.)

Medical experts in the Philippines publicly decry PAO's forensic investigators as unqualified and their findings as utterly wrong.

"They're not even pathologists. They've not had a single day of training," says Raymond Lo, an anatomical and clinical pathologist who is board certified in both the U.S. and the Philippines. "They were conducting autopsies in public, in full vision of television cameras, exhibiting all these bloody organs. You could spread disease. They made a mockery of the whole thing." (As a former administrator at a hospital that procured Dengvaxia for the government immunization drive, Lo has been charged by the PAO with reckless imprudence resulting in homicide; he is fighting the charges.)

Lo has reviewed thirty-three of PAO's forensic reports—all of which, he says, cited viscero- and neurotropic-like disease as causes of death, despite clinical notes, death certificates, and hospital pathology reports indicating the child in question died of natural causes. The Philippine Society of Pathologists has also challenged PAO's findings, as have the Danses. Antonio Dans notes that the PAO's forensic investigators have based their conclusions all on two basic observations—organ swelling and hemorrhaging. "Those simple things you can find in almost every child who dies," says Dans.

The parents whose children were autopsied by the PAO offered radically different descriptions of their sicknesses and deaths. For some, the events had been sudden; in other cases, multiple hospital stays and surgical procedures were involved. Some had died weeks after vaccination, and others years. What the stories had in common was a list of general symptoms—fever, headaches, cough, dizziness, UTIs, irritability, fatigue, swollen limbs. And also a shared belief that before Dengvaxia, their child was healthy and normal—and after, he or she had died.

Many of the parents didn't initially suspect Dengvaxia as the cause of the child's death or illness but reached that conclusion after talking to someone—the kid's teacher, a bystander at the funeral, a nurse at the hospital, who then connected them with the Dengvaxia Victims Facebook group. It had never made sense to these parents that their once healthy children were dead, and after hearing about other kids, it made more sense that it had been Dengvaxia than what was diagnosed or written on the death certificate: leptospirosis, rabies, leukemia, an enlarged heart, and so on.

"One Death Is One Too Many"

In March, the Filipino government indicted a wide range of individuals for their alleged roles in the so-called Dengvaxia deaths. They included former health secretary Garin and six Sanofi employees, but also a cast of more peripheral figures—Julius Lecciones, executive director of the Philippine Children's Medical Center, which procured the vaccine; Rose Capeding, the researcher who investigated Sanofi's dengue trial in the

Philippines; and a handful of career employees at DOH. They were all charged with "reckless imprudence resulting in homicide," which is punishable by up to six years in prison. All of the accused deny any guilt. Sanofi says it strongly disagrees with the DOJ's findings and it is "vigorously defending" its employees.

When I spoke with some of the defendants in July, they were having a hard time. Many had left their jobs and were struggling to reconcile their situation with the fact that they had spent their lives serving the public. Facing a trial was expensive and stressful; it also made them public targets. One of the accused, Lyndon Lee Sy, a former Health Department spokesperson, died of a heart attack in September; his family and friends blame the weight of the case. Others noted the prosecution of researchers set a chilling precedent.

Richard Anthony Fadullon, the senior deputy state prosecutor for the Department of Justice, told Fortune that linking the deaths to the vaccine and the administration's "rushed" implementation will be difficult. The PAO's methods and findings, he admits, may complicate his efforts. But he says prosecuting the cases filed by the PAO is a worthy pursuit. "We cannot close our eyes to the deaths that happened," said Fadullon. "One death is one too many. It matters a lot to the family, and it matters a lot to government."

So how many children died as a result of Dengvaxia? That remains a controversial question. Sanofi's answer: "There is no clinical evidence that any reported fatalities were causally related to vaccination."

While the PAO has been publicizing every "Dengvaxia" death and autopsy, a DOH-sanctioned task force has been quietly reviewing cases of Dengvaxia recipients who have died. Of the 891,295 individuals vaccinated in the government program, there had been 315 deaths as of October 25, according to the DOH. And 41 of those cases were due to dengue. (There have been a total of 6,171 cases of dengue and 124 severe dengue among those vaccinated.) While the work is ongoing, DOH says that at present it has not directly linked any deaths to Dengvaxia itself, as the PAO asserts or to "severe" cases of dengue precipitated by the vaccine, as Sanofi warned about. As for the 41 deaths due to dengue, there is currently no clear way to determine if they were related to the immune-enhancement effect according to the DOH and the WHO.

As for the number of people who may die from dengue without the protection of a vaccine, well, that too is unknowable for now—but the number is likely to be many, many times larger.

"You've got a vaccine against this disease, which has an enormous public health burden. The population benefit is clear, but there are a small number of people who would be exposed to more severe disease," says Jeremy Farrar, the director of the Wellcome Trust, who cochaired the SAGE committee that recommended Dengvaxia's use in 2016.

"There are people that argue the public health benefits are the most important issue, and the numbers are hugely in favor of vaccination," he adds. That said, many people, Farrar included, believe there is an obligation to test prior to vaccination if it's possible to identify those at risk. To not, many point out, is a violation of medicine's do-no-harm principle.

The seemingly easy answer is to give Dengvaxia only to those who are not at risk of harm, as in those who have suffered a previous dengue infection. This is not an easy thing to do, though.

An estimated three-fourths of dengue infections are asymptomatic—meaning the majority of people who get dengue will never know they had it. There are tests that can tell you, but they are relatively expensive, not sufficiently accurate (they can't reliably distinguish Zika from dengue, for instance), and can take labs days or weeks to process. That's not a feasible solution for a government that hopes to protect its population against an epidemic.

And that's precisely what the Philippines' dengue outbreak became this August. The escalation forced a short-lived and somewhat awkward national conversation: Was it time to bring Dengvaxia back?

Many in the medical community thought so; the vaccine could be used responsibly and benefit many in the private market. There also seemed to be demand—a smattering of Filipino celebrities and politicians had made news by visiting Singapore and Thailand for dengue inoculations.

Despite the cases the government had filed over Dengvaxia-related deaths, President Rodrigo Duterte expressed openness to the possibility. Though he had been silent on most Dengvaxia matters, he told reporters he trusted that local experts knew what to do.

The Health Department didn't reinstate Dengvaxia's license, but in mid-August it said Sanofi Pasteur could reapply, which the company is in the process of doing. Jean-Antoine Zinsou, Sanofi Pasteur's general manager in the Philippines, expresses confidence that the product will be back eventually.

This year's epidemic, meanwhile, has proved worse than any before in the country, with some 360,000 cases and 1,373 deaths through September. Among the infected was Duterte's teenage daughter Kitty, who had reportedly received Dengvaxia. She was hospitalized in October but made a full recovery.

A Brief History of the Dengvaxia Scare

- 1993: French pharma giant Sanofi begins its pursuit of a dengue vaccine.
- 2009: Still years away from launching the vaccine, Sanofi builds a $398 million plant outside Lyon to produce it.
- 2011: Sanofi begins its two Phase III trials of its vaccine, involving 31,000 children in ten countries.

- December 2015: Now named Dengvaxia, Sanofi's vaccine wins first approvals in Brazil, Mexico, and the Philippines.
- February 2016: Eminent researchers Scott Halstead and Philip Russell publish a paper in *Vaccine* arguing Dengvaxia should not be given to people who have not had a previous infection.
- April 4, 2016: The Philippines launches the first-ever public vaccination program against dengue, targeting one million schoolchildren.
- April 15, 2016: The World Health Organization recommends Dengvaxia for highly endemic dengue countries.
- November 29, 2017: Sanofi issues an "update" on Dengvaxia, recommending the vaccine no longer be given to people who have not had a previous dengue infection.
- December 2017: The Philippines suspends its Dengvaxia program as well as Sanofi's ability to sell the vaccine in the country and calls for a refund from the pharma company.
- March 2019: The Philippines' Department of Justice indicts twenty individuals, including six Sanofi executives, for their roles in the Dengvaxia immunization program.
- August 2019: The Philippines declares a dengue epidemic. President Duterte says he's open to a return of Dengvaxia.

The Believer

FINALIST—FEATURE WRITING

"Two months after hearing a story about the borderlands debutante ball where Mexican American girls dress up in full period costume and pretend to be Martha Washington, I arrived in Laredo from the north," writes Jordan Kisner in "Las Marthas." She is there, in "a city that's American on its north side and Mexican on its south side," to witness the Martha Washington Colonial Pageant and Ball. But she is also there to explore what she describes as her own "in-betweenness," both as the daughter of an "undetermined WASP mix" father and a Mexican American mother and as a woman "in love with a woman." The National Magazine Award judges said that Kisner writes "with humanity and wisdom as she considers the complexities of ethnicity, femininity, identity and class." A nine-time National Magazine Award finalist, The Believer *was founded in 2003 and is now published by the Black Mountain Institute at the University of Nevada, Las Vegas.*

Jordan Kisner

Las Marthas

The dresses take a year to sew, and the girls spend a year learning how to wear them: how to glide, how to float their arms out so they never touch the skirts, how to hold their heads under the weight of the coiffure. The look is Marie Antoinette in her let-them-eat-cake days, and the dresses, like Marie's dresses, weigh so much—up to one hundred pounds—that they hurt the girl. They leave bruises at the shoulders and hips where the dress bones pull down on girl bones. The dresses, like the gestures, are passed down from mother to daughter.

Each girl needs five dressers, who first lace her into her corset, then affix the "cage" of the hoop skirt to her waist, sneaking a pillow between the cage and her body so her skin isn't rubbed raw. Then come petticoats, and the dress on top. The dressing occurs over a tarp with a hole cut into its center, and once everything is in place, the women pick up the girl and the tarp together and walk her to the stage so that the dress never touches the ground. If it is raining, they wrap her in plastic too.

When she walks, she takes the smallest steps possible so she appears to be borne along on a current of air. Large steps make the giant hooped skirt slap back and forth, and, anyway, a stately, exhibitive gait is key. Her arms remain at attention, hovering lightly above the hips of the dress, elbows soft, wrists tilted, hands in the Barbie claw. These subtle positions are a staple of the contemporary pageant: the ritual gestures, all bodies made to form the same shapes—back rod-straight in the corset, head erect, smile mannered.

For the girls, the hardest task is the curtsy, learning to sink to the floor gracefully and then rise again as if the monument on their hips were only a trick of light. They teach me to do it in a little group in the salon, all of them laughing in flip-flops and sweatpants with their toenails and lip liner already done. You go slowly onto one knee, they explain, and then, while remaining motionless from the waist up, tuck the other knee underneath for extra support. Slowly, we sit down and back on our heels and bow magisterially over our imaginary skirts, keeping our chins up, up, up until the last moment, when we finally accede to the skirt, turning the right cheek. It looks in this final phase like the girl is cocking one ear to her dress, listening for what's underneath.

Why? I ask. Why is this the bow?

They shrug. It's always been this way. That's how they taught it to us.

• • •

There are many debutante balls in Texas and a number of pageants that feature historical costumes, but the Society of Martha Washington Colonial Pageant and Ball in Laredo is the most opulently patriotic among them. In the late 1840s, a number of European American settlers from the East were sent to staff a new military base in southwest Texas, a region that had recently been ceded to the United States after the Mexican-American War. They found themselves in a place that was tenuously and unenthusiastically American. Feeling perhaps a little forlorn at being so starkly in the minority, these new arrivals established a local chapter of the lamentably named Improved Order of Red Men. (Members of the order dressed as "Indians," called their officers "chiefs," and began their meetings, or "powwows," by banging a tomahawk instead of a gavel.)

The Improved Order of Red Men fashioned itself as a torch-bearer for colonial-era American patriotism, and its young Laredo chapter was eager to enshrine that culture down at the border. So it formed the Washington's Birthday Celebration Association (WBCA). For the inaugural celebration, in 1897, they "laid siege" to the Old Laredo City Hall, pretending to be a warring native tribe conquering the city. (The optics here must have been confusing, as the order was made up of white men, while most of the city's residents were either Mexican by birth or indigenous.) A young woman was appointed to play Pocahontas, and after brokering peace between the tribe and the city, she received the keys to Laredo in appreciation of her efforts.

The siege was done away with long ago, but every February since 1898, the WBCA has thrown a massive festival—America's largest, most elaborate party for its first president. Lately, the festival includes a Comedy Jam for George, a Founding Fathers' 5K Fun Run, a Jalapeño Festival, a Princess Pocahontas Pageant and Ball, an Anheuser-Busch-sponsored citywide parade, and so on. The prestige event of the season is the pageant and debutante ball hosted by the Society of Martha Washington, which was started by WBCA wives in 1940 with the aim of adding glitz to the festival. Their daughters dress up in what is creatively imagined to be Martha-like attire (in fact, the dresses are not much like what Martha Washington would have worn), playacting historical figures who might have known her. Each year, one adult Society member is chosen to play Martha herself, and a man from the WBCA is asked to play George.

The WBCA was started by members of Laredo's mostly white upper class, but in the almost one hundred years since the association's founding, the city has become almost entirely mixed-ethnicity: on the 2010 census, 96 percent of the population identified as Hispanic. Through intermarriage, the upper class of

Laredo has come to include not only the Lyndeckers and the Bunns (two original WBCA families still prominent in the Society) but also families named Rodriguez, Gutierrez, Martinez, and Reyes. Today, Martha, George, and the girls are mostly Mexican Americans. Many of them descend from the original WBCA families, but just as many are descended from the people who were categorically oppressed—and, in several instances, massacred—by an American colonialist expansion set in motion by the Founding Fathers they dress up to honor.

In Nahuatl, there's a word for in-betweenness: *nepantla*. The Aztecs started using the word in the sixteenth century when they were being colonized by Spain. *Nepantla* means "in the middle," which is what they were: between a past they wrote themselves and the future that would be written by their conquerors, in the middle of the river between who they had been and who they were allowed to be now. Twentieth-century theorists have used the word *shattered* to describe the liminal existence of *nepantleras*, indicating both brokenness and the possibility of making something radically new. The word has also been used to describe the borderlands experience, the mixed-race experience, the experience of anyone who lives both in and outside their world of origin. As Gloria Anzaldúa wrote, *nepantleras* are "threshold people."

Two months after hearing a story about the borderlands debutante ball where Mexican American girls dress up in full period costume and pretend to be Martha Washington, I arrived in Laredo from the north. I'd flown into San Antonio, where my grandmother lives, and driven the 150 miles of interstate down to the border. When I checked into my hotel, the front desk attendant warned me not to miss the last exit on the freeway. If you don't get off at the last exit, she said, there's no turning around and you'll wind up across the border in Nuevo Laredo and need a passport to get back. "It's OK," I assured her. "I'm from a border city too."

Laredo and Nuevo Laredo are often described as neighboring cities, but geographically they are one city, the Laredo–Nuevo Laredo Metropolitan Area, bisected by the U.S.-Mexico border and the Rio Grande. It's a city that's American on its north side and Mexican on its south side. The river is narrow as a straight pin at this portion of its journey from Colorado to the Gulf of Mexico, and only fifty yards across. It's a city of bridges: there is the Juárez-Lincoln International Bridge, the World Trade Bridge, the Colombia Solidarity Bridge, and the Gateway to the Americas Bridge, all roughly a thousand feet long. Thousands of people cross from one place to the other each day, to work or to school or to see family. Laredo's adopted nickname is "the Gateway City," though the border is tightly regulated. Of the major ports for trade, trafficking, and immigration between the United States and Mexico, Laredo is among the very busiest, often outranked only by San Diego, where I am from.

In this country, major border towns share some common features. They contain armies of immigration and customs enforcement officers; if you drive down near the border, you'll see ICE vehicles ferrying migrants between detention centers. Everyone knows people who are undocumented, which lately means that everyone knows someone who has vanished without warning or notice. The radio traffic reports always include estimates for the delays at each of the crossings. And then there's the fence.

Unlike Laredo, San Diego County remains majority white and segregated in ways designed by city planners and codified by city councils decades ago. Speaking generally, white and affluent people—categories that blur in San Diego—populate the west and north of the county, the parts that have the beaches. While all the beaches in California are public land, people who own beachfront property own the views of the ocean. They own the right to see horizon. With some exceptions, lower-income families, immigrants, and most Mexican Americans live to the south and east, on the sides of the county that face the desert and the border.

I was a teenager when I first went to the beach at Border Field State Park with some friends and we wandered until we ran into the fence. I was startled to see the wooden posts jammed deep into the sand and extending out into the ocean. I'd never known that the border went beyond the water's edge. This reveals more than I wish it did about the teenager I was and the city I lived in.

But every Easter, we would travel as a family to Mission, Texas, which is a border town an hour southeast of Laredo, farther down into the Valley, as Texans call it. Hidalgo County—which contains Mission, where my great-grandparents lived, where my grandparents were raised, and where my mother spent long periods of her childhood—is consistently ranked among the poorest counties in the United States. My earliest memories of Mission are of my great-grandmother Carmen Garcia, whom everyone called Grandma Carmen; billboards with letters missing; a dusty pickup with its bed full of watermelons.

All the Garcias would gather each Easter at my great-grandparents' house. There were always so many people that we'd have to go to a park for a proper picnic—aunts and uncles, second and third cousins, in-laws, and dozens of grandchildren. It is a tradition among Mexican families in South Texas to do the Easter egg hunt with *cascarones*, eggshells that have been hollowed out, filled with paper confetti, and resealed with colorful tissue paper. Once the children had hunted down all the *cascarones*, there'd be a smashing melee, where everyone ran around and broke the eggs over one another's heads so the confetti exploded in showers around you, settling into your hair and sandals. At the end, everyone would be in stitches, and inevitably one child would be bawling and the ground in that corner of Mission would look as if a parade had blown through. As a child, I spent a lot of time playing in the colorful, littered dirt of that park and understood it to be, in some important ways, dirt that belonged to me, and me to it.

Still, I always felt slightly out of place in Mission. My father is a somewhat undetermined WASP mix by way of New Jersey, and when I was young I looked mostly like him. The last time we went to stay with Grandma Carmen, I was a teenager, and I spent the whole time feeling pale and giant. There's a photo of us standing outside her front door: Grandma Carmen and my brother and me. He's thirteen and I'm fifteen, and next to us she looks like a child, not even five feet tall, barely ninety pounds. My brother looks plausibly related to her; I look like a guest. We didn't talk much, but she would grasp me by my arms and peer into my eyes and smile. I remember her in her kitchen, holding my mother's hands and laughing, saying, "*Mi'ja, no sé lo que les gusta comer.*" Always, we would get on a plane and fly back to the ocean.

• • •

I met 2018's Martha Washington at a strip mall in north Laredo, where we had agreed to have lunch between her nail appointment and her hair appointment. The Martha, a blonde woman in her fifties named Tami Summers, was two days away from concluding her duties.

"Right now I'm kinda nervous because of all the stuff that's going on," Tami said, waving vaguely at her stomach. She ordered bone broth and a piece of chicken. "I don't want to sound silly, but I try to get things organized because I'm a teacher, and I plan. And then everything goes to hell." After decades of teaching middle and high school, she was teaching a class called Race in America at Texas A&M International University in Laredo but had gotten her classes covered for the week to handle the appointments, houseguests, and other tasks. The Martha Washington–themed T-shirts she'd ordered hadn't arrived until eleven o'clock the night before, which delayed the arrangement of the welcome baskets she'd planned for the few dozen family members arriving from out of town to see her in the pageant. "So that's running late. And then I had a mani, so my nails are done, and I have to be back at the Civic Center at three, because we're putting on the dresses to see how they work onstage. And then we practice tonight with the dresses on." She heaved a little sigh and took a sip of coffee.

Tami is gregarious and forceful, a short woman with wide blue eyes, a broad, friendly face, and the demeanor of someone who's made a career corralling teenagers. Her hair was, for the moment, bright blond, which isn't how she normally wears it. The stylist who does hair for the pageant wanted her to go platinum for Martha. (Martha's hair was brown, but that's not the point.) "I kind of like it," Tami said, patting her head. "I think I might keep it this way."

She wore a crisp white button-up embroidered with the blue crest of the Society. Across from her sat her childhood friend Carole, also a member of the Society, and to her right sat her teenage daughter, Bailey, who apologized right away for how much she would be yawning through lunch. She'd flown in from Florence, where she'd just started a semester abroad.

Most women are members of the Society because someone in their family was in it—a mother, an aunt—or because they've married into it. Tami's husband's aunt was a founding member, his father played George in 1987, and he played George in 2006. Tami, who is a joiner and naturally enthusiastic, was admitted into the group in 1998. Bailey began practicing the elaborate curtsy of the Martha Washington debutantes when she was three years old.

The number of members of the Society of Martha Washington is limited to about 250 at any given time, and openings are always outpaced by demand, so women are encouraged to apply for membership long before their daughters are of debutante age. For their first two years in the group, new members must sell fifteen thousand dollars' worth of advertisements in the pageant's annual program, which is the size, shape, style, and layout of a high school yearbook.

I asked the three women how they understood the Society's role in the community more generally. Tami paused, chewing and thinking. "It's interesting here because we're such a Hispanic population. At least 95 percent. It's really a Hispanic base, which is how the WBCA started. We were so Hispanic and so Mexican and so far away, located on the border—we were saying to America, *We are American, and we're going to celebrate Washington's birthday!* We are dual culture. We embrace our Mexican roots."

This hadn't been my understanding of the origins of the association—that it was started by Mexicans hoping to be brought into the feel-goodery of the American body politic—but as I was considering a next question, Carole chimed in, pointing out that, in her view, the crowning event of the Washington's Birthday Celebration is something called the Abrazo Ceremony, which takes place the morning after the pageant, before the parade. Four children, a boy and a girl each from Laredo and from Nuevo Laredo, cross the Juarez-Lincoln International Bridge from their respective sides, dressed in colonial-era costumes and accompanied by the mayors of their cities. When they reach one another in the middle of the bridge, over the waters of the Rio Grande, they hug.

"This whole celebration is about unification and friendship, especially with our neighbors to the south," said Carole. "I think for you, knowing you," she said, nodding at Tami, "the number one thing about this celebration is connection and family. I mean, for god's sake, Bailey is here from Italy."

Tami agreed. "I just think the connection and the continuation of the thing—"

Carole interrupted: "It's roots. Not connection."

"But what does a root do?" Tami asked. "It connects you to the ground. It connects you to the earth. It connects you to other people."

Bailey nodded, looking at her mom. "It makes you a part of something."

• • •

I spent most of the next two days in salons, particularly in the Regis Salon at the Mall del Norte, where Tami and a number of the debutantes were having their hair prepared for the various events of the weekend: the dress rehearsal, the pageant, the parade, the cocktail reception. When I arrived, the salon's rather stern-looking owner, a woman named Grace, was in the middle of back-combing Tami's hair sky-high. Blond extensions lay like coiled rope on a metal tray nearby.

Tami grinned as a greeting, careful not to move her head. Her iPhone was in her lap, and she was steadily fielding questions and handling minor crises from the various people needing her attention. She had arranged for her female family members who'd come in from out of town to have their makeup professionally applied for the occasion, but coordinating their schedules was proving complex. Next to Tami, a dark-haired, skinny sixteen-year-old named Sydney was further along—the young stylist working on her was already pinning her extensions into a pompadour. Sydney's mother was negotiating with a makeup artist about the day's schedule. I asked her what it was like to have a daughter presented.

She smiled. "It's been a beautiful experience. She's loving it: she gets pampered, she shines at the parties." Sydney's mom leaned forward to show me a picture of Sydney in her dress for the November father-daughter dance, one event on the slate of social obligations that precede the pageant. It was a long, white satin gown, off the shoulder. "It's actually a wedding gown," she said. "You have to buy a wedding dress. And because I have an older daughter, too, I now basically own two wedding dresses." She laughed.

I asked if the Society paid for these appointments, since she was the Martha.

Tami shook her head and pointed at her chest.

"You pay for it."

"Yes. The Society pays for—" She paused. "Nothing."

"Not the dresses?"

"No, no. That's why you'll see all levels of dresses. They can get really crazy and be really reasonable just depending on what the person's budget is. We have to sponsor our float in the parade. We pay for our tickets; we pay for our dress. There are yearly dues."

"Are there scholarships for members who want their daughters to be presented but don't have the money to do it?"

"No, no, no. No. No, they just either don't do it or they borrow a dress. And some people will say, 'We just can't do it.' If it comes down to either you're gonna get a car or you're going to college or you're going to get presented, you don't do it."

I asked whether they had to wear a different outfit for every party.

Tami laughed. "Oh, yeah! And shoes."

Bailey chimed in. "And hair and makeup."

"And we bought ninety-five seats for friends and family."

I did the math: that morning, I'd paid Tami two hundred dollars for a spare set of tickets to the pageant, ball, and cocktail party. Seeing the look on my face, she snorted in agreement.

"Head up," commanded Grace.

I turned to Sydney. "What's your favorite part of this?"

"Well, I really love the dress," she said. "I'm really in love with it."

"And what's the hardest part?"

She gave a little sigh and said that the hardest part was wearing the dress. "The weight is on my hips and it's more than sixty pounds," she said. "It really hurts."

• • •

Before I arrived in Laredo, I'd begun researching the local economy. While the city is one of the least white cities in America, a University of Toronto study named Laredo as America's most economically segregated small city. In 2014, Laredo processed twenty billion dollars in trade with Mexico, but nearly 40 percent of the city's population lives below the poverty line. Wealthy Laredoans live in neighborhoods like Plantation, Regency Park, and Lakeside. Poor Laredoans live in neighborhoods like El Rincon del Diablo and El Trompe. The per capita income in Laredo is $16,462, and the median household income is $41,403—which is, if your tastes run opulent, roughly the cost of a new dress for a Martha.

For the month of February, Texas A&M International University in Laredo loaned gallery space to the Society of Martha Washington for a museum of retired dresses. Between salon appointments, I drove over to have a look. The room was on the second floor of the fine arts center and shaped like a fishbowl. Several dozen mannequins stood silently in full regalia.

It was like standing among the discarded, gleaming exoskeletons of eighteen-year-olds as they existed throughout the twentieth century. I could see how short- or long-waisted the woman was, the set of her hips, the approximate fleshiness of her upper arms. One dress, with mint-green satin and aurora crystals, holds the shadow-body of Molly LaMantia, who was eighteen in 2011, and of her four older sisters before her. Another holds the echo of Evelyn Bruni Summers, a distant in-law of Tami's, who in 1988 had thin wrists and sloping shoulders. An especially beautiful gown made of plum brocade with cap sleeves, held a girl who was uncommonly long-legged and slender.

Viewed up close, the dresses are more beautiful than they need to be. While it is a point of pride to have a dress that has been worn by many generations, mostly because it indicates a long Society lineage, it's also customary to dramatically redesign an inherited dress for each new girl so it feels uniquely hers. This is a way of making sure a dress keeps up, as the gowns trend more extravagant and splendid each year. One series of photographs showed the transformation of a single gown as it was handed down through a set of five sisters: The oldest sister, Reina Ann LaMantia Cullen, had a pearlescent gown with large pink roses embroidered on the bodice and skirt; the next year, her sister Morgan changed the body of the dress to a sea-foam green and added a wide, tongue-pink ribbon; the third sister added a giant bow and replaced the sleeves; the fourth sister threw out all the pink and added olive-green velvet trim; the final sister tore off all the ribbon, added puff sleeves, and let the beadwork, which had been growing steadily more elaborate, shine for itself.

Each night, back in my hotel room, I turned on the television and was greeted by *Say Yes to the Dress*, which appeared to have been granted its own 24-7 channel by the state of Texas. *Say Yes to the Dress* is a reality show, based at a bridal boutique in Manhattan, that follows brides who are in search of "the dream dress." In this search, they are stewarded primarily by a man named Randy Fenoli, who has an immaculately gelled crew cut. Randy credits his success as both a bridal-wear designer and bride handler to his former life as what was then called a "female impersonator" by the name of Brandi Alexander, who was crowned Miss Gay America in the 1990 pageant. Participating in drag pageantry, Randy once told a journalist, is how he learned to speak to women preparing to be on display.

The camera zooms in and out of fitting rooms, stockrooms, and the grand showroom, where women stand on pedestals in front of small committees of girlfriends or sisters or gay male friends or occasionally a father and almost always a mother. There is invariably one member of the committee deputized to have narrowed eyes and an unpleasant demeanor, and to say things like "I don't think it's doing great things for your ass" or "I think tuck ruffles are whorish."

The show's premise is that a wedding marks the most important day of a woman's life, not because she's going to marry the person of her dreams but because she is going to wear the dress of her dreams.

I love this show.

I wish I didn't love this show. Women as creatures in pursuit of a princess fantasy or a supermodel fantasy; gay men as effete handmaidens to and quiet manipulators of straight women's vanity; weddings as a performance of heteronormative habit and class aspiration and unbridled consumption . . . What a nightmare. Still, I can't get enough of it, and part of the reason I love it is because I like to imagine what it might be like to be the woman in that dress. In this show, I see a path not taken, much as I see a path not taken in the pageantry of the debutante. I do not want to be her, and yet I like watching her pick out her gloves.

As a little girl, I was carefully combed and dressed, with bows in my hair that matched my outfits. I went to cotillion with my friends. I learned to fold my hands in my lap. I was enthusiastic about most of this, having been the kind of little girl who liked princesses and sparkly shoes. I enjoyed feeling pretty. I felt fancy eating crumbling grocery store cookies in white cotton gloves.

When I hit adolescence and the rituals of femininity became social requirements rather than play, I chafed against them, and my mother and I began to argue more over my appearance. By and large, women inherit their habits and neuroses about femininity from their mothers, and mine were inherited from my own Texan mother and, by extension, hers. The rituals of female beauty are deep-rooted in Texas, as is pageant culture—the desire to commodify the beauty of young women, and the sense that it is the moral duty of the mother to teach her daughter the rules of tasteful and advantageous self-display.

My mother is not the kind of woman who would enjoy *Say Yes to the Dress*, being both a self-proclaimed feminist and the person from whom I learned the devastating implications of the word *ostentatious*. (She also taught me the word *gauche*.) Her personal style was constructed as a rebuke to the big-hair-and-blue-eye-shadow stereotype of a Texas woman. Still, she is uncommonly beautiful—so much so that it's often the first quality of hers people remark upon—and she has stewarded that beauty vigilantly, in part because I think she understands appearance as a reflection of both character and aspiration, an occasion to demonstrate not just beauty but intelligence about who you are and where you belong. She has since told me that she wanted to equip me and my brother to move comfortably and inconspicuously through any kind of social space—that's why we went to cotillion. It was with that in mind that she dressed us as children.

As a teenager, I balked at learning to blow-dry my hair with a round brush, or at being told not to go out without earrings. I argued, citing all the times she'd told me that what mattered most was my mind and character, saying that I shouldn't have to look pretty if I didn't want to, that how I looked wasn't the important thing about me. She argued that I should look "like I cared."

Still, there was a sliver of time, when I was twelve, when I might have been a debutante. We had moved to Northern California, and in an attempt to make some friends, my mother let someone put her in touch with the local chapter of the National Charity League. My mother was skeptical from the beginning because, she said, societies like this were less about charity than about social climbing—a phrase that, because I was twelve, I needed her to define. Most mothers joined because they wanted to debut their daughters, which, she suggested, was a pretty antiquated and sexist ritual of declaring your daughter to be "on the market" to men. Nevertheless, she went ahead with our application, reasoning that she might be willing to deal with it if it would help us build a social life in this new place.

My mother had a phone interview with the mother in charge of the chapter, whose questions gave her the prickling feeling that having a last name like Garcia might be a stumbling block with the league ladies. Our application was refused.

• • •

They were breathtaking all together, and blinding, roughly a quarter of a million sequins and crystals catching the light. They looked more like a squadron of ships than of girls. Their traffic patterns were elaborate and cautious. The disembodied voice of the emcee would later declare to the thousand people watching out there in the darkness, to the mayor and his pretty wife, to the Texas senators who had traveled to see them debut, that they were "the best of Laredo."

The enormous stage of the Jesus Martinez Performing Arts Complex had been arranged with backdrops painted with bursting, fecund cherry trees surrounding a Palladian manor house: Mount Vernon. Three tiers of risers led up to painted double doors, attended by two young pages, both outfitted in breeches and false ponytails clipped into their crew cuts. Before George, Martha, or any of the girls emerged, the bishop of the Diocese of Laredo prayed over the event, and the Junior ROTC band played the national anthem, and all one thousand audience members, dressed in their own best formal wear, rose and placed hands over hearts.

The most common form of pageantry in America is the beauty competition, but this show is a pageant more in the medieval or religious sense of the word. Medieval pageantry was like ritualized communal theater, put on seasonally or to celebrate particular saints' days. This kind of pageant has plot, elaborate costumes, and a rank assigned to each participant, denoted by her place in the procession. (Historically, the closer you were to the king, the higher your rank; here, it's about being close to George.) Medieval pageants held in honor of Corpus Christi reenacted the entire history of the world, starting with Genesis 1 and hauling all the way through to the Apocalypse. The 2018 Society of Martha Washington Colonial Pageant reenacted a fictional dinner party hosted by George and Martha in Mount Vernon with a party theme of, inexplicably, literacy.

The girls arrived one by one, in order of the status of their families within the Society. First came Andrea Victoria Gutierrez, daughter of Mr. and Mrs. Albert Gutierrez III. Andrea had been chosen to lead because her ancestral line within the Society is the longest and most distinguished, according to an elaborate and strictly maintained hierarchy: The girls with mothers who are members always come first, and within each group the girls are ranked in order of the length of time the family has been in the Society. Next come the girls whose connection is not through a mother but another female relative, subranked again in order of the date of membership. After them come two or three girls who have been invited as the Society's "guests" for the year. It's tradition to invite a girl from a neighboring city in Texas whose family has ties to the Society. It is also customary to invite a girl from Nuevo Laredo to debut with the Society. The non-Laredoan Americans are presented after the Laredoan girls; the Mexican girl comes last.

This is the order in which their portraits appear in the yearbook-program, the order in which they are presented at the November father-daughter dance, the order of their names in the paper. In the citywide parade, at which each girl has her own corporate-sponsored float, blue-eyed Andrea Gutierrez's float will drive through first, at nine-thirty a.m. Those farther back will wait their turn in the heat until finally Angela Moreno of Nuevo Laredo passes by, sometime after noon.

I don't know what I had imagined would happen during the pageant. Maybe a little play? Maybe elaborate choreography? Instead, when each girl was announced, as she appeared in silhouette in the plywood double doors and began descending to the stage, hand firmly gripping that of her escort for balance, the emcee read aloud an account of her breeding. Whether she was in boarding school or on the honor roll, where she would be attending college, which tony activities she excelled at. More time and emphasis were devoted to who her mother was, who her father was, who their mothers and fathers and aunts and uncles were; what important positions, associations, or distinctions they had enjoyed, as far back as possible. Two girls' bios made proud mention of genealogical connections to people who were involved in the Revolutionary War. One triumphantly traced her ancestry back to Patrick Henry, information that was received with excitement.

While her social stats were being announced, each girl walked a slow oval around the stage, smiling widely, moving carefully so that she could be admired from every angle. I understood, suddenly, why the girls had been so nervous about falling, wobbling, and tripping. Though their order of appearance identified the innate hierarchy, which was out of their hands, each girl's promenade was her moment of evaluation before her community, much like the purebred's turn in the arena at Westminster. This slo-mo one-woman parade was her opportunity to be judged or celebrated for her beauty, grace, breeding, and accomplishments.

All the members of the Society I spoke to were nervous that I would portray this enterprise as elitist. They pointed out that anyone is welcome to apply for a membership and that in the past several years they've welcomed a number of members who had no family ties to the organization. They pointed out as well that any woman, once a member, has the right to present her daughter as a debutante when she is eighteen, and that, conversely, it's perfectly common and acceptable not to debut your eighteen-year-old.

It was important to them that I know they are mostly working women. Nearly a dozen women I interviewed told me that the membership is full of "judges and doctors and lawyers and professors." The list was always the same: judges, doctors, lawyers, professors—indicating, I suppose, hardworking careerism and advanced education. Furthermore, they pointed out, the Society spends quite a bit of time and money on local philanthropy. It pays the fees for low-income Laredoan teenagers to go to a week-long civic-engagement program in Washington, DC, every year. And furthermore, they told me, the pageant contributes millions of dollars to the local economy. Out of their own pockets they pay hundreds of thousands of dollars to hairdressers and seamstresses and caterers, jewelry designers and florists. The pageant effectively spreads their wealth.

Leaving aside the critique of trickle-down economics that notion might invite, it seemed what they were trying to convey was that though they may be wealthy and interested in exclusive memberships based around traditional definitions of "high society" as a group of people with special value (related to but not exactly synonymous with their special wealth), they're not unkind or unprincipled.

It is true that they were kind. I wrote again and again in my notebook that the women and girls (and orbiting young men) I interviewed were warm. They were skittish about having a reporter around because they felt they had been betrayed and misunderstood by other journalists, who had painted them as frivolous elitists, but still they were welcoming. They seemed motivated by love of family, love of tradition, and love of country. They spoke over and over again about inclusivity, standing for unity with their "brothers and sisters in Nuevo Laredo." They mostly didn't speak the name of the president, but they often declared meaningfully that Laredoans believe in building bridges, not walls.

Neither did they seem to be rude about their wealth, unless you think public celebrations of one's wealth and status are inherently rude—which, granted, some people do. The children were unfailingly polite and well spoken. The mothers were anxious but reasonable. In general, they seemed to be a group of people aware of being on view, setting an example. They adhered, perhaps, to an old-fashioned notion of gentility.

It may be true that the millions of dollars spent on the Colonial Pageant and Ball stimulate the local economy, and it may be true that the members of the Society do not intend to place themselves unpleasantly above the people who cannot participate. But it is also true that exclusivity is predicated on someone being excluded. It is also true that when you designate a group of young women to be the "best of Laredo," you are saying something about all the young women who have not managed to make their way into that glittering formation.

Throughout the pageant, I kept thinking of a moment from earlier in the day in the makeup salon, after Tami left. I was hanging around chatting with a makeup artist while she did another debutante's makeup, and she told me that years ago, when she was first starting to do makeup for the pageants, the hardest thing for her was remembering that the girls in the Society have different coloring.

"Most people in the Society are lighter?"

"Yes," she said. "Most are. Or they have European blood in them. And that's what it is, the pageant. They're telling you all their lineage, and that's European blood." She smiled a little smile. "I call them Martians. Because they look good in greens."

I asked about the other pageant that happens at this time of year: the Princess Pocahontas Pageant and Ball. It started around the same time as the Colonial Pageant and Ball, but it carries on by honoring Pocahontas's original role in the festivities. As it's described on the WBCA website, this pageant celebrates the "regal Indian maiden" and "presents the Native Americans in a setting that is both mystical and natural." I wondered aloud whether the girls who played Pocahontas and her court were also Martians.

She shook her head. "No. The Society is . . . the crème de la crème, so to speak. It's—you're born into that."

She told me that this year, Tami had invited her to one of her parties for the Society. "Tami is so down-to-earth, and so nice," she said. "But are you kidding me? I don't have anything to wear; I don't even know what to wear. I shop at Target and Walmart, and there's just no way I can be there and feel comfortable." She shook her head, her expression somewhere between amused and grimacing. "You realize, *Oh, wow, there's a really different world out there.* It's not my world."

I recalled this as I watched one winsome young woman after another arrive at the top of the stage and float down the stairs to applause. *This is your world*, their community was telling Andrea Gutierrez and Bianca Martinez and Jordan Puig and Rebeca Peterson and Rebecca Reyes and Lauren Moore and Azul Martinez and Leticia Garcia and Marissa Gonzalez, and all the rest. *This whole beautiful world is for you.*

When my mother was five years old, my grandmother tried to put her in a pageant. Specifically, my grandmother entered her in a contest to select the Court of Queen Citrianna for the Mission Texas Citrus Fiesta, the pageant that still takes place every year in my great-grandparents' hometown. Mission is one of the primary producers of citrus in the country, specifically of ruby red grapefruits, and my mother's grandfather was a foreman for one of the citrus producers. "I didn't even know what I was doing," my mom said when she told me about her audition for the littlest citrus girl. "I had to learn to curtsy and all that. It was probably the blonde girls who were selected." She made a sound between a laugh and a sigh. "My mother came from a really nothing family, right, but she had these aspirations."

While I was in Laredo, we had been talking on and off about a dynamic at work on the stage at the Jesus Martinez Performing Arts Complex, a dynamic that I'd seen play out before: an equation of Americanness with middle-class "whiteness" that's exerted so powerfully on brown people that they eventually begin to accede and conform.

After finishing high school in Mission, my grandfather enlisted in the army and spent his career as a helicopter pilot, in part to facilitate getting out of Mission. My grandparents left the Rio Grande Valley and raised their children while traveling between San Antonio and far-flung military bases throughout the United States and in Italy and Turkey, where they lived mostly among white people. It seemed important to my grandmother to fit into these spaces and for her children not to seem too Mexican, too "from the Valley."

Though Spanish was both of my grandparents' first language, they only spoke English to their children because they believed that speaking Spanish would do them no favors in Texas. My grandmother would punish my mother if her words ever took on the melodic singsong intonation of Spanglish from the Valley. "*Do not speak like that*," my mother says, imitating her mother's voice, which is itself accented. "*You're going to sound like you're Mexican.* As Mexican Americans, you pretty much wanted to subsume your racial identity. And there was no 'Mexican-American' when I was growing up! You didn't hyphenate. You lost that. You were just American."

All of my grandmother's seven children married white people. None of her fourteen grandchildren speak fluent Spanish. It is a source of great pride and patriotism in our family that one of my uncles and several of my cousins and cousins' husbands followed my grandfather into the armed forces. No family is more American than a military family, the logic goes. Everyone who had an opportunity to change their last name through marriage did, with the exception of my mother. The parts of the family history that included poverty or immigration or the "wrong" kind of Mexicanness or any other perceived stain were dropped from conversation so that my generation would never know them.

But why? I'd always wanted to know. This was all totally antithetical to the kind of pro-multicultural America I was told I lived in as I was growing up. When I asked my mother, who hasn't typically wanted to talk about this kind of thing, she was quick to point out that in the areas where she grew up, Mexicans and indigenous people were enslaved. In the early decades of the twentieth century, the same thirty years between the founding of the WBCA and my grandparents' birth, Texas Rangers tortured and executed Mexicans en masse down in the borderlands. A Texas newspaper defended the killings as a reasonable response to "a serious surplus population that needs eliminating." Prominent Texas politicians were calling for "all those of Mexican descent" to be sent to concentration camps.

When my grandmother was young, there were still teachers who were against speaking Spanish in public school, and so she was punished for speaking her first language on the playground. There were separate drinking fountains. My mother recalls that in Mission, the train tracks really were the dividing line between the white neighborhood and the Mexican neighborhood, and that the roads on the Mexican side went unpaved until the late seventies.

My grandparents grew up in a geographically and culturally marginal part of the country that was desperately economically depressed. My grandmother in particular was raised in poverty. Neither of them went to college. In the decades between their coming-of-age and mine, American politics has developed a new term for people who fit my grandmother's description in the moment when she was making decisions about who and how to be. They're called "vulnerable populations." What would a refusal or failure to assimilate have cost her?

In the months after I visited Laredo, the news broke that the U.S. government had begun separating migrant children from their parents at the Mexican border. Between May and June 2018, two thousand children were taken from their families and put into detention centers, and by July news outlets were estimating that nearly twelve thousand immigrant children were in U.S. custody. Several thousand were in a new tent camp in the desert outside El Paso. The youngest children, many of them still infants, some of them taken away from their mothers as they were breastfeeding, were sent to "tender age" shelters in South Texas. Laredo's detention center, which is about seven miles northeast of the bridge where the Abrazo Ceremony takes place, holds mostly parents, but the press released photos of children being held in cages in McAllen, the city next to Mission, which was widely credited as the epicenter of the family separation policy. "They treated us as though we were animals," said one woman in a letter to her lawyer. In August, a man massacred twenty-two people in a Walmart in El Paso minutes after publishing a manifesto online that explained, "This attack is a response to the Hispanic invasion of Texas."

Writing about the particular ferocity of anti-Mexican racism and violence on the border, historian Greg Grandin suggests that the border is where so-called white Americans have felt marginalized, most vulnerable to becoming the "other" they fear. If borders signify "domination and exploitation," he writes, "they also announce the panic of power, something that overcomes a political state similar to the way dread comes over an individual with the realization that their psyche isn't theirs to control alone, that it's formed in reaction to others." He quotes Freud: "The phobia is thrown before the anxiety like a fortress on the frontier."

I'd always had the sense, formed subliminally or even innately, that it was better to erase the past. My grandmother carried and then pushed her children as far as possible from her upbringing toward an imagined ideal of power, affluence, credibility, respectability, and safety. And my mother, in turn, carried and pushed me as far from her own upbringing as she could, clear across the country to California, then to the Ivy League, and then to New York, to the life I lead now.

In ways I don't like to contemplate, my life as an excellently educated, widely traveled, white-passing American woman was the dream behind that erasure. What could be more ungrateful than to redraw in public what was so carefully and privately elided?

Still, my mother took steps to preserve the parts of herself that her mother wanted gone. She learned Spanish in her youth, and, in the eighties, began referring to herself as Mexican American. "That's very much the reason I didn't change my name when I got married," she said. After a beat, she added, "Though going to Rosette Kisner would have been the ultimate success, in a way."

When people inquire after my mother's ethnicity now, she tells them that she's "as Mexican as you can get" because her father was a Garcia and her mother is a Martinez, which, she always adds, are like the Smith and Jones of the Mexican world. "Both my parents are Mexican and *completely* Mexican," she says.

I'd been sort of puzzled by the emphasis, particularly because it's not categorically true: the most Mexican you can get, in one sense, is to be from Mexico. This gestures toward a key—if confusing—element of the second- or third-generation experience: your cultural rootedness isn't always constructed based on your relationship to your family's actual country of origin. When I asked her about it, she said, "I feel like I have to sort of convince people that I'm Mexican. I don't feel Mexican enough." She moves through mostly white social spaces, and it bothers her that her features are ambiguous enough that all her life people have been asking her where she's from.

This shouldn't have surprised me, but it did. My mother is often the yardstick by which I estimate myself, and I had always assumed that I didn't feel Mexican enough because I was not enough like her. When I was growing up, she used to tell a story about how she and my father moved to Paris shortly after they were married, and when I was born she began to take me to the park near our apartment, in an affluent neighborhood. Most of the women at the park during the day were foreign au pairs tending to the babies of the white women who lived nearby. I was a fair baby with gold hair; my mother was mistaken for my au pair.

I always heard this story as an example of racial bias: my mother, a young, olive-skinned woman, was assumed to be the help rather than the mother. I also noted it as the first time that I was "not Mexican enough" to be recognizable. Subliminally, I understood it as a story about the deepest form of intergenerational betrayal: a daughter who doesn't resemble her mother. It strikes me now that my mother might not have thought of it that way at all—that she might simply have felt lonely in the park, caught between the mothers and the au pairs.

I hesitate to draw parallels between my life and my mother's because they are not the same life—by her design. My mother raised me with the hope that she could be my threshold, that her sacrifices and mistakes, her proximity to oppression, would deliver me to a different life, a life of being inside, where there was no space I wouldn't occupy comfortably, where the whole beautiful world was for me. But I am *nepantla*, in my ways, too. I, too, know what it feels like to pass without exactly wanting to.

It does not seem like a coincidence that a pageant devoted to celebrating a Eurocentric story about the American project should involve corsets and false eyelashes and elaborate, perfectly uniform curtsies—given that modern pageantry is a kissing cousin to drag or given that sites of extreme pressure to conform racially or nationally tend to beget even greater pressure to conform along lines of gender and sex. The pageant girl reflects an ideal that's being championed: wealth, national pride, a precise if exaggerated performance of traditional femininity, young beauty on the arm of a man. All that is in the dress.

There was a period in my twenties—when I'd begun dating women but hadn't yet told my mother—when we started arguing more than usual about my clothes. My wardrobe was migrating toward grays and tans, loose shapes, long necklaces, and clunky boots. There were minor tussles whenever I was home and tried to leave the house without earrings. I recall thinking that she looked at my clothing with distrust. I was becoming a different kind of woman than she is, and though I've never asked her about it, I think she could sense it from the cut of my shirts.

When I told my mother, finally, that I was in love with a woman, she was shocked and not a little outraged. I had always dated men, she reminded me. I'd been with one man for five whole years. Had I just been lying my way through that?

No, I tried to explain. I was attracted to men and women. I was choosing to be with women. I was in love with this woman.

"Don't," she said. "Just don't." She couldn't understand why, if I could be straight, if I could be safely inside the majority, I'd choose to be outside it. Furthermore, she couldn't understand why, if I wasn't going to be straight, I couldn't just go ahead and be gay—why I was insisting that I was some kind of in-between thing.

I was angry about this conversation for a long time. It wasn't until later that I realized she might have been expressing the kind of fear that comes from experience—it's not an easy thing to live as not quite one thing and not quite another when it's not a circumstance you have chosen. But if you are lucky enough to be able to choose—if someone has made you feel safe enough to choose—it can feel like freedom.

Once or twice, I tried to explain to my mother the feeling I had when I was watching the Marthas onstage. Even though I saw the forces of what constrained her and her mother and her mother's mother, even though I saw the corsets and the money and the bald desire to fit into a jingoistic idea of Americanness that contorts the people it touches—even though I saw all that, it also made my stomach flip. Because there was bilingual Leticia Garcia, "daughter of Mr. and Mrs. Hector Garcia," beaming before a thousand people while the names of her parents and grandparents were read as honorifics. You could say that it was simply because her family had money and that this is just a continuation of the pathological "right kind of Mexican" self-policing, and you'd be right. I'd just never gotten to see a girl named Garcia from South Texas stand in front of a room of the most powerful people in that state's government and society and be celebrated specifically for her "excellent" lineage. It was like seeing an alternate history. And I was ashamed, but I was moved.

• • •

The morning after the pageant, I woke up early and drove down to the Juarez-Lincoln International Bridge to see the Abrazo Ceremony. George Washington, an affable guy named Tim, had assured me that I could park downtown by the historic San Agustin Plaza and then walk the two blocks to the bridge.

Coming into Laredo near the main border crossing, you see first the mostly abandoned colonial structures of the old city: a tiled plaza rimmed with stylish Spanish stucco buildings that now sit mostly empty. The library was abandoned and emptied decades ago, and aside from a boutique hotel fashioned out of one of the renovated colonial buildings and the San Agustin Cathedral, which still holds Mass in Spanish, the historic downtown has a derelict quiet about it.

The streets downtown were empty. I parked near an abandoned office building and walked the couple blocks of uneven pavement to the bridge entrance, only to find it, too, empty except for three ICE officers hanging around near their booths. Juarez-Lincoln isn't a pedestrian bridge; it's a five-lane highway, so I hopped a little gate and walked across the quiet pavement toward the officers.

"I'm trying to see the Abrazo," I said.

The young man squinted at me. "Who are you? Are you with the mayor's office?"

When I explained, he shook his head. "The Abrazo Ceremony isn't open to the public."

I'd believed, based on the way that everyone from the Society had talked about the Abrazo, that it was a moment of mutual public celebration. I'd foolishly imagined that the Laredoans would walk onto the bridge from the north side and the Nuevo Laredoans would walk out from the south side, and they would meet in the middle. I'd pictured the two cities behaving as one city, the bridge open, cheers and music as the children hugged.

But there was nothing to see from the American side except the implacable faces of the ICE officers and nothing to hear at all. Of course, the bridge is never left wide open in Laredo to whoever wants to cross, not even on this day. The children are escorted out by the mayors and city officials, their parents, ICE officers, and military from both sides. A dais is set up in the middle of the bridge, garlanded in red, white, and blue, and the children are called forth by a dignitary. They approach one another, the four of them alone on the road. The little girl from Laredo is dressed like a mini Martha, the little boy like George. The children from Nuevo Laredo are dressed as was fashionable during the Spanish colonial period, with the girl in a mantilla and the boy in a sombrero, and each girl hugs the boy across from her.

I listened to it on the radio in my rental car. Driving back north, the city still seemed to be sleeping.

By the time I arrived near the parade grounds, it had awoken. It's hard to explain the mood of a town on the morning of an event like this: Every elevator held a man carrying a ruffled shirt in a garment bag. There were squads of kids in dance costumes camped out on the floor of my hotel lobby. Outside, ball-capped fathers had staked out positions on the bleachers with umbrellas and thick coolers full of beer and snacks.

The Anheuser-Busch Washington's Birthday Parade is for the whole city, and everyone—from the local children's dance studio to H-E-B supermarket employees riding on a fourteen-foot-tall grocery cart—participates. In between them all, paced every five floats or so, are the dresses on display, each with a girl inside it, each dress and its girl on its own corporate-sponsored parade float.

It is customary for the girls to have attendants ride with them on their floats and throw little gifts to the crowd. It is also customary for the people standing on the sidelines, catching the trinkets, to shout for the girls to lift up their heavy skirts and show their shoes. "*Muéstranos tus zapatos!*" This seems like an almost philosophical response to spectacle: an audience looking at young women in a state of exquisite display, corseted and contoured, fake hair piled high, and demanding to see what they're hiding.

Up come the manteau, the petticoats, the hoop, and when everyone sees what's underneath, they cheer.

This is the moment that former debs talk about as their fondest memory, the part when the whole city gets to see and admire their dresses. For most of them, it will be the only time in their lives that this many people will look at them all at once and applaud.

In *Say Yes to the Dress*, the moment always comes when, after trying on and discarding dozens of gowns, the woman approaches the mirror in The One. This is the denouement of the episode, and it's always the same. She steps up onto the pedestal in the showroom, sees her reflection, and is bewitched, thrilled, her own dream of herself coming true. Her mother, who perhaps has had reservations about some of the other options, immediately weeps.

"Are you saying yes to this dress?" Randy asks.

"Yes," the woman whispers or shouts or sobs. "Yes!" Everyone cheers, even the bitchy sister. This, in the logic of the show, is the happy ending. (The wedding, if they show it in the closing credits, is simply the occasion where she displays this achievement.)

So American, this show. You just go to the store and choose yourself off a rack at your preferred price point. As a metaphor—only as a metaphor—the Marthas' dresses are much more realistic: your mother or your sister or an aunt hands you a hundred-pound corseted structure and says, "Walk in that," and then you make a lot of decisions about what parts of the gown you want to keep, whether you'll change its color, cut off the weird embellishments the last wearer put on, or strip it to its bones, which cannot change.

I stayed at the parade for a while, weaving between the children jumping for beads and the fathers in lawn chairs who'd rise and angrily tap the shoulder of any passerby who paused and blocked their view. Marching bands and baton twirlers sandwiched the local Catholic bishop, who was riding on the back of a convertible like a teenager. Princess Pocahontas and her court, dressed in giant feathered headdresses and ornately beaded suede, rode skittering horses to great applause. ICE had a large formation of armored vehicles.

The last girl I saw that day was Sydney, the sixteen-year-old from the hair salon, who, despite the pain the dress was causing her, was beaming and waving. She wants to be a lawyer when she grows up. You could hardly tell she was sitting on a stool until the crowd yelled for her to show them her shoes. She smiled obligingly, gathered her skirts in each hand, heaved them upward, and kicked. There was a swirl of color: the peach and lavender of her dress reared back, revealing petticoats and then a splash of sequins. She was wearing six-inch platform go-go boots with another five inches of heel, covered toe-to-knee in sequins. Custom-made and star-spangled, red, white, and blue.

An appreciative roar went through the crowd. When Sydney saw me, I gave her a wave and then turned and began the walk back to my hotel, kicking the confetti in the dirt.

New York Times Magazine

WINNER—FEATURE WRITING

"I spent one month in the camps in Bangladesh listening to stories of rape and destruction, but nothing prepared me for the genocide of the mind," writes Sarah A. Topol in this account of the the Rohingya who fled persecution in Myanmar. "A people can survive a mass murder; those who remain can rebuild their lives. But what happens when a people's identity is taken from them?" The judges who chose "The Schoolteacher and the Genocide" as the recipient of the 2020 National Magazine Award for Feature Writing said that this "is a story whose distinctive, masterful approach to storytelling and structure sets it apart from any work of narrative journalism in recent memory." A writer at large at the New York Times Magazine, *Topol has spent the last decade reporting from overseas. The* New York Times Magazine *also won the award for Feature Writing in 2017 for "I Have No Choice but to Keep Looking," by Jennifer Percy.*

Sarah A. Topol

The Schoolteacher and the Genocide

When he was in primary school, Futhu read a story about a girl who named her flowers. She wrote their names in a diary, logged when she planted and watered them, and charted how they grew. The story was in a book Futhu's uncle brought to their village in Myanmar's western Rakhine State from across the border in Bangladesh—the words in English and in Bengali. Futhu was the first in his extended family to attend school—the first of twenty-two uncles, countless aunts and cousins—and though he excelled at Burmese and English class, he could not really understand the book on his own. His father was himself illiterate, as were most people in their community. So Futhu asked a village trader who often visited their home to read him the stories in the book, one by one.

Futhu followed along, practicing his English. Over time, the pages of the book tattered, until Futhu was able to read it himself. He thought the girl had a good idea and started keeping a diary of his own daily chores. He could not write in Rohingya, the language of his community, because it has had no written form, so he wrote in a mixture of English and Burmese.

The book told another story, too: The girl who kept the flower diary lived through a period in history known as World War II, when, as Futhu understood it, there was a fight between Hitler and the Jews. The girl's entries about flowers became a diary of what was happening at that time. When Futhu looked around his village, he thought there were many similarities between this story and what he saw in his own Muslim community. He decided he should write the incidents of Rohingya oppression, because maybe someday, in the future, people might want to know about what happened.

Ever since Futhu was small, he knew that the government did not consider Rohingya to be of this place but instead thought of them as illegal immigrants from Bangladesh. As far as Futhu knew, none of his family had migrated from Bangladesh. They'd only been driven there as refugees after one of the many armed operations against the Rohingya—of which there have been roughly a dozen since 1948, though Futhu did not know the exact number. Futhu had learned that there were 135 recognized ethnic groups in Myanmar, called *taing-yin-tha*, which is often translated as "national race" but literally means something like "offspring of the land," or indigenous. Those 135 groups, including the neighboring Rakhine and the country's main ethnic group, the Bamar, had the rights and citizenship that went along with official recognition, but the more than one million Rohingya did not.

Futhu began to write down some of the things he saw around him. The Rohingya, he noted, had to register all their livestock with the government. They required government permission to repair their homes. They needed permission from the government to marry, often paying hefty bribes and waiting for as long as two years to do so. They were unable to enroll in certain majors in college—they could not study to be lawyers or doctors. They could not join the army or the police or serve as heads of governing bodies or run for public office. They were not allowed to have more than two children. Women were forced to take birth control or seek illegal abortions. Families paid bribes to register additional children or hid them from the authorities. Over time, almost every Rohingya had their nationality cards taken from them. They had to give the authorities their chickens and cows, to lend them their motorcycle or their bodies for forced labor when it was demanded, and received no compensation. Many doctors refused to treat them. Getting to a hospital would require so many travel permissions and so much time that Rohingya often arrived half dead and eventually did die. Families cast the blame on the hospitals themselves—they were sure the doctors intended to kill them. Many stopped going. More died of preventable causes.

Futhu did not know why the government focused on the Rohingya with such ferocity, only that they were unwanted. While the Burmese government maintained that the Rohingya were Bangladeshi and the government of Bangladesh said they were Burmese, a question hung over the community: How could we not be offspring of this land? Did we fall from the sky?

• • •

When Futhu set about writing down the story of his village back in the late 1990s, he did not have grand ambitions. He wanted to know about his community, about his family and his neighbors, to understand their own roots in this tiny sliver of earth. Dunse Para, as they called it—Koe Tan Kauk in Burmese—was nestled on a narrow stretch of flat, verdant land with the gray Bay of Bengal on one side and the rocky Mayu Mountains looming on the other. Each morning, the men of the village would wake in the darkness, walk to the shoreline, and climb into boats, setting off for their daily catch. The boats—small wooden rowboats and twenty-two larger vessels with motors—belonged to a few wealthy villagers who employed shift workers to go far out to sea. When men weren't fishing, they were farming their rice paddies or growing chiles. They tended to their animals—chickens, water buffaloes, cows, and goats. The community was deeply conservative. Women stayed at home, far from the lingering eyes and hands of the Burmese security services, who often harassed them.

Futhu peppered his grandfather and village elders with questions about Dunse Para's founding. His grandfather explained that their forefathers lived on a nearby hill where the community now grazed buffaloes. Futhu's great-great-grandfather donated part of the family's land there to make a cemetery, but after its construction, people started getting sick, and so they fled down the hill, to a village they called the Village by the Mountain. When it got too crowded there, people migrated, slowly moving closer to the surf. They set up the Big Village, then the Village by the Sea and then the Big Village Transferred by the Sea, where Futhu and his family lived. Dunse Para was composed of these four smaller villages, the roughly 1,000 homes arranged around straight, neatly plotted footpaths running through groves of trees. Dunse Para sat about a mile away from the nearest Rakhine settlement of about one hundred households, also called Koe Tan Kauk, with a security checkpost stationed between. As far as Futhu had been able to verify, the land they lived on had been theirs for generations.

Once Futhu was satisfied with his documentation of the land, he turned to the stories of the people themselves. He went back to his grandfather and the elders in order to diagram the village's family trees. He listed names and birth villages: a mother's village, a father's village, and the children they had, the siblings of the mother and the father, backward and forward in time, until his chart sprawled across several villages. He found that in some cases, people who lived in the same village were actually related to one another through blood, though they did not know it. Or in others, that people were related by blood, but not in the way they thought. This was true in his own family. A girl whom Futhu had grown up calling his sister was in fact his cousin. Her father's grandmother and Futhu's mother's grandmother were sisters, and then she was married off to another family. Futhu also found people who had relatives in different villages whom they had never met. Futhu would follow one little family's bloodline until it grew like vines across the mountains.

The residents of Dunse Para did not always understand the value of Futhu's inquiries. They asked him why he was always writing things down—was it perhaps for some kind of sorcery? But when they needed a question answered, about who was related to whom and how and when, they came to ask him, and he would explain. Slowly, as Futhu's notebooks filled, then multiplied, these small proofs wove a larger web of authenticity—a document of roots in this earth, of offspring, ownership, and belonging.

• • •

Dunse Para had no books that could have explained to Futhu that outsiders had documented the presence of the Rohingya community as far back as the eighteenth century. In 1799, Francis Buchanan, a Scottish physician living in India, visited what was then called Arakan and wrote that two groups populated the area—the "Yakein" and the "Rooinga." (This record is crucial and as such highly contested in the debate over who was or wasn't in Burma before the British arrived and, thus, who is and who isn't "offspring of this land.")

Futhu knew that the British began to wrest control over Rakhine State's present territory in 1824, but he did not know that it would take them six decades to take the rest of Burma, which became a province of India, with open borders between the two. The British encouraged migration from India, which at that time included present-day Pakistan and Bangladesh, rewarding Muslim arrivals with high posts that drew the envy and ire of locals. Still, everyone in the community talked about life under the colonizers as a time of prosperity and peace.

Futhu's grandfather explained that when the Japanese invaded Arakan in 1942 during World War II and battled the

British in the mountains, the fighting did not touch the people of Dunse Para. His grandfather never told him that when the war broke out, the Rohingya and Rakhine took opposing sides. These communal strains would reverberate through generations. The Buddhist Rakhine backed the invading Japanese, who promised independence from the British, while the Muslim Rohingya supported the British colonizers, who treated them well. His grandfather said only that at that time of the great war, both communities took long knives and rocks and massacred each other.

Many Rohingya, like Futhu's family, fled to the north of the state for safety, while the Rakhine congregated in the south to protect their own lives. Futhu knew that his grandfather's grandmother, who was very old at the time, could not run fast enough and died in those battles, cut down with a knife. His grandfather told him that the family stayed in the north for a month and when they returned, they found their houses smashed, their cows vanished. It was the first of what would be several violent upheavals in recent history, all distinct in origin yet all following a grim pattern of displacement and return.

Before Burma's independence in 1948, the country was rocked by anti-Indian and anti-Muslim riots. The rioters demanded that those who had come with the British leave with them. Many people fled, making their way to what was then East Pakistan, now called Bangladesh. In the 1950s, Burma's first elected government under Prime Minister U Nu announced that anyone who lived within Burma's borders before the British colonizers arrived would be granted citizenship. Many Rohingya, like Futhu's family, were issued papers. There were promises of future autonomy and more rights.

But the coup of Gen. Ne Win in 1962 put an end to these plans. Ne Win believed that the identity of the state should be Buddhist and that all ethnic minorities agitating for rights should be suppressed in favor of national consolidation. His ire focused particularly on Muslims, whom he saw as transplants and feared would have more children, shifting demographics in their favor. In Rakhine State, the junta imposed travel restrictions on the Rohingya and tasked the Buddhist Rakhine with enforcing the new orders. More Rohingya fled—including Futhu's grandfather, who took refuge in Bangladesh in 1963. He seldom spoke about those years, but Futhu knew that in exile he learned to read Bengali. When Futhu was very small, after evening prayer, he watched his grandfather read long Bengali poems, almost like music; people from the village would come, listen, and make requests.

Beginning in 1977, the Burmese military, known as the Tatmadaw, carried out a major operation called Naga Min, or Dragon King, designed to drive "illegal immigrants" out of Burma. The army descended on Rohingya villages, corralling people—including Futhu's mother and father—and forcing them to roll up their sleeves to show if they had received vaccinations, claiming Bangladeshis had scars on their right arms while Burmese citizens had them on their left. During this campaign of intimidation, Rohingya had their citizenship papers confiscated. The soldiers burned villages, destroyed mosques and herded people into fenced stockades. They raped and murdered. More than 200,000 Rohingya refugees were crowded into ramshackle camps on the Bangladeshi side of the Naf River, which separates the two countries. The Bangladeshi authorities, who also didn't want them, withheld food rations in an attempt to force the Rohingya back. Less than six months after they fled, the Rohingya were forcibly repatriated. Three years later, the military government passed the 1982 Citizenship Law. The act would be used to effectively bar Rohingya from citizenship. The Rohingya became the largest stateless population within a country in the world.

Futhu had just started primary school when his older sister and the family joined thousands of Rohingya walking to Bangladesh in 1992, all of them trying to escape a new drive to conscript the

Rohingya, including his father, into forced labor. The family fled, trekking six days along paths already worn by earlier exoduses. That wave was made up of 270,000 people. They lived in the Bangladeshi refugee camps for four years. During that time, unknown to them, the Burmese government started a program of building "model" Buddhist villages on their soil. They lured poor Rakhine or Bamar prisoners from other parts of the country to repopulate the state, offering tempting deals of ample land, a pair of oxen, and a house.

In the camps, Futhu's father did not give up on his son's education. Futhu attended private classes in an unused shack, where he learned English and Burmese in a small group taught by another Rohingya refugee. One morning, the family was informed that the next day they had to go back to Myanmar. They had no choice. Refugees who protested were beaten. Some were killed. The family boarded a speedboat that deposited them back to the land that did not want them. When Futhu's mother stepped onto the shore, she saw the Tatmadaw and the Rakhine people and grew sick to her stomach. Nothing of their house remained. They would have to start from scratch, collecting timber from the hills.

Futhu walked to the Rakhine village to finish primary school then boarded in a nearby Rakhine town for middle school. But the fear never left. It asserted itself in a variety of ways. His father was terrified every time he saw the military. He shook and worried, even if Futhu did not see the danger. The trauma carried over to the next generation even if history's dates and details did not. Children absorbed it through their mother's embrace or their father's anger. It was present in the way their fathers flinched when they saw an approaching patrol or the way the men of the village sometimes ran away, spending nights in the hills, thinking the security services were after them. It was erasure without eradication, the inability to conceive of a peaceful future. Some refused to build nice houses. Others made do and continued to invest in a land that did not want them. All of them, one by one, generation by generation, had no choice but to survive. They grew up to live their parents' traumas themselves. They never knew the origins or when something might come again to throw them violently off the earth.

• • •

Futhu's father did not have the funds to send him to university. Education was expensive—between 1.8 million and 2 million kyat ($1,250) to put a child through one year of high school. Families usually could afford to educate only one son while his brothers worked.

After he finished high school, Futhu began keeping another journal, a special smaller red notebook, where he documented incidents in which the government's brutal frontier force, the NaSaKa, came to the village from their nearby outpost—bribes, extortion, beatings, fines, arrests. Futhu's father offered to loan him money to start a small shop, but he wanted something more. A friend of his, who taught Quranic school in the morning and afternoon at the mosque, suggested that Futhu hold a small class teaching children English and Burmese during the day. There were so many children who wanted to learn, the friend said. Together they collected two dozen students. Futhu visited parents to explain that they needed to try to save money for textbooks. When some families couldn't find the funds, Futhu asked wealthier people for donations. If those weren't enough, he paid for the students' books himself.

Futhu made deals with traveling traders to bring him the weekly newspaper from Maungdaw to better understand the world. He loved history and languages. He was obsessed with writing down the lyrics to English songs. He collected books. He read about World War I, Winston Churchill, and Bill Clinton. From the start, he loved to teach. He sang his students songs and read them poems so they would better remember. He translated the Burmese curriculum into Rohingya, so it was easier to understand. Like the history in his notebooks, he started every explanation at the very, very beginning.

Within a few months, his students were reading and writing. Within two years, they started passing exams for middle-school placement. The teachers at the nearby primary school in the Rakhine village were surprised when Rohingya started scoring better than their Rakhine peers. How did you do it? they asked.

In the country's 2010 elections, when the Rohingya still had the right to vote, the candidate from the Union Solidarity and Development Party (USDP), known for its ties to the military, held a campaign event in Dunse Para. The junta was loosening its reins after the "saffron revolution"—a series of antigovernment protests in 2007 led by Buddhist monks calling for political reforms. The election was boycotted by the party led by Daw Aung San Suu Kyi, the Nobel Peace Prize recipient, and international observers would slam the vote as unfair, but in Dunse Para, the USDP promised the Rohingya rights for votes. They offered seven million kyat for local development. Instead of dividing it among the residents, which would net each family enough to buy a cup of tea, Futhu thought they should establish an official school. Until that point, Rohingya students who wanted to attend a registered government primary school had to walk to the one Futhu himself attended in the Rakhine village. For middle school and high school, they had to board in larger villages, as Futhu had.

The village chief, Foyaz Ullah, agreed with Futhu, but the community took some persuading. For weeks, Futhu went door to door. He met with parents. He held community meetings. He noticed differences between his community and the *taing-yin-tha* groups. They might say: "My son has a BA" or even "My son has a master's," but in Futhu's community, people said things like "I have seven kani of land," or "I have two cows and a goat." He thought the Rohingya should measure the value of their lives differently.

Not everyone was convinced. If we send our children to Burmese schools, will they forget their culture? they asked. Will they ignore the values we taught them? Will they start to drink beer like the Rakhine people? And even if a child could pass primary school, middle school, and secondary school, what was the point? They could not go to college or get good-paying government jobs or join the police or the army. Children were needed for labor and errands. Why spend money on bribes, books, and exams when the future was already predetermined?

But, Futhu argued, if the Rohingya were educated, they could put an end to these rules. More of their community could run for Parliament. If they had a dozen members of Parliament, even if the authorities killed one or two of them, the rest would remain, and they could come up with new ideas for how to cast light into their darkness.

Together with prominent members of the community, Futhu eventually persuaded the town. He organized the school's registration with the government. He tabulated and retabulated the budget in his diary. He realized that the promised money wasn't nearly enough: A properly built school would cost ten times the USDP contribution. He put together a committee to figure out how to build it more cheaply. To avoid paying laborers for construction, they collected twenty-five volunteers. They needed coconut trees for wall beams, but to buy a whole coconut tree and carry it from the hills would cost a huge sum. Futhu had another idea: Many people in the village had coconut trees on their land that had not given fruit in years. He mapped those trees and went to their owners. Could they not buy their useless trees for a reduced price? Within a week, all barren coconut trees of the village became stumps.

During construction, to attract more free labor, they put up speakers at the site and loudly played Hindi and English pop songs. When people gathered, drawn by the commotion, they asked: Can you help us? Students made fires and tended stoves;

they fetched water from the well and made tea for the laboring guests. They built fences to block the school grounds from the nearby stream, so the kids wouldn't stumble and fall in. They strung up tarpaulins for walls, taking care to make sure fresh air could come in to the classrooms. They blocked the view of the road, so children would not be distracted.

In 2010, when they were done, the first official government school in Dunse Para had space for four classes, blackboards, and 260 pupils. Starting one village school, which may seem so simple, was actually so difficult and so monumental, it was like changing the course of a deep river.

In 2013, Futhu married his wife in a big ceremony attended by many people from the village. She was beautiful, with soft round features, sparkling eyes, olive skin, and a laugh that sounded like little bells chiming. Futhu had loved her since they were children and had won her heart secretly over time. When Futhu's parents came to her house to officially arrange the match, her mother and brothers were keen: Futhu was educated, and he spoke English. Her mother blessed the union.

By then, Futhu's red logbook was full of short entries about the punishments meted out by the NaSaKa, which he wrote in Rohingya but spelled in a mixture of English and Burmese—a code only he could decipher. He also kept his daily diary, writing in it every night in the bed he now shared with his wife. Sometimes she grew angry with him for keeping their kerosene lantern on long into the darkness. The Rohingya were not allowed to have the lights on late at night. About this, their conversations grew heated and sometimes verged on fights. Futhu explained to her that the information he was writing was more valuable than money; if something happened to him and he died, the knowledge he was collecting would live on forever.

By the time Futhu and his wife had their own sons, he had more than forty diaries. He lived in the house he shared with his parents and three brothers, and he kept the diaries in a wooden chest he'd paid a small fortune to build. They were mixed in together with other schoolbooks and papers like camouflage.

• • •

Two years after the school's founding, the structure needed repairs, and Futhu organized a soccer tournament to raise the money. In early June 2012, after the final match, the villagers saw many Rakhine people passing along the road. Futhu thought they were going to a nearby mountain, where they held a yearly festival to celebrate the end of the Rakhine year with songs and dramas. But that evening, as the people of Dunse Para were deconstructing the field and stands, they heard rumors that Rohingya houses in nearby towns were being burned.

Over the next few days, Rohingya began showing up in Dunse Para with stories of fires swallowing their villages and Rakhine mobs out to kill them with sticks and knives. The communal violence eventually led to the deaths of several hundred people, including dozens of children who were hacked apart, as the security services either looked the other way or joined in the bloodletting on the Rakhine side. Futhu had heard about times like these, the interethnic riots of the past, though he had never witnessed them himself. Only later did he learn that it began when a Buddhist woman had been raped and killed, and there was a rumor that Muslim men had committed the assault. The story had spread online, and in retaliation a bus of Muslim men was set upon by a Rakhine mob numbering hundreds. Ten Muslim men were killed in revenge.

Though Dunse Para was far from the violence, it was not immune to the fallout. Villagers' land was commandeered to house those displaced. After running over the mountains in hordes to Dunse Para and a nearby village called Chein Khar Li, the newly homeless never left. The villagers heard that in Sittwe, the state capital, Rohingya were herded into a few city blocks, ensnared by barbed wire, and couldn't leave. They had been living in a ghetto ever since.

As the Rohingya were stripped of their rights, the outside world didn't seem to notice. In 2012, President Barack Obama eased sanctions on Myanmar after by-elections netted Aung San Suu Kyi a majority of the seats in Parliament. The first sitting United States president ever to set foot in Myanmar, Obama arrived shortly after the 2012 communal violence. He only briefly mentioned the Rohingya in a glowing speech that focused on the nation's new democratic future.

Two years later, Futhu used a mobile phone with internet access for the first time, and it changed everything. He was struck by the wealth of information this tiny object held—the weather in Delhi or diseases in other parts of the world. When he opened Facebook, he saw something else: posts disparaging his community, calling them *kalar* (a derogatory term for foreigners), dogs, and rapists and agitating for them to leave Myanmar. Muslim-owned shops burned in other parts of the country. Muslims were killed in the street. A group of fanatic monks, who called their organization 969, and then MaBaTha, had been preaching violence for years. Though Futhu knew about these incidents, they did not form any kind of early warning pattern in his mind. In 2015, he began teaching at the first official middle school in Chein Khar Li, shared by the two Rohingya communities. His focus remained on his students.

• • •

On October 9, 2016, in the early morning hours, when Futhu was sleeping in the middle-school dormitory in Chein Khar Li, the sound of bullets ripped across the paddy fields and through the thatched houses of Dunse Para. Men rushed outside to try to figure out what was going on. Robbers? Thieves? A gang? They trampled the dirt paths to ask their village chief, Ayub, for surely he would know. Ayub had been in the position for two years, serving under the head chief from the Rakhine village, who was often referred to as Chairman. Ayub, short and stocky, was a wealthy businessman. He had a good relationship with the authorities and had been doting on them for far longer than his current term. His house was made of tin, and the door was locked from the inside. The villagers pounded until he answered. "What is happening?" they demanded. He had no idea.

The men stayed together until dawn broke. The gunfire had subsided, and the anxious crowd shifted from Ayub's house to tea stalls next to the Big Village's main mosque. By the time Futhu returned, Dunse Para was undulating with fear. Ayub and his deputy chiefs, who headed the smaller villages, had been called to the checkpost by the Myanmar Border Guard Police, known as the BGP. A security-service detachment had surrounded the village. Women were told to stay indoors while men clustered here and there, trying to figure out what was going on.

At the post, Ayub was taken inside to see the BGP sector commander, who showed him a captured militant, presumably among those responsible for the violence.

"Do you know him?" he asked.

Ayub said he did not.

They showed him a dead militant's body.

"Do you know him?"

Ayub swore he did not. The imprisoned man seconded Ayub's claim under interrogation. The militant said that the men had come to attack the checkpost, with no help from the local community.

In the afternoon, the sector commander told Ayub to bury the dead body in secret. The man had a beard; he was obviously a Muslim. "It'll be better if you bury the dead body in a Muslim graveyard. Take three people. Make sure nobody sees it."

When Ayub returned to the village, he informed two town criers—*saingom*—that the authorities had handed down additional rules. The men walked the dirt paths of the villages, calling out the orders: Curfew from dusk to sunrise! No more call to prayer! Men cannot gather in groups greater than four! Quranic school is suspended! Fishing and going to the mountains for timber are forbidden! All house fences must be torn down!

In an instant, the men's livelihoods were taken. No one understood what had happened. Two days later, a video was posted online by a group claiming responsibility for the October 9 attack. They called themselves Harakah al-Yaqin, the Faith Movement, and would later take the name the Arakan Rohingya Salvation Army, ARSA. Suddenly, everyone in Dunse Para was talking about them, even the small children. They wondered who these people were and which village they had come from. The group, led by a committee of Rohingya émigrés in Saudi Arabia, used their language. In the video, they explained that they were spurred to act after the 2012 oppressions. They had launched simultaneous strikes on two BGP checkposts and the BGP headquarters in Maungdaw township. It was not a major offensive, but it had come as a surprise. In total, nine policemen and eight militants were killed. ARSA fled with 62 firearms and more than 10,000 rounds of ammunition. The government estimated that the total attackers numbered 400 and accused the local community of helping.

As the ARSA video circulated online, the security services returned to Dunse Para. Officers fanned out through the village on patrol. A cluster approached Futhu's house. They told everyone to come outside and bring their household list, an official record of every member of their family. Anyone missing during a security check could be crossed off the list and banned from ever returning.

The family came down into their yard. Other than Futhu's older brother, who had fled more than a decade before and eventually settled in Malaysia, braving the risky sea journey in which thousands of Rohingya have died over the years, everyone was present. Seemingly satisfied, the officers said they could go back inside. They were at the edge of the family's property when the commander turned back and called for Futhu.

"Where were you on October 9?" the commander asked.

Futhu explained he was at the middle-school dormitory. If they had any questions, they could speak to the Rakhine chairman. The commander eyed him, reached up, and grabbed him by his hair. "Why are you trying to fight against the Tatmadaw?" he spat. "Why are you doing this violence?"

"I'm not involved in any kind of violence," Futhu said. "Why would I? You're like our brothers."

Futhu recognized one of the BGP officers. He was stationed at the checkpost Futhu crossed every day as he went to the school. They often exchanged greetings and sometimes played soccer together. "I know that man," Futhu pleaded. "He knows me. Why do you suspect us? We all help each other, we do each other favors. I've never been involved in this kind of work. I am a teacher."

The commander continued pulling Futhu's hair at the root. "Why are people coming from Bangladesh fighting with the police and military?" he said. Futhu managed to keep himself quiet. The commander released his grip and strode away. Before the officers left, they kicked down the family's outhouse fence.

In the days after the ARSA attack, men of the village were plucked out for interrogation. The village chief's brother, who was an Islamic teacher, was beaten, and then Ayub himself was taken. The two deputies who accompanied him on the day he was detained fled to the hills, terrified that they would be next.

• • •

A few weeks later, the Rakhine chairman sent word that an international delegation would be coming to several towns, including Dunse Para, to learn about their situation. The villagers did not know what to expect. After the 2015 elections, when Aung San Suu Kyi became de facto head of the country, no one pushed the new leadership to account for previous sins. They used many excuses to abdicate "the lady" from responsibility for the apartheid that had flourished for years, including that the Tatmadaw, not the government, was actually still in control. But the ARSA attacks focused international attention on the state, as the Tatmadaw launched "area clearance operations."

Futhu was getting ready for prayer at the mosque when he saw a cluster of elders and young students sitting on the ground, discussing what the community should do when the foreigners came. The group was debating making signs in English about their oppression—they could write "RAPE, GENOCIDE, KILLING, TORTURE" in big letters. Someone suggested asking a teacher to write the words in English correctly.

Futhu wasn't sure what he thought of the idea. There had been no trouble in their village during the 2012 riots. Was it wise to be writing such things when they lived in peace and harmony with their Rakhine neighbors? Futhu never said he was a brave man. He was helping to oversee the reconstruction of the primary school, which had been wrecked by a cyclone in 2013. They had jury-rigged the roof. He kept his head down; he avoided eye contact; he hurried to finish his prayers.

The foreigners came during harvest. The rice at the top of the stalks in the paddies was hard and yellow, ready to be cut, threshed, and dried in the sun. When the helicopter landed, everyone working in the fields gathered on the dirt roads. Some held placards, while others strained for a glimpse, as if at a soccer match. One sign read, "How long we suffer mass killing, rape Rohingya mothers and sisters from Rakhine and BGP and government." Futhu thought his students had looked up the correct English spellings on Facebook.

There was a foreign woman and a few foreign men wearing clothing from their own countries. The villagers believed they really had come to help. Delegations usually brought their own translators, but more often than not these translators could not speak Rohingya, and most villagers could not speak Burmese. The Rakhine chairman was charged with translating, but he was having trouble with the words.

The authorities asked if Futhu could help. He stepped forward, along with another teacher. An older woman was crying and crying. The delegates asked what was wrong. She wanted to explain that her brother had been arrested and she had no idea where he was, alive or dead. Other villagers tried to explain their situation: We are not recognized with our real ethnicity. We don't have permission for anything. We don't have freedom to move from here to there. We need to receive permission to marry. We don't have rights. They say that we are foreigners. They say we're Bengali, and we're not. All our ancestors, fathers, and grandfathers have been living here for a long time. Why do they not accept us as citizens? Please, you, delegation of different countries, please, try to fix this problem and give us recognition.

When the meeting ended, the members of the delegation began walking back to their cars, but the Rakhine chairman lingered. He turned to the villagers with anger: "You complained about us and shamed our government," he told them. "There will be a big problem waiting for you."

• • •

Several mornings later, the village found a dozen BGP trucks parked on the main road. Futhu and his father raced to hide his diaries, shoving them in a sack and stowing it in a rice paddy next to some bushes. Hurrying home, they saw the officers making their way to the Big Village. By eleven a.m., they heard the calls of the *saingom*: All males over twelve years old, report to the Big Village!

When they arrived, they saw their neighbors, hundreds of them, maybe a thousand, seated in a formation of rows in identical, unnatural positions. The men had their legs straight in front of them, their hands clasped behind their necks, heads bowed. The BGP lined the path. As the new arrivals approached, the officers hit them with sticks or kicked them with their boots. They forced each man to take off his watch and put them in a big, shiny pile. Futhu handed over his watch—a wedding gift from his wife's family that had come all the way from Yangon, the former capital. But before he could take his place, he was called out of the line. Officers tied his hands behind his back and started beating him. There was no explanation, just a torrent of blows that fell on his head and his body. Futhu fell over. The beating continued. He was bleeding, dizzy. He saw that his father was bleeding from the mouth. He lost consciousness and woke intermittently. He was being dragged now. The sharp points of knives were piercing his skin. A cigarette smoldered his arm. As the villagers watched Futhu's torment, no one was surprised. They all knew what happened to the educated when the authorities came.

When Futhu woke up, his arms were still tied behind him. Everything—his back, his stomach, his arms, and his head—hurt. He had been dragged a short distance from the group. If anyone protested or looked up, they were beaten harder. The BGP officers lit cigarettes, smoked, and chatted. One man recorded the detention on his mobile phone, turning it around to film his face, as if he were taking a vacation selfie. An officer barked at Futhu to get up. He could barely stand, but he followed the officer to a clearing, where three higher-ranking officials sat under the shade of betel nut trees.

"You did the translation for the delegation?" one of them asked.

Futhu confirmed that he had. "This is not your country," Futhu remembers him saying. "You're Rohingya. Your ancestors came from Bangladesh. You claim that you're indigenous of this country, and you demanded rights? How dare you."

Futhu saw that one of the officers in the group was the highest-ranking officer from the nearby BGP post. Another was a man he had played soccer with. He looked to him as he spoke. "I'm the schoolteacher here."

"Who wrote the placards?" the officers asked him.

"I don't know," Futhu responded. "I don't know."

The officer Futhu had recognized from the checkpost came over and smashed him in the head with a rifle. They wanted to know about ARSA. Futhu said he knew nothing about them. The Rakhine chairman was there, and the officers turned to him: "What kind of person is he?"

"I know his parents and his ancestors," the chairman said. "He is a good man. He goes to school straight and comes back. Maybe he was involved in the placard writing, but he is not involved with any bad people."

It was as good of a character reference as Futhu could have hoped for. "Ask the other military and police soldiers how good a relationship our relationship was," he begged, unable to stop himself from talking. "They see me going to school and coming back directly from the school! Morning and evening, every day! I don't know any of those people. I have never been involved in this work!"

Futhu was ordered to return to the others, his life spared.

By the evening, it had started to rain, turning the ground the men sat on to mud. The officers told the soaking mass to get up. They were herded into a two-story thatched house with the interior walls removed. Hundreds of men were pushed in and piled on top of one another.

In the morning, women and children appeared, having been told that they could bring food for the captives. Futhu's mother arrived with fish curry and rice, but her son could not swallow through the pain. As the men ate, the BGP came for the women. In the Big Village, they stormed into their homes. They rooted through their things. They ripped the gold ornaments off their necks and the mobile phones from inside their blouses. They chased women, and if they caught them, they touched all of their bodies.

At Futhu's house, his wife, along with one of Futhu's sisters and his eleven-year-old brother, sat under a tree watching the officers toss their belongings outside. They began to tear apart Futhu's chest and collect his papers. The papers were useless to everyone except Futhu; even his careful father hadn't thought to hide them. Futhu's wife was eight months pregnant with their second child. She had never known her mother-in-law to be particularly forceful, but she charged up to the officer. "What are you doing?" Futhu's mother demanded. "Why are you going through my son's papers?" Having just come from seeing her son's wounds, how much more could she take? Futhu's wife watched in shock as she tried to grab some of the papers from the officer's hand. The man did not let go. The officers took all the papers except one, which she picked up off the ground and slid next to her heart. Futhu's diaries, which he and his father hid that morning, remained safe.

The BGP commander explained that because Ayub was detained and his two deputies had fled, they needed new leadership. He asked Futhu if he wanted the job. "I am only a teacher," Futhu said. "I don't want to be responsible for this."

The commander told the group to pick their new leaders. Everyone looked to Foyaz Ullah, because he had held the job before Ayub. Foyaz Ullah was crestfallen. He had no choice but to accept.

"This time we are letting you go, but next time we will burn your houses and turn them into ashes," the commander said. "Now, we are warning you orally. Next time, this will talk!" He turned his rifle on the crowd.

The officers brought Futhu a blank paper. On it Futhu was instructed to write: "The BGP came to our village. They did a check. They did no harassment or looting. They took good care of us." The men signed their names.

In the days after the mass detention, men who had run up into the mountains returned to Dunse Para. Those who sheltered in the paddies crept back by night. In the end, the village counted ten men who had been arrested, including the other translator for the foreign delegation. Relatives would spend months trying to figure out where these men were held and whether they had been hurt. For those who remained, their already small world was shrinking—the restrictions were still in place. Men could not fish or cut timber from the hills, but they had families to feed, marriage fees to pay, bribes to register children outside the two-child law. What happens to men when they are powerless? What happens to women who live in fear? Some got desperate and sneaked into the mountains to forage for wood scraps. Others, forbidden to fish with boats or nets, ran into the sea with plastic bags tied to their bodies.

Since the October 9 attacks, ARSA was growing in strength. They set up cells within dozens of villages, led by local leaders, usually imams. They recruited young, frustrated men, promising money and rights. They revealed a more menacing side. ARSA began targeting Rohingya they suspected of being informants—they killed more than a dozen village heads and other local administrators. For Foyaz Ullah, the pressure would be coming from all sides—if he received ARSA pressure and reported it, he could be executed for collaboration. The military, meanwhile, demanded ARSA updates, even if he had none to give. The community swore they'd never seen or heard from actual ARSA members, but who could be sure what was happening high in the mountains, where they weren't technically even allowed to tread.

Ever since the village detention, schools had been closed. With no students to teach, Futhu thumbed his books, read his newspapers, and listened to the radio, but he began losing patience. The children were falling behind their Rakhine peers. He heard members of the community say that even if the schools reopened, they would not send their children back. The middle school was about an hour's walk to Chein Khar Li from Dunse Para, past the checkpost, and parents did not want their children anywhere near the officers.

Futhu saw that the video taken by the officer at the village detention had been posted to Facebook. A commission came to Dunse Para to "investigate"—the villagers later heard that some officers, including the one Futhu knew, were put in jail. It would be one of the only cases in which the military or the police charged its own with crimes committed against the Rohingya. But nothing in the village changed. The men detained that night were still missing. The villagers heard that one had died in custody. By the summer, Ayub was still in detention. His family had retained a lawyer who told them that with enough money, she could get him released on August 30, but they would have to wait. Futhu had spent the spring focused on rebuilding the primary school. They had collected all the materials, and by August 2017, they were almost done with the new roof.

• • •

In the dark early hours of August 25, everyone in Dunse Para and Chein Khar Li woke together and at once to a barrage of bullets, so many that it sounded like pounding rain. Futhu's wife, who had given birth not long ago to their second son, told her brother-in-law to call Futhu, who was sleeping at Chein Khar Li, but the line would not connect. The sounds were coming from that direction, and they began to fear for his life. A crowd went to see Foyaz Ullah, who was unsure of what they should do. Though the nearby village was being attacked, perhaps the military would not come to Dunse Para. We are innocent people, they repeated to themselves.

Awake in Chein Khar Li, Futhu could think only of his family. One of his friends told him to stay put, that there could be danger on the road. As the hours dragged on, the bullet rain kept falling. By dawn, Futhu decided to risk it. In the morning light, he could see the security services and gunfire on the main road. To the north, the beach was calm, waves lapping at the shore. He ran. When he arrived home, the house was empty. His thoughts, normally so ordered and rapid, now broke apart and scattered: How will I find my family? What will I do now? How will I save myself? He hurried to the Big Village to check his in-laws' house, with the thought that his family could have fled there. At his mother-in-law's place, he found a woman he did not know taking refuge. She had not seen his wife or his parents.

The bullet rain was now joined by the thunder of heavy weapons and explosions. Futhu picked his way from one house to the next, asking for his family. At the main mosque, he spotted a crowd of men making their own calculations: Those with small children were running to the hills, while older people were staying put. They told Futhu to check his aunt's house. They thought they'd seen his family there.

When Futhu finally saw them—his father, mother, wife, and children all together, all safe—there was the briefest moment of relief. They had fled that morning, not knowing how to pass him the message that they were seeking shelter. Futhu filled his father in on what he'd seen along the way.

"What should we do?" his father asked.

"We don't have a choice," Futhu decided. "We follow the crowd."

The path to the mountains crossed the road on which the military trucks traveled. Though they were parked outside Chein Khar Li, they could move at any moment. Futhu and his family agreed to run fast. They could only hope the trucks did not shudder to life.

When the family set out, they tried to stay together, but the young couple were weighed down by two babies. Futhu's wife carried their youngest, and Futhu carried their toddler. Soon they lost each other in the scrum of people scrambling up the hills, jagged with rocks and slippery with monsoon mud. Futhu's sandals got stuck immediately, so he threw them off. All he had was a red T-shirt, trousers, and a raincoat. The tiny cluster collided with other families picking their way up the mountains, everyone using any limbs they could to cling to the land while moving toward the sky. When they got above the village, they cast their eyes below. In Chein Khar Li, smoke and red flames danced in unison. Bodies were strewn on the ground. Dunse Para appeared empty. A few young men braved the route down to Chein Khar Li to scavenge food and returned with burned rice and tales of burned bodies. Darkness came. Futhu and his family decided they would sleep there. There were about two dozen people sheltering under a tiny scrap of tarp.

The next morning, an ethereal, unnatural calm settled like mist. In Dunse Para, Foyaz Ullah held out hope. Maybe the military wouldn't come. First one day passed, then two. Soon the people in the hills would return. Their village would again be spared. Futhu and his family walked to another village, Boshora, where they slept two nights. They ate and prayed it was all over. They collected a few pots, dried meat, and a larger tarp, in case they would have to run again.

On August 28, in the early morning, the security services entered Dunse Para and Boshora, weapons firing. Instantly, the residents knew they had never been safe. Futhu and his family ran again. They heard explosions at their backs. They clambered up the mountains again, higher and higher, and sheltered under the trees. When the military entered Dunse Para, those who had remained tried to run up the same paths. Foyaz Ullah's family dashed out of their house. As they ran, a bullet tore through Foyaz

Ullah's torso. He was murdered by the same people he'd tried to appease, in front of those he'd tried to calm. There was such chaos, such surprise, that mothers let go of their children. They left elderly grandparents who could not run behind. Those bodies would burn in the houses they'd built with their own hands. One mother's body was found charred, tied, dragged to a boat, and mutilated.

From the heights of the hills, just as the security officer had prophesied, Futhu watched his world turn to ashes. He could see half a dozen villages below. All were bathed in bright red flames topped with plumes of black smoke. He thought about the school he had built and almost rebuilt. The books and newspapers he had read and collected. And the diaries. The knowledge and stories and proofs he'd painstakingly chronicled, which he believed would outlast him no matter what happened to his body, vanished to soot.

• • •

Across Rakhine State, in the early hours of August 25, ARSA had launched thirty simultaneous attacks on checkposts, but the government response did not distinguish between civilians and militants. It was as if the authorities had been waiting for an excuse. Troop buildup had been underway for months. At least twenty-seven army battalions, joined by the BGP and civilian Rakhine militias, began to cleanse the land.

The military had seeded Facebook with anti-Rohingya propaganda, taking cues from the ultrafanatic monks who had propagated anti-Muslim sentiment. Massacres spread like waves. At least 10,000 men, women, and children were slaughtered—stabbed, beheaded, quartered, set on fire, shot. Babies were pried from their mothers' arms and tossed in fires. Some were cut into pieces. Women were abducted, locked in houses, bitten, and gang raped, their breasts cut off, before they, too, were set aflame. (U Tin Thin Soe, the Rakhine village administrator for the Koe Tan Kauk village tract, denied that ten men had been arrested; he said the Rohingya were terrorists who burned down their own houses and fled.)

For days, the hills were a jumble of confusion and rumors. Families set off in one direction, thinking it was safe, only to reverse course and walk back upon seeing destruction or a new checkpost. Bodies, alive and dead, were everywhere. If you could not see them, you could hear them talking through the trees. By night, young people gathered and planned to make trips down to their villages, to scavenge for food, to look for and bury their dead. Futhu wanted to join them and look for his diaries, but his father forbade it. "If we die, we die here without eating. You don't need to go down there to die again."

On the fifth night, there was a new rumor—the military would come into the mountains soon, so everyone was fleeing into Bangladesh. Futhu and his family followed, walking all night through the mud and crossing a small river the following day. When they came upon the white sandy beach of the large Naf River, they saw a never-ending collection of people. The most crowded marketplace Futhu had seen did not compare. People were pitching tarpaulin tents, spreading their meager belongings on the sand.

Boatmen came and went, ferrying families. Futhu did not want to go to the nearest Bangladeshi shore. The government might set rules about who could enter, and they might end up stranded on the water. He wanted to go to Cox's Bazar's main port, deeper into Bangladesh. When the boatman wanted an exorbitant fare, he didn't bother negotiating. The night of their trip, it rained more than Futhu had ever remembered it raining. Fourteen hours later, on September 7, thirteen days after they fled their village, the boat stopped in chest-high water, and Futhu helped his mother and wife off to the shore.

Futhu's family was among the 700,000 Rohingya who arrived to Bangladesh in one of the largest, most precipitous exoduses of refugees in recent history. They slept along a main highway, stringing up tarps as a tent. On their third morning on the road, the Bangladeshi military commanded them to all move away into the dense jungle. They trudged through the trees, forming the biggest and most congested refugee settlement on Earth. As if overnight, the jungle was cleared. Bamboo and tarp shacks upon shacks sprang up along the muddy hills, which shifted under their weight. Monsoons caused landslides; new arrivals were unable to find even a small patch of earth to tolerate them. Endangered Asian elephants now found their paths brimming with endangered human bodies. They trampled tents, killing thirteen refugees and injuring dozens.

One night, that first hectic week, Futhu sat down and started a new diary. He tried to write down what happened to him as carefully as he could—the dates of fleeing the village, the nights spent in the hills—but he found that his usually orderly brain had broken. His thoughts seemed to disintegrate: Had it been this day or that one? The images of death, flames, and violence were strong, but the facts and dates were hazy. It was as if his brain had not recorded the memories in order. He drafted the timeline for a week, starting and stopping, and then beginning again.

Because everyone from Dunse Para fled at roughly the same time, they lived in roughly the same patch of camp—an entire village transported. Every time he met a familiar face on a muddy path, he inquired about the person's family. He asked how many relatives were injured or if anyone had died. If the person's family survived, he asked what they had heard about their neighbors. Futhu decided he needed another document. Where once he had mapped the lives of his villagers, he now chronicled their deaths. He wrote in English and titled it "List of Died." With each name, a face swam through his mind. In the end, there were twelve names on his list. Futhu reminded himself that he was lucky: He was alive. He had not written any of his own family members' names. Still, he knew all of these souls—mothers, children, and sons. It was important to keep track of history.

• • •

I met Futhu one afternoon almost a year to the day after the August carnage, next to the largest metal bridge in the camps, which had been donated by the Japanese government, its inscription now reading, "From th e ple of Japan." The news from the summer of 2017 had been pornographic in its misery, shocking the world. A United Nations fact-finding mission has since levied charges of war crimes, crimes against humanity, and genocide against Myanmar's military commanders. But for anyone who had been following the plight of the Rohingya, what happened in August was inevitable. How had the Rohingya lived every day in a country that did not want them, through generations that have been marked by exodus as steadily as the seasons? I met an old man who had been a refugee four times. How did he return each time? How could he start again and think it would end any differently? How do you live every day on borrowed time?

With the help of a translator, I interviewed more than two dozen people to understand what had happened in Dunse Para, and Futhu, still in his early thirties, was referred to me as one of the most knowledgeable members of the community. He asked that his name not be used and offered a childhood nickname to protect him from retribution in the case of repatriation. Futhu's story tumbled out in a torrent. He often started years before the event I had asked him about. His explanations went on for hours. Futhu worked during the day, and foreigners could not stay in the camps after dusk, so we met at his work, at his shack and in the huts of his family members, snatching hours when we could, spending the days he had off together. Other people I spoke to called their own community "miserable," "pitiful," and "wretched"—but Futhu did not speak this way. He lived in Myanmar as he meant to, as anyone would, believing things could change if you just tried hard enough, not because it was some grand idea he had, though he did have it, but because ultimately he had no other choice.

Life in the camps was at once better and worse than life in Myanmar. Unlike in their village, they could sleep through the night without worrying about being killed. But they were forbidden to leave the camps and needed permission to travel to proper hospitals outside its boundaries. Forces far outside their community controlled their fate. Myanmar and Bangladesh are negotiating for repatriation. Many Rohingya say they will refuse to go without official ethnic recognition, but they have no elected leaders or representatives at the table. ARSA, meanwhile, has made its presence known in the camps, and executions of those who speak out against them continue. The United Nations refugee agency is trying to arbitrate. But who knows how suddenly this place too would again cast the Rohingya off.

Bangladesh does not allow Rohingya to enroll in government schools. UNICEF had set up "child-friendly spaces"—but children went there to play and draw pictures, not to learn. Aid agencies also set up some "learning centers" without a set curriculum. Futhu scoffed at the uselessness. Private tutoring schools cropped up, like the kind Futhu attended as a refugee, but they covered only basic math and language instruction, not history or science or anything else children would need to pass exams. Classes were held for just an hour a day. Another generation living in a grave. They were still teaching to the Burmese education system, hopeful as ever that their situation would change and they would return to their land.

Day to day, Futhu survived, and you could even say he prospered. He volunteered for the World Food Program and received promotions to become the manager of an aid-distribution site.

But he stopped teaching, and he stopped keeping his diaries. Sometimes he wrote down the dates and times of a few events on his cell phone—an International Committee of the Red Cross delegation visit or the birth of a baby—but his nightly chronicles had ceased. He told me that it was because the camps were crowded and humid, that there was no peace in which he could put together his thoughts, but I wondered if there wasn't something else, if this life was not really the one he wanted to document.

• • •

In all the hours we spent talking, Futhu only ever asked me one question: What did I think would happen to the Rohingya? I told him I didn't know. I asked what he thought about returning to Dunse Para. One day he told me he wanted nothing more than to return with his rights; another day he decided he would rather perish in the sea.

I'd read that the Burmese government was building a model village on Dunse Para's lands, which now were nothing more than unkept fields with burned stumps. When I mentioned this to Futhu, he told me he had heard the same but did not want to believe it. It seemed too much—to cast them off their earth and then just take it? The events of October 9 and August 25 played regularly in his mind. When he dreamed, he saw only his father, who died several months earlier, buried in the camp graveyard, far from the land he sprang from. "Everyone will die one day," he told me. "I will also have to die. I convinced my mind of that. But about the hardship we went through, I failed to convince myself to forget about them."

On my last night in the camps, at around eight p.m., well past the dusk curfew, Futhu was kneeling in the bamboo hut as the darkness stretched its arms through the cracks in the thatch, his face silhouetted against a single solar-powered light bulb.

Something happened in him then—I still don't know what—but Futhu, who had always been so optimistic and purposeful, suddenly crumbled. The hut had filled with relatives and neighbors, and in front of his family and villagers, he started weighing his life.

"Is this a life anybody can look forward to? Why live such a life full of hardship?" he asked. "My kids, my father. . . . My father died, my grandfather died. Nothing has changed. Now it's my turn. I have kids. This is the time, I have to try to support my kids. I don't even want to have kids anymore. Thinking about it is useless. We are just trying to survive here, and also I don't know what will happen to my future. My head gets messed up if I think about it. All the things I used to do. That time I was very much into this campaign for education, but right now I don't want to think about it. My heart is in so much turmoil."

He sat on his knees, his face in anguish. He looked at me, calling me "sister," as he had begun to after our first week together.

"Sister, your parents supported you for better education, they suffered for your literacy, spent hard-earned money to make you an expert. Now you are using that expertise to help your relatives, your country, or maybe other countries too. If someone doesn't get that type of opportunity to use this expertise, what's the use of doing all this hard work and making your parents suffer through this the whole time?" he asked.

"My parents supported my education. It would have been better if they hadn't. I would have been saved from all the trouble and the beating. It's like that, sister. If you die, it's the end. Or maybe if we died . . . many people died . . . it would have been the end. Instead, we came running with our lives. Sometimes when I think about it, it feels so painful. I feel like letting go of everything."

I spent one month in the camps in Bangladesh listening to stories of rape and destruction, but nothing prepared me for the genocide of the mind. A people can survive a mass murder; those who remain can rebuild their lives. But what happens when a people's identity is taken from them? When for years they are repeatedly erased from their earth? When for generations they are told that they do not exist? And what about when the brightest among them give up, stop writing, stop teaching, and stop thinking? Is this not what the Burmese government was seeking all along? How useless was all the work Futhu put into educating people, when the goal of one man was subject to forces so far beyond his control?

Before I left that night, I gave Futhu a present, a notebook I thought he could use as a diary if he ever found the inspiration. Our parting was heavy and clumsy. Futhu told me he was sure that if they went back, they would all be killed.

We kept in touch over WhatsApp when Futhu could get signal—the network in the camps was terrible at best. After I left, he messaged me and told me he had started keeping his diary again. He told me he dreamed of saving enough money to buy a computer. A few weeks later, he messaged to say that he was involved in a new project, planting trees in the camp to help stop landslides—to cement roots into the earth. A few weeks after that, he messaged again, saying that he was working with other community leaders to open a new school. It would teach Burmese, English, and math. It aimed to reach 1,000 students.

In December, they finished building the school—a large bamboo shelter with blue tarp. By January, it needed repair. Futhu explained that they did not have money for proper construction. They were collecting money from students' parents, but those refugees did not have jobs, and there was no real income to pay for education. The landslide project had moved forward, and he often sent me photos of trees and plants. He messaged me about the dreams he had of his father. Sometimes they were running from the Burmese military; sometimes they were just talking about his life. He most often messaged me lamenting his diaries, the destruction of his carefully collected histories. He asked frequently about this article. He wanted to know how people in America felt about the Rohingya. He wanted to know if he could hold a copy of this magazine. He begged me not to forget to send it to him. He said he wanted to keep it for the future.

New Yorker

FINALIST—FEATURE WRITING

For readers who did not grow up eating pimento-cheese sandwiches or playing a quick nine holes before dusk, the appeal of Augusta National Golf Club and the Masters tournament it hosts may seem beyond comprehension. But fear not. Nick Paumgarten is here to explain it to you. From the piped-in birdsong that plays alongside the course to the near-papal regard in which the chairman of the club is held, Paumgarten describes the dreamworld that is Augusta National in mesmerizing yet skeptical detail. Or as the National Magazine Award judges put it: "Paumgarten's dead-on reporting about the club's secrecy, elitism and idol worship exposes the allure of still-powerful myths about wealth and power." The New Yorker, *where Paumgarten has worked as a staff writer since 2005, has received twenty-five nominations in Feature Writing since the category was introduced in 1988 and won the award five times, most recently in 2019 for "A Theory of Relativity," by Elif Batuman.*

Nick Paumgarten

Unlike Any Other

Beneath Augusta National, the world's most exclusive golf club and most venerated domain of cultivated grass, there is a vast network of pipes and mechanical blowers, which help drain and ventilate the putting greens. The SubAir System was developed in the 1990s by the aptly named course superintendent Marsh Benson in an effort to mitigate the effects of nature on this precious facsimile of it. When the system's fans blow one way, they provide air to the densely seeded bent grass of the putting surface. This promotes growth. When the fans are reversed, they create a suction effect and leach water from the greens. This promotes firmness. The professionals who arrive at Augusta every April to compete in the Masters Tournament, the event for which the club is known, expect to be tested by greens that are hard and fast. Amid all the other immodesties and peculiarities of Augusta, the greens, ultimately, are the thing. Herbert Warren Wind, who for decades covered the sport at this magazine and at *Sports Illustrated*, once asked a colleague, on arriving in Augusta, "Are they firm?" The antecedent was understood. In 1994, Gary McCord, a golf commentator for CBS, the network that has televised the tournament for sixty-three years, said on the air, "They don't cut the greens here at Augusta, they use bikini wax." He was banned from the broadcast.

It is by now hardly scandalous to note that Augusta National—called the National by its members and devotees and Augusta by everyone else—is an environment of extreme artifice, an elaborate television soundstage, a fantasia of the fifties, a Disneyclub in the Georgia pines. Some of the components of the illusion are a matter of speculation, as the club is notoriously stingy with information about itself. It has been accepted as fact that recalcitrant patches of grass are painted green and that the ponds used to be dyed blue. Because the azaleas seem always to bloom right on time, skeptics have propagated the myth that the club's horticulturists freeze the blossoms, in advance of the tournament, or swap out early bloomers for more cooperative specimens. Pine straw is imported. Pinecones are deported. There is a curious absence of fauna. One hardly ever sees a squirrel or a bird. I'd been told that birdsong—a lot of it, at any rate—is piped in through speakers hidden in the greenery. (In 2000, CBS got caught doing some overdubbing of its own, after a birder noticed that the trills and chirps on a golf broadcast belonged to nonindigenous species.)

You hear about this kind of stuff before your first visit, just as you get the more commonplace spiel that everything is perfect, that the course is even more majestic in real life than it is on TV, and that, in spite of all the walking, you'll put on five pounds. Pimento-cheese sandwiches, egg-salad sandwiches, peach-ice-cream sandwiches, MoonPies, underpriced beer. You are urged to adopt the terminology favored by the tournament hosts and embraced by CBS. Spectators are "patrons." The rough—longer grass that lines the fairways—is the "second cut." (And it is controversial, because its abundance contravenes the wishes of the patriarchs, who designed the course to have a dearth of rough. Gary McCord may have been onto something.) The traps are bunkers, and what appears to patrons and television viewers to be the whitest sand in golf is technically not sand but waste from feldspar mines in North Carolina.

Augusta National is sometimes likened to Oz. For one thing, it's a Technicolor fantasyland embedded in an otherwise ordinary tract of American sprawl. Washington Road, the main approach to the club, is a forlorn strip of Waffle Houses, pool-supply stores, and cheap-except-during-the-Masters hotels. In the Hooters parking lot during tournament week, fans line up for selfies with John Daly, the dissolute pro and avatar of midround cigarettes and booze. But step through the club's metal detectors and badge scanners, and you enter a lush, high-rent realm, where you are not allowed to run, talk loudly, or cheer a player's mistakes. Order is maintained by security guards, who for decades were provided by the Pinkerton detective agency. (Though Pinkerton was acquired by a Swedish company called Securitas in 1999, many patrons still refer to the guards as Pinkertons.) In 2012, a fan who stole onto a fairway to take a cup of bunker sand was thrown in jail.

I showed up on a Monday afternoon before the tournament, just as a series of storms swept in and as the spectators, there to witness the first rounds of practice, were being herded off the grounds. Owing to the threat of lightning, play was suspended for the day, and the club was closed to visitors. The throngs poured out of the gates into the real world, just as I was leaving it. I took refuge in what the club calls the press building, a recently constructed Taj Mahal of media mollycoddling. This columned, ersatz-antebellum megamansion, in operation just ten days a year, has got to be the fanciest media center in sports. It has state-of-the-art working quarters, radio and television studios, locker rooms, a gratis restaurant with made-to-order omelets for breakfast, and a bountiful hot lunch, as well as a grab-and-go counter with craft beers, artisanal cheeses and jerkies, and a full array of Augusta's famous sandwiches, each wrapped in green paper.

Such generosity and care for the journalists reflects the role that so many of them have played in burnishing the mythology of the Masters; it also suggests an effort to keep them away from the course and the clubhouse. The press is provided with every disincentive to venture out. The gang's all there. Even the bathrooms are capacious and staffed with attendants. Each member of the media has a work station with a brass nameplate, a leather swivel chair, a pair of computer monitors, and a surfeit of real-time tournament footage and information—far more data than one would be able to gather out on the golf course, especially because, outside the press building, reporters are not allowed to carry cell phones. (The phone ban, strictly enforced and punishable by immediate removal from the grounds, applies to patrons and members, too. One morning during the tournament this year, a story went around that the club had done a spot inspection of staff headquarters and found that an employee had hidden a cell phone between two slices of bread.) The golfers and the tournament officials appear dutifully for press conferences; why bother heading out to the clubhouse to hound them for quotes? No phones are allowed at the press conferences, either. The club wants control over sounds and pictures—the content. The club can tell who's who and who's where by RFID chips affixed to each press badge.

The working area faced the practice range, which the players had abandoned once the rain began hammering down. As dusk approached, the rain briefly let up, and a battalion of men in baggy white coveralls—the official caddie costume at Augusta—fanned out across the range, to retrieve the hundreds of balls that the players had struck there earlier in the day. In the gloaming, these white jumpsuits, moving irregularly amid the deep green of the manicured grounds, brought to mind an avant-garde film about a lunatic asylum: the inmates, in their hospital gowns, out for a constitutional.

• • •

The course was still closed the next morning. I caught a ride to the clubhouse on a golf cart with a member, a so-called green jacket, named John Carr, an oil magnate from Ireland, who told me that he was on the media committee.

The members in attendance during the tournament (and at dinner, whenever they visit) are required to wear their green blazers. The club's founders decreed, in the earliest years of the tournament, that any members present had to make themselves available to patrons who might be in need of assistance. The jackets tell you who the members are. It is an oddity of the place that its members insist on secrecy—there are some three hundred, but there is no public list, and omertà is strictly enforced—and yet here, at the biggest golf tournament of the year, they parade about in uniform, wearing name tags: Roger Goodell, Sam Nunn, Rex Tillerson.

The jackets themselves never leave the grounds; they hang in the members' lockers. Each winner of the Masters gets a green jacket, too, which is presented immediately after the victory by the club's chairman and the previous year's winner, in an awkward ceremony staged for television in the basement of a house called the Butler Cabin, near the eighteenth hole. The solemnity surrounding this perennial observance suggests the initiation ritual of a really square fraternity. Jim Nantz, the longtime host of the CBS broadcast and of the Butler Cabin sacrament, has perfected an air of unctuous self-satisfaction that signals even to the casual viewer that there is something batty about the whole enterprise. The way that Nantz repeats the tag line—"A tradition unlike any other"—assumes a sinister, cultish edge. Everyone associated with the club seems to take all this very seriously. On the official Masters podcast, the host, Marty Smith, said to the celebrity chef David Chang, as though reciting a prayer, "The respect for the grounds and the reverence for the event permeate us as human beings and we thereby disseminate that same respect to our peers."

"It's a beautiful thing," Chang replied. "It almost restores my faith in humanity." As one long-standing media-badge holder told me after he'd spent ten minutes singing the club's praises on the record, "These guys are out of their fucking minds. They think it's supernatural."

A friend who used to play at Augusta every year during non-tournament weeks (his father was a member) told me that, at dinner in the clubhouse, you could see the power of the green jacket in the body language of the guests, as they fawned over their host. Yet there was also a certain gelding effect: "Dad was not a humble man, but he was always nervous at Augusta. He didn't want to break a rule. The club turned these high-powered men into boys."

Carr seemed free from such concerns. He led me straight to the clubhouse, into the grill room, where other green jackets were milling about. The clubhouse dates back to the 1850s, though it has been renovated and expanded through the years; its dimensions are modest, its décor restrained. It sits atop one of the finest wine cellars in North America. Soon Carr was greeting others, and then he was gone. I did not feel welcome, so I kept going, through the first door I saw, which opened onto a patio that looks out toward the first tee. The patrons massed and flowed on the other side of a rope line, some thirty yards from the porch; in the space between stood an immense oak, its trunk some twenty feet in circumference, its branches cabled up and sprawling into a canopy that created a swath of shade. So this was the famous Tree, the default meeting place and schmoozing ground. The area, though closed to the public, bustled with members, managers, agents, journalists, players past and present, caddies, and a range of VIPs. "This is the gathering of golf," Jerry Tarde, the editor of *Golf Digest*, here for his fortieth consecutive year, told me. "Under the Tree, all of golf passes you by."

Beyond the Tree, out in the sun, the air was thick with moisture baking out of the ground. The course was evidently playable, but the spectators' paths through it and along the fairways were slick and shiny with mud. Amid the squelch, you could hear the low roar of the SubAir system. Here and there, vents in the ground emitted a rush of warm exhaust. A patron stood astride one, a little obscenely, drying his pant legs. Where there was pitch, patrons in less sensible shoes wiped out in ways that made my ligaments wince. Descending the right side of the tenth fairway, while following the practice round of a Mexican amateur named Álvaro Ortiz, a large older man went heels up and splashed down in the mud. Nearby, another man—a lawyer, apparently—said to his wife, "I'd file in a heartbeat. Take about twelve minutes to get a settlement." The mud, or maybe the drying agent, gave off a reek of sewage. Years of watching the Masters on television had not prepared me for the smell of shit.

• • •

By the following morning, the air had dried out, and the grounds sprang into a kind of sharp autumnal relief—a pretense of perfection. At the driving range (which, like the press center, is new, sprawling, and used pretty much only during the tournament; the members warm up elsewhere), the pros, many with a coach or a manager present, hit balls. Behind them was a wide grandstand, at the rear of which patrons made half-whispered comments, knowing or otherwise, about the array of swings and flight paths. To look from face to face was to regard a study in contentment or even, thanks to the pervasive cigar smoke, self-satisfaction. Everyone there, it seemed, knew that this was the place to be; the aura was all the more intense because of the unquenchable desire to take and post look-where-I-am cell-phone photos.

Tiger Woods was at the far-right end of the line, in a mint-green shirt and gray pants. He had his driver out—the club that hits the ball the farthest, the one you use off the tee. He has had intermittent trouble with it through the years. Errant drives make life difficult. Still, Woods had been playing better and better since last year's Masters, after a decade in the weeds with injuries (most notably his back, on which he'd had four surgeries), painkiller addiction, the collapse of his marriage, and the subsequent sordid revelations of all the philandering that had occasioned it. Some golf writers talked about his career in terms of pre- and posthydrant, a reference to the night in 2009 when his now ex-wife, going through his phone, found out about one of his affairs and chased him out of the house. He fled in his SUV but, zonked on sleeping pills, immediately crashed into a fire hydrant, whereupon she smashed the back window of the car with a golf club. From there, his life went off the rails.

Some commentators thought or wanted to believe that Woods could contend at the Masters this year—he'd won four times already—and even a casual know-little like me couldn't help noticing that, on the day before the first round, he was roping his drives, one after another, each soaring toward the water tower on Washington Road on a clean, almost identical trajectory—a slight draw, right to left, which suits the doglegs of Augusta. Occasionally, after a drive, he wandered ten yards or so out onto the range to fetch his tee. With the others hitting nearby, this looked heedless, like a movie colonel not flinching amid a mortar barrage. Utterances of "Tiger" popped up out of the murmur of the crowd—hundreds of white people just standing there staring at him.

After a while, he went to work on his wedges. The crowd moved with him, while some broke off to line the path he'd be taking from the range to the clubhouse and the course. Momentarily averse to such gawkery, I hung back and watched a couple of golfers I'd never heard of; I recognized, not for the first time, that the mechanics and variables of the golf swing are a mystery to me.

Still, it was a soothing place to hang out. I'd been told that the recorded birdsong played on a loop, and so for a few minutes I listened intently, but I didn't have the ear for it. Earlier, I'd been told by a guard that there was a bird speaker in a nearby magnolia tree. Now I followed one chirping sound to a holly bush. I eased my head carefully into a gap in the prickly leaves and, to my surprise, scared up an actual bird. Pulling my head out, I saw that I was being watched closely by a couple of Pinkertons. "A real bird!" I said to them. The Pinkertons remained expressionless.

The Masters is the only one of the four major tournaments that is staged at the same place every year. The other three—the U.S. Open, the PGA Championship, and the Open Championship (known as the British Open)—are organized by various governing bodies and rotate among an evolving roster of courses, some of which are open to the public. The Old Course at St. Andrews, in Scotland, the so-called home of golf and an inspiration for the layout at Augusta, is a public course. So is Bethpage Black, on Long Island, the site of two recent U.S. Opens as well as last month's PGA Championship. The 2019 U.S. Open, which took place last week, was at Pebble Beach in California, also a public course.

Augusta is obstinately private. Its leadership, embodied by its chairman, who serves for an indefinite term as a kind of sovereign and is the only person authorized to speak about the Masters, invariably deflects questions about club matters by saying that they are club matters. The club operates as a for-profit corporation. No one knows how much money it makes or has—except that it's a lot, judging by the investments the club continually makes in the tournament, the course, the physical plant, and the expansion of its real-estate holdings. No one, anyway, is pocketing cash. Still, the high profile of the Masters, as an athletic competition and a cultural event, has often made Augusta National's desire to be otherwise left alone seem risible, especially in light of the prominence—in business, in politics, in public life—of so many of its members. It's a remarkable if dodgy achievement that the club has managed to maintain the private-public charade for as long as it has.

Augusta National opened in 1932. Its founders were Bobby Jones, the amateur golfing champion, and Clifford Roberts, a Wall Street stockbroker. Jones, an Atlantan and a lawyer, with an English degree from Harvard and an engineering degree from the Georgia Institute of Technology, was, except for Babe Ruth, the era's most revered sports figure and is still considered, in the precincts where such mythologies pertain, the quintessence of the humble and graceful gentleman-athlete. As he grew disenchanted by fame and by competitive golf, Jones sought to establish a world-class private club in his home state—a winter course. Roberts, a flinty, fastidious martinet with a hardscrabble background and a knack for making himself indispensable to powerful men, befriended Jones and took up the cause. In Augusta, they found 365 acres of a defunct commercial nursery called Fruitland, which had been owned and operated by a Belgian family called Berckmans. (The owner before that was a slaveholder, and some evidence suggests that slaves were housed on the property.) Jones and Roberts hired a British designer named Alister MacKenzie to lay out a course, and Roberts set about building a membership. At first, he had a difficult time getting more than a handful of men to join, owing both to the remote location and to the Depression. In the first decade, the operation was basically broke. The failure to attract members led Roberts and Jones to abandon grander plans—for squash and tennis courts, a "Ladies' course," a new clubhouse, and the development of estates adjacent to the links.

The tournament, first held in 1934, was Roberts's gambit for attracting attention, members, and money. He persuaded Jones to come out of retirement to compete in it—an instant lure to fans and players alike—but at first Jones wouldn't agree to calling it the Masters, finding the word too grandiose. A pivotal development, in the life of both the club and Roberts, was the membership of Dwight Eisenhower, who, at Roberts's behest, first vacationed there with Mamie in 1948 and was thereafter besotted with the place, despite a rickety golf game. Jones's health was declining, and Roberts adopted Eisenhower as his (and the club's) principal means of advancement. Roberts served as Ike's financial adviser and executor and, after Roberts helped arrange his run for president, as his bagman. During his presidency, Eisenhower made the club his Mar-a-Lago, visiting twenty-nine times; Roberts had a house built for him on the property. Eisenhower and his son were shareholders, along with other members, in a lucrative international Coca-Cola-bottling venture called Joroberts, run by Roberts and Jones, who were set up in the business by the Coca-Cola chairman and early Augusta member Robert Winship Woodruff, known as the Boss. Augusta National is still Coke country, although, in keeping with a Roberts edict of yesteryear, no brand names are visible at the concession stands.

The golf establishment tends to remember Roberts as a sour figure, a charmless tyrant, and a canny sycophant—the bad cop to the faultless Bobby Jones. Given access to the club's archives, my colleague David Owen, in *The Making of the Masters*, from 1999, painted a more nuanced portrait of Roberts, from his dismal, itinerant farm-boy childhood to his death, by self-inflicted gunshot, on the grounds of Augusta National in 1977, next to Ike's Pond, which he'd had built for Eisenhower to fish in. Owen dismisses or, at least, parses some of the nastier Roberts legends. But, clearly, the club and the tournament owe their exacting standards and often peculiar, now widely venerated traditions to Roberts's obsessive attention to detail and stubborn insistence on a certain way of doing things.

Because of him, the Masters is probably the best-run sporting event in the world. "They have established the gold standard in terms of the conditioning of the golf course," Brandel Chamblee, the commentator and former pro, told me. "I've yet to encounter anyone who is curt or rude. I don't know how you can find fault with this place." A standard of etiquette, attributed to Jones and strictly enforced, is printed on the sheets that patrons carry around, with groupings, tee times, and a course map: "'Most distressing to those who love the game of golf is the applauding or cheering of misplays or misfortunes of a player'—Robert Tyre Jones, Jr. (1902–1971), President in Perpetuity." The concession stands run smoothly, and the prices are famously modest: a buck-fifty for a soda or a sandwich, four dollars for a beer. You could say that it's a prelapsarian paradise, a dream of a bygone America of good manners and affordable delights. You could also say that this America never really existed, except as a figment of privilege and exclusion, and that the conjuring of it, on such a scale, is a kind of provocation.

As a televised event, the Masters is peerless. You don't have to be a golf fan to enjoy it or to enjoy napping in front of it. The apparatus for all this footage—the camouflaged camera towers, the buried cables, the hidden microphones—is hardly noticeable when you're there. The club maintains tight control over the broadcast and has been awarding one-year contracts to CBS since 1956. The Masters could fetch more on the open market, but Roberts and subsequent chairmen have exchanged higher rights fees for control, which, in the end, has enhanced the event's prestige and ultimately its earning power. Originally, only the final four holes were broadcast. Later, coverage expanded to include the "second nine," as the back nine is called at Augusta. (Jones felt that "back nine" evoked an image of one's rear end.) Now the entire tournament is televised, and this year an app carried every shot by every player in the field. Because the players compete on what is more or less the same terrain, year after year, they do so in the context of bygone feats and failures, a folklore of shots made or missed, so that the way each successive champion tackles, say, the par-three twelfth is analogous to the way generations of folk musicians interpret "Long Black Veil."

And yet they do so in an oligarchs' playground rather than in coffee shops. Augusta National has more in common with the Bohemian Grove, the exclusive men-only encampment in the California Redwoods, or the World Economic Forum in Davos than it does with Wimbledon or Fenway Park. From the beginning, even though subscription fees were modest, it was a club for the rich and powerful. The majority of the members, then as now, were from outside the South. In the early days, the eastern WASP establishment prevailed. Now it's the CEO class, which, of course, remains mostly white and male. Many of those CEOs are Southerners, and supposedly the Atlanta contingent still holds sway. "The Masters is a Southern institution the way the Vatican is an Italian one," Tarde said.

The chairmanship certainly has some of the pomp of the papacy. The writers used to get an audience with the chairman, but now there's usually just a press conference in an auditorium. On Wednesday, the current chairman, Fred Ridley, a real-estate lawyer from Florida and a former amateur golf champion, submitted to his, with a few dozen members assembled at the back of the hall, like a convocation of cardinals—all in their green jackets. Ridley was onstage, flanked by two committee members. The reporters addressed him as Mr. Chairman, or Chairman Ridley. He talked for a while—about the recent death of the writer Dan Jenkins, the rainy winter, future construction projects, and the success of the final round of the women's national amateur championship, which Augusta had hosted the week before for the first time—then opened the floor to questions.

The first came from a reporter right in front of him: "Chairman Ridley, when I watch other tournaments on television, I notice lots of cell phones, I notice lots of yelling. Will you please talk about the decorum in place at Augusta National that sets the Masters apart?"

"Thank you," Ridley said. "I think that's something that does set us apart."

So it was that kind of a press conference. Only one question, occasioned by the women's championship, came in with a little bite: "In hindsight, was it a mistake to be so restrictive for so long?"

"We can always look back and say we could do better," he replied. "I don't think it's particularly—well, it is instructive. It's always instructive to look at the past."

The history of the club, like that of so many institutions in the Deep South/United States/world, is fraught with backwardness and bigotry. Charles Sifford, a prominent black golfer in the sixties, once quoted Roberts as saying, "As long as I live, there will be nothing at the Masters besides black caddies and white players." No one has been able to corroborate this statement, but it does describe the state of things there for decades. (Owen, for what it's worth, unearthed examples of Roberts expressing his hope that black golfers would soon qualify for the tournament.) It wasn't until 1975 that a black player, Lee Elder, made the field, and only in 1990 did Augusta invite its first black member, Ron Townsend, an executive at the Gannett Television Group, to join. (One does not apply for membership; the invitation just comes when it comes, though there are back channels for communicating a desire to be considered.) Among its early members were Jock Whitney, who financed *Gone with the Wind*, and Freeman Gosden, best known for performing, in black-voice, on the radio program *Amos 'n' Andy*.

But it wouldn't be entirely accurate to chalk this up merely to geography. The game of golf has its own ugly history with regard to African Americans; the Professional Golf Association, which governs touring golfers in the United States, had a whites-only rule until 1961. There are plenty of private clubs in the Northeast, for example, that have fewer black or Jewish members than Augusta National does, and there are still a handful of prestigious clubs that do not accept women—but those clubs do not put on the world's most prestigious professional tournament.

This was the core of the argument made by Martha Burk, the head of the National Council of Women's Organizations, in her campaign, prior to the 2003 Masters, to pressure the club's chairman at the time, a South Carolina banker named Hootie

Johnson, to accept women as members. Johnson, insisting on the club's right to privacy and self-governance, and citing such single-sex organizations as the Boy Scouts and the Junior League, dug in, as did the media, most notably the *Times*, which made Augusta National an A1 staple. In an editorial, "America's All-Male Golfing Society," the *Times* urged Tiger Woods, who had won the previous two Masters, to boycott. "It's frustrating, because I'm the only player they're asking," Woods said. "They're asking me to give up an opportunity no one ever has—win the Masters three years in a row."

One finds now, in the back and forth of this saga, foreshadowings of the cancel-culture wars of today. As Alan Shipnuck recounts, in *The Battle for Augusta National: Hootie, Martha, and the Masters of the Universe*, published in 2004, the club hired a Washington consulting company, WomanTrend, run by Kellyanne Conway, which produced a survey whose finding was that Augusta National's membership policies were not topmost on the list of women's concerns. Burk—reasonably, once you see the questions—derided it as a "push poll" and "highly unethical." Two days later, Jesse Jackson entered the fray: "We strongly support the movement to end gender apartheid at Augusta National Golf Club." In the end, Woods, too, came out in favor of admitting women. In a press conference, Johnson replied, "I won't tell Tiger how to play golf if he doesn't tell us how to run our private club."

Eventually—and somewhat amazingly, looking back from the reputation-strewn battlefields of 2019—it all just sort of went away. To let its sponsors off the hook, the club announced that it would stage the 2003 Masters by itself, without them—opting, once again, for control over short-term profit. And then, nine years later, the first two women were admitted: Condoleezza Rice, the former secretary of state, and Darla Moore, a financier from South Carolina.

Around midnight on the eve of the first round, while killing cockroaches in my room at the Rodeway Inn, I got a text message from an acquaintance who works in finance. A client of his had canceled at the last minute, which left him with a spare pass to Berckmans Place. He offered it to me.

Berckmans is the Oz within Oz, a lavish dining-shopping-and-drinking complex accessible only to those who have been approved by the club to buy passes, at a cost of ten thousand dollars for the tournament. The club built Berckmans seven years ago, behind a wall of greenery southwest of the fifth fairway, to give favored patrons and corporate friends a sumptuous refuge from the elements and the throngs, and presumably to capture some of the revenue it had been ceding to off-campus entertainments.

The Masters may be America's top corporate-hospitality event; because it's a golf tournament, it attracts a clubbier cohort than the Super Bowl or the Final Four, and because the competition lasts four days rather than two minutes, like the Kentucky Derby, it can please more of them. Kenny Dichter, a founder of the jet-lease company Wheels Up, called the tournament "Coachella for CEOs." "This is where we entertain our premium-experience guests," Andrew Chason, an executive at Creative Artists Agency, told me. "The prestige, the privacy, the beauty of the grounds, the traditions, the quality of the production—it can't be beat."

Wheels down: out pour the premium-experience guests. A certain kind of Instagram feed fills up with photographs of rich people, famous people, lucky people, flashing the Gulfstream grin. The catch is that the hotels, restaurants, and caterers of the city of Augusta (known to many Georgians, however unfairly, as "Disgusta" and to Roberts as a "little tank town") aren't really up to the task of taking care of all these people in the manner they may be expecting. And so a luxury pop-up culture has sprung up outside the gates. Augusta homeowners cover their annual mortgage payments and landscaping bills by renting their houses to the out-of-towners, who, in turn, host clients and friends for spectation by day and dinners and other festivities by night. Celebrity chefs are flown in. Even the journalists get in on it. The press building's bigger names often have a full slate of paid appearances, entertaining diners with pro-level patter and off-the-record scuttlebutt. This practice may explain why journalists are so deferential to the tournament—it's their meal ticket, too. CAA, which represents a number of top golfers, produces a dinner series; this year's, managed by Danny Meyer, featured nine chefs and a sommelier and staff, for a group of just thirty people. Mercedes and the other two domestic tournament sponsors, IBM and AT&T, are provided with so-called cabins (which could as easily be called mansions) on club property, down by the tenth fairway. Various fixers and event planners put together elaborate itineraries, which sometimes include a round of golf at a nearby club, such as Sage Valley, across the South Carolina border—a highly regarded Augusta National clone founded in 2001 by a real-estate magnate who had given up on being invited to join the real thing.

A Berckmans badge might be part of the program. Just after sunrise, I arrived at the acquaintance's rental house, not far from the club, and boarded a van with some of his clients, the executives of a large entertainment company. Not long afterward, the van pulled up to a pavilion, where a dozen or so attendants stood smiling and waving to us. "Welcome to Berckmans!" a security guard called out. "Bird songs too loud? I can turn them down for you." Signs indicated that phones and photography were prohibited inside.

At the metal detectors, two men behind me, whose golf shirts identified them as employees of a prominent private-equity firm, asked if I'd carry an extra folding chair of theirs through security. Everyone is allowed one chair. Presumably, these two were carrying additional ones for their superiors, or else—could it be?—angling for an unfair advantage. As soon as the grounds open each morning, chair holders—first members and their guests, then the general public—fan out across the course and secure their viewing spots; you leave a chair behind, usually with a name tag or a business card affixed to it, then wander around in the expectation that it will be vacant, or immediately vacated, when you come to claim it. Sometimes the chairs stay empty, like barely used country houses.

Berckmans operates for just one week of the year. This is astonishing to contemplate: it's a small indoor village, reportedly ninety thousand square feet. There are shrines to various touchstones of Augusta National lore and a vast, immaculate store that sells Masters merchandise, one of several on the grounds. Sweaters, hats, shirts, jewelry, club covers, platters, pens. You can buy official merch only on site; Augusta National sells nothing online or outside the gates. You might guess that this restriction would cut into sales, but scarcity fuels desire, or so it appears, judging by the queues at the shops and by the patrons lugging around clear-plastic shopping bags stuffed with purchases for the people back home. The club doesn't share sales figures—it doesn't even reveal how many tickets are sold—but a popular estimate is that it moves fifty million dollars of merchandise in that one week.

In some ways, Berckmans is just a food court, but exclusivity can be mind-altering. A badge holder pays for nothing. People who can afford a meal at any restaurant in the world derive a thrill from dining without being handed a check. There are five restaurants: Ike's; Calamity Jane's, named for Bobby Jones's putter; MacKenzie's Pub, for the course architect; the Pavilion, outside; and Augusta's, a sprawling Art Nouveau palm-frond-and-tin-ceiling seafood emporium, where you can get raw oysters, étouffée, and bananas Foster. For breakfast, our host chose Ike's. There were hooks under the table on which to hang our ball caps. "The little things," he said. A TV on the wall carried a live feed of Jim Nantz, off air but on site, having his hair strategically restructured. At the buffet, we heaped our plates with biscuits, grits, eggs, French toast, and candied peaches. I thought guiltily of my colleagues at the press center, having to make do with omelets and no hooks for their hats. As I hid in a john to jot down a few notes, I noticed that the restroom attendants cleaned the stalls after each patron's use. (Later, I overheard a man talking to his wife on a courtesy phone: "Guess what: every time you go, there's a guy who runs in and cleans the toilet.")

Berckmans guests occasionally find themselves staying all day: oysters, Bloody Marys, air conditioning, golf on TV. Why bother going out to watch the disjointed, partial, live version? The clincher, for many, is the Putting Experience, along the northeast side of Berckmans—replicas of the seventh, fourteenth, and sixteenth greens, with Augusta National caddies on hand, in their coveralls, to help the civilians manage what, up close, look like preposterously hilly putts. After breakfast, there was a queue of people waiting their turn to test the greens. Condoleezza Rice, in green jacket and tan slacks, was there to greet them one by one. (The man on the courtesy phone: "A former secretary of state out there saying hi to everybody? Honey, it's crazy!")

Depending on your area of interest or expertise, you might recognize prominent citizens in golf-fan disguise. A patron who knew his hockey Hall of Famers, for example, could introduce himself to Chris Chelios and Lanny McDonald. One who knew his media magnates might note that Fred Ridley was having lunch with Brian Roberts, the chairman of Comcast and the head of the club's digital-technology committee.

One Berckmans badge holder I didn't recognize but whom a younger patron pointed out later, by the sixth green, was a thirty-one-year-old social-media personality named Bob Menery, who has made a name for himself by posting profane mock-narrations of sports highlights, in a dead-on sportscaster's voice. Towering over him was his girlfriend, Katie Kearney, a swimsuit model and former Miss Missouri. Menery and Kearney had been invited to the Masters by a Lebanese businessman named Ahmed Tayeb. There were dinners (one hosted by a Saudi golf magnate, another with Ireland's fifth-richest man); parties (at CAA's, Menery had a rough go of it after mistakenly eating a housemate's pot gummy); a round at Sage Valley (Menery shot his best-ever score, a seventy-five); and multiple late-night sessions at Hooters. As I chatted with Menery and Kearney, we were joined by their friend Jena Sims, an actress and former Miss Teenage Georgia, and the girlfriend of Brooks Koepka, the number-one golfer in the world, who had recently lost twenty pounds in advance of an appearance with her in the Body Issue of *ESPN the Magazine*. Menery and Koepka liked to kid around with each other about their attractive girlfriends. When Menery, outside the ropes, heckled Koepka about this during an early round at the Masters, Koepka laughed, but Menery got the Pinkerton glare. "You don't fuck around here," he told me. Last year, Menery posted a video on Instagram in which he crank-called the club pretending to be Bill Gates (who is a member), ludicrously demanding a tee time in the midst of the tournament. Now he was hoping that no one remembered this stunt; he was having too good a time, making too many connections, and, like nearly everyone at Augusta, sorely hoping to be invited back. On Sunday, he watched the final round on the flatscreens at Berckmans, leaving vacant the folding chairs that a runner had placed for him and his housemates by the eighteenth green early that morning.

• • •

Right outside Berckmans, you slip into the flow of regular patrons, a river of well-to-do white people in golf clothes. But what had previously appeared to be the most homogeneous crowd I'd ever seen suddenly seemed to contain some intriguing variety, relative to the clientele at Berckmans. The frat boys and young jocks, with stacks of empty beer cups (the cups are collector's items); the slightly dotty elderly golf fanatics, with their binoculars and old Masters badges and long-standing viewing spots at the sixteenth hole; the sunburned Brits on boys' trips, smoking 100s in the shade. Still, you see a lot of khaki shorts, ankle socks, and golf shirts. Sometimes you can tell people apart only by the corporate logos on their left breast: Hitachi Chemical, Mercy Care, Strategic Wealth Specialists, Newton Center Chiropractic, South Bay Construction, Arborguard, True Temper, Twisted Dune, the Citadel. Everyone had the look of someone who was used to telling other people what to do.

Here and there, I struck up amiable conversations with well-mannered men from all over the country. A carnival concessionaire from Austin. An art-frame conservator from New Haven. A white-water kayaker from the Smokies. I eavesdropped on greetings and farewells:

"What's up, General?"

"Good to see you, Bud."

"You guys be safe."

Tim Jones, a senior project manager at a steel company in Louisville, told me, "Never been anywhere like this, where everything's A1, from the hand towels in the bathrooms to the grass. I called my son. I told him, 'This isn't a golf tournament. It's a cultural event where the Southern United States has its chest stuck out and is saying come down and visit.' It's been a hundred and fifty-five years since the Civil War, and yet we want to let people know we're a strong people, a hardworking people, a proud people."

A guy named Rick Foor, from Fort Mill, South Carolina, on hearing that I was from New York, asked, "Are you left of Trump?" He let me know that he was busting my chops. "So, but seriously, what's the deal with AOC?"

I had another conversation about Ocasio-Cortez and the perils of single-payer health insurance with a large-bodied fund manager from New York. We met at a concession stand as we were both reaching greedily into a freezer for peach-ice-cream sandwiches, the last two in stock. (An old Augusta hand had given me some advice: "Follow the fattest fucker you see and he'll lead you to the peach-ice-cream sandwiches.") After a couple of bites, the trader threw his out. "It's too mushy," he said. "Yesterday I had one, and it was the best thing I ever had." (Another pro tip: remove the cutlet from a chicken sandwich, put it in a pimento-cheese sandwich, then, before eating the new sandwich, carry it in your pocket for a few holes.)

At one point, a young man told me, "My uncle dropped dead last year on eleven. This is the one-year anniversary of his death." Then the uncle introduced himself. Johnny Pruitt, age fifty-four, from Bluffton, South Carolina. He'd gone into cardiac arrest in the gallery and was out for twenty-five minutes before paramedics revived him. The family were gathered here to celebrate his resurrection. "I bow down at Amen Corner," he said. "I had goosebumps coming through the gate this morning."

• • •

Amen Corner, so named by Herbert Warren Wind, is the crux of the course, comprising, strictly speaking, the eleventh green, the twelfth hole, and the tee shot at thirteen. A stand of pines juts into the course here and provides a sociable vantage over hallowed ground and consequential golf. On Friday afternoon, fans watched balls arrive suddenly from the left and land on or near the eleventh green. Then came the players. The scoreboard—updated by men standing behind it using placards featuring each competitor's name—would tell you whom to expect, if you didn't have the grouping sheet. No matter where you were, Tiger Woods approached as if on a rising tide, behind the leading edge of the throng that was following his round. Agents from the Georgia Bureau of Investigation preceded him, and then, as shouts of "Tiger!" rippled out ahead, the man himself came striding along, with his familiar air of purpose and annoyance. He was in the second-to-last group and near the top of the leader board, and a buzz was starting to build that he might in fact be in the running.

To great fanfare, he birdied eleven and walked toward the grandstand, and the twelfth tee. Twelve is a famous, picturesque par three, Augusta's Matterhorn. To land a ball on the green, you have to hit it over a creek and short of an embankment of azaleas. Great players have come to grief here. Woods, though, hit his tee shot to within a half-dozen feet of the flag. Pandemonium. And then, from seemingly everywhere, came the sound of a siren. There was lightning in the area, and everyone had to evacuate the course. The crowd groaned. *Puttus interruptus.* Woods rushed across the bridge to the green, marked his ball, and disappeared offstage, behind the azaleas, as the multitudes emptied out of the grandstand and the glades of Amen Corner and streamed back toward the exits—there was no place on the grounds for them to take shelter, in the event of a storm, unless they had passes to Berckmans. The sky darkened.

A few patrons lingered among the pines. "I'm staying here till they make me leave," one man said. He smoked a cigarette and admired the vivid slaty light. After half an hour, far off, a cheer went up, and suddenly the crowds were returning, some people at a run, to reclaim choice spots in the pines. The atmosphere had got rowdy, strangers striking up conversations like old friends.

A start horn rang out. Woods was waiting by the twelfth green, where he was soon joined by his partners. But after a long delay he missed his birdie putt. Soon a heavy rain arrived, and the SubAir system kicked in.

• • •

On Sunday, a threat of afternoon storms, possibly even of tornadoes, prompted the club to make the unprecedented and therefore surely agonizing decision to move the start times to early morning, and to send the groups out in threesomes, rather than the usual pairs. Woods lucked into the final group, a tactical advantage.

The patrons in the galleries had a range of rooting interests. Some cheered for Rickie Fowler, who is widely acknowledged to be the American contingent's leading young mensch, or for Phil Mickelson, whom many writers privately described as its reigning jerk. I stood next to an executive from Adidas and his fiancée, whose interests were best represented by the rising star—and Adidas athlete—Xander Schauffele. Go, Xander! A South African contingent went berserk for Louis Oosthuizen. But the contender who inspired the roars was Woods.

Early that morning, in the press building, I was flipping through a recent biography of Woods, by Armen Keteyian and Jeff Benedict. Skipping, as one will, to the dirty bits, I alighted on a section describing his serial infidelities of a decade ago and some text messages he'd sent to a porn star named Joslyn James, the first of which read, "Hold you down while i choke you and Fuck that ass that i own." The rest were worse. This was the man whom everyone was roaring for. There was something Trumpean about it all—a suggestion not of redemption and forgiveness but of indulgence or abandon.

It can seem weird how enthusiastically the golf world roots for Woods, even though so many of its citizens, especially the ones closest to the tour, aren't especially fond of him. People like to witness greatness, maybe, or to partake of excitement. He's good for business, people said. One golf executive told me, "It's easier for everybody when Tiger is winning." This, too, seemed Trump-y: forbearance, in the name of lucre. It's perhaps worth noting that Woods and Trump, who is closing in on two hundred rounds as president, have been both playing and business partners; Woods is designing a course for Trump's property in Dubai.

In 1996, a year before the first of Woods's Masters triumphs, his father, Earl Woods, told *Sports Illustrated*, "Tiger will do more than any other man in history to change the course of humanity," including Mandela, Gandhi, and the Buddha. He referred to Woods as "the Chosen One." It was soon clear that the son's ambitions didn't align with the father's. One can argue, and many have, that no man is duty-bound to lead the struggle or that merely by dominating a mostly white field, often in places that have historically been closed to people of color, Woods is doing more than his share to advance the cause. It's always been hard to parse the extent to which his popularity is a function of his being a pioneer, as a black man in a white world, or of his reticence about this.

Now, two months after the Masters, as Woods and most of the rest of the field have teed it up at the U.S. Open at Pebble Beach, we know that the people got what they wanted. We may even remember what happened on Sunday. On the twelfth hole, the steady Italian Francesco Molinari, ahead of Woods by two strokes, hit his tee shot into the creek. The patrons, now more like a mob, avidly cheered his mistake, in violation of Bobby Jones's rules of comportment. In the CBS control room, a producer exclaimed, "Game on!" And then Woods lofted his tee shot safely onto the fat part of the green, made par, and walked onto the next tee box in a tie for the lead. This time, there was no siren, no lightning. Overhead, the private jets were coming in low, presumably to fetch the premium-experience guests. As Woods made his way down the thirteenth fairway, Amen Corner emptied out for the last time, the crowds following him, shouting his name.

Almost two hours later, Woods sealed the victory with a bogey on eighteen, then made his way to Butler Cabin, to retrieve his green jacket. In a sitting room inside the clubhouse, his mother, his children, and his girlfriend had assembled to watch the ceremony on TV. Pinkertons guarded the door. In the grill room, a semicircle of members, still wearing their own green jackets, stood rapt before a flatscreen in the corner. They applauded when

Woods slipped his arms into the jacket—the same one he'd won in 1997. He'd get to take it off the premises for another year.

In the parking lot, a group of reporters interviewed Woods's caddie, Joe LaCava, who was leaning against the back of a courtesy Mercedes SUV. "I'm happy he won today," he said. "It might've bought me a couple more months." Fans and commentators spoke of Tiger's miraculous comeback. Mostly, in their telling and certainly in his, what he'd come back from was debilitating back pain and other injuries, rather than the collapse of his marriage, his public image, or his emotional well-being. But it was all there, as subtext. Knowing what we do about America's capacity for forgiveness or for willful forgetting, we can maybe allow, with some ruefulness, that the restoration of his body was more astonishing, after all. A few weeks later, at the White House, Trump draped the Presidential Medal of Freedom around Woods's neck. The ribbon got twisted, and no one thought to straighten it out.

Georgia Review

WINNER—PROFILE WRITING

"Jerry's intentional art of living was a centrifugal force we couldn't escape," writes Jacob Baynham as he recalls the life and death of his father-in-law, Jerry McGahan, in his cabin in western Montana. "He lived a life that was true to himself, packing twice as much living into every minute and filling his days with the things that he loved. His was a rare and alluring existence, even if it made few accommodations for anyone else—including the people who loved him the most." The National Magazine Award judges described this story as "a timely meditation on living fully and a moving portrait of dying well." Baynham is a freelance journalist in Missoula, Montana, who writes "about people: the things that unite us and divide us, the places we live, and the food we eat." Founded in 1947, the Georgia Review *has received twenty National Magazine Award nominations and previously won the awards for Fiction, in 1986, and Essays, in 2007.*

Jacob Baynham

Jerry's Dirt

I. The Cabin

Jerry McGahan was not well when he stepped out of his Montana cabin on a gusty mid-September afternoon in 2016. His hair was wiry and white. Steroids had swollen his face, rounding the usual angles of his jaw. He elbowed open the front door and slowly crossed the porch. His feet had memorized the distance.

The cabin was older than he was, but solid. In 1973 he found it for sale at the foot of the Mission Mountains just north of here. He paid three hundred dollars for it and gathered some friends to help take it apart. Jerry numbered the logs, loaded them onto a truck, and reassembled them here along the Jocko River with his first wife, Libby. Using skills he learned from carpentry books and an eighth-grade shop class, he framed the windows, wired the outlets, plumbed the pipes, and built the cabinets. By the end of the summer, it became a home in this sylvan oasis. His closest neighbors were the swaying ponderosas, junipers, and cottonwoods of the river-bottom forest.

The cabin looks at home in these woods. Like a nest, it is built of the materials that surround it. The cabin's roof is shingled with hand-split cedar shakes, which are dusted with pine needles. The gutters are trimmed with gray, lichened wood. The doors have no locks.

The cabin has a way of arresting people. Whoever comes down here, whether a deliveryman or—once—the poet Allen Ginsberg, knows they are seeing something rare and beautiful, the fruits of an autonomous life. When a hospice doctor visited, he stepped out of his car, swept his gaze over the house, the mossy rock gardens, and the corkscrew hazel out front, and said: "It looks like a hobbit lives here."

Jerry lived here for two-thirds of his life. At seventy-three years old, he was neither tall nor short, and his body was sinewy from a lifetime of walking and work. He wore glasses and a bristly white moustache. His nose protruded from his face like a beak. It was large enough, the story goes, that a kid once ran over it with a bicycle when Jerry was lying on his side on the school playground, inspecting a bug.

As he walked across the porch, Jerry didn't stoop or wince. He smiled. Laughed, even. The only clue that something was amiss was the tiny aberration in his daily uniform—his collared shirt wasn't tucked into his Levis.

If he was in pain, his face didn't betray it. Comfort rarely guided his decisions, anyway. He did his work by hand, preferring the manual to the automatic. He cut his own wood, fixed his own cars, brewed his own beer, and butchered his own game. If his life was aesthetically beautiful, woodsy, and romantic, it was seldom comfortable. So whenever he had a headache or a wound, he endeavored to overcome his pain mentally. "I try not to attend to it," he'd say.

But this current sickness was greedy for his attention. By now the cancer was accumulating. I imagined it welling up inside his body like a bruise-colored summer thunderhead, the kind of storm that smells of dust long before it ever smells of rain.

• • •

There wasn't a cloud in the sky, figuratively or literally, when I first met Jerry, one spring morning in 2007, shortly after I had fallen in love with his daughter in Missoula. Hilly first described her father to me as a writer and beekeeper who never ate fruit out of season, refused to own a cell phone, bought almost nothing, and knew a lot about birds. In person, I found him to be self-possessed and encyclopedic, but simultaneously humble. He listened more than he spoke, and he was always learning. Our interests in writing, travel, and mountains overlapped. I admired him immediately; in time, I loved him.

Hilly and I married in 2012, in the shade of trees Jerry planted behind the cabin. Then, in 2014, Jerry was diagnosed with prostate cancer. Hilly was pregnant with our first son. The cancer was the type that could have been removed if Jerry had gone in sooner, but he thought of doctors the way he thought of mechanics: the more you saw them, the more they found to fix. So, he prescribed his own health regimen of fresh food and manual labor, radiating the immortality of a tree, for which death is possible, but implausible. Jerry never scheduled the checkup that could have sounded the alarm, and his truancy came with a price: by the time a doctor found it, the cancer was aggressive and inoperable. His oncologist said he might have months to live.

Almost three years passed. The cancer seeped into his organs and bones, the mutated cells proliferating within him like dandelion seeds blown into a breeze. Metastatic growths were starting to fracture his ribs and spine. The cancer's progression was excruciatingly painful, but irreversible. Without the need for more ultrasounds, hormone treatments, radiation, or chemo, he stopped making the half-hour drive into Missoula to see his oncologist. Instead, the hospice nurses came to him. It was just as well. Standing here outside his house, a man in his domain, Jerry clearly had no desire to leave.

Still, the pain was mounting. His first true pain crisis terrified everyone. He was upstairs in his bedroom, writhing and moaning in his bed. When we rushed to him, he looked at us in a panic, sobbing. His eyes flashed like those of a trapped coyote and he said he hoped he would die. For the first time since I had known him, he looked defeated.

Defeat didn't come easy for Jerry. One spring afternoon in 1985, a giant, root-rotted cottonwood fell across the cabin right above the front porch, smashing most of the house. The insurance would have paid a contractor to repair it, but Jerry got to work using borrowed house jacks, come-alongs, and a fence stretcher to hoist away the tree and resurrect his home from its bare, broken bones. In the end, he fixed it for a fraction of the insurance claim and used the extra money to pay off his debts. The cabin was as good as new, and it was *his* cabin, now more than ever.

Cancer, though, was an act of God that no amount of resilience could negotiate, one that promised only diminishment and then erasure. After that initial pain crisis in his bedroom, a hospice nurse increased the dosage on the portable morphine pump installed directly into his abdomen. As Jerry descended the porch steps that September afternoon in 2016, he cradled the pump in his left hand like a Walkman. Every ten minutes or so it delivered a dose with a whirring noise as if it was fast-forwarding to the next song.

Jerry scarcely took a Tylenol in his whole life and in the days to come, these narcotics would dull his wits. But on that day his head was clear and his direction was intact. Janet, his second wife for thirty-five years, took his arm. Her body was riddled with cancer, too: a third round of breast cancer had metastasized to her bones. Until recently, they scheduled oncologist appointments together the way they once went to the movies. For a while, they seemed to be lockstep in a race to the end. Now it looked as though Jerry would finish first.

But before then, he had one bit of business left to attend to in the orchard, one final decision to make before the cancer pulled the rafters down around him. So, with all six of his children and some grandchildren alongside, Jerry slowly stepped down from the porch and started walking.

II. The Birds

He used to run. Every morning, for years, he climbed out of bed, laced up his sneakers, and ran out the front door, down this driveway, into the hills and home again in a seven-mile loop. But a lifetime of movement had worn away the cartilage in his left knee, so by now he walked with a limp. Janet spent years trying to persuade him to get a replacement, and we all chimed in to bolster the case. *You walk so much*, we'd tell him, *why do it in pain?*

Now that was no longer a concern. We watched Jerry walk with his customary cadence, listing from left to right like a windshield wiper.

He walked along river rocks that he set into the earth years ago as a driveway to the outbuilding he called the Honey House, where the family—Jerry, Janet, and all the kids—extracted honey from their hives. In 2012, before Hilly and I got married, Jerry started unearthing each of these stones, clearing the grass around them, and resetting them into the ground, where they looked brand-new. There are hundreds of stones and the job took all summer, but he approached it the way he tackled every task: with daily, incremental work. He applied the same strategy to writing his stories and novels, pruning trees, oil painting, and learning French. In the case of these stones, he knew the grass would grow back between them within a few seasons, but that didn't matter. Like Sisyphus, Jerry rolled his rock up the hill. If it cost him some sweat, it also rewarded him with purpose.

Walking along the stones, he cocked his head toward the forest and for a moment he seemed young again, feeling the cool September air on his cheeks, scanning the trees for birds. Throughout his life, Jerry was most at home when he was outside.

• • •

Jerry McGahan was born in the winter of 1943 in Dillon, a small railroad town in southwestern Montana. His biological father was a well-liked drunk and loose cannon named Johnny Harr. According to a story Jerry was told, Johnny once shot a black bear, ran out of shells, and then tracked it down and killed it with a hammer. Jerry's mother, Alice, divorced Johnny when Jerry was young and moved to Livingston with her new husband, Chuck. Together they opened a restaurant called The Coffee Shop and the family lived above it, in the windowless rooms of an abandoned hotel. In one of his stories Jerry describes it as "a big, dark, hollow place."

Jerry was a scrawny, awkward boy with freckles and few friends, so he learned to entertain himself. He liked climbing the buildings around the hotel. On one building he found a baby pigeon, which he brought home and named Sapphire. The bird became his companion, riding on his cap when he delivered the *Park County News*. Jerry soon became infatuated with birds. He would borrow his mother's car and drive to hike the sloughs and climb the cliffs of Paradise Valley, where he found marsh hawks, falcons, and great horned owls. Along the way, he suffered scrapes with rattlesnakes, badgers, coyotes, bears, and other animals. His childhood was punctuated with tetanus shots.

When Jerry was a teenager, he and his best friend, Jay Sumner, saw a book for sale in Livingston. It was a translated copy of *The Art of Falconry*, the first modern zoological treatise, written in 1250 by the Holy Roman Emperor Frederick II. Jerry and Jay coveted the book, but neither of them had the twenty-five dollars to buy it. Then they caught wind that the owner of an agate shop south of town was willing to pay twenty-five dollars to anyone who could exterminate the skunks under his building. Jerry and Jay took the job.

Knowing little about skunks, they consulted the local government trapper, who suggested they bury a fifty-gallon drum and put a swinging platform on top, baited with a rotten fish. The skunk would step out onto the platform and then—*whoosh*—swing down into the drum.

Jerry and Jay rummaged through the town's garbage piles, attracting some attention from the police, until they found a suitable drum. They cut off its top in Jay's back yard, rigged up a platform, and found a fish. They set the trap below the agate shop and came back before school the next morning to check it. Sure enough, a big skunk hissed up at them from the bottom of the barrel. They killed it, brutally and inefficiently, with rocks and a skewer, but not before it soaked them both in sulfur. When it was dead, they fished it out of the drum and dropped it down a hole, which they learned later was the well of a church.

After that, Jerry and Jay tried a new technique with a steel leg trap attached to a length of wire. When they caught a skunk, one of the boys would grab the wire and run, dragging it out from under the shop. Then the other boy would take aim and shoot the animal with a shotgun. They dispatched eight skunks that way, enough to satisfy the shop owner. They took his money and bought the book. Even into their adult lives, the book spent a year at Jerry's house, and then a year with Jay. Both friends developed a lifelong passion for birds of prey.

One day in high school, Jerry found a fledgling golden eagle in a nest on a cliff outside of town. He lifted the bird out of the nest and brought it home so he could train it to hunt rabbits. He named the eagle Torrey, and he kept her in a large cage outside and fed her prairie dogs that he stored in the freezer. When Jerry went to the University of Montana in Missoula in 1961, he brought Torrey with him. She lived in an enclosure behind the gym. Jerry trained her to fly to him when he blew a referee's whistle and swung a ball of meat in the air.

Jerry was flying Torrey on the mountain behind campus one day while the university football team practiced on a field below.

Alerted, perhaps, by the coach's whistle, Torrey started tracking the football, then swooped, grabbed it, and perched on it near the fifty-yard line. The players all stood around her, hands on hips, maintaining a healthy distance. Jerry had to scramble down the mountain to get her off the ball before the team could resume practice. A photographer snapped a picture of the scene that appeared in the next day's newspaper.

Jerry was a natural student. At UM he compiled his fastidious field research into a paper about the hunting habits of golden eagles around the state. It's still one of the most complete studies on eagles in Montana. He spent summers observing wildlife in the mountains. And he met Libby, a liberal arts major from Missoula who liked to hike as much as he did. They married in 1966, at Soldiers Chapel in Gallatin Canyon outside Bozeman, an elegant log and stone church at the foot of Lone Mountain. Jerry had driven by it one day and determined that one day he would get married there.

That same year, Jerry finished his master's in wildlife biology at UM. Then he and Libby moved to Madison, where Jerry got a doctorate in zoology at the University of Wisconsin. As part of his graduate research, he received a grant from the National Geographic Society to study Andean condors in South America. He and Libby spent two years in Colombia and Peru, scaling cliffs and hunkering in blinds to observe the birds. Jerry filmed a documentary and wrote a story for the May 1971 issue of *National Geographic*. Libby took the pictures, including the cover photograph of Jerry with a giant Andean condor perched on his arm, almost ten-feet-worth of wings flared, seemingly ready to peck off Jerry's nose. Jerry named that condor Gronk and brought it home with him to Montana, before donating it to a zoo.

All of this research was ample groundwork for a career in academia. Jerry was passionate about science, and as a professor he could have stoked the curiosity of another generation of wildlife biologists—but he was a reluctant teacher. When he taught his first class as a graduate student, he was so nervous that he raced through two lectures on the first day. After the bell rang, he ran back to his office to start planning more lessons.

The grandstanding of higher education put him off, too. Ultimately, he decided that he would rather retain his freedom in obscurity than nurture a scientific reputation on a concrete-bound campus. In 1973, he returned to western Montana and settled on the river-bottom land in the little town of Arlee, on the Flathead Indian Reservation just north of Missoula. He and Libby had adopted their first child in Colombia. They named him Jay, after Jerry's old friend Jay, who bought land and built a house just up the Jocko River from Jerry. In 1974, Jerry and Libby had a daughter named Jordan. With a new family to provide for, Jerry bought a flatbed pickup, built some hives, and started a honey business that he called Old World Honey. He kept his hives on ranchland throughout the Mission and Flathead valleys and he valued the work that busied his body but cleared his mind.

Because Jerry spent so much time outside, birds still inhabited his days. He could identify most of them by sight or sound, and the woods around his cabin teemed with them. In spring, he dutifully recorded his first sightings of songbirds, welcoming them as friends. Over time, he taught me the songs of his favorites. When he hiked in the mountains, he listened for the olive-sided flycatcher's jovial call, "*whip three beers*." The shy Swainson's thrush would arrive in late June, thrilling him with its ascending, fluting spiral of a song, like a garden hose spinning through the air. The incessant chatter of the catbird followed him through his summer garden chores while tiny ruby-crowned kinglets chittered at him from the treetops.

One morning in 2010, he walked out of the cabin and heard a song he didn't recognize. He found the bird in a bush and went back inside to consult his field guide. It was a Carolina wren. He reported the sighting to the wildlife department at the University of Montana, but they were skeptical; the Carolina wren is common in the eastern United States, but had never been seen in Montana. Until now.

Birders drove from as far away as Oregon to add it to their "life lists." When they arrived, brandishing spotting scopes and telephoto lenses, Jerry would stop what he was doing and introduce them to the bird.

He paid attention to birds when he traveled, too. Later in life he spent his winters traveling with Janet, and sometimes alone, to India, Haiti, Cuba, and elsewhere. He watched for the honeyguide bird in Mali and Senegal, where he spent several weeks working with local beekeepers. And he tramped around the Guatemalan highlands searching for the resplendent quetzal while visiting Hilly, who worked there for a year after college. She remembers her father walking through the jungle, enraptured, saying things like, "Jesus, that's a barbet! I've never seen a barbet before. No, wait. That's a white-whiskered puffbird. Well, aren't you pretty?"

• • •

There weren't many birds around the afternoon that Jerry walked away from the house with his family trailing behind. It was fall, and most had flown south. Those that remained were the common ones most birders ignore—finches, chickadees, ravens, and turkey vultures. But Jerry found something to admire in every one. The way nuthatches always creep down a tree trunk. The uncanny intelligence of magpies. The way you can distinguish a pileated woodpecker's cry from other woodpeckers because, as he put it, "it's just a little more unhinged."

Jerry had a special affinity for woodpeckers. Like them, he was industrious. He was hardheaded. He was a flash of color in the monochrome woods.

III. The Dirt

Fall in Montana is a period of battening down. For Jerry, it was a season of closure before the dark days of winter. "Fall is chaos," he wrote, "everything wanting attention." There was fruit to pick and gardens to till and food to put up. But at its end, fall was the catharsis of summer, a sigh before sleep.

By mid-September the harvest was complete in the gardens that surrounded the house. As we walked away from the porch that day in 2016 we could see that an early frost had sucked the life from the tomato plants, leaving them limp and brown, slumped against their cages. With Jerry's guidance, Hilly and I had gouged open the potato patch with shovels, stashing the muddy reds, russets, and fingerlings in the root cellar. The cool earth lay ravished around us.

Gardening was one of Jerry's greatest passions. "What you love is what you keep your eye on," he wrote in one of the dozens of short stories he published in the *Georgia Review*, *Gray's Sporting Journal*, *Ploughshares*, and other magazines. "And that's the trick, because what you are isn't much more than what you think about."

In that case, Jerry was part plant.

The first flower he loved was a narcissus bulb a neighbor gave him in graduate school in Wisconsin. He poked it into some pebbles inside a glass of water, set it on a windowsill, and waited. Eventually it sprouted, and then bloomed. The creamy blossom smelled like honey and lit up the house like a lantern in the melancholic mid-winter.

When Jerry had just bought the river-bottom land in Arlee, his step-cousin Clifford, who was like an uncle and a mentor to him, gave him a Queen of Hearts dianthus. Jerry treasured it, but as he was putting the roof on the cabin he dropped a piece of lumber and crushed the plant. He felt terrible and told Clifford he couldn't take any more plants until the house was finished.

At that time this land was barren, gravelly, and overgrazed, but to Jerry it was a living canvas. Over the years, he built his small honey business here and he helped raise his blended family.

When I first met Hilly, it took me some time to understand her family tree. Jerry had the two children, Jay and Jordan, from his marriage with Libby. Janet had two sons, Simon and Duncan, with her first husband, Scot. (I was impressed to learn that Scot, his new wife Philippa, Janet, and Jerry all remained close friends.) Janet and Jerry married in 1981 beneath a willow that Jerry had planted behind the cabin. Together, they had two daughters, first Romy and then Hilly, the youngest of the six. They were both born in the cabin and, like their siblings, grew up weeding the gardens and pulling honey alongside their father.

From the moment he got here, Jerry cultivated a sense of belonging to this land. He filled it with trees, flowers, and vegetables. Over time he became so fond of the place that it was nearly impossible to coax him from it. He went into town reluctantly, and when he attended parties he reliably slipped out early and undetected and headed for home on foot. After almost fifty years of accumulating this dirt under his fingernails, of transforming its molecules into food, there was no longer a clear separation between this land and the man himself. One smelled of the other, elemental and eternal, like smoke and leather and loam.

When the house was built, the land around it had no topsoil. Jerry was working four jobs at the time—keeping bees, teaching biology at a local high school, conducting a biological survey of the Blackfoot River for the Nature Conservancy, and working as a state bee inspector. He didn't have time for landscaping, but he spread sawdust around the house and scattered grass seed. When the grass took root, he mowed it and left the clippings. As years of this went by, the clippings decomposed and manufactured dirt.

By the end of Jerry's life the grass grew thickly around the cabin and the topsoil was two knuckles deep.

Jerry appreciated the value of the dirt in his vegetable beds, too. As a gardener, he considered dirt his most precious currency. When he pulled weeds, he shook the soil off their roots. When he rinsed his potatoes, he poured the watery sludge back into the patch. At the end of the season, he shoveled out the chicken coop and tilled this compost into the soil by hand. After four decades of devotion, the dirt in Jerry's gardens was fine and dark, the color of possibility.

Whenever the earth wasn't frozen, Jerry had his hands in it. He developed growing systems for a cornucopia of vegetables—parsnips, asparagus, squash, beans, garlic, Jerusalem artichokes, and more. It was all food for the table. But Jerry spent equal time with his flowers, growing food for the eyes.

He was always scouting for new plants. Walking along the Clark Fork River in Missoula one afternoon, he noticed a flower he liked. He stopped and pinched off part of it to plant in one of his rock gardens, where it thrived. Later, he was walking along the same trail when he noticed the original plant had died. So he returned with a clipping from his own garden and replanted it. He figured the plant wanted to be there.

That was the sort of man he was. A naturalist friend of his taught him to put a coin in the earth whenever he took a wildflower out of the mountains. It was a measure of gratitude. Jerry spent his life searching out beauty, and when he found it he knew how to acknowledge it. He smuggled rock fig seeds across the border from Mexico. When Hilly and I lived in Cincinnati, he and Janet visited us and flew home with cuttings of mulberry and shagbark hickory wrapped in dampened paper towels. A friend gave Jerry a rosebud tree from Wisconsin and he planted it next to an oak in the backyard. Toward the end of his life, Jerry and Janet placed a conservation easement on their land to protect it from future subdivision or development, to ensure it remained the refuge that they knew it to be.

Jerry spent so much time working this land that its geography became a sort of map of himself. To dispose of accumulated garbage—old kitchen timers, the children's trophies, and other unwanted flotsam—he put piles of the stuff in the yard and covered it all with big, naturally sculpted, lichened rocks that he and Janet quarried in the mountains themselves. Then he filled in the gaps with soil and planted flowers. Each flower in these gardens tells a story. The gentians that bloom in June—with a blue "so deep you could fall into it and never come up again," he told me once—also grow on one of his favorite hiking trails in the Missions. The black tulip was a gift from a long-time friend. We all urged Jerry to get out more, to come to this party or that event, but he only needed to walk his gardens to be among all the people and places he loved.

For the rest of us, the flowers were a fireworks display in slow motion. Even when our visits were regular, the palette of his gardens was constantly changing. One week the place would be covered in delicate purple-pink daphne, thickening the spring air with its fragrance. The next week Jerry would have conjured crocuses from the dirt, grape hyacinths, and hepaticas in delicate bouquets. As spring turned to summer, peonies, coral bells, and foxgloves budded and burst. When you were interested, and sometimes even when you weren't, Jerry would lead you to his favorites and insist that you see them, smell them, *know* them. If you cared about the man, you cared about his flowers and felt honored by these introductions. Like the birds, they were among his closest friends.

During his last summer, Jerry started writing treatises about gardening, short Word documents that offer wry guidance on how he grew raspberries, potatoes, string beans, and sugar snap peas.

In the peas treatise, he describes how he dries his peas and freezes them to kill a tiny leafcutter called a sharp shooter that would otherwise destroy his seeds. In the one on raspberries, he explains his method for catching and releasing porcupines that depredate the canes: the technique involves chasing a fleeing porcupine through the undergrowth before diving in front of it with a wire cage and a broom. Jerry caught and released half a dozen this way.

The pole bean treatise offers haiku-like wisdom: "Don't wear corduroy shirts in the bean patch. Leaves stick like appliqués." He goes on to suggest picking the beans early: "Otherwise, lumpy, leather-tough beans proliferate out there like chunks of hose."

• • •

The season of closure was on our minds that mid-September afternoon as Jerry led us to the orchard. We passed a rock garden where a feeble fall poppy swayed on a slender stem. Nothing much was growing now, with the exception of the strawberry patch, back by the beehives. There, in spite of the cold, shortening days, fat September strawberries spilled out beneath serrated leaves. Occasionally, when the sadness welled up inside the house and threatened to pour out the windows, I'd take my two-year-old son, Theo, out to the patch. We filled our mouths with berries and carried handfuls back to the house, depositing them on the kitchen table with red-stained fingers.

Fruit growers prize fall strawberries, which aren't as prolific as the spring crop but taste better because the plants are stressed. It's as if, knowing that the winter freeze is imminent, the plants empty themselves into their final fruit, this sugary, red proof of life, this small revolt against the inevitable.

With the spirit of a September strawberry Jerry walked to the orchard, as his hours of clarity diminished, and a small procession of his family followed closely behind.

IV. The Subarus

Jerry walked along the side of a rock garden and under a black walnut tree to the circular turnaround where the cars were kept. The family had always owned Subaru station wagons; they are the most fuel-efficient, snow-worthy cars that are also big enough to haul an elk during hunting season. Jerry learned their engines and dutifully changed the oil every three thousand miles.

Of course, Jerry scarcely drove at all. He was too practical for joyrides and he walked into town every morning to collect his mail. However, every Tuesday for more than twenty years, he faithfully drove into Missoula to visit his daughters and have dinner with Janet at the home of a history professor and his wife, their long-time friends. After dinner, more friends would arrive—a lawyer, a linguist, a vet, and others—and Jerry would join these men at a circular table in the basement to take stock of each other's lives and play poker. Jerry would go down carrying a green and white cooler filled with bottles of beer he had brewed in his bathroom, with his own hops and habaneros. He'd drive home late those nights, often drunk. Sometimes he'd eat a spoonful of mustard from the fridge before climbing the stairs to join Janet in bed.

In the years that I knew him, his car was a sky-blue 1987 Subaru station wagon. Rust nibbled at the wheel wells, and there was a dent in the back from a day we went goose hunting and he uncharacteristically reversed into a stop sign. Whatever the car, Jerry always left it unlocked, with the key in the ignition. As I understood, this habit was partly an incentive to never own a car worth stealing. It was also a declaration of his trust in people.

That contract wasn't always honored. One summer day in the 1990s, Jerry walked out into the driveway to find his car missing. The car, Hilly says, was a lousy silver and brown Subaru whose sides were so rusted they looked as if they had been peppered with birdshot. The interior smelled like a dead animal, and the family called it "Rat Car." Jerry reported its disappearance to the police.

Six days later he got a call from a sheriff's deputy in Pocatello, Idaho. They'd found the car. The young teenage boys who stole it had been pulled over by an officer who noticed the driver was barely tall enough to see over the steering wheel.

The next day, Jerry boarded a bus for Idaho. He found the car in the impoundment. The attendant took one look at the car and winced. "Did you say they only had it six weeks?" he asked.

"No, six days," Jerry said.

The man let out a low whistle. "They did a real number on it," he said.

In truth, it looked no different from when it was stolen. The boys had thrown out Jerry's public radio recordings and left an Eazy-E cassette in the tape deck. Jerry was scandalized by the hardcore raunch-rap as he drove the four hundred miles home.

Jerry also drove to go hunting. During bird season, he would tie an old rubber dinghy to his car's roof, load up his black lab, Annie, and drive out to the Flathead River to stalk pheasants and geese. In big game season, he would wake up before dawn and drive to his favorite haunts to look for deer and elk. He hunted the same places so long that every ridge and draw had a story for him. The land knew his footsteps.

But Jerry put the bulk of the miles on his Subarus in winter, when he, Janet, the young children, and usually a black lab piled into the car and drove to Mexico. The migration suited Jerry's personality and occupation. The bees hibernated in winter, and Jerry grew restless and gloomy amid the sunless inaction of the season. They drove down to the Sonoran Desert, where they camped along the Sea of Cortez. The family spent their days reading, painting, writing, and walking. Jerry taught the kids the constellations of the winter sky. He fished for corvina along the rocky coast. The family dug for razor clams, which they grilled over the campfire and ate with a squeeze of lime and a slash of hot sauce.

I joined the family on one of those trips, a year after I started dating Hilly. It took three days to get there. Jerry drove the entire way, ensuring optimal fuel-efficiency by never exceeding the Carter-era fifty-five miles per hour. He stopped only for gas. We'd all rush in to use the bathroom, and Janet would heat up food in the convenience store microwave.

Because he drank almost nothing between his morning coffee and his evening beer, Jerry seldom had to pee. He filled the tank and then sat in the car, eating sunflower seeds and tapping the steering wheel, impatient to be moving again. If we were slow, I found myself anxious that Jerry would be irritable. He was clearly the captain of these trips, and it felt important to abide by his schedule. In his family, travel happened on his terms and at his pace. I could sense that Janet and the children sometimes tired of his rigidity, but for me he was an exhilarating guide. New to the family and eager to please, I fell in line like a solicitous sailor.

Jerry had the habit of pushing even his finest qualities to the extreme. His frugality, for example, bordered on the obsessive. I borrowed his fishing rod one day in Mexico and got snagged on a rock on the ocean bottom. I broke off the lure and walked back to camp. I frequently lose my own lures when I fish, but Jerry looked disappointed, as if I hadn't tried hard enough to get it back, which reflected poorly on my character.

He was passionate in a debate, which made him a colorful conversationalist but also an intimidating one if he disagreed with you. His nightly beers made him even more emphatic.

"Jerry didn't have opinions," his friend Steve once said. "Jerry was just right."

He would wag a condescending finger at you and dismantle your logic with withering efficiency. He clung to his beliefs so tightly that arguments sometimes precipitated fallings-out with friends and even family members.

His views of gender roles could be antiquated, too. He didn't cook, and never changed a diaper. Later in life he expressed admiration for the way my male friends and I cared for our children, and he said he wished he'd learned to cook. As a father, he had focused on providing for his family, even if he didn't always attend to them. He was like that at home, and he was like that on the road.

But for me, and others, Jerry's intentional art of living was a centrifugal force we couldn't escape. He lived a life that was true to himself, packing twice as much living into every minute and filling his days with the things that he loved. His was a rare and alluring existence, even if it made few accommodations for anyone else—including the people who loved him the most.

• • •

I couldn't tell if Jerry noticed the parked cars as we all walked past them. There would be no more trips to Mexico. At this final stage of his sickness, Jerry wasn't driving anywhere. The narcotics had dulled his reflexes, and he didn't have anywhere he wanted to go. He was left to walk now, which had been his preferred mode of transport since he was a kid, and so we followed this charismatic, complicated man on foot past the rusting hulks of his cars and on up the driveway, adding still more mileage to the seemingly limitless odometer of his legs.

V. The Pit

Beyond the clearing where the cars were kept, we came to a gate. It wasn't much of a gate, just a length of wire fencing with a rotted log nailed to the bottom. Janet and Jerry always kept it open, even during Arlee's summer powwow, when RVs and teepees crowded the grounds above the cabin, and campers ambled through the property to swim in the river while young lovers had trysts in the woods. The only time Jerry closed the gate was in fall, when the bears come down from the mountains to fatten up before winter. This particular fall, a black bear sow and her two yearlings had noticed the fruit trees on the property. They seemed to be circling the place, waiting for their chance.

Beekeepers working hives in bear country have ample cause for concern; some even carry handguns to protect themselves. But Jerry respected bears more than he feared them. During summer breaks in college, he put radio collars on grizzlies in Yellowstone National Park with his mentors, the late wildlife biologists John and Frank Craighead. He watched a grizzly attack a car with filmmakers in it, shaking it like a tambourine. Once, Jerry and another biologist shot a boar grizzly with a tranquilizer dart, and then pulled a premolar from the animal's jaw to help determine its age. The bear was surprisingly alert, but they managed to take the tooth. When they got back to the truck, they realized their dart had contained only half the required dose of tranquilizer.

Jerry knew he'd be living alongside bears here on the river bottom. Bears use the Jocko River like a highway, and growing up Hilly and her siblings saw plenty of them in the yard. Once, when the kids were outside doing chores, Jerry set up a prank. He crept into the bushes near them and started woofing and snorting and snapping sticks like a bear. They were scared all right, and Jerry was in stitches until his eldest son, Jay, ran into the house and emerged with a rifle.

Given a chance, the black bears would pillage the dog food, raid the chicken coop, and snap off the thin, grafted branches of his fruit trees. So in the fall Jerry hooked up an electrical line that ran along the top of his fence. Every summer, before he turned it on, he walked the fence perimeter, clawing through the thick undergrowth, to clear out any bushes or trees that would touch the line and short it out. It was an arduous task, but it kept out the bears. Best of all, the fence itself was almost invisible. Jerry never liked to draw conspicuous lines between the animals' territory and his own.

• • •

On our way to the orchard, we passed through the gate and walked toward the garbage pit. Once the rock gardens were built, everything Janet and Jerry couldn't recycle, burn, compost, or reuse ended up here, in a yawning hole beside the driveway. An old fridge is buried in there, along with broken windowpanes, a mattress, and more. Like a midden, it's filled with the archaeology of a family's life here.

After Jerry learned that his cancer would kill him, he started making trips to this hole to dump the assorted documents of his life. Not wanting to leave any sorting to his survivors, he systematically organized his old stories, letters, and other papers, throwing away almost everything. Jerry said he thought about things by writing about them, and a fictional account of this end-of-life audit appears in a short story he published in the *Georgia Review*, "The Longing of Men." In it, Jerry describes a woman with cancer dumping boxes of her possessions into a pit: "She was exhilarated to be free of all those self-imposed illusions about having a history, about preserving anything, about ever mattering. When she hoisted the wheelbarrow handles to let the boxes fall and bounce into the bone pit, they made sounds like animals getting the wind knocked out of them."

If Jerry was conflicted about erasing the paper trail of his history, he didn't mention it. But one day at Deer Camp he did wonder aloud to me about his legacy. He had just read a review of a book called *Sum: 40 Tales from the Afterlives*, in which neurologist David Eagleman describes the three deaths we all face: the first is the moment life leaves our body, the second is when our body is consigned to the earth, and the third and final death occurs when someone speaks our name for the last time.

This third death haunted Jerry the most. He asked me, "How much do you know about your great-grandfather?" Jerry had a nasal timbre to his voice and squinting, inquisitive eyes that made me aim to answer his questions squarely. I wanted to think a man like Jerry would always be remembered, but I had to admit to him I didn't know much about my great-grandfather.

"You see?" he said. "It only takes a couple generations to be forgotten."

In time, he seemed to come to peace with his cosmic insignificance. In his final years, he sat down with a family friend, a writer named Candice, to tell her some of his stories. She recorded these and later transcribed them, and their details helped furnish this essay. During one of those sessions, Jerry told her this:

> Camus said that Goethe would be forgotten in ten thousand years. He'll probably be forgotten in one thousand years, maybe in a hundred. The point is we're all going to be forgotten.
>
> I once wrote a book all about death, to explore it, and I read everything I could get my hands on. I learned that you can't live like you're going to die tomorrow and you can't live like you're never going to die. People who die well are people who lived well. That seems right to me. By living well, a person learns about grace, and that would have to extend to dying.
>
> One of the best ways to live is with despair, in which you've made peace with how little you can do. But that doesn't change how hard you work. I've related that to having cancer. I want to get the gardens tilled and dug up. I may not be here next spring, but it doesn't matter. It's what you do this time of year. Like the parable about St. Francis: he was out hoeing his garden and an acolyte came to him and asked, "What would you do if you knew God was coming in an hour?" St. Francis said, "I'd hoe my garden."

VI. The Apples

The orchard is at the far end of the garbage pit. When we finally reached it, Jerry knelt to unhook the electric fence from the truck battery that powered it. He stretched the wire gate, unfastened it, and pulled it aside to let us in.

In total, Jerry planted fifty-four apple trees on this land. He began soon after he settled here, and the process was slow. First, he planted the rootstock, which he covered with sawdust and dirt. He waited a year for them to sprout, then drove to experimental orchards on Flathead Lake and in the Bitterroot Valley to taste their apples. The *next* spring, he returned to cut wood from the varieties he liked and grafted that wood onto his young trees. Slowly the rootstock and the grafts matured into trees and after a decade or so, Jerry picked his first apples.

They were wonderful, unusual apples, with names like Incarnation, Star Song, and Priscilla. He had Sansa apples from Japan, and an English variety called Ashmead's Kernel that originated in the eighteenth century. An apple called New Jersey 46 has soft pink flesh that tastes like strawberry soda.

Unsatisfied to stop here, Jerry then selected his favorite varieties and crossed them, hoping to combine one apple's flavor with another apple's texture, for example, or its storability. To do this, he tied a sack around the blossom of the parent apples while they were still buds. When the blossoms opened, he fertilized them by hand with pollen from his chosen apple parent. Once the petals had fallen, he removed the sack, labeled the location, and waited for the fruit. The seeds within the resulting apple would be genetic crosses of the two parents.

When that apple was ripe, he picked it and planted its seeds in his greenhouse. Each seed had different traits, like children in a family. The following year, he planted these seedlings in his garden. Several years later, when the wood was pencil thick, he would graft a section of it onto one of his trees. Then he waited several more years for the new branch to mature, flower, and produce fruit of its own.

After four decades, Jerry's trees contained 175 different kinds of apples—eighty-two standard varieties and ninety-three of his own crosses. (Because the process is so glacially slow, only eight of his own crosses bore fruit before he died.) Without the ability to control which qualities each parent apple contributed, some of the crosses were terrible and Jerry sawed these branches off his trees. Those apples made Jerry think of the anecdote in which the dancer Isadora Duncan wrote to George Bernard Shaw, "Will you be the father of my next child? A combination of my beauty and your brains would startle the world." Shaw declined, misogynistically, on the grounds that the child was just as likely to have his beauty and her brains.

But some of the crosses were successful. One of them, between a Blushing Golden and a William's Pride, Jerry called Morning Sky. The crowning achievement of his orchard, though, was his fourth attempt at crossing a Sweet 16 with a Gold Rush. He called it the Jocko—after the river that flowed past his house. This variety has a clean crunch, it stores well, and its flavor is delicately sweet, with a faint note of fennel. It was a worthy dividend to decades of tinkering.

Late in Jerry's life, I learned that he never actually ate his apples. He'd take a bite now and then to feel the texture and enjoy the flavor, but he spat out the pulp. He made sure every last one of them was picked, at peak ripeness, and distributed to friends, family, or the food bank. Jerry's chief incentive as an orchardist was the creation of something unique. To me the utility of an orchard was its fruit, but to Jerry an orchard was a laboratory in which the apples were the incubators for the seeds. The fruit would ripen and rot in a season. But the seeds? They were eternal.

• • •

We all filed into the grassy orchard, where Jerry pointed out a limb of Jocko apples. They weren't ready yet, but we hadn't come to eat. Instead, we watched as Jerry swiveled his torso around the orchard, looking for something. Wind whistled through the tops of the pines as Jerry still clutched the morphine pump in his left hand.

"What about this spot here?" he finally asked. "You like this end? I kind of like this end, too. You come in the gate, and you have this spot to go to. You have to walk."

He walked over to the spot and scanned the ground.

"If it were camp, I'd kinda like my head to go here," he said, pointing to the earth. Duncan, his forty-two-year-old stepson, set a large rock on the ground.

"My sleeping bag would come down this way," Jerry said. "Hey Dunc, move that rock two inches to the left."

Jerry was looking down now, making small measuring steps, as if he were about to dive into water. Then he got down on his hands and knees and flattened his back against the earth. His palms lay flat on the grass, his head rested on the rock like a pillow, and his pain pump whirred beside him.

"How do you like it, everybody?" he asked. "Okay?"

It wasn't okay. Not to any of us, no matter how long we'd known it was coming. Death for Jerry was still inconceivable, oxymoronic even. But if he had to be assigned to a single patch of soil, there was no better spot than this. Duncan gently sank a shovel into the grass on either side of Jerry's head, and again at his feet, upturning four divots of sod. Hilly and Janet took Jerry's hands and helped him stand.

"It's a little easier going down," he said.

No one talked. We were all staring at our feet and this plot of grass, beneath an apple tree, next to a garden hose; this ordinary piece of dirt that death would sanctify.

"What a strange bit of knowledge to have in my head," Jerry said. "Wow. It's a gulper. It's a gulper."

We stood there, shifting our weight, awkward under the uncertain certainty of it all. Jerry read the mood and did the kindest thing he could. He walked over to a tree and shook a limb so that ripe Noreen plums rained down on us. It felt as if he'd shaken us, too. Soon we were all stooping down to pick them up. They were tart and sweet. The flesh was bright red and the juice dribbled down my chin. Janet walked over to her husband and wrapped her arms around his waist.

"A graveyard and an orchard," Jerry said. "They go well together."

VII. The Hole

With his decision made and his energy waning, Jerry turned back toward the house and we followed. As we walked down the driveway, some of Jerry's older grandchildren and one great-grandchild were already returning to the orchard with shovels. No one knew how much time we had, but it seemed sensible to dig the hole before the ground froze.

Jerry stopped to offer them some advice.

"You might want to pile it on a tarp," he said. "It'll be a huge amount of dirt. You'll be shocked. A little planning won't hurt."

His fourteen-year-old grandson, Colton, was carrying a pry bar.

"There's a bigger bar," Jerry told him. "I've got the perfect bar for the job."

As we approached the house, we paused for a moment at the foot of a sugar maple by the woodshed. Jerry planted many trees on this land—oaks, lindens, willows, and walnuts. He planted a tree that's a cross between a mountain ash and a pear. Most of the trees are tall and mature now, a diverse arboretum that complements the native grandeur of this forest. But in fall, no tree is more breathtaking than this sugar maple.

It's about as tall as the house, with a trunk forking off into twin branches that reach skyward like raised arms. We had been watching its leaves turn from green to yellow to orange to red. They were like an hourglass of the season.

Before long, the leaves would fall. But at this moment, the tree glowed like an ember. I learned from his stepson Simon that Jerry used to tell the kids something at Deer Camp, when they circled around a warming fire under a glittering November sky. "The heat of that fire," he'd say. "That's sunlight burning." Matter and energy are never created or destroyed, he'd explain. They just change state.

In the same way, sugars in these maple leaves were igniting the last of the summer sun into a Technicolor display. The transformation incurs a metabolic cost to the tree, and botanists still aren't exactly sure why it happens. Whatever the reason, the tree pulled our eyes toward it like moths to a lightbulb.

By the time we reached the porch, the digging had begun. The earth in the orchard is riddled with rocks and we listened to the shovels sing out against them. Jerry walked into the house and sat down to a bottle of beer and a game of cribbage with his old friend Jay. On alternating evenings before dinner, Jay and Jerry would drive to one another's house, up or down the river, to share beers, curse at each other, and play cribbage. They did this almost every day for more than twenty-five years, passing a crumpled dollar bill back and forth to the night's victor.

When he finished this night's game, Jerry tiredly ascended the stairs and crawled into bed. Hilly brought him a Lorazepam to help him sleep. "How are they doing on that hole?" he asked her. "Do they want me dead by morning?"

• • •

In the end more than a dozen family members dug the hole, including young grandchildren and Philippa, the wife of Janet's first husband, Scot. The job took several days. The physicality of the labor and the simplicity of the objective were a refreshing escape from the anguish in the cabin. After one spell of digging, I returned to the house sweating and Jerry looked up at me from his pink recliner with soft eyes. "Thank you," he said quietly.

Meanwhile, Simon and Duncan built a box. They scavenged scraps of wood from the Honey House—the old sides of Jerry's honey truck, pieces of his bee hives, and the colorful remnants of a sign Janet once painted for the local café. The sign became the lid of the casket. Inside, the boards read: soup & salad, espresso, breakfast. The casket sat outside on the porch, a thing of beauty, with handles of purple-grained juniper and a soft, sanded lid. Theo and his three-year-old cousin, Selah, would bang on it gleefully, like a drum.

In the midst of these preparations also came new beginnings. One afternoon, Jerry's daughter Romy gave birth to a daughter, Opal. Duncan drove Jerry into Missoula to see her, arriving just minutes after she was born. Jerry looked gaunt and exhausted, but his face glowed several watts brighter when he sat down and cradled his newest granddaughter.

"You look handsome holding that baby," Janet told him.

His dry lips smiled. "It's just reflected light," he said.

VIII. The Descent

Five days before Jerry's death, my father and I were caring for him upstairs in his bedroom. He was lying in a whorl of blankets, pillows, and cream-colored sheets. His cheeks were unshaven, and his smile—when he could summon it—was apologetic. He lay diagonally on the bed, one knee cocked, like a weather vane swiveled into a storm.

The bedroom was crafted of rough-hewn pine. Hoya vines hung from the ceiling. Books were stacked beside the bed: James

Baldwin, Howard Zinn, and Giuseppe di Lampedusa. A dried-up sea horse was propped on a shelf. Soft light pooled in the north-facing window, and through it we could see the black-eyed Susans atop the root cellar, the blazing sumac, and the rusty trunks of ponderosas. Beyond them the Jocko River tumbled relentlessly westward.

My father and I hovered over Jerry, holding his hand, lifting water to his lips, feeding him morsels of egg, tomato, and toast. Pain and morphine had muddied his mind and it was difficult to know what he was thinking.

"Chavez," he announced at one point, into the stale stillness of the room. "Chavez. He was such a major figure for so long. Now it's a different deal."

He slowly looked around, caught my eye, and raised an eyebrow.

"How many of us are in here?" he asked. "Three? So I can fart."

He was dressed in baggy black sweats and a white undershirt that Hilly and I bought for him at Target. The clothes were too sloppy to suit him, but comfort was our final prayer.

I tried to make conversation.

"The golden eagles are migrating over the Big Belts," I said. "I read it in the paper. They're heading south."

"Hmm, that's funny," he muttered. He looked skeptical, like I had the timing all wrong. He glanced at the window. A few days ago he asked his friend David to measure it and then measure his chair. He wanted to be sure of his exits.

Suddenly his concentration tightened around some unspoken purpose. Spurred by the muscle memory of a lifetime of movement, he pulled himself to the edge of the bed and rose on his weakened legs. But then he forgot his intention. So he just stood there, an island unreachable even to himself.

We took his arms and guided him to his chair at the foot of the bed, where he slumped down and exhaled. The family had agreed that it was time to move him downstairs. Left up here he might fall, and downstairs he'd be closer to the bathroom. The other night he climbed out of bed to pee into a red jug that Janet had bought for him. But he kept trying to unscrew the head of his penis instead of the lid of the jug.

My father and I told him that we'd help him down the stairs.

His chair was next to his shoe shelf. For almost fifty years, he sat here each morning to lace up whatever footwear the day required. His dog would crowd his feet, yawning and stretching in anticipation. Jerry was a dog's ideal human: always outside, active, and punctual. He looked at the shelf now and took inventory. There were his hunting boots, his town shoes, his muddy gardening boots, and the old sneakers he used when he went fishing. His feet were in slippers now.

"My stuff is looking at me with funny eyes," he said. "Like, 'Why don't you do something?'"

He put his hands on his knees.

"That's the plan, then?" he asked. "Going downstairs?"

He seemed to know that he wouldn't see this room again, that every death was its own kind of descent.

IX. The End

We moved him down to a hospital bed that hospice had erected in the living room. Janet oriented it to face the window and the flaming maple outside. The room was filled with curiosities Jerry and Janet had collected. There was a handmade violin from Mexico's Copper Canyon, a whale vertebra they'd found on a beach, an obsidian hunting knife, an aluminum pot punctured by the teeth of a grizzly. The house hummed with stories.

Hospice sent out waves of nurses, pharmacists, and social workers—even a massage therapist and a harpist. The nurses managed the dosage of the pain pump, which purred next to Jerry on the bed. Janet kept his belly plastered with Phentynol patches. And in the evenings, when the nurses had gone, she climbed into bed with him and they ate ice cream and watched Trevor Noah.

I was in the room on one of these evenings, sitting on the sofa. I watched Jerry look over at Janet, his companion of thirty-five years, the patient, gregarious artist, the right brain to his left. Jerry called her "one of life's customers." Different as they were, they were similar in the ways that mattered. Jerry liked to say they were cut from the same rock. (Unbeknownst to us then, Janet had developed a new cancer in her bladder that would kill her less than two years later, in this very room.)

"Let me hold your hand," Jerry said to her. "Just to hold it, I guess. It's you and me, okay? And that's what happened. What's happened has happened."

"No getting out of it," Janet said. "I love you."

"I love you, too."

"Get some rest now. Close your pretty blue eyes."

"It's always going to be what it was."

"That was pretty fun, wasn't it?" Janet said. "At the dinner table, with the kids, talking to them?"

"Yeah. We did what we did."

"That's all you can do in this life, and then you don't do anymore. You get a break. You get a rest."

Jerry closed his eyes. "I love you," he said. "Good night."

Janet kissed him on the forehead. "I love *you*. Good night."

In the corner of the room, the fish tank released bubbles of air.

• • •

While Jerry could still swallow, he ate half a piece of a cherry pie made by Jay Sumner's wife, Janna. His eyes had a faraway look, and he ate small bites slowly and gratefully. It was the last thing he ate.

Eventually he began to cough. The cough turned into a rattle and then a gurgle, like the sound an irrigation pipe makes right as the water chases the last of the air out of it.

Now and then his body convulsed, as it does when you're drifting off to sleep and suddenly you dream that you're falling. He started to sweat, and asked politely if we could turn the heat down, even though it wasn't on. Janet put a cool washcloth on his brow. When his lips cracked, we smeared them with Bee Balm—the lotion he once made out of the beeswax from his hives.

We held vigil over his bed, shuffling seats around him, ceding chairs to our superiors in the hierarchy of closeness. The grandchildren entertained themselves outside, throwing leaves at each other under the maple. Duncan's wife, Jana, sang Norah Jones. For long stretches, Hilly sat at the old saloon piano and played: Satie's "Gymnopédies," "Ave Maria," and a piece called "Ode to Life," written by the jazz pianist Don Pullen after the death of his friend.

Jerry's eyes brightened with the music. "Wow," he whispered. "Wow." They were his final words.

The gurgle in his chest took on the sound of a coffee percolator right before it's finished brewing a pot, like the sound of gravel falling into a hole. His body was a tool he was not quite ready to set down. I took a seat at his writing desk, beside his bed, and found a scrap of paper with his handwriting. "Let the great world spin," it read.

• • •

And then the spinning stopped. It was four o'clock in the morning, and Janet was sleeping next to him. The silence woke her, she said, when the drone of his labored breathing shut off like a switch. Hilly, Theo, and I were sleeping nearby in the kids' cabin. When we reached him he looked like he was still sleeping, with his mouth slightly open. Crying, Hilly nudged it closed.

"He looks more like himself than he did yesterday," she said.

The rest of Jerry's children arrived, along with other family and Jay Sumner and his friend David. A hospice nurse came to pronounce the death. Looking tired but stoic, Janet brought down fresh clothes: his best pair of dark Levis, a rust-colored corduroy shirt, a vest, and his sun hat. We washed and dressed him, wrestling his stiffened arms through the sleeves.

From the kitchen came the hiss of bacon and the smell of coffee as Duncan cooked breakfast. The whole house seemed to exhale as we gathered around the kitchen table and ate. Jerry had built this table, a sturdy oval of blond pine, as a Christmas present for Janet a few years after they married. If you look closely, you can see the wood is streaked blue and pitted with small tunnels, the handiwork of the beetles that killed the tree. Jerry filled each beetle tunnel with resin; he layered epoxy on the table's surface, sanded it, and then layered again. The job required immense perseverance.

More than thirty years later, the table remains the heart of the home. Hilly grew up around it, canning vegetables in summer, butchering venison in the fall, debating with her father over dinner and learning to distinguish herself from him. At family gatherings, the table was always laden with food—garden salads, Janet's braided cardamom bread, wild geese, and elk steaks fried in tamari, garlic, and thyme. Now the family crowded around it once more and filled their plates, allowing this small relief to precede our impending grief.

• • •

We carried his body out to the casket and laid him on a bed of sugar maple leaves inside. Somehow his expression had shifted. He looked chagrined when we washed him, and contemplative when we dressed him. Now a faint smile had crept into his lips. He looked peaceful and a little bemused, maybe even proud.

Janet knew he shouldn't go into the earth alone. She put a bottle of his homebrew into the box, a pair of his hand-dipped beeswax candles, and a stack of their old love letters. David put in a raven's skull and a bison hoof. Jay Sumner contributed a crumpled dollar bill, a miniature cribbage board, and the game's best hand: three fives and a jack. Hilly picked a ripe Jocko apple and set it into her father's palm. Some grandchildren arranged a bouquet of purple asters on his chest. Janet bundled his decades-old, duct-taped parka under his head as a pillow. The casket was now a kind of message-in-a-bottle, a testament to the future of who this man was, and what he loved.

"Some of the best things in life are in that box," David said.

We walked with Jerry to the orchard one last time and slowly lowered him into the earth. Duncan said a prayer. Jana sang a song. Swarms of woolly blue aphids hovered in the air like electric-blue storm clouds. Then, under a gray sky, everyone began filling in the hole, and the most alive person I've ever known disappeared into the dirt. Even his trees seemed to kneel.

• • •

The following spring, when the crocus bulbs were poking out of the soil again as if by magic, almost-three-year-old Theo asked Hilly and me, "Where's Grandpa?"

We were out in Arlee visiting Janet, and just then we were driving past the orchard. Hilly said, "Well, his body's in the ground, right there."

"But not his face?" asked Theo.

"No, his face too," Hilly said. "His whole body."

After a moment, I said: "I guess the answer is that we don't know where Grandpa Jerry is. His body is in the ground, but some people believe we have souls and that when we die our bodies stay on earth, but our souls go up to heaven."

"Or they become a mountain," said Hilly.

"Yeah," I said, "or they live in that person's favorite places."

Theo considered this. Then he said, "I think he's an apple."

And neither of us could say anything for a while.

Coda

One May morning, the year before he died, Jerry took me fishing. He wanted to show me a hole that held a big brown trout. He knew this because he had caught and released it, twice, in successive years. It was a twenty-three-inch hen, with a rounded nose, that he called Big Mama.

Jerry wasn't a trophy sportsman. In his eyes, if a bull elk or a lunker trout outwitted the world long enough to become this grand, it earned a pass. He felt lucky just to see such creatures, and when he did, he savored them.

We left his Subaru on the side of the road and waded through a field of waist-high grass and wild rose toward the river. Jerry walked as though some unseen hand was on the small of his back, thrusting him forward. Forty-one years his junior, I had to quicken my pace to keep up. The morning was bright and the yellowthroat warblers called *wichity wichity* from the riverbank. A trio of deer sprang away from us in bounding arcs, their tails waving like white flags behind them.

As we navigated a patch of thistles, Jerry slowed long enough to turn back and say, "You know you're excited when part of you is almost afraid to get there."

Jerry grew up fishing the Yellowstone River and the spring creeks of Paradise Valley. Now, he still fished like a kid, in a pair of Levis and sneakers. He used an old fiberglass rod that he rigged with a leader knotted together from scraps of monofilament. Ever since I lost his lure in Mexico I had made sure to tie him an ample supply of flies. (He liked woolly buggers best.) I didn't have to tie many, because he hardly ever changed flies, even after fish had mangled them beyond recognition.

The poverty of his equipment didn't impair his results. He usually fished alone, but I saw enough to know that he cast his rod like a wand, jigging his fly through the current in just the right seams at just the right speeds to solicit the swirling flash of a striking trout. I was eager to watch him catch Big Mama.

At last we came to the river's edge, and Jerry showed me the hole. It wasn't much to look at, just a sunken log on the far bank where a fast riffle had carved out a pocket that was a promising shade of pewter. The pool was the size of a stovetop.

Jerry held his rod behind his back. "Go for it," he told me.

"What? No, this is your hole," I said. "This is your fish. You try."

He insisted, so I waded out to my knees and dropped my fly upstream of the log. I let it sink and felt the current pull it quickly through the deep water. I picked up my line and cast again. I could sense Jerry's anticipation behind me, and I wanted to catch this fish for his sake as much as mine. I cast again and again but never got a strike. Either I couldn't catch Big Mama, or she was gone.

Jerry didn't seem disappointed. We continued fishing downstream and caught a rainbow apiece, which we kept for dinner.

It was late afternoon by the time he turned his Subaru down the driveway to the cabin on the river bottom. Janet and Hilly were there, and we all cooked dinner together. Janet poached the fish in soy, onions, and curly garlic scapes. I cooked pasta with peppers. Jerry cut some fresh asparagus, and Hilly made a chimichurri sauce with cilantro and parsley from the garden.

Finally, we sat down to eat at the picnic table in the back yard where Janet and Jerry and then Hilly and I had married, thirty-one years apart. The food in front of us was fresh and green and vital, and the warming spring sunshine filtered down through the leaves with the promise of growth and goodness to come.

We sat around the table, enchanted. I watched Jerry raise his fork to his mouth. He was wringing the glory out of every second. His face tilted like a flower's toward the sun, his eyes were closed, and he chewed his food slowly, as if it were altogether too precious to swallow.

New York

FINALIST—PROFILE WRITING

Published in August 2019—when there were, as Rebecca Traister noted at the time, "a historic number of female candidates in contention for the Democratic nomination"—this profile of Elizabeth Warren examined her candidacy in the context of her work as a teacher. "In doing so," said the National Magazine Award judges, "Traister explores the politics of gender while illuminating the challenges powerful women confront as they strive to communicate on the campaign trail." The nomination of "Elizabeth Warren's Classroom Strategy" was Traister's fourth in the last six years. Nominated in Columns and Commentary for her work for the New Republic *in 2015 and in Feature Writing for* New York *in 2017, Traister won the award for Columns and Commentary for* New York *in 2018 for her columns on #MeToo. Under the leadership of Adam Moss and now David Haskell,* New York *is one of the most celebrated magazines of our time, this year alone earning nine Ellie nominations.*

Rebecca Traister

Elizabeth Warren's Classroom Strategy

The story of Elizabeth Warren's career in education—at least in legal education—begins with one word: *assumpsit*. It is literally the first word of the first case she had to read for the first class she ever took as a twenty-four-year-old law student at Rutgers University in 1973. She has recalled, in vivid detail, the fear and confusion she'd felt as a young mother, former public-school teacher, and unlikely law student when her first law professor walked into the room and called on a student whose name began with *A*, asking her, "Ms. Aaronson, what is 'assumpsit'?" Ms. Aaronson had not known, and neither had the next several students he called on after her. Ms. Warren also had not known what *assumpsit* meant, despite having done the reading for the day.

Since her last name was at the end of the alphabet, Warren was spared public humiliation, but she left her first law-school class badly shaken, with a degree of clarity about how she must move forward: "Read all the words and look up what you don't know."

In the following years, Warren became a law-school professor: first teaching night classes at Rutgers and eventually landing at Harvard, where she worked for sixteen years before becoming a U.S. senator from Massachusetts in 2013.

In 1999, more than twenty years after Warren attended her first law class at Rutgers, Jay O'Keeffe, who now works as a consumer-protection lawyer in Roanoke, Virginia, attended his first law class at Harvard. It was taught by Warren. "She did not say anything like 'Hello' or 'I'm Liz Warren, and welcome to Contracts,'" O'Keeffe recalled. "Instead, she put her books down, looked over her glasses at her seating chart, and said, 'Mr. Szeliga, what's 'assumpsit'?'"

Assumpsit—which, Warren told me, "means that the action is in contract rather than in tort"—became Professor Warren's calling card, though she says no matter how widely advance warnings spread, 96 percent of new law students would walk in unprepared for it. When Joseph Kennedy III introduced Warren at the Democratic National Convention three summers ago, the Massachusetts representative and grandson of Robert Kennedy recalled his "first day of law school, my very first class" in 2006, during which he had been the unlucky mark: "Mr. Kennedy, do you own a dictionary? That's what people do when they don't know what a word means; they look it up," he recalled her saying during his public immolation. "I never showed up unprepared for Professor Elizabeth Warren ever again."

"Yes, I do to my students what my teacher did to me," Warren said gleefully, as she drank tea on her Cambridge sunporch in July. She spoke in the present tense, as she often does, about her teaching career, even though it's been more than eight years since she has commanded a classroom.

So much of Warren's approach to pedagogy can be understood via the assumpsit gambit: With it, she establishes direct communication and affirms that she's not going to be doing all the talking or all the thinking; she's going to be hearing from everyone in the room. By starting with a question that so many get wrong but wind up learning the answer to, she's also telegraphing that not knowing is part of the process of learning.

Warren's work as a teacher—the profession she dreamed of from the time she was in second grade—remains a crucial part of her identity, self-presentation, and communicative style. Her 2014 book, *A Fighting Chance*, opens with these sentences: "I'm Elizabeth Warren. I'm a wife, a mother, and a grandmother. For nearly all my life, I would have said I'm a teacher, but I guess I really can't say that anymore."

But just because she's not in the classroom these days doesn't mean that those she's talking to can't smell it on her from a mile away. Leading up to the first round of debates, the *Onion* ran a headline reading, "Elizabeth Warren Spends Evenings Tutoring Underperforming Candidates." And during a June episode of *Desus & Mero*, the two Bronx hosts did a riff on how Warren "definitely gives you teacher swag, but the teacher-that-cares-a-lot swag," imagining her being the kind of teacher who comes to your house to tell your mom you have potential. "You came all the way to the Bronx for this? Wow . . . that *blanquita* cares."

Warren has won multiple teaching awards, and when I first profiled her in 2011, early in her Senate run and during what would be her last semester of teaching at Harvard, I spoke to students who were so over the moon about her that my editors decided I could not use many of their quotes because they were simply too laudatory. Many former students I interviewed for this story spoke in similarly soaring terms. One, Jonas Blank, described her as "patient and plainspoken, like an elementary-school teacher is expected to be, but also intense and sharp the way a law professor is supposed to be." Several former students who are now (and were then) Republicans declined to talk to me on the record precisely because they liked her so much and did not want to contribute to furthering her political prospects by speaking warmly of her.

Yet it remains an open question whether the work Warren does so very well—the profession about which she is passionate and that informs her approach to politics—will work for her on the presidential-campaign trail.

Plenty of our former presidents have been teachers. Some of them, including William Howard Taft and Barack Obama, taught law; some, including Millard Fillmore, primary school. Warren has been both law professor and primary-school teacher, and as a person who ran for office for the first time in her sixties, her four decades as a teacher define her in a way Obama's stint as an instructor in constitutional law never did. Here, as in all else, it matters that she's a woman. Teaching is a profession that, in postagrarian America, was explicitly meant to be filled by women. That means teachers historically were some of the only women to wield certain kinds of public power: They could evaluate and punish, and so it was easy to resent them.

In 2019, we have a historic number of female candidates in contention for the Democratic nomination. But many of them have approached politics via traditionally male paths: Kamala Harris and Amy Klobuchar were prosecutors, Kirsten Gillibrand worked at a white-shoe law firm, Tulsi Gabbard was in the military. Elite law schools were historically the domain of powerful men, but on the campaign trail, Warren is determined to establish herself not simply as an educator of the elite but also (with an anecdote she trots out often) as a kid who used to line up her dolls and pretend to assign them homework. The candidate's presentation of her teaching career—from kids with disabilities at a New Jersey public school to fifth-grade Sunday-schoolers in Texas to Kennedys in Cambridge—as key to her identity means she is hurtling toward the White House as a specific kind of feminized archetype.

It's a risk. *Schoolmarm*, after all, is a derogatory descriptor, one that was deployed against Hillary Clinton, also a former law professor, and one that flicks at the well-worn stereotype of the stern lady who can force you to recite your times table. The phrase has already been used to critique Warren's political demeanor, perhaps most memorably by Boston Democratic consultant Dan Payne. In 2012, Payne wrote a radio segment quoting women complaining about Warren's "hectoring, know-it-all style"; he claimed she treated delegates to the Democratic convention "as if [they] were her pupils" and advised her to "stop the finger-wagging; it adds to her strict schoolmarm appearance and bossy manner." Back in 2005, when Warren was testifying in front of the Senate on bankruptcy reform, challenging then-senator Joe Biden on stripping protections from families, Biden dismissed her with a slick, back-row smirk: "Okay, okay, I got it; you're very good, professor." More recently, Democratic adviser David Axelrod observed to the *New York Times Magazine*'s Emily Bazelon that one of Warren's drawbacks is that "she's lecturing . . . people feel like she's talking down to them."

Much of this is uncut, misogynistic claptrap, but Axelrod's swipe edges toward a legitimate concern: If the election of our current president makes anything clear, it's that many Americans do not want high-minded talk from their leaders. There is fair reason to worry that a candidate who is literally a professor runs the risk of alienating rather than energizing voters. In the primary field, Warren polls far higher with college-educated voters than she does with voters without a college degree.

And that doesn't begin to touch on what would happen should she get out of the primary: In February, Donald Trump Jr. offered a preview of how his father will likely frame a fight against an educator, telling the young conservatives at one of his father's rallies, "You don't have to be indoctrinated by these loser teachers." It's obviously a broader Republican line of argument. In July, former Wisconsin governor Scott Walker tweeted about "left-wing college professors" embracing socialism and showing "disdain for America." Of course, Walker lost his 2018 gubernatorial reelection bid to former public-school teacher and administrator Tony

Evers, in the same election cycle that Jahana Hayes, once named Teacher of the Year by Barack Obama, became the first black woman to represent Connecticut in the House of Representatives.

In fact, with waves of teachers' strikes politicizing voters in many states, it seems possible that 2020 could easily be framed as a contest between teachers coming for Republicans and Republicans eager to vilify teachers. The role our current president would play in such a setup takes no imagination: He is the ultimate back-of-the-class bully, mocking and menacing the woman with the answers standing at the front. We have seen this before.

When I asked Warren whether these are dynamics she worries about, she answered with an emphatic *no*: "Nobody wants to be talked down to—nobody. That's true whether we're talking about big national audiences or law students or fifth-graders or little tiny kids." But, she said, this is not at all at odds with the work she has done as an educator, because "that's not what teaching, good teaching, is about."

Instead, she said, "good teaching is about starting where you are and the teacher having the confidence in you to know that if you had a little bit more information, a little bit more time on this, if you thought about this from a little different perspective, you might move a little bit."

• • •

It should probably go without saying that, as a child growing up in Norman, Oklahoma, Warren, then called Betsy Herring, loved school. It was an era in which not many paths were open to ambitious young women. But her second-grade teacher, Mrs. Lee, "of ample bosom and many hugs," Warren said, took her aside and said, "'You know, Miss Betsy, you could be a teacher.' And *bam!* I was sold. It changed my whole vision of myself."

Mrs. Lee put the eight-year-old in charge of a less advanced reading group. The experience of helping struggling readers string letters together into words was intoxicating. Speaking to me in Cambridge, wearing an oversize button-down and baggy chino shorts, her hair bobby-pinned out of her eyes, Warren recalled the process of breaking words into their parts until "that flash, that spark, that *I went from not knowing to knowing.* It happens in their face, and it happens then in my heart, instantly. My brain. It's enormously intimate."

After that day with the reading group, Warren has written, "I harassed the neighborhood children to read out loud so I could play teacher, and when I couldn't get any takers," that's when she began to map out that rigorous curriculum for her dolls.

But just because Warren's ambitions had been electrified didn't mean her path was clear. "My mother wanted me to get married to a good provider and have babies and be safe; she didn't want me to do anything else," Warren said. Her three older brothers joined the military, worked in construction, started a business. "But me? My fortunes would be tied to the man I married."

By the time Warren was in high school, whenever her mother heard her discussing a teaching career, she would, as Warren tells it, "break into the conversation and explain to whomever I was talking to, 'But she doesn't want to be an old-maid schoolteacher . . . Right, Betsy?'" The mother-daughter battle was so intense that one night, after interrogating Betsy about why she thought she was so special that she should go to college, her mother hit Betsy in the face.

Warren won a full-ride debate scholarship to George Washington University, where she majored in speech pathology and audiology so she could teach students with speech and hearing impairments. But her mother's dire view of the world for unmarried women had a deep enough impact on Warren that when her old high-school boyfriend proposed to her just before her junior year, she promptly said yes, dropping out of school and giving up that scholarship. "For nineteen years I had absorbed the lesson that the best and most important thing any girl could do was 'marry well,'" Warren has written. "And for nineteen years I had also absorbed the message that I was a pretty iffy case—not very pretty, not very flirty, and definitely not very good at making boys feel like they were smarter than I was."

Warren and her husband settled in Texas, where she finished her undergraduate degree, then moved to New Jersey, where she found a job as a special-needs teacher for public-school students with speech and learning disabilities. But at the end of one term, she was visibly pregnant with her first child, Amelia; the principal did not ask her back. She enrolled at Rutgers University Law School in Newark, then one of the most diverse and progressive law schools in the nation.

Warren graduated nine months pregnant with her son, Alex, and there were no firms eager to hire a new mom of two. That's when one of her Rutgers professors suggested she might teach a night class at the school. That first year of teaching law school, she has recalled, was the second-grade reading group all over again: "I watched faces, and it felt like a victory every time I saw the *click!* as a student grasped a really hard idea."

From Rutgers, Warren secured a tenure-track job at the law school at the University of Houston and taught Sunday school. She divorced her husband and later married Bruce Mann, a law professor and historian whom she had met at a law conference. Warren proposed to Mann in a classroom after watching him teach a class in property law. "It was the thing I needed to know," she explained to me. "I couldn't be married to another teacher if I didn't respect his teaching. And watching him teach, he was good and engaged, and he cared and he was cute and I was already pretty crazy about him. But it was really important for me to know that." What Warren especially appreciated while watching Mann teach was his clear belief in his students. "That's the heart of really great teaching," she said. "It's that I believe in you. I don't get up and teach to show how smart I am. I get up and teach to show how smart you are, to help you have the power and the tools so that you can build what you want to build."

The pair's struggle to find double teaching appointments led them from Houston to the University of Texas at Austin to Penn and finally to Harvard, where she was hired in 1995 and where Mann came on as a professor of law and history in 2006. By the time she arrived, Harvard Law School was in the midst of a controversy over diversity in hiring; Professor Derrick Bell had taken an unpaid leave in protest of the fact that none of the school's sixty tenured professors were women of color (in 1990, only five were women, all of them white). And while much attention has been paid to the question of whether Warren's self-identification as Native American on a variety of forms during her career had any impact on her hiring trajectory, it is quite likely that, as a white female law professor in a massively male-dominated sphere in the 1980s and '90s, she did benefit from affirmative-action policies. White women have been affirmative action's disproportionate beneficiaries.

Warren was an odd duck at Harvard, not just because she was one of only a handful of female professors; she was also among the only faculty whose degree had been issued by a public university. She began to speak to the masses in more direct ways, about the research she was doing on why families were going into bankruptcy, on television programs like *Dr. Phil* and *The Daily Show*. She didn't publish academic books but ones about bankruptcy and personal finance coauthored with her daughter Amelia.

Warren believed that the law and its remedies should not be simply the domain of the already powerful, and her approach to communicating with her students—and later, as a more public figure, with a wider audience—came back to her drive to make seemingly complicated concepts available to those who didn't already have an expertise, specifically by decluttering the language she feels is meant to drive people away from engagement with the policies that shape their lives, rather than drawing them in and making them full participants.

A perfect example, she told me, was the lead-up to the financial crash in 2008, "where the smart boys, as the economy is tumbling over the edge, only wanted to talk in terms of reverse double-half-nelson derivatives and said, in effect, 'The rest of you aren't smart enough to understand this. We the elite will take care of this.' And they were wrong."

In the wake of that crash, Warren stepped into her role as America's teacher, defying those "smart boys" by explaining to big audiences what had happened with a clarity that felt as comforting to some as Mrs. Lee's hugs had felt to Warren back in the second grade. In 2010, Bill Maher told her, "I just want you to hold me," before putting his head in her lap and embracing her. The same year, Jon Stewart took a hot-for-teacher route, telling her, "I wanna make out with you." In fact, for all the reasonable concern about how men especially may rear back from schoolteachers, the reception Warren has sometimes earned offers plenty of evidence that some of them take deep solace, in perilous times, in the plainspoken educator who can tell a straight story about how we got here and where we need to go next. After her second debate performance last week, CNN commentator Van Jones told Warren, "You make me feel like help is on the way . . . You make me feel good." What she's offering is belief—in her students, the audience, voters.

It's the same, in Warren's view, as nudging people to understand that they can read: "We can all understand this, and we can all demand some oversight and accountability and then make some real changes so it doesn't happen again." Conveying information; inviting in people who feel shut out; making stories, syllables, letters clear and legible—this is precisely, Warren says, "what a good teacher does."

• • •

Chrystin Ondersma was a second-year transfer student at Harvard Law School in the fall of 2005 and did not feel at home. The working-class daughter of a waitress and a father who filled vending machines, she had grown up in the conservative Dutch Christian Reformed community in Grand Rapids, Michigan, attended Calvin College (alma mater of Betsy DeVos), and taken her first year of law classes at Arizona State. Ondersma had come to Harvard to take classes in constitutional law and civil rights, with an eye to becoming a gender-studies professor. She'd also hoped to study with the civil-rights theorist Lani Guinier, who in 1998 had become the first woman of color appointed a tenured professor at Harvard Law and, in the 1990s, had levied a critique of how law-school classes were taught. Guinier particularly took issue with the Socratic method—whereby professors cold-called students in large lecture halls, asking them to cough up information about case law in front of their peers—as being fundamentally unfriendly to the least-privileged students in a classroom.

Ondersma agreed with Guinier about the limitations of the Socratic method, and when, during her first semester at Harvard, she saw a notice about a lunchtime lecture on the Socratic method offered by Elizabeth Warren, a professor she'd never heard of, she decided she'd go and argue her case. By phone, Ondersma remembered how, in a small conference room packed with students, Warren had laid out a case "for how, if you really care about equality in the classroom, if you care about racial justice, gender justice, and you just rely on voluntary discussion in classrooms, you're only going to hear from the two white guys that love to talk." For Warren, the Socratic method did not further inequities; it was a tool to mitigate them.

Warren reiterates this argument today, suggesting that "what Lani was criticizing was the Socratic method done really badly." She said to me, "The reason I never took volunteers is when you take volunteers, you're going to hear mostly from men. 'Cause they have a lot more confidence, and they'll get those hands up."

Several of her students mentioned the rumor that she targeted only guys with the assumpsit query because Warren was determined not to kick off her class by putting her more vulnerable students on the spot. (It was, perhaps, not accidental that Joseph Kennedy III found himself her prey.)

Troy Schuler, a tutor now working on an education start-up, took Warren's contracts class the last semester she taught it, in 2011. He remembered another way she obsessed about equal access: In the run-up to exams, when people came to her office with questions, "she made everyone write up those questions and send them to her, then she wrote up her answers and sent them back out to the entire class. Because if one person has a question, it probably means that a lot of people had the same question, and it was very important to her that people were not going to have any structural advantage because they were the kind of person who knew to come to talk to a professor in office hours."

Warren's argument about her commitment to inclusion was so persuasive that Ondersma put aside her plans to challenge her on the Socratic method and, as soon as the lunchtime session was over, wrote Warren an e-mail that began, "I went to your lecture and feel like a convert." Warren responded right away, asking her to come to office hours and noting, "I always love to talk to students interested in commercial law."

Ondersma was slightly embarrassed—she had zero interest in commercial law—but was so grateful that a professor who didn't know her would take time to meet her that she went anyway. She explained herself to Warren. "I didn't care about how corporations were structured, and I didn't care about financial intricacies between creditors and debtors," she related to me recently. "I didn't think that was crucial to the mission of social justice."

Warren listened for a long time, Ondersma remembered. "And then she said, 'If you really care about social justice, you should think about focusing on commercial law and bankruptcy.'"

The professor told her it was a shame that so many of those who were committed to fighting injustice went into public law, leaving private, commercial practice dominated by more-conservative young lawyers. (Warren had herself been a conservative and moved to the left through her research into how Americans were going bankrupt.) "'Economic law has a huge impact on women and folks of color,'" Ondersma remembered Warren telling her. Ondersma ended up taking every class Warren offered and became her teaching assistant in the first-year contracts class.

In this position, Ondersma remembered, she had one job: to make sure everyone got called on equally. "The whole idea was that she wanted everybody in the classroom to participate." Ondersma would sit with the class list and check off every student who'd gotten a cold-call question. Then, in the last ten minutes of the class, "I'd hand her a notecard with the names of all the students she'd not yet called on," and Warren would try to get to them all.

Jed Shugerman, now a law professor at Fordham, recalled coming to Harvard as a brand-new hire in 2005. He had been advised to attend other teachers' classes to get a feel for how things were done. Observing Warren, he said, was a little scary: "She knew every one of eighty students by name. She used no notes. She had the day's material memorized in her head as she walked around the room and asked detailed questions about the cases."

It sounds impossible, Shugerman said, to call on more than two dozen people during a class. "Calling on more than fifty people sounds absurd, and like the questions and answers must have been superficial," he said. "But she was so responsive and such a good listener that she could build on the last person's answer with someone else afterward so it would build up to more complicated and sophisticated points that would go deeper."

After class, Warren asked Shugerman to lunch. When he told her that watching her had intimidated him, Warren asked him, "Do you think I could do that when I was your age? I had no clue.

It takes years to find your own teaching style." But she explained to him the thinking behind hers: ninety minutes, she said, is a long time to sit and be talked to. The Socratic classroom as she handled it forced everyone in it to pay close attention not only to what she was saying but also to what their fellow students were saying. She was not the leader of conversation; she was facilitating it, prompting the students to do the work of building to the analysis.

It's a pedagogical approach that Warren sees as linking all of her experiences of teaching. "It's fundamentally about figuring out where the student is and how far can I bring them from where they are." Her biggest lesson in this, she said, came not in a law school but in teaching Sunday school to fifth-graders in Texas. Asked by her Methodist preacher to take over a group of unruly kids, she thought it would be simple: "You teach them a little lesson, you do a little art project, you give them cookies and juice, you say, 'Thank you, Lord,' and then the hour's over." But for weeks, things were bad: "They cut each other's hair, they cut each other's clothes; the boys climbed out the window." So she thought to herself, *Okay, you know how to teach. Teach them like you teach them in law school.* She brought in a kids' version of the story of Noah and told them to read it, because she was going to ask them some questions.

Her first question was "How do you think Noah felt when he heard this voice?" They giggled. "'He thought he was going crazy. He had a worm in his ear.' But they actually got interested in the question: What would it be like to be somebody who had a job, who had a family, and hears God talking to him? Does he know it's God? Would you really sell your stuff? Before you knew it, it was time for juice and cookies and then everybody went home," she said. "I thought, *Dang, that worked.* I loved my fifth-graders. They showed me, in all my cases of teaching, it's about figuring out where they are, adding a little to it."

Ondersma sees Warren's Socratic approach at work on the campaign trail: "There's a lot of listening happening. I saw that in classrooms, and it happens in town halls, too. She's telling them her ideas, but I bet she gets ideas from them, too." Among other things, Warren has vowed, if elected president, to appoint a public-school teacher to be secretary of education, an idea she said she first heard from a voter—a public-school teacher—at a town hall.

Of course, presidential debates aren't a forum that lend themselves to the Socratic approach—she doesn't get to tussle at length with moderators or opponents (let alone the audience) to really break down ideas or build a case. But you can see her applying it around the edges, and watch her expertly poke holes in bad arguments. After the second debate, Warren was pressed by MSNBC's Chris Matthews to say that her health-care plan would raise taxes. Warren refused again and again to cede to Matthews's frame, which takes as its basis a right-wing obsession with taxes as the only measure of costs to voters.

Warren has not enjoyed a warm relationship with the political press. She has too often been clipped, defensive, uneasy—the experienced teacher who cannot for the life of her figure out how to get a room full of fifth-graders to listen to her. She is perhaps coming closer to finding her footing, in part by engaging reporters with more assuredness, honed via her Socratic training: Her ability to wrestle through an argument with Matthews made her seem authoritative and in control.

Warren agrees that her belief in Socratic dialogue informs how she instinctively engages with people professionally. In part, she said, Socratic teaching is about that back-and-forth, a breaking down of ideas and examining them from all angles. So when she and her policy team began discussing a wealth tax, she said, "I kept taking the side of the opposition: Wouldn't this create a problem?. . . We're pulling it apart to stress-test it, see if it would work."

When she was first doing town halls, after proposing a wealth tax, she said, "I'd look at the faces and think, *I don't think everybody is connecting. It's not quite gelling.* So I tried a couple of different ways, and then it hit me. I'd say, 'Anybody in here own a home or grow up where a family owned a home?' A lot of hands would go up. And I'd say, 'You've been paying a wealth tax forever. It's just called a property tax. So I just want to do a property tax; only here, instead of just being on your home, for bazillionaires, I want it to be on the stock portfolio, the diamonds, the Rembrandt, and the yachts.' And everyone kind of laughs, but they get the basic principle because they've got a place to build from."

Warren has also remained a "cold-caller" in other corners of her professional life, running offices as she ran a classroom. Corey Stone, a former assistant director of the Consumer Financial Protection Bureau, worked with her for six months as she built the agency; he recalled that her former students who worked at the bureau had warned him that she was "the queen of the cold call and had high expectations that people have their facts in order." In small meetings, he said, she'd ask direct questions of the people present, "and if we didn't have the answer, it was not necessarily that we were dumb, just that there weren't data to answer those questions. So it made us make sure that we had the research to answer the questions we couldn't answer."

Consider too that, by some measures, Warren has brought the process of cold-calling into her fund-raising strategy: After vowing not to do closed-door fund-raisers with big donors, she began phoning small-dollar donors at random, mercifully not to ask them about case law. But it's the same principle: The people coming in with structural advantages—money, confidence, experience navigating intimidating institutions or plying the powerful—should not have more access than those who don't.

One of Warren's former students who declined to be named had a theory about the seeming paradox of a woman known as a bold political progressive adhering to an old-fashioned, rule-bound approach to teaching. It reminded him, he said, of Thurgood Marshall, who was known for being punctilious about civil procedure even as he broke revolutionary ground on civil rights. This student talked about how Marshall understood that rules could be used to enforce equality, and that as soon as you introduced flexibility and discretion, those with more power would take advantage of the wiggle room. Regulations, calling every name in a classroom, could serve as a set of guide rails, a system it would be harder to take advantage of. It's easy to see how Warren's fondness for just this kind of formal system jibes with her view of regulations in the financial industry. It is also true that teachers love rules.

Along with the rules, there were the dogs. Good Faith (given to her by students and named after "good-faith purchasers," those who didn't use a contract and who, she had explained in class, were like golden retrievers: "empty head, good heart") used to sit with Warren during office hours. After Faith came Otis. Alison Schary, who graduated in 2008 and is now an intellectual-property lawyer, recalled that Warren used to post office hours for Otis. "You could sign out Otis and take him for a walk around campus."

Her current dog, Bailey, has become a staple on the campaign trail, doing the work of any good politician's pet: making the candidate more accessible to those she might otherwise intimidate.

• • •

For years, Warren served on Harvard Law School's admissions committee. Shugerman briefly served alongside her and noted "how focused she was on giving special consideration to people who'd been first in their families to go to college, students who had been in the military, who'd had work experience outside of the academy." Shugerman said it was striking that Warren chose the admissions committee, since big law-school muckety-mucks often preferred the hiring committees.

This is part of how Ondersma came to Harvard and wound up in Warren's office hours. It wasn't pure serendipity: Warren headed the committee that had decided to admit Ondersma as a second-year law student from Arizona State. Warren knew exactly whom she was talking to when Ondersma first came to her office and, once she was there, took great satisfaction in persuading the young radical to focus her fight against injustice on the study of commercial law.

When I asked Warren about her wooing of progressive students into her own traditionally more staid field, she rubbed her hands together, a cheerful spider in full command of her web. She told me a story about how she performed the same trick with Katie Porter, a student who flubbed an early answer in class, came to beg Warren not to give up on her, and blurted out, "I don't care about any of this bankruptcy stuff!" Porter not only went on to study bankruptcy with Warren; she wound up teaching it as a professor and, in 2018, flipped an Orange County California House seat blue. Warren wants progressives, she said, "armed with maces and spears and sticks" in their fights for economic equality. Porter now performs viral eviscerations of bankers and bureaucrats on the House floor, reminiscent of what her mentor does in the Senate.

Porter isn't the only elected progressive to have emerged from Warren's classes. Boston city-council member Michelle Wu was a Warren student; so, of course, was Joe Kennedy. And both Warren's chief of staff, Dan Geldon, and her former policy director, Ganesh Sitaraman, are former students. She has, by some measures, used her time in the classroom to build a small army, which also includes prominent bankruptcy professors Dalié Jiménez and Abbye Atkinson.

But there's another student of Warren's who now sits alongside her in the Senate: the bloodred Tom Cotton from Arkansas.

Cotton once told Chuck Todd that, while he knew from her scholarship that she was a liberal, he hadn't been able to divine her politics in class.

Warren and Cotton appeared together at a 2017 panel at Harvard for senators associated with the school (at which Warren was the only woman and the only panelist without a Harvard degree in the all-white group). During the discussion, Warren was describing why she'd come to teach at Harvard, how "every day I got to walk into the classroom where [there was] such privilege, such opportunity, such incredible tools, but to say to people, 'Come on, get better at what you've got and widen it out, because the only mistake you can make is not to get out there and do something with passion.'"

Cotton interrupted her: "That's not exactly the way I remember it," he deadpanned, explaining that "she was teaching us that lesson by being very hard on us."

Warren leaned over and looked at her former student. "And are you sorry?" she asked him.

Cotton backed down. "She was probably the best professor I had," he conceded.

• • •

Writing about Warren in the *Times Magazine* earlier this summer, Emily Bazelon, herself a lecturer at Yale Law School, wrote that "Warren didn't sound to me like a law professor on the trail, but she did sound like a teacher." Bazelon worried, a bit, that "trying to educate people isn't the easiest way to connect with them."

In a presidential context, the question of how women might make themselves "likable" looms large and perpetually unsolvable. Warren, like every other woman who speaks loudly in public, has already been tagged for being imperious and inauthentic, for faking her love for beer, for being too elite or too folksy. Male paths to presidential endearment—academic genius, a facility for languages, shows of muscularity, business acumen, bellowing, football jokes, and the plausible enjoyment of beer—are apparently off the table. So what are women going to do?

The conviction that teaching—being a literal teacher—might be an answer feels, on some level, far-fetched. First, it is hard work when part of the education means schooling the public on the bias and exclusion that have left nonmale, nonwhite candidates on the margins to begin with. Warren's colleague and competitor Kamala Harris recently observed—after engaging in a back-and-forth with Joe Biden over the history of busing—"there's still a lot of educating to do about who we are" and acknowledged that those efforts can be draining. "In my moments of fatigue with it all, I'm like, 'Look, I'm not running to be a history professor,'" Harris said.

Then there's the fact that it's a very short step from clarifying truth teller to the emasculating scold who shames you or puts you in a time-out. I felt a shiver of dread when, during the second debate, she stared at a distracted and giggling audience in the midst of her story about activist Ady Barkan's struggle to pay for his ongoing ALS treatment and admonished, "This isn't funny. This is somebody who has health insurance and is dying." *Eep*, I thought. But everyone shut up and listened.

Here's the thing: since there aren't a lot of other easy models for powerful women to authoritatively communicate with masses of people they've never been encouraged to lead, why wouldn't it make sense that the model by which a woman could emerge in a presidential sphere might be the same as the one that permitted women entry into the public sphere to begin with?

It is, after all, no coincidence that many of the few women to have made serious approaches toward the presidency in the past found their first professional foothold in a classroom: Shirley Chisholm was a director of nursery schools and an early-education consultant who made early education central to her political agenda; Hillary Clinton was the second female law professor at the University of Arkansas; Margaret Chase Smith and Elizabeth Dole also did stints as teachers.

It's true that people may resent teachers. It's also true that people are *primed* to resent teachers, because they resent women who might wield power over them, and it is still new and uncomfortable to think about women having political—presidential!—power. And yet: People who have had great teachers love them in ways that are intense and alchemical and irrational and sometimes difficult to convey—which is also, oddly enough, how some people love the politicians they believe in and choose to fight for.

Ondersma, who was going to teach women's studies and critical race theory, now teaches bankruptcy and commercial law at Rutgers, where many of her students are working-class children of immigrants and were first-generation college students. She cold-calls them, using the Socratic method to draw them in. Ondersma is still in touch with Warren, whom she talks about the way many people talk about the teachers who changed their lives. "Every time I messaged her, she always wrote back and said, 'I'm proud of you,'" Ondersma said, calling those "the four most important words I've heard from almost anyone in my life."

It may be true that we don't want a president who asks us to do homework. But we might want one who manages to see in us, somehow, potential.

Poetry

WINNER—ESSAYS AND CRITICISM

"We have DeafBlind artists, but do we have DeafBlind art?" asks John Lee Clark in this essay for Poetry. *Clark answers in part by describing his encounters with objects admired or created by sighted people and then offers a more-meaningful alternative for DeafBlind people like him: tactile art. "True tactile art must have language," writes Clark. "It should express and extract meaning. Texture, contour, temperature, density, give, recoil, adsorption, and many other elements are units in this language." The judges who chose "Tactile Art" as the winner of the 2020 National Magazine Award for Essays and Criticism praised the keen intensity of Clark's writing and described the essay as "startling and revelatory." Clark is a poet and essayist whose most recent book is* Where I Stand: On the Signing Community and My DeafBlind Experience. *Founded in Chicago in 1912,* Poetry *previously won National Magazine Awards for General Excellence, in 2011 and 2014, and Podcasting, also in 2011.*

John Lee Clark

Tactile Art

i

Downtown St. Paul is home to one of the most extensive skyway systems in the world. The sprawling maze connects buildings via enclosed bridges above the streets. The skyway solves one of our challenges as DeafBlind people traveling through a city: crossing busy intersections. My family lived there for as long as we could afford to because it was such a joy to be a mouse racing inside and out, up and down, plying my long single whisker. Following my nose, I found all the best places to eat and, following other instincts, I infiltrated all the cleanest bathrooms hidden away from the masses.

One day my partner, Adrean, an ASL Deaf artist, came home to tell me about something she'd spotted. It was a sculpture of a giant open Braille book. She had never gone that way before, but I'd passed by it several times. It stood in a building's courtyard, some paces from the street. You had to see it to see it.

A few days later friends from out of town were visiting. We took them out to our beloved Ruam Mit Thai, and after our feast we gave them a tour of the city. I remembered Adrean's sighting and asked her to show us the public work.

It turned out to be a huge sheet of metal propped up, its bottom edge near the ground and its top edge a foot taller than I.

Each Braille dot was the size of a golf ball. This made it impossible to read the text, which was supposed to be a passage from a Walt Whitman poem. Although the sheet mimicked the open face of a book, with two facing pages, each line ran across both pages.

There was a plaque with the title, artist name, perhaps a statement. Did the statement pay tribute to Braille? This information was not available in regular Braille.

As I struggled to read what the golf balls had to say, a security guard trundled out of the building. He spoke no sign language but we got the message. One of the nice secret restrooms was close by, and we hurried there to wash our hands.

ii

Museums are difficult to get to. They don't want me to touch anything. They require that I make an appointment—by phone, no less. So my information about mainstream aesthetics has largely come from ducks.

They rule over gift shops, Goodwills, and garage sales. Squeaking rubber versions have long been infants' first encounter with artifice. Minnesota's state bird is the loon, and many homes and stores here feature wooden, ceramic, metal, stone, plush, and glass loons. Waterfowl are a favorite of woodcarvers. There is even a DeafBlind Canadian who whittles, paints, and sells ducklings. What they all have in common is a flat bottom. A goodly portion of their natural anatomy is taboo. They are meant to appear floating on the still waters of a tabletop, a windowsill, or a bookshelf.

The hitch is that were I to handle a live duck paddling across a pond, I would be able to feel it as a whole, for water is not a tactile barrier as it is a visual one.

Small wonder, then, that one of my definitions of beauty is a certain stuffed wood duck in the nature center at Richfield,

Minnesota. A piece of ordinary taxidermy, its feathers are ridiculously soft. "Wood duck," I was inspired to write in a slateku, a form I invented using the Braille slate, "I feel for you / You never had hands to stroke / Your own wings." Even more bewildering are its round velvet bottom and granular webbed feet, which bespeak a master creator.

iii

"Here, you can touch my face."

"Thank you, no."

"No, it's fine. Really."

"Nah. I just—"

"I want you to."

Well, I want to tell them, what you are offering for my inspection is just a skin-covered skull.

"A head," jokes the eighteenth-century British comedian George Alexander Stephens, "is a mere *bulbous excrescence*, growing out from between the shoulders like a wen; it is supposed to be a mere expletive, just to wear a hat on, to fill up the hollow of a wig, to take snuff with, or have your hair dressed upon."

A friend once showed me a prized possession of his, an egg-shaped sculpture. I could feel its eyebrows, nose, and mouth, but they conveyed nothing. For my sighted friend, it had an exquisite expression of serenity. *Peace*, it's called.

At least it was bald. The bust of Mark Twain in a museum I visited in New York had him wearing a futuristic helmet, with fantastical whorling grooves. A terrible tumor grows under his nose. Ulysses S. Grant was similarly helmeted but had an iceberg stuck up his jaw.

Helmets notwithstanding, sculptors were onto something with nudity and gesture until the Victorians began to manufacture a statue for every philanthropist and politician. Of these "leaden dolls," G. K. Chesterton grouses, "Each of them is cased in a cylindrical frock-coat, and each carries either a scroll or a dubious-looking garment over the arm that might be either a bathing-towel or a light great-coat."

iv

You are the best one
in the museum. You don't
try to be real. You
are wise not to attempt
hair. You have no face.
Your clothes make you. You
were inspired by a youth
famous for pretending to be
a statue. He would die
five years later. But you
are still here. We touch
you. You do not flinch.

—*Cubist Statue*, by John Lee Clark,
after Jacques Lipchitz's *Matador*, 1914–1915

v

We will call her Allie. Shortly after her death I learned from friends that she was a fake. It was one reason she had relocated some years earlier, to leave a local DeafBlind community that had caught on to her.

I had known—or, rather, not quite known—Allie for many years as a fellow member on multiple listservs in our community. I'd met her in the flesh only once. The posthumous revelations were not that shocking; we've always had DeafBlind wannabes or compulsive sympathizers in our midst. For better or for worse, they are part of our lives. Whatever it is that any of them gets out of it, many do give of themselves in return.

In Allie's particular case, she also gave me the most tactile work of art I own. It is a marvelous mosaic of seashells, judiciously arranged so to have it rise and fall by turns from roaring densities to quieter rumblings. Though just two inches at its tallest point, it is a work of such soaring lyricism that I begin to understand what is meant by the sublime.

A long-distance DeafBlind friend of Allie's had lovingly put it together for her. It was the first time the artist had made something with a fellow DeafBlind person in mind. Allie explained to me that, unfortunately, the artist's other work is visual, primarily concerned with color, with only feeble tactile features. So it was a DeafBlind fake who had challenged a real DeafBlind person to make an intentionally tactile piece for the first time.

I cannot stop running my hands over it. When Allie knew she was going to die, she sent it with a note saying, "This piece cried out to be enjoyed by Mr. Tactile so it goes to you. Love, Allie."

vi

When I attended Deaf school growing up, I learned about a sickness that infects many hearing people. It keeps them awake at night unless they do something to bring music into our supposedly silent world. Dance troupes, bands, orchestras, and ex-hippie sound engineers invaded our campus every year.

I would later learn that sighted people were often afflicted in the same way. Only their desperate mission is to make visual art accessible to blind people. One victim of this malady is John Olson, a photojournalist and war photographer who made his mark dispatching images from the wars in Vietnam. After an illustrious career spanning five decades, he found himself wondering

> what it was like for those who didn't have access to art, to photography. I wondered what it was like for the blind community, who couldn't access visual information. It was at that

> moment, on a Labor Day weekend of 2008, that I set out to develop a means by which blind people could see art, could see photographs, and could acquire visual information.

For the past decade, he has been busy with his company 3DPhotoWorks, creating raised representations of art, photography, maps, and graphics. As he told a convention of the National Federation of the Blind in July 2018, "it has been my goal from the very beginning to create a worldwide network of museums, science centers, libraries, and institutions willing to provide the world's blind population with visual information using this tactile medium."

No one seems to have asked whether we want access to visual information. Why would we want a representation of a representation of something? Why not a tactile representation of that something, bypassing visual representation altogether? Why force visual art to be what it is not? We accept that most visual art is meant to be visual alone. Sighted people and institutions are the ones having trouble reconciling themselves with this fact.

vii

What shall we call it—tactile grammar, semiotics of touch, Protactile aesthetics, tactiletics? True tactile art must have language. It should express and extract meaning. Texture, contour, temperature, density, give, recoil, adsorption, and many other elements are units in this language.

Most things made by sighted people that we touch fail to make sense. Heft is one common grammatical unit they get wrong.

There are many toy tanks, for example, that replicate the shape and many of the moving parts of a real tank. Visually, it looks exactly like the real thing, and is thus able to exude some of its menace.

In the tactile realm the toy tank is a joke, because it is made of flimsy plastic parts and is light, being hollow and without ballast. If I wished to install an exhibit about the terrors of totalitarianism, tanks rolling over protestors like so much cardboard, I would need tanks with real heft. The protestors can be made of, well, cardboard, and can even be taller than the tanks. But the power is with the heft, and the tanks have it.

Or if I wanted to send a more hopeful message, I could reverse things. The tanks are made of cardboard, while the protestors possess the gravity of rock. The tanks could be much bigger, but the power, again, is with the heft. Visually, the power is with size; tactilely, size is much less important. That's grammar.

viii

One winter, not long ago, your parents invite you and your boys to join them at the Minnesota Landscape Arboretum to visit its greenhouse. It is lovely to inhale the heavy air, which makes your lungs giddy. Smiling, you reach out—

Cacti.

So much for unfettered intercourse with nature.

As you tiptoe deeper into the garden, you find where the proper plants are and begin to examine them. There, among the pencil trees and ferns, you meet the most beautiful flowering plant.

It has a fan of smooth arching blades, and from the fist that holds this fan sprouts stems stretching out at odd angles. A matte-like human skin covers these stems, and it reminds you of a warm handshake.

Excited, you look for someone to read the label, because nothing is in Braille here. The first sighted person you find is your mother. You tug her to meet your new friend and you ask her its name. She looks and says there is no label. "Why," she then inquires of you, "do you want to know the name of such an ugly plant?"

Taken aback, your mind slips inside its library and pulls out Mary Shelley's 1818 novel *Frankenstein*. It is the story of a tall, loose-limbed gentleman who had been assembled in a laboratory. When he emerged into the world, however, he could find no one willing to be his friend—except for a blind man. They were engaged in a productive conversation when the blind man's sighted family returned from their outing. Seeing the tall gentleman, they screamed.

Poor fellow, so unjustly treated! Well, you would be this plant's friend. You decide that its name is "Frankenstein's Handshake."

ix

We have DeafBlind artists, but do we have DeafBlind art?

The potters carefully glaze for visual effect. Legos are easy to build with, but are hideous to the touch. Many attend painting and drawing classes at centers for the blind. There are dancers who spin into empty air. Actors hope they are aimed in the right direction. Hundreds have beaded or woven or quilted tapestries that are tactilely blank. Artists ask sighted assistants "What color is this?" and "Does it look all right?"

Sir Joshua Reynolds, the eighteenth-century Deaf British portraitist, provides a crude but helpful formula. "The regular progress of cultivated life," he wrote, "is from necessaries to accommodations, from accommodations to ornaments." We don't have all our necessaries in place as tactile people. As yet we own very little of the material world and are forced to make do with sighted things.

But it isn't true that we haven't made much art. We have an incredibly rich literature. We probably have more writers per capita than any other community in the world. It is because there is one space within which we have gone from necessity all the way to art: our traditional virtual space. Our correspondence networks and access to books began in the middle of the nineteenth century and have served as our home until we could begin to make claims on the corporeal world.

The goal of the Protactile movement is for us to get, do, and make everything in our own way. After we peeled our language away from visual sign language and remade it completely, reciprocally, and proprioceptively tactile, Protactile storytelling, Protactile poetry, and Protactile theater quickly emerged. It makes sense that those forms would come first, as they do not require that we buy anything or lug equipment around or hammer something together. Just ourselves and each other. Protactile theater, though, is starting to play with costumes and props. Does this mean Protactile art is next?

x

I once dreamed about installing an exhibition of assemblage art, using familiar objects that my friends would recognize immediately. The only glue I use is gravity. They can lift anything, handle it in their hands.

Some of the pieces were:

A 1970s cassette player with the slot popped open. Inserted within is a sticky toy wind-up brain that pulsates. *The Brain Implant.*

A Midwestern-sized cereal bowl filled with hearing-aid earmolds. Silver spoon. *Breakfast of Champions.*

A coffin made of old and used white folding canes. At rest inside, surrounded by a few lilies, is a wrecked Franklin Mint replica of a car. *Accident.*

In another dream the exhibit is called *Buried Treasures*. Each box is filled with a hand-sinkable substance—sawdust, popcorn, glass beads, and, my favorite, quinoa. Buried inside these boxes are surprise objects that juxtapose with the materials we dig through to get at them.

In another dream, a museum has lovely railings that take us from one exhibit to another, following the poetry of conavigation. But another dream shoves it aside because the museum is now a gloriously walled labyrinth. It leads into a burrowing tunnel. This, in turn, cedes to a dream of water.

In another dream, I meet Genghis Khan. Most DeafBlind people have Usher syndrome, whose genetic history can be traced back to the Mongolian juggernaut. I realize from this wonderful statue in the dream that wood is so suggestive of living flesh; that most statues should be naked and then covered with clothing or representations thereof, for we feel right through clothes in real life; and that foam is a fine way to represent hair. Beneath his armor and linens I could feel Genghis Khan's love handles and the loins whence we came.

In another dream I am in a vast library of tactile objects. Millions of objects are housed there. They have an acquisitions department and a replica-making department. Things too small to feel with my hands are magnified. Things too large to grasp are reduced to the right scale for manual inspection. Many of the library's holdings are real objects. Most importantly, the great bulk of the collection is mailable. I can order anything, and a few days later, a box arrives.

xi

Since most of what may be understood as tactile art doesn't exist yet, there are no master strokes. But this doesn't mean there haven't been lucky strokes. My friend Robert Sirvage, a DeafBlind architect and design consultant, stumbled upon two such examples while traveling in Norway in the fall of 2017.

Norway had then recently legislated the separation of church and state. The formerly official national Lutheran Church had seven Deaf churches—called Døvekirken—that provided many services to the Deaf and DeafBlind communities. Now that these churches would no longer administer these programs, the seven Døvekirken realized that they would need to reinvent themselves. Sirvage was hired to help them reimagine their role and their spaces.

Upon entering the Bergen Døvekirke, Sirvage's cane rapped against the base of the first of two extraordinary works. A priest at the Døvekirke in Stavanger named Georg Abelsnes had created them with DeafBlind parishioners in mind. He gave the pieces to the new Døvekirke in Bergen when it opened its doors on December 10, 1989.

The first piece, *God Bless You*, rests on a board about three feet from the floor. The main portion is a sectional cut of a tree trunk, a section where it starts to spread its roots. The grains are pleasantly rough, and the middle grain is studded with gemstones.

Sirvage found himself moving his hands downward and outward, his thumbs bumping across or wiggling past the gemstones. He turned to ask his host how they said "bless" in Norwegian Sign Language. It was as he thought—the piece indeed invites hands to follow its grains and in doing so say the word "bless."

By returning to the top, this time beginning properly with closed fists, he discovered that the piece has another feature. Cleverly placed along its downward planes is a stick. When Sirvage moved his hands downward, he felt the stick gently opening up his hands. He marveled and later told his friends that the artwork is "all about motion and tempo, not static at all."

As wonderfully interactive as this piece is, nothing could have prepared Sirvage for what he encountered next. He was later given to understand that the second piece is called something like *God Loves and Protects You*. Standing about four feet tall, it is made of rounded, polished, and unevenly shaped wood. It has subtle suggestions of a head, neck, and torso. Just below and in front of the torso-trunk of the figure, the wood becomes hollow, and within this is another piece of wood with a different texture. It includes a handle carved to slide into one's grasp.

His host suggested that he walk around to hug the figure from behind. When he rested his head on the crook of the figure's neck, he told me,

> My heart jumped. *Holy*—Remembering that I was in a house of worship stopped me from completing the thought. It felt like I was transgressing big here, but in a good way. It felt like I had found a whole new way of knowing God.

What he had done was to temporarily assume the place of God, leaning over to hug the figure, which now represented Sirvage himself, his hand the Hand of God holding the handle, perhaps the hilt of a sheathed sword.

Shaken, Sirvage stepped back to ask his host more about this "performative artwork." He learned that the DeafBlind parishioners and many others would, upon entering, commune with both pieces and go through the whole motions of simultaneously performing and receiving the messages.

"After my host became distracted talking with someone else," Sirvage went on to share,

> I turned back to interact with it again. This time I let myself relax and hug the figure. To make the message clearer, I allowed my heart and physical being to radiate with tenderness and love. After a while, I stood up and caressed my body. Somehow I knew that I would retrieve myself if I said something, and I was instantly retrieved when I whispered, "Thank you."

The Nation in partnership with Type Media Center

FINALIST—ESSAYS AND CRITICISM

Originally presented as the Jonathan Schell Memorial Lecture on the Fate of the Earth at Cooper Union in New York City in November 2019, "India: Intimations of an Ending" describes a democracy surrendering its founding principles. "From the denial of citizenship to Muslims to the rise of state-sanctioned lynch mobs, Arundati Roy sharply and decisively catalogues the tightening grip of Hindu nationalism," said the National Magazine Award judges. "In a sweeping essay, pulsing with incandescent, furious prose, Roy issues a harrowing warning as India moves ever closer to fascism." Arundati Roy is the author of two novels, The God of Small Things, *which won the Booker Prize, and* The Ministry of Utmost Happiness, *as well as several collections of nonfiction. Her new book,* Azadi: Freedom. Fascism. Fiction., *was published in September. She lives in New Delhi. Founded by abolitionists in 1865 as a voice for progressive causes,* The Nation *is the oldest continuously published weekly magazine in the United States.*

Arundhati Roy

India: Intimations of an Ending

While protest reverberates on the streets of Chile, Catalonia, Bolivia, Britain, France, Iraq, Lebanon, and Hong Kong, and a new generation rages against what has been done to their planet, I hope you will forgive me for speaking about a place where the street has been taken over by something quite different. There was a time when dissent was India's best export. But now, even as protest swells in the West, our great anticapitalist and anti-imperialist movements for social and environmental justice—the marches against big dams, against the privatization and plunder of our rivers and forests, against mass displacement and the alienation of indigenous peoples' homelands—have largely fallen silent. On September 17 this year, Prime Minister Narendra Modi gifted himself the filled-to-the-brim reservoir of the Sardar Sarovar Dam on the Narmada River for his sixty-ninth birthday, while thousands of villagers who had fought that dam for more than thirty years watched their homes disappear under the rising water. It was a moment of great symbolism.

In India today, a shadow world is creeping up on us in broad daylight. It is becoming more and more difficult to communicate the scale of the crisis even to ourselves. An accurate description runs the risk of sounding like hyperbole. And so, for the sake of credibility and good manners, we groom the creature that has sunk its teeth into us—we comb out its hair and wipe its dripping jaw to make it more personable in polite company. India isn't by any means the worst, or most dangerous, place in the world—at least not yet—but perhaps the divergence between what it could have been and what it has become makes it the most tragic.

Right now, seven million people in the valley of Kashmir, overwhelming numbers of whom do not wish to be citizens of India and have fought for decades for their right to self-determination, are locked down under a digital siege and the densest military occupation in the world. Simultaneously, in the eastern state of Assam, almost two million people who long to belong to India have found their names missing from the National Register of Citizens (NRC), and risk being declared stateless. The Indian government has announced its intention of extending the NRC to the rest of India. Legislation is on its way. This could lead to the manufacture of statelessness on a scale previously unknown.

The rich in Western countries are making their own arrangements for the coming climate calamity. They're building bunkers and stocking reservoirs of food and clean water. In poor countries—India, despite being the fifth-largest economy in the world, is, shamefully, still a poor and hungry country—different kinds of arrangements are being made. The Indian government's August 5, 2019, annexation of Kashmir has as much to do with the Indian government's urgency to secure access to the five rivers that run through the state of Jammu and Kashmir as it does with anything else. And the NRC, which will create a system of tiered citizenship in which some citizens have more rights than others, is also a preparation for a time when resources become scarce. Citizenship, as Hannah Arendt famously said, is the right to have rights.

The dismantling of the idea of liberty, fraternity, and equality will be—in fact already is—the first casualty of the climate crisis. I'm going to try to explain in some detail how this is happening. And how, in India, the modern management system that emerged to handle this very modern crisis has its roots in an odious, dangerous filament of our history.

The violence of inclusion and the violence of exclusion are precursors of a convulsion that could alter the foundations of India—and rearrange its meaning and its place in the world. Our constitution calls India a "socialist secular democratic republic." We use the word "secular" in a slightly different sense from the rest of the world—for us, it's code for a society in which all religions have equal standing in the eyes of the law. In practice, India has been neither secular nor socialist. It has always functioned as an upper-caste Hindu state. But the conceit of secularism, hypocritical though it may be, is the only shard of coherence that makes India *possible*. That hypocrisy was the best thing we had. Without it, India will end.

In his May 2019 victory speech, after his party won a second term, Modi boasted that no politicians from any political party had dared to campaign on "secularism." The tank of secularism, Modi seemed to say, was now empty. So, it's official. India is running on empty. And we are learning, too late, to cherish hypocrisy. Because with it comes a vestige, a pretense at least, of remembered decency.

India is not really a country. It is a continent. More complex and diverse, with more languages—780 at last count, excluding dialects—more indigenous tribes and religions, and perhaps more communities that consider themselves separate nations than all of Europe. Imagine this vast ocean, this fragile, fractious, social ecosystem, suddenly being commandeered by a Hindu-supremacist organization that believes in a doctrine of One Nation, One Language, One Religion, One Constitution.

I am speaking here of the RSS, the Rashtriya Swayamsevak Sangh, founded in 1925—the mothership of the ruling Bharatiya Janata Party. Its founding fathers were greatly influenced by German and Italian fascism. They likened the Muslims of India to the Jews of Germany, and believed that Muslims have no place in Hindu India. The RSS today, in typical RSS chameleon-speak, distances itself from this view. But its underlying ideology, in which Muslims are cast as treacherous permanent "outsiders," is a constant refrain in the public speeches of BJP politicians, and finds utterance in chilling slogans raised by rampaging mobs. For example: "*Mussalman ka ek hi sthan—Kabristan ya Pakistan*" (Only one place for the Muslim—the graveyard, or Pakistan). In October this year, Mohan Bhagwat, the supreme leader of the RSS, said, "India is a Hindu Rashtra"—a Hindu nation. "This is nonnegotiable."

That idea turns everything that is beautiful about India into acid.

For the RSS to portray what it is engineering today as an epochal revolution, in which Hindus are finally wiping away centuries of oppression at the hands of India's earlier Muslim rulers, is a part of its fake-history project. In truth, millions of India's Muslims are the descendants of people who converted to Islam to escape Hinduism's cruel practice of caste.

If Nazi Germany was a country seeking to impose its imagination onto a continent (and beyond), the impetus of an RSS-ruled India is, in a sense, the opposite. Here is a continent seeking to shrink itself into a country. Not even a country, but a province. A primitive, ethnoreligious province. This is turning out to be an unimaginably violent process.

None of the white supremacist, neo-Nazi groups that are on the rise in the world today can boast the infrastructure and manpower that the RSS commands. It says it has 57,000 *shakhas*—branches—across the country, and an armed, dedicated militia of over 600,000 "volunteers." It runs schools in which millions of students are enrolled, and has its own medical missions, trade unions, farmers' organizations, media outlets, and women's groups. Recently, it announced that it was opening a training school for those who wish to join the Indian Army. Under its *bhagwa dhwaj*—its saffron pennant—a whole host of far-right organizations, known as the Sangh Parivar—the RSS's "family"—have prospered and multiplied. These organizations, the political equivalents of shell companies, are responsible for shockingly violent attacks on minorities in which, over the years, uncounted thousands have been murdered.

Prime Minister Narendra Modi has been a member of the RSS since he was eight years old. He is a creation of the RSS. Although not Brahmin, he, more than anyone else in its history, has been responsible for turning it into the most powerful organization in India and for writing its most glorious chapter yet. It is exasperating to have to constantly repeat the story of Modi's ascent to power, but the officially sanctioned amnesia around it makes reiteration almost a duty.

Modi's political career was jump-started in October 2001, just weeks after the 9/11 attacks in the United States, when the BJP removed its elected chief minister in the state of Gujarat and installed Modi in his place. He was not, at the time, even an elected member of the state's legislative assembly. Five months into his first term, there was a heinous but mysterious act of arson in which fifty-nine Hindu pilgrims were burned to death in a train. As "revenge," Hindu vigilante mobs went on a well-planned rampage across the state. An estimated 2,500 people, almost all of them Muslim, were murdered in broad daylight. Women were gang-raped on city streets, and nearly 150,000 people were driven from their homes. Immediately after the pogrom, Modi called for elections. He won, not despite the massacre but because of it—and was reelected as chief minister for three consecutive terms. During Modi's first campaign as the prime ministerial candidate of the BJP—which also featured the massacre of Muslims, this time in the district of Muzaffarnagar in the state of Uttar Pradesh—a Reuters journalist asked him whether he regretted the 2002 pogrom in Gujarat. He replied that he would regret even the death of a dog if it accidentally came under the wheels of his car. This was pure, well-trained, RSS-speak.

When Modi was sworn in as India's fourteenth prime minister, he was celebrated not just by his support base of Hindu nationalists but also by India's major industrialists and businessmen, by many Indian liberals, and by the international media as the epitome of hope and progress, a savior in a saffron business suit, whose very person represented the confluence of the ancient and the modern—of Hindu nationalism and no-holds-barred free-market capitalism.

While Modi has delivered on Hindu nationalism, he has stumbled badly on the free-market front. Through a series of blunders, he has brought India's economy to its knees. In 2016, a little over a year into his first term, he announced on television that, from that moment on, all 500 and 1,000 rupee banknotes—over 80 percent of the currency in circulation—had ceased to be legal tender. Nothing like it had ever been done on such a scale in the history of any country. Neither the finance minister nor the chief economic adviser seemed to have been taken into confidence. This "demonetization," the prime minister said, was a "surgical strike" on corruption and terror funding. This was pure quack economics, a home remedy being tried on a nation of more than a billion people. It turned out to be nothing short of devastating. But there were no riots. No protests. People stood meekly in line outside banks for hours on end to deposit their old currency notes—the only way left to redeem them. No Chile, Catalonia, Lebanon, Hong Kong. Almost overnight, jobs disappeared, the construction industry ground to a halt, small businesses simply shut down.

Some of us foolishly believed that this act of unimaginable hubris would be the end of Modi. How wrong we were. People rejoiced. They suffered—but rejoiced. It was as though pain had been spun into pleasure. As though their suffering was the labor pain that would soon birth a glorious, prosperous, Hindu India.

Most economists agree that demonetization, along with the new goods and services tax that Modi announced last year—promising "one nation, one tax"—was the policy equivalent of shooting out the tires of a speeding car. Even the government's own data show that unemployment is at a forty-five-year high. The 2019 Global Hunger Index ranks India 102nd out of 117 countries. (Nepal comes in at 73rd, Bangladesh 88th, and Pakistan 94th).

But demonetization was never about economics alone. It was a loyalty test, a love exam that the Great Leader was putting us through. Would we follow him, would we always love him, no matter what? We emerged with flying colors. The moment we as a people accepted demonetization, we infantilized ourselves and surrendered to tinpot authoritarianism.

But what was bad for the country turned out to be excellent for the BJP. Between 2016 and 2017, even as the economy tanked, it became one of the richest political parties in the world. Its income increased by 81 percent, making it nearly five times richer than its main rival, the Congress Party, whose income declined by 14 percent. Smaller political parties were virtually bankrupted. This war chest won the BJP crucial state elections in Uttar Pradesh and turned the 2019 general election into a race between a Ferrari and a few old bicycles. And since elections are increasingly about money, the chances of a free and fair election in the near future seem remote. So maybe demonetization was not a blunder after all.

During Modi's second term, the RSS has stepped up its game. No longer a shadow state or a parallel state, it *is* the state. Day by day, we see examples of its control over the media, the police, the intelligence agencies. Worryingly, it appears to exercise considerable influence over the armed forces, too. Foreign diplomats and ambassadors have been hobnobbing with Mohan Bhagwat. The German ambassador even trooped all the way to the RSS headquarters in Nagpur to pay his respects.

In truth, things have reached a stage where overt control is no longer even necessary. More than four hundred round-the-clock television news channels, millions of WhatsApp groups and TikTok videos keep the population on a drip feed of frenzied bigotry.

This November the Supreme Court of India ruled on what one judge called one of the most important cases in the world. On December 6, 1992, in the town of Ayodhya, a Hindu vigilante mob, organized by the BJP and the Vishwa Hindu Parishad—the World Hindu Council—literally hammered a 460-year-old mosque into dust. They claimed that this mosque, the Babri Masjid, was built on the ruins of a Hindu temple that had marked the birthplace of Lord Ram. More than 2,000 people, mostly Muslims, were killed in the communal violence that followed. In its recent judgment, the court held that Muslims could not prove their exclusive and continuous possession of the site. Instead, it turned the site over to a trust—to be constituted by the BJP government—tasked with building a Hindu temple on it. There have been mass arrests of people who have criticized the judgment. The VHP has refused to back down on its past statements that it will turn its attention to other mosques. This can be an endless campaign—after all, everything is built over something.

With the influence that immense wealth generates, the BJP has managed to co-opt, buy out, or simply crush its political rivals. The hardest blow has fallen on the parties with bases among the Dalit and other disadvantaged castes in the northern states of Uttar Pradesh and Bihar. Many of their traditional voters have deserted these parties—the Bahujan Samaj Party, Rashriya Janata Dal, and Samajwadi Party—and migrated to the BJP. To achieve this feat—and it is nothing short of a feat—the BJP worked hard to exploit and expose the hierarchies within the Dalit and disadvantaged castes, which have their own internal universe of hegemony and marginalization. The BJP's overflowing coffers and its deep, cunning understanding of caste have completely altered the conventional electoral math.

Having secured Dalit and disadvantaged-caste votes, the BJP's policies of privatizing education and the public sector are rapidly reversing the gains made by affirmative action—known in India as "reservation"—pushing those who belong to disadvantaged castes out of jobs and educational institutions. Meanwhile, the National Crime Records Bureau shows a sharp increase of atrocities against Dalits, including lynchings and public floggings. This September, while Modi was being honored by the Bill & Melinda Gates Foundation for building toilets, two Dalit children, whose home was just the shelter of a plastic sheet, were beaten to death for shitting in the open. To honor a prime minister for his work on sanitation while tens of thousands of Dalits continue to work as manual scavengers—carrying human excreta on their heads—is grotesque.

What we are living through now, in addition to the overt attack on religious minorities, is an aggravated class and caste war.

• • •

To consolidate their political gains, the RSS and BJP's main strategy is to generate long-lasting chaos on an industrial scale. They have stocked their kitchen with a set of simmering cauldrons that can, whenever necessary, be quickly brought to the boil.

On August 5, 2019, the Indian government unilaterally breached the fundamental conditions of the Instrument of Accession by which the former princely state of Jammu and Kashmir agreed to become part of India in 1947. It stripped Jammu and Kashmir of statehood and its special status—which included its right to have its own constitution and its own flag. The dissolution of the legal entity of the state also meant the dissolution of Section 35A of the Indian Constitution, which secured the erstwhile state's residents the rights and privileges that made them stewards of their own territory. In preparation for the move, the government flew in more than 80,000 troops to supplement the hundreds of thousands already stationed there. By the night of August 4, tourists and pilgrims had been evacuated from the Kashmir Valley. Schools and markets were shut down. By midnight, the internet was cut and phones went dead. In the weeks that followed, more than 4,000 people were arrested: politicians, businessmen, lawyers, rights activists, local leaders, students, and three former chief ministers. Kashmir's entire political class, including those who have been loyal to India, was incarcerated.

The abrogation of Kashmir's special status, the promise of an all-India National Register of Citizens, the building of the Ram temple in Ayodhya—are all on the front burners of the RSS and BJP kitchen. To reignite flagging passions, all they need to do is to pick a villain from their gallery and unleash the dogs of war. There are several categories of villains—Pakistani jihadis, Kashmiri terrorists, Bangladeshi "infiltrators," or any one of a population of nearly 200 million Indian Muslims who can always be accused of being Pakistan lovers or antinational traitors. Each of these "cards" is held hostage to the other and often made to stand in for the other. They have little to do with each other and are often hostile to each other because their needs, desires, ideologies, and situations are not just inimical, but end up posing an existential threat to each other. Simply because they are all Muslim, they each have to suffer the consequences of the others' actions.

In two national elections now, the BJP has shown that it can win a majority in parliament without the "Muslim vote." As a result, Indian Muslims have been effectively disenfranchised, and are becoming that most vulnerable of people—a community without political representation, without a voice. Various forms of vicious social boycott are pushing them down the economic ladder and, for reasons of physical security, into ghettos. Indian

Muslims have also lost their place in the mainstream media—the only Muslim voices we hear on television shows are the absurd few who are constantly and deliberately invited to play the part of the primitive Islamist, to make things worse than they already are. Other than that, the only acceptable public speech for the Muslim community is to constantly reiterate and demonstrate its loyalty to the Indian flag. So while Kashmiris, brutalized as they are because of their history and, more importantly, their geography, still have a lifeboat—the dream of *azadi*, of freedom—Indian Muslims have to stay on deck to help fix the broken ship.

(There is another category of "antinational" villain—human rights activists, lawyers, students, academics, "urban Maoists"—who have been defamed, jailed, embroiled in legal cases, snooped on by Israeli spyware, and, in several instances, assassinated. But that's a whole other deck of cards.)

The lynching of Tabrez Ansari illustrates just how broken the ship is, and how deep the rot. Lynching, as you in the United States well know, is a public performance of ritualized murder, in which a man or woman is killed to remind their community that it lives at the mercy of the mob. And that the police, the law, the government—as well as the good people in their homes, who wouldn't hurt a fly, who go to work and take care of their families—are all friends of the mob. Tabrez was lynched this June. He was an orphan, raised by his uncles in the state of Jharkhand. As a teenager, he went away to the city of Pune, where he found a job as a welder. When he turned twenty-two, he returned home to get married. The day after his wedding to eighteen-year-old Shahista, Tabrez was caught by a mob, tied to a lamppost, beaten for hours and forced to chant the new Hindu war cry, "*Jai Shri Ram*!"—Victory to Lord Ram! The police eventually took Tabrez into custody but refused to allow his distraught family and young bride to take him to the hospital. Instead, they accused him of being a thief, and produced him before a magistrate, who sent him back to custody. He died there four days later.

In its latest report, released earlier this month, the National Crime Records Bureau has carefully left out data on mob lynchings. According to the Indian news site *The Quint*, there have been 113 deaths by mob violence since 2015. Lynchers and others accused in hate crimes including mass murder have been rewarded with public office and honored by ministers in Modi's cabinet. Modi himself, usually garrulous on Twitter, generous with condolences and birthday greetings, goes very quiet each time a person is lynched. Perhaps it's unreasonable to expect a prime minister to comment every time a dog comes under the wheels of someone's car. Particularly since it happens so often.

Here in the United States, on September 22, 2019—five days after Modi's birthday party at the Narmada dam site—50,000 Indian Americans gathered in the NRG Stadium in Houston. The "Howdy, Modi!" extravaganza there has already become the stuff of urban legend. President Donald Trump was gracious enough to allow a visiting prime minister to introduce him as a special guest in his own country, to his own citizens. Several members of the U.S. Congress spoke, their smiles too wide, their bodies arranged in attitudes of ingratiation. Over a crescendo of drum rolls and wild cheering, the adoring crowd chanted, "Modi! Modi! Modi!" At the end of the show, Trump and Modi linked hands and did a victory lap. The stadium exploded. In India, the noise was amplified a thousand times over by carpet coverage on television channels. "Howdy" became a Hindi word. Meanwhile, news organizations ignored the thousands of people protesting outside the stadium.

Not all the roaring of the 50,000 in the Houston stadium could mask the deafening silence from Kashmir. That day, September 22, marked the forty-eighth day of curfew and communication blockade in the valley.

Once again, Modi has managed to unleash his unique brand of cruelty on a scale unheard of in modern times. And, once again, it has endeared him further to his loyal public. When the

Jammu and Kashmir Reorganization Bill was passed in India's parliament on August 6 there were celebrations across the political spectrum. Sweets were distributed in offices, and there was dancing in the streets. A conquest—a colonial annexation, another triumph for the Hindu Nation—was being celebrated. Once again, the conquerors' eyes fell on the two primeval trophies of conquest—women and land. Statements by senior BJP politicians and patriotic pop music videos that notched up millions of views legitimized this indecency. Google Trends showed a surge in searches for the phrases "marry a Kashmiri girl" and "buy land in Kashmir."

It was not all limited to loutish searches on Google. In the weeks after the siege, the Forest Advisory Committee cleared 125 projects that involve the diversion of forest land for other uses.

In the early days of the lockdown, little news came out of the valley. The Indian media told us what the government wanted us to hear. The heavily censored Kashmiri papers carried pages and pages of news about canceled weddings, the effects of climate change, the conservation of lakes and wildlife sanctuaries, tips on how to live with diabetes and front-page government advertisements about the benefits that Kashmir's new, downgraded legal status would bring to the Kashmiri people. Those "benefits" are likely to include projects that control and commandeer the water from the rivers that flow through Kashmir. They will certainly include the erosion that results from deforestation, the destruction of the fragile Himalayan ecosystem, and the plunder of Kashmir's bountiful natural wealth by Indian corporations.

Real reporting about ordinary peoples' lives came mostly from the journalists and photographers working for the international media—Agence France-Presse, the Associated Press, *Al Jazeera*, the *Guardian*, the BBC, the *New York Times*, and the *Washington Post*. The reporters, mostly Kashmiris, working in an information vacuum, with none of the tools usually available to modern-day reporters, traveled through their homeland at great risk to themselves, to bring us the news. And the news was of nighttime raids, of young men being rounded up and beaten for hours, their screams broadcast on public-address systems for their neighbors and families to hear, of soldiers entering villagers' homes and mixing fertilizer and kerosene into their winter food stocks. The news was of teenagers with their bodies peppered with shotgun pellets being treated at home, because they would be arrested if they went to a hospital. The news was of hundreds of children being whisked away in the dead of night, of parents debilitated by desperation and anxiety. The news was of fear and anger, depression, confusion, steely resolve, and incandescent resistance.

But the home minister, Amit Shah, said that the siege only existed in peoples' imaginations; the governor of Jammu and Kashmir, Satya Pal Malik, said phone lines were not important for Kashmiris and were only used by terrorists; and the army chief, Bipin Rawat, said, "Normal life in Jammu and Kashmir has not been affected. People are doing their necessary work. . . . Those who feel that life has been affected are the ones whose survival depends on terrorism." It isn't hard to work out who exactly the government of India sees as terrorists.

Imagine if all of New York City were put under an information lockdown and a curfew managed by hundreds of thousands of soldiers. Imagine the streets of your city remapped by razor wire and torture centers. Imagine if mini–Abu Ghraibs appeared in your neighborhoods. Imagine thousands of you being arrested and your families not knowing where you have been taken. Imagine not being able to communicate with anybody—not your neighbor, not your loved ones outside the city, no one in the outside world—for weeks together. Imagine banks and schools being closed, children locked into their homes. Imagine your parent, sibling, partner, or child dying and you not knowing about it for weeks. Imagine the medical emergencies, the mental health emergencies, the legal emergencies, the shortages of food, money, gasoline. Imagine being a day laborer or a contract worker, earning nothing for weeks on end. And then imagine being told that all of this was for your own good.

The horror that Kashmiris have endured over the last few months comes on top of the trauma of a thirty-year-old armed conflict that has already taken 70,000 lives and covered their valley with graves. They have held out while everything was thrown at them—war, money, torture, mass disappearance, an army of more than a half million soldiers, and a smear campaign in which an entire population has been portrayed as murderous fundamentalists.

The siege has lasted for more than four months now. Kashmiri leaders are still in jail. They were offered release under the condition of agreeing not to make public statements about Kashmir for a whole year. Most have refused.

Now the curfew has been eased, schools have been reopened, and some phone lines have been restored. "Normalcy" has been declared. In Kashmir, normalcy is always a declaration—a fiat issued by the government or the army. It has little to do with people's daily lives.

So far, Kashmiris have refused to accept this new normalcy. Classrooms are empty, streets are deserted and the valley's bumper apple crop is rotting in the orchards. What could be harder for a parent or a farmer to endure? The imminent annihilation of their very identity, perhaps.

The new phase of the Kashmir conflict has already begun. Militants have warned that, from now on, all Indians will be considered legitimate targets. More than ten people, mostly poor, non-Kashmiri migrant workers, have been killed. (Yes, it's the poor, almost always the poor, who get caught in the line of fire.) It is going to get ugly. Very ugly.

Soon all this recent history will be forgotten, and once again there will be debates in television studios that create an equivalence between atrocities by Indian security forces and Kashmiri militants. Speak of Kashmir, and the Indian government and its media will immediately tell you about Pakistan, deliberately conflating the misdeeds of a hostile foreign state with the democratic aspirations of ordinary people living under a military occupation. The Indian government has made it clear that the only option for Kashmiris is complete capitulation, that no form of resistance is acceptable—violent, nonviolent, spoken, written, or sung. Yet Kashmiris know that to exist, they must resist.

Why should they want to be a part of India? For what earthly reason? If freedom is what they want, freedom is what they should have.

It's what Indians should want, too. Not on behalf of Kashmiris, but for their own sake. The atrocity being committed in their name involves a form of corrosion that India will not survive. Kashmir may not defeat India, but it will consume India. In many ways, it already has.

• • •

This may not have mattered all that much to the 50,000 cheering in the Houston stadium, living out the ultimate Indian dream of having made it to America. For them, Kashmir may just be a tired old conundrum, for which they foolishly believe the BJP has found a lasting solution. Surely, however, as migrants themselves, their understanding of what is happening in Assam could be more nuanced. Or maybe it's too much to ask of those who, in a world riven by refugee and migrant crises, are the most fortunate of migrants. Many of those in the Houston stadium, like people with an extra holiday home, probably hold U.S. citizenship as well as Overseas Citizens of India certificates.

The "Howdy, Modi!" event marked the twenty-second day since almost two million people in Assam found their names missing from the National Register of Citizens.

Like Kashmir, Assam is a border state with a history of multiple sovereignties, with centuries of migration, wars, invasion, continuously shifting borders, British colonialism, and more than seventy years of electoral democracy that has only deepened the fault lines in a dangerously combustible society.

That an exercise like the NRC even took place has to do with Assam's very particular cultural history. Assam was among the territories ceded to the British by the Burmese after the First Anglo-Burmese War in 1826. At the time, it was a densely forested, scantily populated province, home to hundreds of communities—among them Bodos, Cachari, Mishing, Lalung, Ahomiya Hindus, and Ahomiya Muslims—each with its own language or speech practice, each with an organic though often undocumented relationship to the land. Like a microcosm of India, Assam has always been a collection of minorities jockeying to make alliances in order to manufacture a majority—ethnic as well as linguistic. Anything that altered or threatened the prevailing balance became a potential catalyst for violence.

The seeds for just such an alteration were sown in 1837, when the British, the new masters of Assam, made Bengali the official language of the province. It meant that almost all administrative and government jobs were taken by an educated, Hindu, Bengali-speaking elite. Although the policy was reversed in the early 1870s and Assamese was given official status along with Bengali, it shifted the balance of power in serious ways and marked the beginning of what has become an almost two-century-old antagonism between speakers of Assamese and Bengali.

Towards the middle of the nineteenth century, the British discovered that the climate and soil of the region were conducive to tea cultivation. Local people were unwilling to work as serfs in the tea gardens, so a large population of indigenous tribespeople were transported from central India. They were no different from the shiploads of indentured Indian laborers the British transported to their colonies all over the world. Today, the plantation workers in Assam make up 15 to 20 percent of the state's population. Shamefully, these workers are looked down upon by local people and continue to live on the plantations, at the mercy of plantation owners and earning slave wages.

By the late 1890s, as the tea industry grew and as the plains of neighboring East Bengal reached the limits of their cultivation potential, the British encouraged Bengali Muslim peasants—masters of the art of farming on the rich, silty, riverine plains and shifting islands of the Brahmaputra, known as *chars*—to migrate to Assam. To the British, the forests and plains of Assam were, if not Terra nullius, then Terra *almost*-nullius. They hardly registered the presence of Assam's many tribes and freely allocated what were tribal commons to "productive" peasants whose produce would contribute to British revenue collection. The migrants came in the thousands, felled forests, and turned marshes into farmland. By 1930, migration had drastically changed both the economy and the demography of Assam.

At first, the migrants were welcomed by Assamese nationalist groups, but soon tensions arose—ethnic, religious, and linguistic. They were temporarily mitigated when, in the 1941 census and then more emphatically in the 1951 census and then every census that followed, as a gesture of solidarity with their new homeland, the entire population of Bengali-speaking Muslims—whose local dialects are together known as the Miya language—designated Assamese as their mother tongue, thereby ensuring that it retained the status of an official language. Even today, Miya dialects are written in the Assamese script.

Over the years, the borders of Assam were redrawn continuously, almost dizzyingly. When the British partitioned Bengal in 1905, they attached the province of Assam to Muslim-majority East Bengal, with Dhaka as its capital. Suddenly, what was a migrant population in Assam was no longer migrant, but part of a majority. Six years later, when Bengal was reunified and Assam became a province of its own, its Bengali population became migrants once again. After the 1947 Partition, when East Bengal became a part of Pakistan, the Bengal-origin Muslim settlers in

Assam chose to stay on. But Partition also led to a massive influx of Bengali refugees into Assam, Hindus as well as Muslims. This was followed in 1971 by yet another incursion of refugees fleeing from the Pakistan Army's genocidal attack on East Pakistan and the liberation war that birthed the new nation of Bangladesh, which together took millions of lives.

So Assam was a part of East Bengal, and then it wasn't. East Bengal became East Pakistan and East Pakistan became Bangladesh. Countries changed, flags changed, anthems changed. Cities grew, forests were felled, marshes were reclaimed, tribal commons swallowed by modern "development." And the fissures between people grew old and hard and intractable.

The Indian government is so proud of the part it played in Bangladesh's liberation from Pakistan. Indira Gandhi, the prime minister at the time, ignored the threats of China and the United States, who were Pakistan's allies, and sent in the Indian Army to stop the genocide. That pride in having fought a "just war" did not translate into justice or real concern, or any kind of thought-out state policy for either the refugees or the people of Assam and its neighboring states.

The demand for a National Register of Citizens in Assam arose out of this unique, vexed, and complex history. Ironically, the word "national" here refers not so much to India as it does to the nation of Assam. The demand to update the first NRC, conducted in 1951, grew out of a student-led Assamese nationalist movement that peaked between 1979 and 1985, alongside a militant separatist movement in which tens of thousands lost their lives. The Assamese nationalists called for a boycott of elections unless "foreigners" were deleted from the electoral rolls—the clarion call was for "3D," which stood for Detect, Delete, Deport. The number of so-called foreigners, based on pure speculation, was estimated to be in the millions. The movement quickly turned violent. Killings, arson, bomb blasts, and mass demonstrations generated an atmosphere of hostility and almost uncontrollable rage towards "outsiders." By 1979, the state was up in flames. Though the movement was primarily directed against Bengalis and Bengali-speakers, Hindu communal forces within the movement also gave it an anti-Muslim character. In 1983, this culminated in the horrifying Nellie massacre, in which more than 2,000 Bengal-origin Muslim settlers were murdered over six hours.

In *What the Fields Remember*, a documentary about the massacre, an elderly Muslim who lost all his children to the violence tells of how one of his daughters, not long before the massacre, had been part of a march asking for "foreigners" to be expelled. Her dying words, he said, were, "Baba, are we also foreigners?"

In 1985, the student leaders of the Assam agitation signed the Assam Accord with the central government. That year, they won the state's assembly elections and formed the state government. A date was agreed upon: Those who had arrived in Assam after midnight of 24 March 1971—the day the Pakistan Army began its attack on civilians in East Pakistan—would be expelled. The updating of the NRC was meant to sift the "genuine citizens" of Assam from post-1971 "infiltrators."

Over the next several years, "infiltrators" detected by the border police, or those declared "Doubtful Voters"—D-Voters—by election officials, were tried under the Illegal Migrants Determination by Tribunal Act, passed in 1983 by a Congress Party government under Indira Gandhi. In order to protect minorities from harassment, the IMDT Act put the onus of disproving a person's citizenship on the police or the accusing party—instead of burdening the accused with proving their citizenship. Since 1997, more than 400,000 D-voters and Declared Foreigners have been tried in Foreigners Tribunals. Over 1,000 are still locked up in detention centers, jails within jails where detainees don't even have the rights that ordinary criminals do.

In 2005, the Supreme Court adjudicated a case that asked for the IMDT Act to be struck down on the grounds that it made the "detection and deportation of illegal immigrants nearly impossible." In its judgment annulling the act, the court noted, "there can be no manner of doubt that the State of Assam is facing 'external aggression and internal disturbance' on account of large scale illegal migration of Bangladeshi nationals." Now, it put the onus of proving citizenship on the citizen. This completely changed the paradigm and set the stage for the new, updated NRC. The case had been filed by Sarbananda Sonowal, a former president of the All Assam Students' Union who is now with the BJP and currently serves as the chief minister of Assam.

In 2013, the Supreme Court took up a case filed by an NGO called Assam Public Works that asked for illegal migrants' names to be struck off electoral rolls. Eventually, the case was assigned to the court of Justice Ranjan Gogoi, who happens to be Assamese.

In December 2014, the Supreme Court ordered that an updated list for the NRC be produced within a year. Nobody had any clue about what could or would be done to the 5 million "infiltrators" that it was hoped would be detected. There was no question of them being deported to Bangladesh. Could that many people be locked up in detention camps? For how long? Would they be stripped of citizenship?

Millions of villagers living in far-flung areas were expected to produce a specified set of documents—"legacy papers"—that proved direct and unbroken paternal lineage dating back to 1971. The Supreme Court's deadline turned the exercise into a nightmare. Impoverished, illiterate villagers were delivered into a labyrinth of bureaucracy, legalese, documentation, court hearings, and all the ruthless skullduggery that goes with them.

The only way to reach the remote, seminomadic settlements on the shifting, silty "char" islands of the Brahmaputra is by often perilously overcrowded boats. The roughly 2,500 char islands are impermanent offerings, likely to be snatched back at any moment by the legendarily moody Brahmaputra and reoffered at some other location, in some other shape or form. The settlements on them are temporary, and the dwellings are just shacks. Yet some of the islands are so fertile, and the farmers on them so skilled, that they raise three crops a year. Their impermanence, however, has meant the absence of land deeds, of development, of schools and hospitals.

In the less fertile chars that I visited early last month, the poverty washes over you like the dark, silt-rich waters of the Brahmaputra. The only signs of modernity were the bright plastic bags containing documents that their owners—who quickly gather around visiting strangers—could not read but kept looking at anxiously, as though trying to decrypt the faded shapes on the faded pages and work out whether they would save them and their children from the massive new detention camp they had heard is being constructed deep in the forests of Goalpara. Imagine a whole population of millions of people like this, debilitated, rigid with fear and worry about their documentation. It's not a military occupation, but it's occupation by documentation. These documents are peoples' most prized possessions, cared for more lovingly than any child or parent. They have survived floods and storms and every kind of emergency. Grizzled, sun-baked farmers, men and women, scholars of the land and the many moods of the river, use English words like "legacy document," "link paper," "certified copy," "reverification," "reference case," "D-voter," "declared foreigner," "voter list," "refugee certificate"—as though they were words in their own language. They are. The NRC has spawned a vocabulary of its own. The saddest phrase in it is "genuine citizen."

In village after village, people told stories about being served notices late at night that ordered them to appear in a court two or three hundred kilometers away by the next morning. They described the scramble to assemble family members and their documents, the treacherous rides in small rowboats across the rushing river in pitch darkness, the negotiations with canny transporters on the shore who had smelled their desperation and tripled their rates, the reckless drive through the night on dangerous highways. The most chilling story I heard was about a family traveling in a pickup truck that collided with a roadworks truck carrying barrels of tar. The barrels overturned, and the injured family was covered in tar. "When I went to visit them in hospital," the young activist I was traveling with said, "their young son was trying to pick off the tar on his skin and the tiny stones embedded in it. He looked at his mother and asked, 'Will we ever get rid of the *kala daag* [stigma] of being foreigners?'"

And yet, despite all this, despite reservations about the process and its implementation, the updating of the NRC was welcomed (enthusiastically by some, warily by others) by almost everybody in Assam, each for reasons of their own. Assamese nationalists hoped that millions of Bengali infiltrators, Hindu as well as Muslim, would finally be detected and formally declared "foreigners." Indigenous tribal communities hoped for some recompense for the historical wrong they had suffered. Hindus as well as Muslims of Bengal origin wanted to see their names on the NRC to prove they were "genuine" Indians, so that the *kala daag* of being "foreign" could be laid to rest once and for all. And the Hindu nationalists—now in government in Assam, too—wanted to see millions of Muslim names deleted from the NRC. Everybody hoped for some form of closure.

After a series of postponements, the final updated list was published on August 31, 2019. The names of 1.9 million people were missing. That number could yet expand because of a provision that permits people—neighbors, enemies, strangers—to lodge appeals. At last count, more than 200,000 objections to the draft NRC had been raised. A great number of those who have found their names missing from the list are women and children, most of whom belong to communities where women are married in their early teenage years and by custom have their names changed. They have no "link documents" to prove their legacy. A great number are illiterate people whose names or parents' names have been wrongly transcribed over the years: a H-a-s-a-n who became a H-a-s-s-a-n, a Joynul who became Zainul, a Mohammad whose name has been spelled in several ways. A single slip, and you're out. If your father died or was estranged from your mother, if he didn't vote, wasn't educated, and didn't have land, you're out. Because in practice, mothers' legacies don't count. Among all the prejudices at play in updating the NRC, perhaps the greatest of all is the built-in, structural prejudice against women and against the poor. And the poor in India today are made up mostly of Muslims, Dalits, and Tribals.

All the 1.9 million people whose names are missing will now have to appeal to a Foreigners Tribunal. There are, at the moment, 100 Foreigners Tribunals in Assam, and another 1,000 are in the pipeline. The men and women who preside over them, known as "members" of the tribunals, hold the fates of millions in their hands, but have no experience as judges. They are bureaucrats or junior lawyers, hired by the government and paid generous salaries. Once again, prejudice is built into the system. Government documents accessed by activists show that the sole criterion for rehiring members whose contracts have expired is the number of appeals they have rejected. All those who have to go in appeal to the Foreigners Tribunals will also have to hire lawyers, perhaps take loans to pay their fees or sell their land or their homes, and surrender to a life of debt and penury. Many of course have no land or home to sell. Several have committed suicide.

After the whole elaborate exercise and the millions of rupees spent on it, all the stakeholders in the NRC are bitterly disappointed with the list. Bengal-origin migrants are disappointed because they know that rightful citizens have been arbitrarily left out. Assamese nationalists are disappointed because the list has fallen well short of excluding the 5 million purported infiltrators they expected it to detect, and because they feel too many illegal foreigners have made it onto the list. And India's ruling Hindu nationalists are disappointed because it is estimated that more than half of the 1.9 million are non-Muslims. (The reason for this is ironic. Bengali Muslim migrants, having faced hostility for so long, have spent years gathering their "legacy papers." Hindus, being less insecure, have not.)

Justice Gogoi ordered the transfer of Prateek Hajela, the chief coordinator of the NRC, giving him seven days to leave Assam. Justice Gogoi did not offer a reason for this order.

Demands for a fresh NRC have already begun.

How can one even try to understand this craziness, except by turning to poetry? A group of young Muslim poets, known as the Miya poets, began writing of their pain and humiliation in the language that felt most intimate to them, in the language that until then they had only used in their homes—the Miya dialects of Dhakaiya, Maimansingia, and Pabnaiya. One of them, Rehna Sultana, in a poem called "Mother," wrote:

> *Ma, ami tumar kachchey aamar porisoi diti diti biakul oya dzai*
> Mother, I'm so tired, tired of introducing myself to you

When these poems were posted and circulated widely on Facebook, a private language suddenly became public. And the old specter of linguistic politics reared its head again. Police cases were filed against several Miya poets, accusing them of defaming Assamese society. Rehna Sultana had to go into hiding.

That there is a problem in Assam cannot be denied. But how is it to be solved? The trouble is that once the torch of ethnonationalism has been lit, it is impossible to know in which direction the wind will take the fire. In the new union territory of Ladakh—granted this status by the abrogation of Jammu and Kashmir's special status—tensions simmer between Buddhists and Shia Muslims. In the states of India's northeast, sparks have already begun to ignite old antagonisms. In Arunachal Pradesh, it is the Assamese who are unwanted immigrants. Meghalaya has closed its borders with Assam and now requires all "outsiders" staying more than twenty-four hours to register with the government under the new Meghalaya Residents Safety and Security Act. In Nagaland, twenty-two-year-long peace talks between the central government and Naga rebels have stalled over demands for a separate Naga flag and constitution. In Manipur, dissidents worried about a possible settlement between the Nagas and the central government have announced a government in exile in London. Indigenous tribes in Tripura are demanding their own NRC in order to expel the Hindu Bengali population that has turned them into a tiny minority in their own homeland.

Far from being deterred by the chaos and distress created by Assam's NRC, the Modi government is making arrangements to import it to the rest of India. To take care of the possibility of Hindus and its other supporters being caught up in the NRC's complexities, as has happened in Assam, it has drafted a new Citizenship Amendment Bill. (After being passed in Parliament, it is now the Citizenship Amendment Act.) It says that all non-Muslim "persecuted minorities" from Pakistan, Bangladesh, and Afghanistan—meaning Hindus, Sikhs, Buddhists, and Christians—will be given asylum in India. By default, the CAB will ensure that those deprived of citizenship will only be Muslims.

Before the process begins, the plan is to update the National Population Register. This will involve a door-to-door survey in which, in addition to basic census data, the government plans to add to its collection of iris scans and other biometric data. It will be the mother of all data banks.

The groundwork has already begun. In one of his first acts as home minister, Amit Shah issued a notification permitting state governments across India to set up Foreigners Tribunals and detention centers manned by nonjudicial officers with draconian powers. The governments of Karnataka, Uttar Pradesh, and Haryana have already begun work. As we have seen, the NRC in Assam grew out of a very particular history. To apply it to the rest of India is pure malevolence. The demand for an updated NRC in Assam is more than forty years old. There, people have been collecting and holding on to their documents for fifty years. How many people in India can produce "legacy documents"? Perhaps not even our prime minister—whose date of birth, college degree, and marital status have all been the subject of national controversies.

We are being told that the India-wide NRC is an exercise to detect several million Bangladeshi "infiltrators"—"termites," as our home minister likes to call them. What does he imagine language like this will do to India's relationship with Bangladesh? Once again, phantom figures that run into the tens of millions are being thrown around. There is no doubt that there are a great many undocumented workers from Bangladesh in India. There is also no doubt that they make up one of the poorest, most marginalized populations in the country. Anybody who claims to believe in the free market should know that they are only filling a vacant economic slot by doing work that others will not do, for wages that nobody else will accept. They do an honest day's work for an honest day's pay. They are not the corporate con men destroying the country, stealing public money or bankrupting the banks. They're only a decoy, a Trojan horse for the RSS's real objective, its historic mission.

The real purpose of an all-India NRC, coupled with the CAB, is to threaten, destabilize, and stigmatize the Indian Muslim community, particularly the poorest among them. It is meant to formalize an unequal, tiered society, in which one set of people has no rights and lives at the mercy, or on the good will, of another—a modern caste system, which will exist alongside the ancient one, in which Muslims are the new Dalits. Not notionally, but actually. Legally. In places like West Bengal, where the

BJP is on an aggressive takeover drive, suicides have already begun.

Here is M. S. Golwalkar, the supreme leader of the RSS in 1940, writing in his book *We, or Our Nationhood Defined*:

> Ever since that evil day, when Moslems first landed in Hindustan, right up to the present moment, the Hindu Nation has been gallantly fighting to take on these despoilers. The Race Spirit has been awakening.
>
> In Hindustan, land of the Hindus, lives and should live the Hindu Nation. . . .
>
> All others are traitors and enemies to the National Cause, or, to take a charitable view, idiots. . . . The foreign races in Hindustan . . . may stay in the country, wholly subordinated to the Hindu Nation, claiming nothing, deserving no privileges, far less any preferential treatment—not even citizens' rights.

He continues:

> To keep up the purity of its race and culture, Germany shocked the world by her purging the country of the Semitic races—the Jews. Race pride at its highest has been manifested here, a good lesson for us in Hindustan to learn and profit by.

How do you translate this in modern terms? Coupled with the Citizenship Amendment Bill, the National Register of Citizenship is India's version of Germany's 1935 Nuremberg Laws, by which German citizenship was restricted to only those who had been granted citizenship papers—legacy papers—by the government of the Third Reich. The amendment against Muslims is the first such amendment. Others will no doubt follow, against Christians, Dalits, communists—all enemies of the RSS.

The Foreigners Tribunals and detention centers that have already started springing up across India may not, at the moment, be intended to accommodate hundreds of millions of Muslims. But they are meant to remind us that only Hindus are considered India's real aboriginals and don't need those papers. Even the 460-year-old Babri Masjid didn't have the right legacy papers. What chance would a poor farmer or a street vendor have?

This is the wickedness that the 50,000 people in the Houston stadium were cheering. This is what the president of the United States linked hands with Modi to support. It's what the Israelis want to partner with, the Germans want to trade with, the French want to sell fighter jets to, and the Saudis want to fund.

Perhaps the whole process of the all-India NRC can be privatized, including the data bank with our iris scans. The employment opportunities and accompanying profits might revive our dying economy. The detention centers could be built by the Indian equivalents of Siemens, Bayer, and IG Farben. It isn't hard to guess what corporations those will be. Even if we don't get to the Zyklon B stage, there's plenty of money to be made.

We can only hope that someday soon, the streets in India will throng with people who realize that unless they make their move, the end is close.

If that doesn't happen, consider these words to be intimations of an ending from one who lived through these times.

Catapult

WINNER—COLUMNS AND COMMENTARY

In their monthly column, "An Unquiet Mind," s.e. smith chronicles the psychological and physical challenges disabled people triumph over daily. Some readers, especially the able-bodied, may find this journey into sometimes uncharted territory emotionally wrenching. Others may be struck by the raw beauty of smith's prose. "With an extraordinary ability for both clear exposition and lyric intensity, smith guides readers to a deeper understanding of communities defined by neuro- and biodiversity," said the judges, who recognized the striking power of Smith's work with the National Magazine Award for Columns and Commentary. Based in Northern California, smith has written for several publications, including Bitch, Esquire, The Guardian, *and* Rolling Stone. *The Ellie for "An Unquiet Mind" was the first for* Catapult, *which describes itself as "an independent daily digital magazine featuring original essays, fiction and art from thousands of contributors and columnists."* A Map Is Only One Story, *an anthology of writing from* Catapult, *was published earlier this year by Catapult Books.*

s.e. smith

When Disability Is a Toxic Legacy *and* The Ugly Beautiful and Other Failings of Disability Representation *and* What We Don't Talk About When We Talk About Mental Health and Medication

When Disability Is a Toxic Legacy

One of my earliest memories involves sitting under the massive, whirling arms of a Heidelberg Windmill, listening to the kiss/thunk of the press, beating in a steady, familiar, comforting rhythm that matched the beat of my own small heart. It was a foil run that day, and the light glittered off the foil, a forbidden banner of gold, as it jerked through the feeder. Someone must have been operating the press but in my memory I am alone, looking up through the forest of machinery, feeling the throb of the press across my whole body.

I didn't know the words for these things, then, foil, platen, rollers, quoin, chase. They were something I knew intimately, in my blood.

Something else was in my blood by then too, although I didn't know it.

• • •

I owe a lot in the direction of my life to a classmate who taught me about two things: military pollution and disability rights. For her, they were deeply intertwined, because her family lived next to a military base when her mother was pregnant, and she was born with arthrogryposis. When I met her, she used a power chair for mobility, and on sunny days she would let us take it on joyrides through the commons. In retrospect, this must have been terrifying, to surrender her legs to a bunch of clueless teenagers, but somehow, we never damaged her chair.

She was a good teacher when she didn't have to be. She taught me to be angry about the families who didn't have the resources to fight like hers, to be angry about the things a disablist world would deny, to be angry about the miscarriages and stillbirths and lives stolen because the military cared so little for its own people that it kept dumping things it knew were toxic where they lived, told people to drink the poisoned water. She taught me to never ever feel sorry for her, to think that people like her shouldn't have been born, to view disability as a tragedy.

Disability is not wrong or tragic or bad, but sometimes it is a symptom of a grave injustice.

Years later I doubt I made much of an impression on her life, but she made a huge impression on mine.

• • •

Now that I spend more time around a small child, I understand, acutely, something I only intellectually knew to be true before: Babies put everything in their mouths. They want to taste the world, to understand it through all their senses, even when those things are small—choking hazards!—or dangerous in other ways. They are allergens Baby should not eat, they are sharp, they are poisonous.

Growing up on the floor of a print shop, crawling and then toddling my way through the maze of presses and type cases, past the giant paper cutter I was forbidden to even think about, let alone touch, there were many, many things to grasp in tiny chubby fingers, to put into a curious mouth. There were wooden blocks satisfying to gnaw on and paper to tear up, empty foil rolls to turn into spyglasses, and lots, and lots, of lead type.

Lead ornaments in a myriad of shapes and sizes, lead slugs, the alphabet writ hundreds of ways across a slew of fonts, slender eight-point periods and chunky eighteen-point Gs. I spent the early years of my life playing with poison and against all odds did not experience developmental delays, vision loss, tremors, numbness in my extremities.

My lead levels were never tested as a child, but I cannot imagine they were in a healthy range.

• • •

I don't remember going to the doctor much as a child, either.

"Sorry, we're not accepting Medicaid patients" was a familiar refrain, and the doctors that did have time for us worked quickly, with limited time for answering questions or listening to hypotheticals and what-ifs. It's unlikely a doctor ever asked if I was exposed to anything hazardous, and if they had, I'm not sure "lead" would have even occurred to my father. It was such a ubiquitous part of my world.

No one ever stopped to wonder if I couldn't do math because something was wrong, assuming instead that I was just lazy; anyway, if someone needed a specialist, it meant going to the City four hours away, and who had a reliable car and that kind of time? Certainly not a single dad tending bar across the street from the main gates of the Mill, the town's largest employer.

In our quiet little town, there was a cancer cluster among people who used to work at the Mill, but I didn't understand it as a disease of place; as a child, I simply understood that this was what happened, that you gave up your life to Georgia-Pacific and it spat you out, sick and trembling. We were too poor and too powerless to fight it.

Years later, I would learn about environmental racism and the children of Flint, of Kettleman City, of military bases crisscrossing the United States. I learned about brownfields and coal ash pits and petrochemical plants belching pollution, chemical spills and oil pipelines, and all the things that blanket communities in insidious evil. Those communities are too poor—an experience acutely familiar to me—but also too Brown and Black, to fight back, even when perpetrators know that what they are doing is wrong, even after they see clusters of miscarriages and children born with congenital disabilities, because it is cheaper for them to keep dumping poison than it is for them to do the right thing, or so they think.

Environmental racism is a deep, grievous harm that echoes for generations through communities of color, and one of the ways it does so is at the cellular level, intervening as one cell becomes two, four, eight. Sometimes those cells peter out and die, or they grow for a time but fail to develop into a baby, become instead a story of heartbreak and blood. And sometimes those cells become children. Children born with neurological, developmental, and intellectual disabilities. Children born with limb differences, cleft palates, ticking time bombs that only become apparent later when they want to have children of their own. Children about whom words like "tragedy" are spoken while no one moves to help their community—we should prevent these disabilities, society says, not understanding that the disability is the consequence of the wrong, not the wrong itself.

It is possible to be privileged on one axis—to benefit from whiteness and all it carries—while lacking privilege on another, to experience the oppression of disablism and all it burdens us with, to be poor and marginalized because people believe we are worthless. Environmental racism—caring little for the communities of color that spring up around military bases to supply their needs—affected my white classmate as collateral damage. The cancer cluster at the Mill sickened white working-class people. Not all sick and disabled people become so because of environmental exposures, of course, and we whites have access to more things than our comrades of color ever will, a stacked injustice that must be confronted.

Talking about how environmental disparities can contribute to disability, though I may never fully know if they caused any of my impairments, becomes complicated as a disabled person who is proud and confident in my identity, surrounded by other disabled people who feel similarly about our bodies and lives—though not all disabled people feel this way. It's hard to say "this disability and the things that follow from it are a sign of injustice" in a way that does not make it sound as though I think the disability itself is a wrongness.

Writing about the thorny subject of acknowledging when disability happens because something has gone wrong in a society in the context of anti-vaccination sentiments, disabled writer and editor Elsa Sjunneson-Henry said: "Threading the needle of not hating myself or my disability but finding the source of my disability utterly reprehensible has been a difficult one . . . I don't believe that anyone should have to live a disabled life—let alone lose a baby—because of bad science and a wrongheaded disbelief in vaccination."

There's nothing wrong with being disabled. But there can be something wrong with the way you *become* disabled, and to pretend otherwise is to perpetuate injustice. Flint still doesn't have clean water and children are paying a high price for that. Flint is not the only community in the United States where children are drinking lead, playing in PCBs, choking on pollution. Most of those communities are low-income and communities of color are heavily represented among them; my community is different now not because people thought better of their misdeeds, but because the Mill closed and it became a playground for rich white people who don't like the thought of their poodles playing in dioxins.

All of these things are wrong, and the disabilities, the miscarriages, the stillbirths, are symptoms of those things. The lack of access to health care to help people affected by pollution lead their best lives is wrong. The failure to include those students in classrooms is wrong. The disproportionate rates of sexual assault, homelessness, poverty, housing and employment discrimination, abuse, and other harms these children will experience over the course of their lives because they are disabled is wrong.

I want those children to grow up knowing disability rights, and disability justice, I want them to grow up affirmed and loved and supported, because they are valued, beautiful people with the world in front of them. And I will keep fighting—as they are—to end the injustice that's ravaging their communities. Not because I think disability is bad, but because I think poisoning communities and perpetuating intergenerational inequality and injustice are bad.

• • •

Years after making a poisonous playground my home, I started to develop some of the symptoms associated with lead poisoning—the numbness, tremors, forgetfulness, irritability. By then, my lead levels were normal, and the cause of my problems remains mysterious, a common experience for disabled people.

Feeling a tension between opposing inequality that expresses itself in the form of disability and experiencing pride in being part of the disability community is also a common sensation for many of us. If we cannot sit in our discomfort, though, we cannot hope to grapple with it authentically, and will fail to make space for the complexity of disabled identities in a disablist world. We will also be failing those who count on us to advocate with them—the children of Flint, the survivors of gun violence, all those with disabilities acquired through cruelty and horror and neglect. The experience of acquired disability can be tremendously isolating, more so when the root causes of the disability make people uncomfortable, but no one should be alone in this troubled world of ours.

The Ugly Beautiful and Other Failings of Disability Representation

A row of vultures showed up this morning on the fence line to spread their wings, stretching them out in the sun and peering curiously at me when I stepped out onto the porch. Vultures always remind me of theater people, with their black turtlenecks and dramatics.

I have a certain affinity for vultures; we are both called ugly sometimes and people dismiss our work. People use the word "vulture" like an insult but all I see is a majestic, glorious creature that cleans up the things people don't want to deal with, soaring the thermals on broad wings, constantly searching for the next project. Vultures gather with equanimity around roadkill of all species, the losers of fights, those who slipped away to die in peace and quiet.

Some say vultures are scavengers preying over the dead; I say someone has to lock up after life has left the party.

Finding beauty, grace, gloriousness in things others find ugly or troubling is a bit of a specialty for some of us, I think. Those who spend their lives in bodies others deem unworthy grow accustomed to building our own self-worth. And we grow accustomed to building each other up. Nondisabled people often seem to believe that bodies like theirs are the pinnacle of accomplishment, that the work of finding beauty is about finding ways to compare ourselves to them, that the greatest goal of all disabled people should be to pass or come close to it. Our bodies should be buttoned up and hidden away from sight when it is impossible to "fix" them to a nondisabled ideal, whether that ideal is a sane mind or mobility.

It is deeply troubling for able-bodied people to learn that, at least for some of us, this is not the case—that we find beauty and pride in ourselves, not in how we can most align with what nondisabled people think human bodies and minds should look like. That rather than hide or minimize disability, some of us want to accentuate it. We want to carry sparkly canes, to sew custom pouches for our medical supplies, to wear crop tops with our ostomy bags showing, to show our facial differences.

Often, though, this kind of reclamation is associated specifically with glamour and conventional beauty; Lauren Wasser, the model with the golden legs, or Mama Cax, a fierce Haitian model with cheekbones that could cut glass and a collection of stunning, bold prosthetic limbs, often in bright patterns and colors, sometimes minimalist and fierce, other times elaborate and lacy. Any one of them costs more than most amputees can afford.

Being pretty is expensive regardless of disability status, but the disability tax—the fact that everything is inexplicably more expensive when it involves disability, whether purpose-built or easily modified for our use, on top of our higher poverty rate and lower lifetime earnings, turning a fashion splurge into little more than a wistful sigh—makes it much more out of reach for disabled people to chase a conventionally attractive dream. For those who want to be "fixed" or blend in, it is well-nigh impossible, not necessarily because of the way bodies and medicine work, but because of the sheer cost, most of which is not shouldered by insurance companies and Medicaid, while remaining well beyond the financial means of most disabled people. And for those who want to stand out, the costs of prettiness, power, fierceness, beauty, can also be well beyond reach; limbs that cost tens of thousands of dollars, innovative mobility devices that one can only imagine using, custom-fit gowns that drape flawlessly on nonnormative bodies. Some manage to find their way through thrift and creativity and washi tape to their own unusual, rebellious beauty, but not everyone has that capacity. For the rest of us, sometimes pride in ugliness feels like a question: Are we making do with what we have, or genuinely turning our backs on societal expectations?

Celebrating disability hints at a future where a cane can be both fashion implement and medical device, not just one or the other. Where mobility equipment doesn't have to come only in that dull medical blue color that speaks of depression and long, cold nights in dull, grim places. Where prosthetics can offer form and function in alignment with the wishes of the wearer, rather than the impositions of society. Where the things that keep us alive are part of our beauty rather than things to be politely ignored, where we can say "nice wheelchair" and mean it. Where the desire for beauty and choice is honored by the entities that hold the purse strings; no longer will we be assigned the basic, dull, cheap "only option."

But we must not forget that there *is* beauty and power in the ordinary. I have a deep love and affection for the beige and "medical blue," the drugstore cane tarted up with some patterned duct tape, the ratty powerchair covered in anarchist stickers that Medicaid refuses to replace. These things are beautiful, and living in them with confidence and defiance is beautiful. I love the fat femme in ill-fitting thrift store clothes who rides her battered scooter with pride, blazing through the streets, refusing to remain hidden. She doesn't look like the glossy magazine features disabled people get thrown occasionally as consolation prizes and this is why I love her.

I love ugly beauty, and what the bearers of it say about how we conceptualize beauty. And I am troubled by the forms of disabled beauty we choose to elevate, not only collectively as a society in "inspirational" coverage of disabled people existing in the world, but as a disability community, for the disability community falls into the same traps our nondisabled counterparts do. We seek out the pretty and shiny and glossy, turn away from the ordinary, even when we do not need to; we are swift to praise any disability representation in media without noting that it often falls in line with nondisabled and racialized expectations of beauty, as though criticizing the depiction also attacks the subject. We applaud photogenic disabled people who grow huge social media followings and politely sidestep the ugly beautiful. Be daring, but not too daring. Don't scare the horses. There are exceptions, of course. There are always exceptions. But that's what makes them exceptional.

We do not talk enough about how money and class weave through the way people are able to present themselves, that some can buy good health care and power and prettiness while others spend hours on the phone every week pleading for prior authorizations and begging to replace ancient wheelchairs, asking for replacements for equipment that is battered, old, held together with duct tape, hair brittle and dull with stress. We see and recognize this financial injustice as a force in our lives, but not necessarily as an influence on our presentation.

I think of Aimee Mullins, a model with the stunningly long legs, blonde hair, and good looks that people think should come with modeling, how she embodies the nondisabled ideal, until she takes her legs off. Then she is an amputee, frightening, other, strange. Stranger still are the legs she can choose to put on: Hand-carved custom Alexander McQueen wooden legs, legs that look like jellyfish floating through the water, cheetah legs for running hard and fast. Legs that mark her as different.

Some might look at women like Mullins and experience a sense of pity, thinking they'll spend their lives pursuing nondisabled perfection and always fail. I look at her and see power, a disabled person who has taken control of her body's destiny, who challenges what destiny should look like. Her prosthetic limbs are not pale imitations of their nondisabled counterparts, she is not trying to pass as nondisabled, she is instead using them as an extension of both her body and her aesthetic. She has achieved something nondisabled people cannot; her stunningly engineered sports legs confer tremendous advantage, and she can casually change her height with a simple equipment switchover. A friend sees her adjustable height as an unfair advantage.

She is unapologetically disabled, though sometimes her public comments reflect deeply internalized disablism, has chosen to accentuate her disability and the mobility devices she chooses to use, has turned disability into art, social commentary, statement. She is beauty. She is power. To see her stride across a stage is to feel a swell of something complicated and almost overwhelming. But she is able to live that way because she has access to privilege, power, money. Because she is white. Because she is able to make her disability relatable, less scary, for audiences, smiling frequently and making jokes. She is approachable.

While it's thrilling to see a bespoke wheelchair on the runway or an attractive and stylish disabled person showing off a robotic arm on a street fashion blog, I do not want us to forget our siblings with less power, privilege, and access. Visibility may elevate the disability community, but it can come at a cost when it is not thoughtful visibility, when it suggests that pretty people can engage in radical embodiment while the rest of us slobs are stuck begging for a seat at the table. Diversity cannot be limited to hashtags that rarely circulate beyond the disability community when we have the whole wide world laid out before us, tantalizing, so close, yet leaving us feeling like we will never touch the sky.

We are vultures soaring aloft, living in precision bodies that are our own, even if they seem grotesque to you, from razor-sharp beaks to naked necks, ragged feathers and gnarled feet. We are as vital and necessary as the swans and peacocks of the world.

We are taught to be humiliated, ashamed of using medical devices. I think of the latest high-profile pretty disability spread in a major magazine, Selma Blair's recent fashion feature, something widely praised in the disability community as a profound moment for visibility. Was it, though? Or was it just a prettification of disability, a celebration of someone with access to considerable resources at the cost of more diverse disability visibility? Or was it a pivotal moment, a Hollywood star flaunting her cane like the fashion accessory and mobility aid and tool of liberation that it is to force nondisabled people to rethink disability identity? Are we so hungry for any representation that we are afraid to demand the beautiful ugly?

What We Don't Talk About When We Talk About Mental Health and Medication

I've spent my entire life being told I'm a reactive person.

Every situation a catalyst for a fiery explosion, a shower of multicolored sparks like the rockets we used to shoot off at the dunes when I was in high school, arcing high into the darkness before inevitably falling down and away, dying out amongst the white-caps. People say "reactive" but they don't mean that, not really. They mean difficult, unpleasant, short, hard to deal with, temperamental, too much. They mean these things in unkind, unpleasant ways but it is hard to take them poorly when sometimes I am the only one saying the things that need to be said. Plain truths are difficult, not the people saying them, but for a long time I believed the people who said these things, that there was something twisted and wrong in me.

When you're mentally ill, many people like to attribute everything about you to your mental illness; if I wasn't crazy, maybe I wouldn't be so *challenging*—as though my mental illness shapes every element of my personality and I am simply pulled along in its wake, unable to make conscious decisions about the person I want to be and how I want to carry myself in the world. They think my mental illness sidles up to me on benches and murmurs, and I do its bidding, holding its hand as it pushes me out into traffic. I must be kept quiet, safe, calm, sane, through chemistry.

"Are you off your meds?" they might ask.

Often, it's a kind of blame. Sometimes it's a well-intentioned excuse, as though they are in the position to determine when my behavior needs to be excused and they're doing me a favor.

But I know true reactiveness, because I have felt it inside my own body—a runaway chain of events that felt wildly uncontrollable and irrational. Experiencing a severe reaction to medication taught me many interesting things about the limits of my own body, but also the limits of the world around me, because it brushed up against some uncomfortable truths about psychiatric medications that many people would rather not discuss—to wit, that they have side effects, and "side effects may include" can apply to anyone and everyone. Pharmaceutical companies are eager to help people overlook that information, rattled off at warp speed in commercials and provided in small print on packaging, but desperation can be a powerful driver too—the willingness to risk anything to make what is hurting you stop. So too can the earnest desire to do good, to encourage people to use medications if they find them helpful, to avoid discussing some of the costs of doing so.

Many of our worst associations with psychiatric medications originate from the moment the pharmaceutical industry first started developing them in force, in the mid-1900s. Powerful antipsychotic drugs that nearly incapacitated patients became the stuff of nightmares and pop cultural lampooning—the drooling, shuffling, slack-jawed "psych patients" depicted in media of that era made a strong impression, as do the calls for haloperidol on contemporary emergency room dramas, turning a screaming, thrashing patient into a compliant, dull-eyed one in minutes. Later classes of drugs have tempered those extreme side effects, designed to allow people to live a full life, not just sedating them into oblivion—but for some patients, the level of sedation can be much higher, by design or happenstance, and it becomes unbearable, creating fog and fatigue that makes it impossible to function.

As ever, the dose makes the poison.

Medication is one among a number of ways to manage mental health conditions and for some of us they can be highly effective, helping us live with, instead of fight, our minds—cultivating space to inhabit the world more fully. It is also deeply stigmatized, intriguingly from almost every imaginable social perspective. Taking meds means you're weak. Taking meds means you're suppressing your body's natural expression. Taking meds means you'll forget your "real" self. Taking meds means you're a tool of big pharma. Taking meds means you'll get dependent and you'll be stuck on them for life. Taking meds means you're not trying hard enough—you should do more yoga, drink more kombucha, go to more crystal healings, think yourself well. Taking

the water bottle I kept by the bed. Mouth hot and dry, prickly. I didn't want to eat, maybe because my stomach was so full of liquid, but maybe because of the fact that my entire body felt like it was in open revolt. I got dizzy, heard ringing in my ears, felt faint.

Something is wrong here, I told myself as the tremor that had started over the summer with a constantly shaking, twitching hand that flapped uselessly against the keyboard and accidentally ripped the pages out of books. It grew more pronounced and spread to my whole body, which jerked randomly and spasmodically, jaw clacking or leg jumping. While driving. At a meeting. While cooking. I slopped boiling water on my foot and looked down with interest as my skin reddened and blistered. Then the vomiting started, on top of visiting the bathroom constantly to pee, having to game every trip out of the house carefully to avoid being caught out, and sometimes I failed at that. I put a pad in front of the toilet to make it easier on my knees, and between bouts I would lie on the couch, hair matted and sweaty, wondering what was happening to me.

I have not been, historically, the kind of person who develops side effects; that laundry list of unwanted events has been largely irrelevant to me. In fact, sometimes medications don't seem to work on me at all; I have yet to encounter an opioid that does anything more than make me care slightly less about pain, not even the fentanyl nurses and doctors kept pushing in the recovery room after my last surgery, for an unrelated matter, in 2017. It took me a moment to realize that this thing, this constellation of miseries that made me want to claw my way out of my body and disappear into the darkness, bobbing away on the waves, was a reaction to medication.

Side-effects happen. Especially if you're adjusting your dosage, which I was. But I am so acculturated to conversations about psychiatric medications that elide side effects and bury truths that it took me over a week of severe symptoms, so notable that even friends were commenting that something seemed off, to connect the dots, to go to the hospital, where the white-haired ER doc, a contractor, because that's all they use these days, said I was in kidney failure because the medication had overcome my body's ability to cope, gave me drugs for the vomiting and the tremor, and told me to talk to my psychiatrist.

That tremor is the medication's little gift to me: It will never go away, and whenever I do go off this medication, when it stops working, which psych meds often do, I'll have to keep taking a different one for the tremor. Maybe if I had known in June what I discovered in September, I wouldn't have been left with such severe damage.

The medication's left me other gifts, ones I could return (I kept the receipt) if I stopped taking it: I am slower than I used to be. I have trouble with deep critical reading, sometimes reading the same passage over and over again and not understanding it. Oddly, I am more impulsive than I used to be, not less, as though my brain has lost a fundamental filter that cannot be restored. I am less observant, a thing I try to turn into a joke, deflecting.

I am not as creative, a thing that seems to have become a bit of a third rail in conversations about psychiatric medications. It goes like this: For a long time, it was broadly accepted that medication "kills creativity" and that, by extension, "true" artists and creators couldn't and shouldn't be on medication, because it would fundamentally reshape their work, that in fact, it was being mentally ill that made people creative. People, rightly, pushed back on that, noting that it's hard to create when you're dead, or spinning out, or feeling overwhelmed by your brain, that medication doesn't necessarily have to mean a dulling of the mind and it shouldn't be described that way. Now, openly saying that one has become less creative as a direct result of taking psychiatric medication can be a dangerous proposition, something author

Heidi Heilig explored in her essay "What We're Born With and What We Pick Up Along the Way."

It is not that my medication killed my creativity, or that managing my mental health with medication makes it impossible to do the work I care about, but that a medication designed to act on the brain acts imprecisely and can suppress certain cognitive activities in some patients, and I am one of them. And yes, there are often other options, some with less suppressive effects, but they're not right for me personally—and patients should absolutely talk to their doctors rather than just suffering, which is something they may not know they can do in a society where admitting these side effects exist is taboo.

This is a tradeoff I have chosen to make, one where I am not as bright and sharp and creative as I used to be, one where developing a transcendent turn of phrase is a fight, not something casual and effortless. I like and value and miss those parts of myself, but I do not like constantly fighting with my brain, feeling wildly tossed like the blades of the dune grasses in winter storms.

Here is a thing I am not supposed to confess: I think about it, sometimes, tapering quietly back down again, letting my mind run free, ending the reaction between the drug and my brain.

Would I have taken the drug at the very start, knowing what came later? Yes, I would have, but I wish I had known, because I would have gotten treatment at the first warning signs, not when it was so severe that I almost had irreversible kidney damage. Refusing to acknowledge that side effects exist doesn't mean they don't happen, it just leaves people marooned without information to make informed choices; to take or not to take, to take a different medication, to get early treatment for side effects. There is nothing wrong with taking psychiatric medication or deciding it is not for you, for any number of reasons. There are no circumstances in which people should be compelled to take it.

We are trying a different formulation, and if that doesn't work, we will try something else, and I will continue on the endless merry-go-round so many crazy people know well as one medication stops working, sometimes dramatically and dangerously, and another one takes its place.

And I will keep talking about side effects, because I am reactive, though not in the way people mean, and failing to be open about it is to set other people up for failure. So many ugly lies and myths swirl around the drugs we take to survive in our minds; when we unmask them, we must not also hide the truth.

New Yorker

FINALIST—COLUMNS AND COMMENTARY

This is where pop culture and emotional frenzy meet. Not Jia Tolentino's—her writing is cool and considered, though often withering—but that of a nation where musicians are sometimes mistaken for spiritual leaders, fans (or is that "stans"?) long to be brutally dispatched by their favorite celebrities, and presidents are accused of rape and no one really notices. The Ellie Award judges praised Tolentino for her "moral conscience and literary flair" while noting that her New Yorker *columns "provide a persuasive and highly readable tour of the American psyche." Now in her early thirties, Tolentino joined the* New Yorker *as a staff writer in 2016. Her first book, a collection of essays titled* Trick Mirror: Reflections in Self-Delusion, *was published in 2019. Since David Remnick was appointed editor in 1998, the* New Yorker *has won fifty-four National Magazine Awards, including three for Columns and Commentary, most recently in 2019 for the work of Doreen St. Félix.*

Jia Tolentino

Kanye West's Sunday Service Is Full of Longing and Self-Promotion *and* Love, Death, and Begging for Celebrities to Kill You *and* E. Jean Carroll's Accusation Against Donald Trump, and the Raising, and Lowering, of the Bar

Kanye West's Sunday Service Is Full of Longing and Self-Promotion

On the first Sunday of 2019, Kim Kardashian West assumed a new position as the unofficial head of communications for a pop-up church experience called Sunday Service, which was created by her husband, Kanye West. She pointed her sixty million Twitter followers to a series of videos that she was posting on Instagram Stories; they showed a seemingly phosphorescent choir, in a large studio flooded with ultraviolet light, singing startlingly beautiful gospel renditions of songs by West ("Father Stretch My Hands," "Lift Yourself"). "Just hearing music as our Sunday Service was super inspiring," she tweeted later, adding "See you next Sunday" and a sparkle emoji. Every Sunday since, West has put on, and his wife has promoted, a small, invite-only musical gathering, sometimes held in a room saturated with monochrome light, sometimes in a verdant field in Calabasas. Attendees have included Katy Perry, Courtney Love, Rick Rubin, Diplo, Busy Philipps, and Tyler, the Creator. (Kardashian West's sisters and their children come, too.) Choir members wear matching outfits, which look like the sweats that West makes for Yeezy, his high-end fashion line; every week, they put on a new color, forming a pulsing block of white or black or periwinkle or "pill yellow." The entire effort has an extravagantly normcore and vaguely cultlike vibe. "There's no praying," Kardashian West told Jimmy Kimmel, on his late-night show. "There's no sermon. There's no word. It's just music, and it's just a feeling." Her sister Kourtney clarified that Sunday Service is, in fact, a Christian thing.

Everyone who attends Sunday Service has to sign a nondisclosure agreement, but attendees seem free to share their experiences through Instagram videos. In one such video, you can—contrary to Kardashian West's description—watch DMX leading a prayer. In March, Courtney Love posted a video of West performing "Jesus Walks," a single from his début album, with the choir stomping and singing the song's a-cappella hook. West sounded good—agile and alert and formidable—which came as a relief to many who have observed his behavior over the past few years with growing worry. Back in 2016, West canceled the second leg of his Saint Pablo Tour and was hospitalized. When he reemerged, he often seemed, if anything, more erratic than before and took to saying things like slavery "sounds like a choice." Last June, he released a slight album, called *Ye*—a diminutive of Kanye—by flying a group of influential people to Jackson, Wyoming, for a listening party; on the way there, he made the album's cover art, a photo of the Tetons with the phrase "I hate being Bi-Polar its awesome" scribbled on it in neon green. "I believe 'ye' is the most commonly used word in the Bible," West said in an interview. It's not, but you see where this is going.

God has always been all over West's music—the gospel-adjacent soul samples, the ever-present sense of glory and revelation—in a way that alternately suggests worship and subsumption. In "Jesus Walks," he positions himself as a prophet as well as a supplicant. The hook samples the Harlem-based Addicts Rehabilitation Center Choir, and West invokes Christ's ministry to all, regardless of their past or their station: "To the hustlers, killers, murderers, drug dealers, even the strippers / Jesus walks for them." West has a blindingly vivid messiah complex; he also has an obsession with iconoclasm that has led him all the way to the idea that slavery was voluntary. A decade ago, he told an interviewer, "I don't wanna fuckin' be Christ-like. I want to be me-like." Later, in an attempt to clarify his remarks, he said, "My entire life, being an African American, Christianity was forced down my throat." In Love's Instagram video, we hear West rap, "I hope this take away from my sins, and bring the day that I'm dreaming about / Next time I'm in the club, everybody screaming out"—"Jesus walks with me," the choir chants. Love tagged the post "#kanye" and also "#jesus #god #calabassas #gospel #holyspirit #transcendent."

• • •

West has suggested that Sunday Service will soon come to an end, but, on Easter Sunday, which was also the last day of Coachella, he held a drawn-out Sunday Service at nine a.m., on a sod-covered hill on the periphery of the festival's campgrounds. The event was live-streamed, in an absurd fashion, through a peephole camera; watching it felt like wandering dizzily around a very luxe cult gathering with two paper-towel tubes glued to my eyes. The choir wore mauve and tramped up the hill in winding single file. As many people observed on Twitter, the morning's aesthetic had a Teletubbies feel, and the choir resembled the Tethered from the movie *Us*. A dense crowd, fenced off from the performance, covered the surrounding grass.

The obvious explanation for Sunday Service is that it's album promotion. Last fall, West announced a ninth album, called *Yandhi*, and he has performed two *Yandhi* tracks at Sunday Service. (West previously shifted his wife's wardrobe from a colorful bottle-service aesthetic to sci-fi-style Yeezy neutrals. It's easy to imagine him issuing monochromatic dress codes for a *Yandhi* tour.) In an interview with TMZ, West explained that *Ye* had been an act of "superhero rehabilitation," meaning, presumably, that it was like the part of an action movie where the avenging champion retreats to his lair to regain his strength. On the *Ye* track "Yikes," he calls his bipolar disorder a superpower; last December, he declared on Twitter that he could not make "dark fantasy level music" when he was taking meds. With *Yandhi*, he said, he was getting "fully back in mode, off of medication." As for the MAGA hat he'd been wearing, he added, it "means I'm being me and I'm punk and I can wear whatever I want 'cause I'm a god."

There's a suspicion in some corners that West, who has recently begun making appearances on *Keeping Up with the Kardashians*, may be borrowing another idea from his wife's family by starting a church. Churches, these days, can be a glossy business proposition. Hillsong, best known for its celebrity-packed Los Angeles congregation—its pastor, Carl Lentz, famously baptized Justin Bieber in the NBA player Tyson Chandler's bathtub—pulls in more than a hundred million (mostly tax-exempt) dollars per year. In 2009, Kris Jenner, West's mother-in-law, cofounded the California Community Church, which operates mostly out of a Sheraton hotel in Agoura Hills. The California Community Church is led by a pastor named Brad Johnson, who resigned from his previous pulpit after revelations that he'd had an extramarital affair. Jenner tracked Johnson down at his subsequent job as a Starbucks barista, persuaded him to lead her new church, and got him to officiate Khloé Kardashian and Lamar Odom's wedding on TV. (When Johnson later married the woman with whom he'd had an affair, Jenner officiated.) The California Community Church, which has already got into some tax trouble, asks congregants to pledge either a thousand dollars per month or, as is typical of many Christian churches, ten percent of their income. In old interviews, Kardashian West has reiterated her commitment to tithing. ("Every year. Absolutely," she told Piers Morgan.) In 2013, she sent her mother's church almost fifty grand.

• • •

Perhaps West is dipping his toe in these waters. It also seems possible that Sunday Service fills a deeply personal need. Though he announced a few years ago that he was fifty-three million dollars in debt, West lives in extremely rarefied circumstances these days—presumably thanks to his wife, whose net worth is estimated to be three hundred and fifty million dollars. A recent *Vogue* video shows their house to be a cavernous, white, near-empty, museum-like edifice; Kardashian West describes it as a "minimal monastery." It is a stark contrast to the Sunday Service videos, which, if nothing else, are loud and full of people.

On the live stream from Coachella, West had purple hair to match his T-shirt. He didn't enter the picture until about forty-five minutes into the performance, and he didn't take center stage until close to the end. The choir ran through gospel standards and through gospel versions of West's music; Chance the Rapper, who speaks and raps often about his Christian faith and shares snapshots of devotional books on Instagram, danced atop the hill. "Jesus Christ is Lord!" Chance shouted into the microphone, rapping his incandescent verse from "Ultralight Beam," which includes the couplet "I made 'Sunday Candy,' I'm never going to hell / I met Kanye West, I'm never going to fail." In the middle of the song, West started crying, and Kid Cudi comforted him. DMX, who, earlier, had said another prayer, wrapped the rapper in a hug. West seemed off while performing—a little slow, a little cloudy. After "Jesus Walks," he sank to his knees in the grass and closed his eyes for a long time.

Like West, I grew up in a community where Christianity was presented as a mandate. I spent years, when I was younger, wishing that church could be wordless and strange; I felt the presence of God more profoundly when I was in a crowd of people listening to music—rap, in particular—than I did while listening to a pastor speak. I also saw, after a decade inside an evangelical megachurch, how quickly a genuine hunger for salvation and community could be converted into cash and self-aggrandizement. West's audience—his curated guests, his festival acolytes—has been primed by our cultural moment to overlook the deep bleakness of invite-only worship, of a 225-dollar bleach-stained sweatshirt that's supposed to promote God and Kanye at the same time. But, even worse, many of them are surely drawn to Sunday

Service out of some sort of meaningful longing: these young people who can afford to pay four figures to behave badly and photograph well in the desert are pursuing absolution, too, in their way. So many things today seem, upon reflection, like a cry for help disguised as a demonstration of cultural capital. At his most courageous, West has seemed hallowed because of how purely he expressed a real hunger. In 2008, he recorded a live album in London, with an all-female string orchestra, called *Late Orchestration*, which includes a rendition of "Jesus Walks." I've been rewatching that performance. It's sublime and agonized, and full of the sort of miraculous devotion that I used to hear about in church.

Love, Death, and Begging for Celebrities to Kill You

The first time I noticed that quite a lot of people on the Internet seemed to be begging celebrities to kill them was a couple of years ago. "Can lana del rey step on my throat already," one person tweeted. "Snap my neck and hide my body," another announced, when Lady Gaga posted a new profile photo. Taylor Swift could "run me over with a tractor and I'd say thank you and ask her if she wants to do it again," another wrote. If you performed a cursory search, you'd find hundreds of such messages, mostly lobbed by young millennials and members of Generation Z. There was an emphatic queerness to much of this discourse, whether or not the person tweeting identified as anything but straight. Many of the messages were about women and sent by women; the subset of men who attracted these tweets tended to be girlish, in a boy-band way. There were lots of appeals to sweetly handsome Korean pop stars, lots of "harry styles punch me in the face" requests, lots of wishes for the still-babyish Justin Bieber to run people over with his car. Nowadays, on Twitter, every hour brings a new crop of similar entreaties.

One takeaway from all this is that young people really love celebrities. Another is that we're craving unmediated connection so desperately that we would accept it in the form of murder. It's also possible that we simply want to die. Earlier this year, at the *Cut*, in a piece about the upswing of "run me over" tweets, Gabriella Paiella observed that the popularity of these jokes can't be separated from the ambient fatalism inculcated by attention to actual real-world problems—"the fact that we're living during a time when we're constantly being reminded that the Earth is going to be virtually uninhabitable by the end of the century, that capitalism is wholly unsustainable, and that we're just one push of a button away from perishing in a nuclear war." Paiella talked to the writer Brandy Jensen, who had recently tweeted that her primary reaction to seeing a hot person was to think "back over me with a truck." Everyone, Jensen said, seemed to be constantly posting about how they were horny and how they wanted to die; it was natural that the two would converge.

Devotion, by its nature, tends to invite agony. "Love has brought me within the reach of lovely, cruel arms that / unjustly kill me," Petrarch writes, in Robert M. Durling's English translation of "Rime Sparse," a set of poems written in the fourteenth century. Shakespeare's "Venus and Adonis," published in 1593, describes Venus as a maiden who "murders with a kiss." In the early seventeenth century, John Donne famously begged, "Batter my heart, three person'd God." (A degraded Internet-era version of the poem, "Holy Sonnet 14," might involve the impassioned poet pleading with God to choke him.) But this language appears to be spilling over. It may originate in a sort of erotic consecration, but love and pain, joy and punishment, seem increasingly convergent, at least in the ways that people express themselves online. Love may be timeless, but the half-ironic millennial death wish has become an underground river rushing swiftly under the surface of the age.

• • •

Earlier this month, I got on the phone with Mistress Velvet, a dominatrix in Chicago with a day job in social work, to ask her what she made of all this. She'd started noticing the prevalence of punch-me-in-the-face talk in 2011, she told me, when she was first coming into her queerness, in her early twenties. "Saying that I'd 'literally let her stab me' was a way of linguistically valuing my queer relationships over my heterosexual ones," she said. "But I've also become interested in it in the context of BDSM." Mistress Velvet told me that, when clients came to her with this sort of intense sacrificial devotion, they often were seeking replacements for powerful people who were absent from their lives. "It reminds me of when I transitioned from Christianity to atheism," she said. "I was suddenly afraid of death—I was nihilistic—and I had to find something else that could fill that gap."

That parallel had never occurred to me, I told her.

"I mean, if we're thinking of it," Mistress Velvet said, "Jesus died for our sins, and believers are supposed to give our lives back to him. My clients sometimes talk to me like this. They'd let me run them over with a truck. I'm like, 'That's not even what I want! Your life is sacred!'"

"Right," I said, suddenly dazed. "Maybe it's a dream of mutuality—of sacrificing yourself for someone in such a way that they would then be permanently tied to you."

I messaged a seventeen-year-old Harry Styles fan whose social-media bio included the sentence "harry can run me over, use my crumpled corpse to wipe his car off and then use me to avoid puddles on the street." She'd been on "stan twitter" since 2012, she explained, and "us stans have always been pretty harsh with expressing our love." (A stan, as the *Oxford English Dictionary* now recognizes, is an obsessive fan of a celebrity; the term comes from the 2000 Eminem song "Stan," and it can be used both as a noun and a verb.) "I say these kinds of things because . . . it would honestly be an honor for Harry to run me over," she wrote. An eighteen-year-old whose Twitter bio was "tom holland could run me over with a truck and I would say thank you" told me, "Even just being near him or in his presence would make me sooo happy, even if it meant he was running me over with a truck."

After perusing the ample and growing archive of tweets in which people ask Cate Blanchett to step on their throats, I messaged a twenty-four-year-old woman who'd posted a photo of Blanchett with the caption "she's so tall pls step on my throat ma'am." Step-on-my-throat language, she wrote back, was all about "the LGBTQ people who just love to love and support women, and get more creative every passing day. its our safe place." Plus, she added, "It's Cate freaking Blanchett, you'd do anything she wants you to do."

• • •

But not all run-me-over tweets direct their sentiment at an object. Plenty of people on Twitter are begging to simply be run over, stepped on, punched in the face. The Twitter user @alwayssad daily, whose name is stated as simply "Anxiety," recently posted a series of emoji snowflakes that formed a giant "F," followed by "*UCKING RUN ME OVER.*" It received twelve hundred likes. "I honestly feel that this new trend of expression is because people in society as a whole these days are becoming more and more numb to life and are losing perspective on the physical part of reality, which in turn causes the brain to react and express things a certain way in order to satisfy the need for feeling in our bodies," the twenty-year-old woman behind the account told me. "Life is becoming increasingly redundant, which makes me iterate these thoughts out loud to myself—hit me with a car, fucking kill me—for psychological satisfaction."

In *Civilization and Its Discontents*, published in 1930, Freud wrote about the unconscious sense of guilt he attributed to his patients, who tended not to believe what he was suggesting; it was hard to become conscious of being unconsciously guilty. "In order to make ourselves at all intelligible to them," he wrote, referring to the approach that analysts took with such patients, "we tell them of an unconscious need for punishment, in which the sense of guilt finds expression." In this framework, masochism is the ego's desire to atone.

In my life—which is mostly, I would say, a vibrant and happy one—this masochistic tendency surfaces constantly, in a sidelong way. About a month ago, while spending a rowdy weekend at a music festival on the beach with nine other people, I started counting the jokes we made about walking into the ocean and dying together. A friend and I kept talking about drowning each other "as a bit." For me, the capacity to experience such unfettered pleasure—the fact of having the time and capital and freedom required for it, at a time when we know that so many people's lives are worsening—is often what instigates the murmur of guilt. I *do* deserve to be run over with a dump truck, I think, at home, opening my delivery packages, thinking about how much plastic I have put on this planet, how much labor I have exploited for the sake of my own convenience. Longing and guilt intertwine every time I think about having children, who, if they exist, will exist in a world defined by manmade crisis and natural disaster. On the beach, flooded with joy, I felt the tug of that familiar undertow. "Fucking kill me," I thought, suddenly desiring a sensation strong enough to silence itself—which is, I suppose, one way of defining love.

E. Jean Carroll's Accusation Against Donald Trump, and the Raising, and Lowering, of the Bar

One of the things I have feared most since the night of the 2016 election is the inevitable hardening of my own heart—and what such hardening might lead to, especially if it were experienced by many other people as well. Specifically, I feared that the Trump era would bring a surfeit of bad news and that I would compartmentalize this bad news in order to remain functional and that this attempt to remain functional would itself be so demoralizing that it would contribute to the despair and distraction that allowed all this bad news to occur.

When I imagined specifics, back in November 2016, I pictured something like last week—or part of it. I imagined that undocumented families would be openly and cruelly persecuted in America and that there would be plans of mass raids and internment and that as this was happening I would not be rioting in the street as I ought to but depressively checking things off my Google Calendar to-do list and probably writing a blog post about a meme. What I didn't imagine, though—and what actually occurred last week—is that a respected and well-known writer would accuse the president of raping her and that I would be so sad and numb, after years of writing about Trump's many accusers, after watching Brett Kavanaugh get confirmed to the Supreme Court in the face of credible sexual-assault allegations, that I would not even have the courage to read the story for days.

• • •

E. Jean Carroll, now seventy-five years old, is a longtime advice columnist for *Elle*. Her approach to life is distinctive: brisk, stylish, tough, compassionate. Her columns provided an early and crucial model for me—when I was little and waist-deep in the mistake of trying to understand life through women's glossies—of never giving my personal problems more weight than was absolutely necessary. The essay that she published last week, in *New York*, titled "My List of Hideous Men"—it's an excerpt from a forthcoming book—performs the tremendous and awful feat of bringing her sharp-edged breeziness to bear on a story about being raped. Carroll's "hideosity bar is high," she writes. A boy who shoved a stick or rock up her genitals when she was a girl doesn't make the list. Hunter S. Thompson, slicing her pants off with a knife in a hot tub, doesn't make it either, because, she writes, "to me there is a big difference between an 'adventure' and an 'attack.'"

Carroll goes on to detail multiple sexual assaults: by a college suitor, by a boss who chased her down a hotel hallway, by the former CBS president and CEO Les Moonves. (Moonves denies the allegation.) "By now, Silent Generation aside, the question has occurred to you: Why does this woman seem so unfazed by all this horrible crap?" she writes. "Well, I am shallower than most people. I do not dwell on the past. I feel greater empathy for others than for myself. I do not try to control everything." Plus, she adds, she's a born cheerleader: she was a cheerleader in grade school, in high school, and was even the winner of a competition called Miss Cheerleader USA. For years, in her advice columns, she cheered for each correspondent to "pick herself up and go on."

But there are two men, she writes, whom she wishes she'd spoken about sooner. One is a camp director who repeatedly molested her when she was twelve. The other is Donald Trump. The incident happened in the fall of 1995 or the spring of 1996, she writes. She and Trump ran into each other at Bergdorf Goodman;

Trump convinced her to help him shop for a present in the lingerie department; Carroll—"and as I write this, I am staggered by my stupidity," she states—went into the fitting room with him; Trump shoved her against the wall, unzipped his pants, and forced his penis inside her. Eventually, Carroll fought him off and ran away. She still carries around the shrapnel of this encounter, myriad pointed details lodged in her mind—such as the fact that, at the beginning of the struggle, she was so shocked that she was laughing. There is a limit, for everyone, to the uses of compartmentalization. Whether it's "my age, the fact that I haven't met anyone fascinating enough over the past couple of decades to feel 'the sap rising,' as Tom Wolfe put it, or if it's the blot of the real-estate tycoon, I can't say," Carroll writes, closing her essay. "But I have never had sex with anybody ever again."

• • •

A lot of hearts seem to have hardened not just in response to Carroll's story but in the long lead-up to it. When the piece appeared online, there was an immediate unspoken sense, I thought—although it's certainly possible that I'm projecting—that it would tell us only what we already knew. Trump accused himself of sexual assault, on tape, in 2005, while filming *Access Hollywood*, and we found out about it just before the election, and, because any man who boasts about grabbing women by the pussy is likely to have done so and worse, repeatedly and with no compunction, it's all been extremely, deadeningly predictable from there. The White House said in a statement that Carroll's story was "false and unrealistic" and was "created simply to make the President look bad." Trump later stated that Carroll was just trying to sell books and claimed that he had never met her, despite *New York* running a photo of the two of them talking at a party. "It is a disgrace and people should pay dearly for such false accusations," he said. On Monday, in an interview with *The Hill*,

Trump, deploying a blatant grotesquerie that was surely intended to play to his base, said, "Number one, she's not my type. Number two, it never happened."

But a public figure accusing the president of rape is news. Even though Carroll is at least the twenty-second woman to accuse Trump of sexual misconduct, she is only the second to accuse him of rape. (The first was Ivana Trump, who later downplayed her story.) Though Carroll received the pride of place at *New York* that she deserved, appearing on the cover of the magazine, her story did not make the front page of the *New York Times*, the *Wall Street Journal*, the *Los Angeles Times*, or the *Chicago Tribune*. The *New York Post* deleted a story about Carroll's allegations on Friday. The *Times* was slow to feature the story online and didn't run its piece in print until Sunday. Weekend talk shows mostly ignored the topic; on Sunday, Brian Stelter, on CNN, discussed the lack of attention the story was getting, citing the possibility—the reality—of media fatigue. There have been so many accusations against Trump that none has been able to receive the undivided attention that it ought to, Stelter suggested. And the news cycle itself is so quick-moving and chaotic that every important story, regardless of its subject, is metabolized too fast.

There are other explanations, too, though none of them are particularly satisfactory. Newspapers tend to prioritize stories that they've broken in house. There are also good journalistic reasons for seeking independent confirmation of a story before giving it prominence. But, on Monday, Dean Baquet, the executive editor of the *Times*, acknowledged that the paper had "underplayed the article." Though Carroll's account was vetted by *New York*—two friends confirmed that she told them the story contemporaneously with the event—it was a first-person account rather than an investigative report. And it gets harder to tell this story over and over and over, as a lesson we learned in 2016 only becomes clearer: there are many people in this country, including, apparently, the majority of Republicans who hold national office, who don't believe that rape is that big of a deal. As we saw during the Kavanaugh hearings, a portion of those people may grow to like a man *better* after he is accused of sexual assault. In her essay for *New York*, Carroll acknowledges the risk that she might make Trump more popular by telling the story of how he raped her. In these cases, the accuser is not so much disbelieved as conscripted into a narrative of women attempting to victimize men by arousing public sympathy. The powerful solidify their power by pretending that they have been threatened and attacked. This dynamic is central to both fascism and abuse.

It has felt impossible, in the Trump era, to hope even for a second that our governing systems will operate on any standard of morality. What we have instead is a standard of consistency. If the president had ever convincingly espoused ideas of respect for people who are not like him or of equal rights for women, it's possible that he would be held accountable for his actions. Instead, he promised mass campaigns of cruelty against undocumented immigrants, and he is delivering. He said that he grabbed women by the pussy, and many women—twenty-two, so far—explained that, yes, he did that, or something like it, to them. Carroll's essay—exceptional, devastating, decades in the making—has made me consider how hard it is to understand right away that you've been exhausted into submission, especially when submission and endurance feel inextricable. It's reminded me of how high I've let my own hideosity bar get lately and also of the fact that no one can lower it again but me.

T: The New York Times Style Magazine

FINALIST—COLUMNS AND COMMENTARY

Listen as Ligaya Mishan describes the experience of eating "crack seed" in Hawaii: "I put one of the hard dark plums in my mouth. It was pure salt. No: It was salt as if I'd never properly understood the word, ageless and engulfing, the world's last gift to a drowning man." Suffused not only with a passion for food but an understanding of history, Mishan's columns for T: The New York Times Style Magazine *take readers around the world and then bring them back home with a new understanding of the small mysteries that grace their dinner plates. Indeed, the National Magazine Award judges described these columns as "learned, elegant and—above all—joyful." Mishan's work has appeared in the* New York Review of Books *and the* New Yorker *as well as the* New York Times. T: The New York Times Style Magazine *won the National Magazine Award for General Excellence in 2018 and 2019 and was nominated again this year.*

Ligaya Mishan

Nothing Sacred *and* An Assault on the Tongue *and* Interlopers

Nothing Sacred

In 1906, the Yokohama-born scholar Okakura Kakuzo published *The Book of Tea*," a brief tract for Western readers on *chanoyu*, the centuries-old, highly ritualized Japanese tea ceremony. He argued that the aestheticization of the humble act of drinking tea—"the adoration of the beautiful among the sordid facts of everyday existence"—must be understood as an ethos underlying an entire culture, from its arts and literature to the "delicate dishes" of its cuisine. His intent was to demystify, but his words had almost the opposite effect, heightening the sense of opacity surrounding both the Japanese approach to food and the island nation itself, which from the early 17th century until 1853 was almost completely closed off from the rest of the world.

More than fifty years after Kakuzo's treatise, the French literary theorist Roland Barthes, in his 1970 monograph *Empire of Signs*, described Japanese cooking in even more esoteric terms, arguing that it privileged the infinitesimal over Western abundance and was practiced "in a profound space which hierarchizes man, table and universe." Today, Westerners remain in thrall to this vision of *washoku*, traditional Japanese cuisine, as forbiddingly precise, each ingredient presented sparely and simply within the narrow window of ripeness in which it has fulfilled its destiny, to reflect the ephemerality of life. (Never mind that this philosophy has only ever applied to *kaiseki*, the most rarefied level of Japanese dining.)

So it's slightly disconcerting to find a bag of Safeway-brand jalapeño cheddar cheese bagels—surely not representative of the beautiful in any culture—in the kitchen at Hannyatou, a tiny sake bar in Seattle helmed by the chef Mutsuko Soma. Lumpy and craggy, the bagels are treated as a serious ingredient: pulverized, then calibrated with salt and *koji* (grains or legumes inoculated with spores of *Aspergillus oryzae*, phylogenetically kin to the mold that turns coagulated milk into blue cheese) and left to turn funky and fetid over weeks. Soma grew up north of Tokyo and came to the United States at the age of eighteen. She is one of several chefs outside Japan—expatriates, immigrants, and nisei and sansei (second- and third-generation descendants of immigrants), as well as gaijin (foreigners), drawn, often circuitously, to the cuisine—who have opened restaurants in the past few years that are pushing Japanese food in unexpected, even counterintuitive directions.

Purists might dispute the idiosyncratic unfolding of *kaiseki* at the haute Odo, half-hidden like a speakeasy at the back of a cocktail bar in the Flatiron district of Manhattan, where Hiroki Odo has been known to forsake tempura in the *agemono* (fried) course in favor of a French croquette heavy with béchamel. There will be quibbles over the *dashi* deployed at the Los Angeles breakfast and lunch spot Konbi, since the chefs, Akira Akuto and Nick Montgomery, leave the bonito shavings to steep and simmer longer than usual, privileging deep, brooding flavor over clarity. And downright bewilderment might greet the melting of Swiss cocoa powder into curry at Tatsu Aikawa's cheekily named Domo Alley-Gato bar in Austin, Texas.

Yet however maverick or heretical on the surface, the work of these chefs is rooted in Japanese technique. Soma treats those jalapeño cheddar cheese bagels as if they were soybeans en route to miso, and the paste they become achieves the same desirable tang of salty-sweet underground rot. Nor is there anything radical about these chefs' attention to seasonality and place, tenets at the heart of *washoku*. It just so happens that the place in question is not Japan but Paris, in the Eleventh Arrondissement, where the American chefs Robert Compagnon and Jessica Yang of Le Rigmarole have adopted Japanese yakitori as, Compagnon says, "a framing mechanism for whatever is in season"—tiny charred tomatoes with puckering skins, leeks daubed with cod-roe mayonnaise—and made variants on the sour-spicy condiment *yuzu kosho* out of French citrus fruits as they come in and out of harvest. In Brooklyn, Patch Troffer, an American chef of Japanese descent who last year took over the kitchen at the farm-to-table institution Marlow & Sons, supplants wasabi with horseradish root grown in upstate New York. "It's the food of the displaced and the diaspora," Troffer says. "What happens when you don't have the right ingredients"—a lesson he learned from his Japanese grandmother, who married a marine during the Korean War and wound up in South Carolina, making *dashi* out of canned clams and writing to Katagiri grocery in New York to beg for shipments of soy sauce and *umeboshi*.

Odo, a native of Kyushu, has had to adjust to the tastes and textures of American ingredients, as well as the bias of the American palate toward more flagrant flavors. The almost ascetic simplicity of classical *kaiseki* can be a cultural barrier; diners here "might feel like they're eating nothing," he says. (His American-born sous chef, Brian Saito, translated for us.) Foraged vegetables from Pennsylvania and upstate New York are delivered to the restaurant once a week. On a recent afternoon in April, they included ramps, whose garlicky punch would be considered too strong for dishes intended to accompany the tea ceremony in Kyoto, where Odo apprenticed in the cuisine. But "this is New York *kaiseki*," he says, so he commits to richness and pairs the ramps with wild Alaskan king salmon, an oily fish that is marinated in bourbon—instead of sake—chosen partly for aroma and partly for provenance: It's made nearby at Brooklyn's Kings County Distillery.

For Aikawa, who at the age of ten was whisked by his mother from Tokyo to a rural Texan commune, food tells the story of immigration and the meeting of cultures. "When I go to a barbecue, I bring a tub of rice," he says. At Kemuri Tatsu-ya, the half-*izakaya*, half-barbecue spot he and the chef Takuya Matsumoto opened in 2017, he categorizes brisket as lean or *toro*, borrowing from sushi vocabulary the designation of fatty tuna. "I want to treat brisket like sashimi—put it on a pedestal," he says. His take on Texas barbecue is straightforward ("out of respect"), but there's a touch of miso in the sauce, and he anoints yakitori skewers of chicken skin with garlic salt and lime to honor his Mexican neighbors.

Within this cohort, several chefs revel in the juxtaposition of Japanese and Italian cuisine—the latter long beloved in Japan, where it is fondly called *itameshi*, and where local chefs obsess over perfecting Neapolitan pizza with kerchief-thin, pliant crusts and cooking spaghetti to the exact second of al dente. Amid the parade of yakitori at Le Rigmarole, Compagnon and Yang present pasta that shows a clear debt to Italy while resembling no codified recipe; even their noodle shapes and names—cushioni, for ravioli that look like doll pillows; faniciulle, from the Italian word for maidens, elaborately folded like demure hoods—are the chefs' inventions. At Blackship in West Hollywood, which opened last December, the New York–raised Keiichi Kurobe presses shiso leaves into housemade noodles and garnishes dishes with them in lieu of basil. And a few miles away, in the Palms neighborhood, the best-known dish at Niki Nakayama's n/naka is the pasta that materializes in the middle of her otherwise recognizably Japanese *kaiseki*: derived from a genre of food called *yoshoku*—dishes borrowed from the West and freely altered with local ingredients to satisfy Japanese tastes—her spaghetti is glossed with *mentaiko* (pickled cod roe), as it might appear in Japan, then strewn with petals of razor-cut abalone and black truffles.

• • •

These dishes confound Western notions of what Japanese food should be, in part because diners who haven't grown up eating the cuisine often encounter it in the limited binary framework of high and low: austere sushi bars where the tab starts at three figures versus quick-turnover ramen shops, with few options in between. In adopting ingredients and techniques from other cultures, the new movement might even uncomfortably recall the Asian-fusion trend that started in the late eighties, which was spearheaded by chefs of European descent. But where those chefs filtered Japanese cuisine through a Western perspective, taking Japanese elements out of context and subsuming and bending them to their will, today's chefs are doing the opposite—viewing the West and its culinary traditions through a Japanese lens. As the thinking on diversity in America has evolved from the metaphor of a melting pot to a mosaic, in which each piece keeps its integrity while enriching the whole, the concept of fusion has become archaic, replaced by a more organic understanding of how food changes when people immigrate and have to adapt to the ingredients on hand.

By refuting rigid orthodoxy—and some inchoate standard of authenticity—these chefs remind us that Japanese cuisine is not some repository of edicts past but a lived and living tradition, as well as a pastiche, one that has borrowed unapologetically from other cultures throughout history, despite the country's long seclusion. Tempura, both dish and word, was a gift from the Portuguese, whose language was brought accidentally to Japan when, in 1543, three Portuguese sailors on a Chinese ship made contact in southern Japan. Jesuit missionaries followed, ultimately passing on a recipe for *peixinhos da horta* ("little fish of the garden"): green beans dusted in flour and deep-fried.

Curry arrived in the nineteenth century, during the Meiji era, from India via the British Royal Navy, when the subcontinent was part of the Raj. It was considered a Western dish and thus pricey until the late 1950s, when Japanese companies started selling instant curry that produced a dish milder and sweeter than either its British or Indian counterpart. Troffer modeled his curry after the best-selling S&B brand but with a lashing of heat; during the colder months, it's served at Marlow as it often appears in Japan, with pork katsu, a cutlet gilded in panko. Aikawa took his Texas version further afield, finding kinship to Louisiana gumbo and Mexican mole as he wrangled more than two dozen spices trying to strike the right balance, recalibrating by the gram in batch after batch. He serves his curry straight or amped up into a near chili, which is stuffed in a brioche bun and topped by a hot dog that's been patted down with panko and deep-fried so it suggests a hard-shell taco.

Ramen, likewise, has no time-honored history. According to George Solt's *The Untold History of Ramen* (2014), the dish is said to have first appeared in 1910 in Tokyo, under the name shina soba (Chinese noodles); almost vanished during World War II, when flour was strictly rationed and street vendors were banned; and revived with imports of wheat under the midcentury U.S. occupation—when Americans hoped to keep the population sated and therefore invulnerable to the promises of communism—to eventually flourish postwar as a hearty and cheap lunch. Of all Japanese foods, it might be "the most open, the most receptive to change and experimentation," the American-born chef Ivan Orkin wrote (with Chris Ying) in the 2013 cookbook *Ivan Ramen*.

Japanese chefs must typically apprentice for years before they get the opportunity to run their own kitchens, but Shigetoshi Nakamura won fame for his ramen shop in Tokyo while still in his twenties. Earlier this decade, he opened an eponymous shop on the Lower East Side of Manhattan, and this year he converted the storefront next door to Niche, focusing on *mazemen*, a version of ramen that largely dispenses with broth. In homage to the neighborhood's historic Jewish delis, Nakamura cold-smokes salmon in-house and drapes it over noodles in a loose sauce of cod roe and olive oil.

Even the California roll, often held up as an example of sacrilege, is believed to have been invented by a Japanese immigrant chef in the late 1960s, who, finding himself in Los Angeles without a reliable supply of bluefin tuna, swapped in an ingredient more plentiful on the West Coast, one with its own richness and heft: avocado.

• • •

As the contours and definitions of Japanese food have expanded, many chefs who are not of Japanese descent have also devoted themselves to this contemporary, freewheeling style, further collapsing and questioning the boundaries between the East and the West. Compagnon and Yang see their Paris restaurant as an ideal compact between cultures equally obsessed with mastery; as Compagnon says with a laugh, "France and Japan are the only two culinary cultures that respect each other while looking down on everyone else." (Some of today's most lauded French restaurants in Paris—including Les Enfants Rouge, Clown Bar, and Abri—are run by chefs from Japan, whose compatriots back in their native country are equally scrupulous in their devotion to French cuisine.) Compagnon came to Japanese food by first studying Japanese language and literature, as did Orkin, who grew up on New York's Long Island and lived in Tokyo for years. These chefs are quick to acknowledge their status as gaijin and students, not masters, of the dishes they've come to love. Orkin and Ying's forthcoming book's title, *The Gaijin Cookbook: Japanese Recipes from a Chef, Father, Eater, and Lifelong Outsider,* addresses it directly while Compagnon and Yang demur from calling Le Rigmarole a Japanese restaurant, speaking instead of a prevailing aesthetic and attention to technique.

For Troffer—whose half-Japanese mother didn't cook Japanese food often but always had nori and a pot of rice at the ready—there is no distance between East and West. "I'm being very clear to myself that I'm not doing Japanese food," he says. "I want to explore what it is to be Japanese American." The results reflect an attunement to the full range of possibility latent in each ingredient: He layers and deepens flavors by using dashi instead of water, "finding every little moment where an ingredient can slip its way in and add something," he says. Nevertheless, his grandmother was skeptical when he showed her a photograph of his *okonomiyaki*, which he calls a sour cabbage pancake on his menu in homage to how she used to make it, with little more than shredded cabbage, soy sauce, and flour. A fried egg is laid over it, in a flop. "She gave me the most disapproving eyebrow," he says.

Yet in Japan, this would hardly be heretical. Freedom is built into the very name of the dish; broken down into *okonomi* and *yaki*, it means whatever you want, thrown on the grill. And although the *okonomiyaki* most commonly found throughout Japan originated in Osaka, there are a number of regional variations, including the Hiroshima style, in which the dish is built one strata at a time: first batter, followed by cabbage, bean sprouts, pork, and noodles and, finally, yes, a fried egg, with the rest of the pancake shoveled over it and then flipped so the egg lands on top.

Sometimes Japanese visitors to Odo's restaurant in Manhattan tell him that they miss the milder flavors of traditional *kaiseki*. But the chef remains firm in his mission. The strict etiquette and radical simplicity of the formal meal are "not very welcoming to Americans," he says, which contradicts the Japanese principle of *omotenashi*, an elevated form of hospitality in which the guest's happiness is the focus of all action and thought. Even in Japan, *kaiseki* can intimidate diners, particularly of the younger generation. To ameliorate this, Zaiyu Hasegawa, the chef of Den, a modern *kaiseki* spot that opened in 2008 in Tokyo, begins each meal with *monaka*, an everyday Japanese treat of adzuki bean paste smeared between *mochi* wafers. While his filling is elevated, studded with foie gras and persimmon, its appearance is not: the dish arrives at the table as the kind of sandwich cookie sold at convenience stores, complete with a paper wrapper. Later comes a salad with carrots cut into the emoji with hearts for eyes and a box evoking Kentucky Fried Chicken that contains wings shucked of bone and stuffed with sticky rice, nestled on a bed of straw.

The food is thrillingly irreverent, so at first you don't notice how fastidious it is, how close to perfection. You laugh, and then you fall silent, the quick visual delight giving way to depths of flavor and something more elusive—a consciousness of food as past and present, at once memory and daily recurrence. The old ways meet the new—not in combat but in continuance.

An Assault on the Tongue

"Crack seed" is less a name than an imperative. In its broadest definition, it is a category of snack, beloved in Hawaii, in which fruit—plum, peach, apricot, cherry, mango, lemon—is dried and shriveled beyond recognition, salted, and sugared, simmered in a broth of sweet medicinal herbs, then served wet or left to shrivel again. But crack seed also refers, more singularly, to preserved fruit in which the stone heart has been split and left embedded in the flesh, a touch of bitterness that makes the taste stronger, keener—a shock to the tongue.

Note that it is never "cracked" seed but always present tense, like another island specialty: shave ice. This reflects the pidgin legacy of immigrants who came from Asia to work Hawaii's sugar-cane plantations in the mid-nineteenth century and had no time for the niceties of conjugation in their new language. There's an immediacy to it; spoken out loud, "crack seed" sounds like what it is, the hard nut breaking under the teeth. In poetic terms, the name is a spondee, two syllables in a row that claim equal force, disrupting the lilt of ordinary speech, like a command or a shout: Shut up, no way, get out.

The custom of eating preserved fruit was passed down by plantation workers from Zhongshan in the Pearl Delta of southern China, who started arriving in Hawaii—then a kingdom—as contract laborers in the mid-nineteenth century. As of the 2010 census, the majority of the state's population was of Asian ancestry; around 15 percent was at least part Chinese, three-quarters of whom can trace their family history back to those early émigrés. Transliterations and adaptations of Chinese words—some Cantonese, some from a Zhongshan dialect—are still used to describe crack seed: "*Kam cho*" signals an infusion of licorice; "*see mui*" is a catchall for dried fruit in general, although the original term refers specifically to the fruit of the *Prunus mume* tree, the drupe of which is commonly called a plum even though it's closer botanically to an apricot, plucked before it's ripe and bracingly sour. (In Japan, the same fruit is fermented to make *umeboshi*.)

But the epitome of crack seed, its quintessential preparation, is *li hing mui*, for which dried plums are plunged in a licorice-laced brew until they take on the root's resinous sweetness. Many calibrations are sold today across the islands, presealed in packets hanging by the checkout at chain pharmacies and grocery stores or, better, fished out of giant glass apothecary jars at one of the few remaining dedicated crack-seed shops. The plums might be sticky or desiccated; armed with seed or pitted; dyed a virulent *char siu* red that stains the fingers or left "white," really a pale rust, like the silt of a river run dry.

These are minor details, a quibble of personal preference. All formulas share the same goal: brazen, maddening flavor, with sweet, sour, and salty in anarchic revel, each taken to the extreme—or "to da max," as *kama'aina* (locals or, literally, "children of the land") might say. This is not so much taste as full-body sensation.

The texture, verging on jerky, can also be a challenge to outsiders. How to maneuver through the fruit's collapsed drapery of flesh? The seed is another complication; you're not supposed to eat it but suck on it as your teeth simultaneously tear at the meat, which resists like leather. The proper technique requires dexterity: it is work, and worth it, and afterward, you spit the seed into the palm of your hand—and then maybe lick the inside of the *li hing mui* bag, for one last hit of salty-sour-sweet.

Almost anything can become *li hing*, from ginger and lemon peel, which are actually whole lemons smashed flat, to "baby seed," a mulberry, to "footballs," a nickname for the so-called Chinese olives (from the *Canarium album* tree) that evoke their Mediterranean counterparts only in shape and sheen, tasting sweet and tart. And *li hing* is no longer confined to preserves: These days, the plums are sometimes ground to powder, which may be strewn over slices of pineapple and rubbed on baby-back ribs, infiltrating gummy bears and vinaigrettes, dusting the rims of margaritas and neon-bright domes of shave ice.

The people of Hawaii are not alone in the West in their devotion to this riotous confluence of flavors. Some 6,000 miles away—almost the distance from Zhongshan to Honolulu—Mexicans likewise anoint mangos and *raspados* (their shave ice) with a salsa known as *chamoy*, whose base is salted plum, amplified by chile. The Chinese voyaged there, too, migrating in the nineteenth century, although it took longer for their culinary notions to enter the culture; only in the past few decades did *chamoy*—the food historian Rachel Laudan has noted the name's etymological kinship to "*see mui*"—become common, first in the form of dried and salted fruit (*saladito*), and then as a ubiquitous condiment, salty-sour-sweet with a quaver of heat, wielded by street vendors and high-end chefs alike.

• • •

In Hawaii, crack seed remains a daily pleasure, but the number of shops dedicated to it have dwindled. One of the loveliest, simply named Crack Seed Store, lies just off the main strip of Kaimuki, a low-slung, unhurried Honolulu neighborhood. Kon Ping Young, sixty-nine, who's run the shop since 1979 with his wife, Fung Tang, is famous for skimming liquid from a jar of *li hing mui* and pouring it into an Icee, a kind of volcanic eruption in reverse and a triumph of salty and sour over sweet. He stocks the shelves with dozens of varieties of preserved fruit, from engorged orbs to near fossils. Some jars, pillaged by previous customers, stand empty save for the inky pickling dregs or with their walls like frosted panes in winter, etched in salt and sugar.

On a recent visit, I pointed to a jar of what looked like ossified plums, tucked away on a back shelf. "That's old-school," Young said. "Not so popular anymore." To be contrary, I bought a quarter-pound, and out on the sidewalk, I put one of the hard dark plums in my mouth. It was pure salt. No: it was salt as if I'd never properly understood the word, ageless and engulfing, the world's last gift to a drowning man. I kept chewing it, thrilled and horrified, until I came out the other side and the salt turned to cooling menthol. My mind felt clean and blank, as if my memory had been wiped; as if I had exhausted the possibilities of taste and was left with nothing but the longing for another bite.

Interlopers

In the hilly Boaco region of central Nicaragua, the turmeric plants on Celia Dávila and Gonzalo González's farm stand over four feet tall—thriving giants, although as natives of South and Southeast Asia, they're actually newcomers to this land. Coffee once ruled these fields, but as its price has grown unstable, smallholder farmers like Dávila and González, fifty-two and sixty-five, respectively, have had to turn to alternative crops, among them this strange arrival that yields knobby rhizomes of shocking orange flesh, rarely eaten unadulterated; instead, the underground stems are dried and pulverized into a musky powder with a throb of bitterness, which is most widely recognized worldwide as the earthy base note and color in many Indian dishes. Nicaraguans have no particular use for the spice, which has yet to make inroads in the local diet. But Americans do, having suddenly and belatedly awakened to turmeric's health benefits, some 3,000 years after they were first set down in the Atharva Veda, one of Hinduism's foundational sacred texts.

It's a story at once old and new, a latter-day spice route making unexpected connections between the grandmother in India, stirring turmeric into warm milk for a sniffily child; the Goop acolyte in California, sipping an après-yoga prepackaged turmeric "elixir," whose makers extol the "body harmonizing" powers of the spice's key chemical compound, curcumin; and Dávila wielding a pickax in rural Nicaragua. She is not alone in her embrace of this new harvest: farmers in Costa Rica, Hawaii, and even Minnesota are planting turmeric with an eye on an expanding market. Nor is turmeric the only spice to flourish far from home. The food writer Max Falkowitz has documented the work of small-scale farmers in Guatemala, mostly poor and of indigenous descent, who now grow more than half the world's cardamom, a crop that belonged for millenniums to India and was brought to the Central American cloud forests by a German immigrant in the early twentieth century. Cardamom is one of the most expensive spices—so valuable that all of it departs Guatemala for sale elsewhere. As with turmeric in Nicaragua, its absence is hardly registered by local cooks, to whom the spice is an interloper.

Spices were among the first engines of globalization, not in the modern sense of a world engulfed by ever-larger corporations but in the ways that we began to become aware, desirous even, of cultures other than our own. Such desire, unchecked, once led to colonialism. After Dutch merchants nearly tripled the price of black pepper, the British countered in 1600 by founding the East India Company, a precursor to modern multinationals and the first step toward the Raj. In the following decades, the Dutch sought a monopoly on cloves, which once had grown nowhere but the tropical islands of Ternate and Tidore in what is today Indonesia, and then in 1652 introduced the scorched-earth policy known as extirpation, felling and burning tens of thousands of clove trees. This was both an ecological disaster and horribly effective: For more than a century, the Dutch kept supplies low and prices high, until a Frenchman (surnamed, in one of history's inside jokes, Poivre, or "pepper") arranged a commando operation to smuggle out a few clove-tree seedlings. Among their ultimate destinations were Zanzibar and Pemba, off the coast of East Africa, which until the mid-twentieth century dominated the world's clove market.

The craving for spices still brings the risk of exploitation, both economically, as farmers in the developing world see only a sliver of the profits, and in the form of cultural appropriation. In the West, we're prone to taking what isn't ours and acting as if we discovered it, conveniently forgetting its history and context. Or else we reduce it to caricature, cooing over turmeric-stained golden lattes while invoking the mystic wisdom of the East. At the same time, a world without borrowing and learning from our neighbors would be pallid and parochial—a world, in effect, without spice.

• • •

Spices are luxuries, ornamental to our lives. They provide little nutritional value and, beyond a few medicinal applications, are entirely unnecessary to survival. What they offer is an escape from tedium—a reason to take joy in food beyond the baseline requirements of existence. Where herbs are often chosen to complement and flatter the ingredients they adorn, spices call attention to themselves, transforming and sometimes even usurping a dish, so it becomes a mere vehicle and excuse for spice itself. Roast spices in a pan before cooking with them, as is done in India, and they seize the air, the fragrance like a liberated genie.

There's righteous bemusement in India over newly converted Americans proselytizing on behalf of turmeric. For centuries, the West ignored it. Other spices from the East were coveted and fetishized, launching a thousand ships, notably cinnamon, nutmeg, black pepper, and cloves. But turmeric languished, overshadowed by its cousin ginger, punchy and sweet, and coming off the worse in its superficial kinship to lofty saffron, the world's most expensive spice, although the two share little beyond the ability to turn whatever they touch the color of gold. (This hasn't stopped spice sellers and cooks throughout the ages from trying to pass off turmeric as a cheaper saffron; even its scientific name, curcuma, comes from an Arabic word that originally meant saffron, *kurkum*, a wistful reminder of its status, in Western eyes, as a dupe.) Meanwhile, *haldi*, "turmeric" in Hindi, manifests in over 95 percent of Indian dishes, according to the Delhi-based food writer Marryam H. Reshii, who writes in *The Flavour of Spice* (2017) that its absence in cooking "is often considered blasphemous or at least idiosyncratic."

Then again, the West has always been late to the party, sidelined geographically from the bounty of the East. Many of the spices used in Western cooking come from the seeds, bark, roots, rhizomes, flowers, and fruits of plants born in Asia. Traders brought cloves north from Southeast Asia to Han dynasty China, where courtiers were not allowed to speak to the emperor unless their breath had been purified by cloves (known as "chicken-tongue spice"), and to arid Arabia, where in the 1970s cloves were excavated, still intact, from a ceramic pot in a house dating back to 1750 BCE in the Babylonian city of Terqa in modern Syria.

Not until Greek and Roman antiquity did the West learn of these treasures, as Arab traders became the intermediaries between the hemispheres. They tried to keep the origins of spices shrouded in mystery to prevent customers from finding or planting them on their own; in the fifth century BCE the Greek historian Herodotus reported tales of cassia gathered from a lake guarded by "winged animals, much resembling bats, which screech horribly, and are very valiant," and of cinnamon sticks knocked out of the nests of enormous birds, both in unknown Arabian locales. To the ancient Greeks, spices were "the product of an exceptional union between the earth and the fire of the sun," the Belgian historian Marcel Detienne writes in *The Gardens of Adonis: Spices in Greek Mythology* (1972)—a literal embodiment of their often tropical origins. They served as emblems of all that lay beyond the known world, be that defined in terms of geographic distance or the more nebulous passage between life and death; the Greeks, Detienne argues, used spices "to mediate between the near and the far-away and to link the above and the below," notably in funeral rites and sacred devotions. In one version of the phoenix myth, when death finally looms after a thousand years, the bird readies a nest of cinnamon and frankincense to help ensure its resurrection. During the Roman Empire, Nero burned a year's supply of cinnamon at the funeral of his second wife, Poppaea, perhaps regretting that, as recorded by early historians, he himself had murdered her. (On a more earthly note, spices were also employed as tools of seduction—Caesar was reportedly beguiled by the cinnamon wafting from Cleopatra's hair—and served practical purposes, mitigating the salt in preserved foods and masking bad breath and odors from poor sanitation.)

The Romans eventually figured out how to bypass the middlemen to find the sources of those spices themselves. Their yearning for these potent scents and flavors drove them into the monsoon winds—an advancement in navigation skills—toward India and its cache of black pepper. In the first century CE, pepper was "bought by weight like gold or silver," as recorded by the Roman historian Pliny the Elder, who worried that the empire would squander its wealth on such spices. At its height, a pound of pepper cost half a month's wages; Alaric the Visigoth, on the verge of sacking Rome in 410 CE, exacted 3,000 pounds of black pepper as part of the city's ransom.

Pepper's value was sustained in Europe throughout the Middle Ages, as landlords accepted peppercorns as rent and daughters were married off with peppercorn dowries. Only in the mid-seventeenth century did Europeans begin to turn away from spices, in part because they had become more readily accessible and lost their ability to confer status on those wealthy enough to afford them but also, as the historian T. Sarah Peterson has argued, because of advances in science and medicine and a new skepticism toward spices' supposed occult capabilities. The historian W. E. Mead, writing in 1931 in *The English Medieval Feast*, dismissed Middle Age diners as "coarse eaters" with palates dulled from overexposure to spices "by which the most innocent meats and fruits were doctored and disguised until the cook himself could hardly distinguish from the taste what had entered into their composition." In the meantime, in the regions of the world where spices were native, they simply continued to be part of the landscape and culture, subjects of neither idolatry nor condemnation—until Europeans brought their new, more minimalist culinary standards to the countries they colonized, suppressing indigenous cuisines and the very ingredients they once fought wars over.

• • •

In Nicaragua, Dávila and González leave their turmeric plants in the fields for two years instead of the typical six to twelve months, and that longer gestation—abetted by partial shade instead of direct sunlight—appears to have boosted the amount of curcumin in the rhizomes as well as deepened their orange hue. Reshii's *The Flavour of Spice* reports a high of 6.5 percent curcumin in turmeric from Kerala, India, compared to an average of 3 to 3.5 percent in the crop from nearby Tamil Nadu; Nicaraguan turmeric has registered at 7.9 percent. It's ideal for a market primarily interested in the spice for its curative rather than culinary properties, even as the health benefits of curcumin remain unproven beyond a few preliminary clinical trials that suggest its potential as an anti-inflammatory and an antioxidant.

Dávila and González's current crop is still in the ground, but the harvest of fellow farmers in their cooperative is available in the United States through Burlap & Barrel, a spice purveyor based in New York. Ethan Frisch, one of the company's founders, visited the couple last spring and was intrigued to find that they had no plans to use their turmeric in the kitchen. He asked if they might try the leaves, if not the spice itself, the way they use banana leaves, to wrap tamales. Eyebrows were raised. A crazy notion, to change the way things have been done for hundreds of years.

It may take time, but the spice could still win converts here. Consider what happened to nutmeg, which once grew only on the Banda Islands of modern Indonesia and now flourishes on Grenada in the Caribbean. In the early seventeenth century, the Dutch slaughtered Banda's indigenous inhabitants to gain control of the spice; out of 15,000 natives, barely 1,000 remained. In London, nutmeg was marked up at more than 60,000 times its Banda price. It was the Frenchman Poivre, again, who smuggled seedlings to the West, where the spice eventually gained a second home in Grenada, nearly 12,000 miles away. Today, it suffuses jams, cakes, ice cream, the batter for fried fish, and a syrup for basting chicken. It even holds pride of place on the country's flag.

Note, however, that nutmeg is considered an intoxicant and is classified by some Muslim jurists as *haram*, as it's laced with myristicin, which has hallucinogenic properties, and safrole, a chemical sometimes used in synthesizing the psychedelic MDMA. Malcolm X wrote in his 1964 autobiography of getting high off nutmeg while in prison in Massachusetts in the 1940s—"a penny matchbox full of nutmeg had the kick of three or four reefers"—and the spice was reportedly banned from New Jersey state prison kitchens at one point. So the connections multiply: from seventeenth-century Dutch colonialists to the Black Panthers of 1960s America and farmers in balmy Grenada—even to the frantic crush and heave of Manhattan, a bit of swampland once called New Amsterdam, which those same Dutchmen saw fit to pawn off on the British in 1667 in exchange for Run, one of the nutmeg-producing Banda Islands and so tiny it's barely visible on a world map. The Dutch didn't care—Run had nutmeg, after all. They thought they'd got the better deal.

New York Times Magazine

WINNER—PUBLIC INTEREST

"Black Americans have . . . been, and continue to be, foundational to the idea of American freedom," writes Nikole Hannah-Jones in this essay, her introduction to "The 1619 Project." "More than any other group in this country's history, we have served, generation after generation, in an overlooked but vital role: it is we who have been the perfecters of this democracy." It is this spirit that courses through "The 1619 Project," a special issue of the New York Times Magazine *that sought, in the words of the editors, "to reframe the country's history by placing the consequences of slavery and the contributions of black Americans at the very center of our national narrative." Now a* Times Magazine *staff writer, Hannah-Jones was nominated in Public Interest in 2015 for "Segregation Now . . . ," published by* The Atlantic, *and won the 2017 award for her* Times Magazine *article "Worlds Apart." The* Times Magazine *won five Ellies in 2020, including the award for General Excellence.*

Nikole Hannah-Jones

Our Democracy's Founding Ideals Were False When They Were Written. Black Americans Have Fought to Make Them True.

My dad always flew an American flag in our front yard. The blue paint on our two-story house was perennially chipping; the fence, or the rail by the stairs, or the front door, existed in a perpetual state of disrepair, but that flag always flew pristine. Our corner lot, which had been redlined by the federal government, was along the river that divided the black side from the white side of our Iowa town. At the edge of our lawn, high on an aluminum pole, soared the flag, which my dad would replace as soon as it showed the slightest tatter.

My dad was born into a family of sharecroppers on a white plantation in Greenwood, Miss., where black people bent over cotton from can't-see-in-the-morning to can't-see-at-night, just as their enslaved ancestors had done not long before. The Mississippi of my dad's youth was an apartheid state that subjugated its near-majority black population through breathtaking acts of violence. White residents in Mississippi lynched more black people than those in any other state in the country, and the white people in my dad's home county lynched more black residents than those in any other county in Mississippi, often for such "crimes" as entering a room occupied by white women, bumping into a white girl or trying to start a sharecroppers union. My dad's mother, like all the black people in Greenwood, could not vote, use the public library, or find work other than toiling in the cotton fields or toiling in white people's houses. So in the 1940s, she packed up her few belongings and her three small children and joined the flood of black Southerners fleeing north. She got off the Illinois Central Railroad in Waterloo, Iowa, only to have her hopes of the mythical Promised Land shattered when she learned that Jim Crow did not end at the Mason-Dixon line.

Grandmama, as we called her, found a house in a segregated black neighborhood on the city's east side and then found the work that was considered black women's work no matter where black women lived—cleaning white people's houses. Dad, too, struggled to find promise in this land. In 1962, at age seventeen, he signed up for the army. Like many young men, he joined in hopes of escaping poverty. But he went into the military for another reason as well, a reason common to black men: Dad hoped that if he served his country, his country might finally treat him as an American.

The army did not end up being his way out. He was passed over for opportunities, his ambition stunted. He would be discharged under murky circumstances and then labor in a series of service jobs for the rest of his life. Like all the black men and women in my family, he believed in hard work, but like all the black men and women in my family, no matter how hard he worked, he never got ahead.

So when I was young, that flag outside our home never made sense to me. How could this black man, having seen firsthand the way his country abused black Americans, how it refused to treat us as full citizens, proudly fly its banner? I didn't understand his patriotism. It deeply embarrassed me.

I had been taught, in school, through cultural osmosis, that the flag wasn't really ours, that our history as a people began with enslavement and that we had contributed little to this great nation. It seemed that the closest thing black Americans could have to cultural pride was to be found in our vague connection to Africa, a place we had never been. That my dad felt so much honor in being an American felt like a marker of his degradation, his acceptance of our subordination.

Like most young people, I thought I understood so much, when in fact I understood so little. My father knew exactly what he was doing when he raised that flag. He knew that our people's contributions to building the richest and most powerful nation in the world were indelible, that the United States simply would not exist without us.

In August 1619, just twelve years after the English settled Jamestown, Va., one year before the Puritans landed at Plymouth Rock, and some 157 years before the English colonists even decided they wanted to form their own country, the Jamestown colonists bought twenty to thirty enslaved Africans from English pirates. The pirates had stolen them from a Portuguese slave ship that had forcibly taken them from what is now the country of Angola. Those men and women who came ashore on that August day were the beginning of American slavery. They were among the 12.5 million Africans who would be kidnapped from their homes and brought in chains across the Atlantic Ocean in the largest forced migration in human history until the Second World War. Almost two million did not survive the grueling journey, known as the Middle Passage.

Before the abolishment of the international slave trade, 400,000 enslaved Africans would be sold into America. Those individuals and their descendants transformed the lands to which they'd been brought into some of the most successful colonies in the British Empire. Through backbreaking labor, they cleared the land across the Southeast. They taught the colonists to grow rice. They grew and picked the cotton that at the height of slavery was the nation's most valuable commodity, accounting for half of all American exports and 66 percent of the world's supply. They built the plantations of George Washington, Thomas Jefferson, and James Madison, sprawling properties that today attract thousands of visitors from across the globe captivated by the history of the world's greatest democracy. They laid the foundations of the White House and the Capitol, even placing with their unfree hands the Statue of Freedom atop the Capitol dome. They lugged the heavy wooden tracks of the railroads that crisscrossed the South and that helped take the cotton they picked to the northern textile mills, fueling the Industrial Revolution. They built vast fortunes for white people North and South—at one time, the second-richest man in the nation was a Rhode Island "slave trader." Profits from black people's stolen labor helped the young nation pay off its war debts and financed some of our most prestigious universities. It was the relentless buying, selling, insuring, and financing of their bodies and the products of their labor that made Wall Street a thriving banking, insurance, and trading sector and New York City the financial capital of the world.

But it would be historically inaccurate to reduce the contributions of black people to the vast material wealth created by our bondage. Black Americans have also been, and continue to be, foundational to the idea of American freedom. More than any other group in this country's history, we have served, generation after generation, in an overlooked but vital role: it is we who have been the perfecters of this democracy.

The United States is a nation founded on both an ideal and a lie. Our Declaration of Independence, approved on July 4, 1776, proclaims that "all men are created equal" and "endowed by their Creator with certain unalienable rights." But the white men who drafted those words did not believe them to be true for the hundreds of thousands of black people in their midst. "Life, Liberty and the pursuit of Happiness" did not apply to fully one-fifth of the country. Yet despite being violently denied the freedom and justice promised to all, black Americans believed fervently in the American creed. Through centuries of black resistance and protest, we have helped the country live up to its founding ideals. And not only for ourselves—black rights struggles paved the way for every other rights struggle, including women's and gay rights, immigrant and disability rights.

Without the idealistic, strenuous and patriotic efforts of black Americans, our democracy today would most likely look very different—it might not be a democracy at all.

The very first person to die for this country in the American Revolution was a black man who himself was not free. Crispus Attucks was a fugitive from slavery, yet he gave his life for a new nation in which his own people would not enjoy the liberties laid out in the Declaration for another century. In every war this nation has waged since that first one, black Americans have fought—today we are the most likely of all racial groups to serve in the United States military.

My father, one of those many black Americans who answered the call, knew what it would take me years to understand: that the year 1619 is as important to the American story as 1776. That black Americans, as much as those men cast in alabaster in the nation's capital, are this nation's true "founding fathers." And that no people has a greater claim to that flag than us.

• • •

In June 1776, Thomas Jefferson sat at his portable writing desk in a rented room in Philadelphia and penned these words: "We hold these truths to be self-evident, that all men are created equal, that they are endowed by their Creator with certain unalienable

Rights, that among these are Life, Liberty and the pursuit of Happiness." For the last 243 years, this fierce assertion of the fundamental and natural rights of humankind to freedom and self-governance has defined our global reputation as a land of liberty. As Jefferson composed his inspiring words, however, a teenage boy who would enjoy none of those rights and liberties waited nearby to serve at his master's beck and call. His name was Robert Hemings, and he was the half brother of Jefferson's wife, born to Martha Jefferson's father and a woman he owned. It was common for white enslavers to keep their half-black children in slavery. Jefferson had chosen Hemings, from among about 130 enslaved people that worked on the forced-labor camp he called Monticello, to accompany him to Philadelphia and ensure his every comfort as he drafted the text making the case for a new democratic republic based on the individual rights of men.

At the time, one-fifth of the population within the thirteen colonies struggled under a brutal system of slavery unlike anything that had existed in the world before. Chattel slavery was not conditional but racial. It was heritable and permanent, not temporary, meaning generations of black people were born into it and passed their enslaved status onto their children. Enslaved people were not recognized as human beings but as property that could be mortgaged, traded, bought, sold, used as collateral, given as a gift, and disposed of violently. Jefferson's fellow white colonists knew that black people were human beings, but they created a network of laws and customs, astounding for both their precision and cruelty, that ensured that enslaved people would never be treated as such. As the abolitionist William Goodell wrote in 1853, "If any thing founded on falsehood might be called a science, we might add the system of American slavery to the list of the strict sciences."

Enslaved people could not legally marry. They were barred from learning to read and restricted from meeting privately in groups. They had no claim to their own children, who could be bought, sold, and traded away from them on auction blocks alongside furniture and cattle or behind storefronts that advertised "Negroes for Sale." Enslavers and the courts did not honor kinship ties to mothers, siblings, cousins. In most courts, they had no legal standing. Enslavers could rape or murder their property without legal consequence. Enslaved people could own nothing, will nothing, and inherit nothing. They were legally tortured, including by those working for Jefferson himself. They could be worked to death, and often were, in order to produce the highest profits for the white people who owned them.

Yet in making the argument against Britain's tyranny, one of the colonists' favorite rhetorical devices was to claim that *they* were the slaves—to Britain. For this duplicity, they faced burning criticism both at home and abroad. As Samuel Johnson, an English writer and Tory opposed to American independence, quipped, "How is it that we hear the loudest yelps for liberty among the drivers of Negroes?"

Conveniently left out of our founding mythology is the fact that one of the primary reasons some of the colonists decided to declare their independence from Britain was because they wanted to protect the institution of slavery. By 1776, Britain had grown deeply conflicted over its role in the barbaric institution that had reshaped the Western Hemisphere. In London, there were growing calls to abolish the slave trade. This would have upended the economy of the colonies, in both the North and the South. The wealth and prominence that allowed Jefferson, at just thirty-three, and the other founding fathers to believe they could successfully break off from one of the mightiest empires in the world came from the dizzying profits generated by chattel slavery. In other words, we may never have revolted against Britain if some of the founders had not understood that slavery empowered them to do so, nor if they had not believed that independence was required in order to ensure that slavery would continue. It is not incidental that ten of this nation's first twelve presidents were enslavers, and some might argue that this nation was founded not as a democracy but as a slavocracy.

Jefferson and the other founders were keenly aware of this hypocrisy. And so in Jefferson's original draft of the Declaration of Independence, he tried to argue that it wasn't the colonists' fault. Instead, he blamed the king of England for forcing the institution of slavery on the unwilling colonists and called the trafficking in human beings a crime. Yet neither Jefferson nor most of the founders intended to abolish slavery, and in the end, they struck the passage.

There is no mention of slavery in the final Declaration of Independence. Similarly, eleven years later, when it came time to draft the Constitution, the framers carefully constructed a document that preserved and protected slavery without ever using the word. In the texts in which they were making the case for freedom to the world, they did not want to explicitly enshrine their hypocrisy, so they sought to hide it. The Constitution contains eighty-four clauses. Six deal directly with the enslaved and their enslavement, as the historian David Waldstreicher has written, and five more hold implications for slavery. The Constitution protected the "property" of those who enslaved black people, prohibited the federal government from intervening to end the importation of enslaved Africans for a term of twenty years, allowed Congress to mobilize the militia to put down insurrections by the enslaved, and forced states that had outlawed slavery to turn over enslaved people who had run away seeking refuge. Like many others, the writer and abolitionist Samuel Bryan called out the deceit, saying of the Constitution, "The words are dark and ambiguous; such as no plain man of common sense would have used, [and] are evidently chosen to conceal from Europe, that in this enlightened country, the practice of slavery has its advocates among men in the highest stations."

With independence, the founding fathers could no longer blame slavery on Britain. The sin became this nation's own, and so, too, the need to cleanse it. The shameful paradox of continuing chattel slavery in a nation founded on individual freedom, scholars today assert, led to a hardening of the racial caste system. This ideology, reinforced not just by laws but by racist science and literature, maintained that black people were subhuman, a belief that allowed white Americans to live with their betrayal. By the early 1800s, according to the legal historians Leland B. Ware, Robert J. Cottrol, and Raymond T. Diamond, white Americans, whether they engaged in slavery or not, "had a considerable psychological as well as economic investment in the doctrine of black inferiority." While liberty was the inalienable right of the people who would be considered white, enslavement and subjugation became the natural station of people who had any discernible drop of "black" blood.

The Supreme Court enshrined this thinking in the law in its 1857 *Dred Scott* decision, ruling that black people, whether enslaved or free, came from a "slave" race. This made them inferior to white people and, therefore, incompatible with American democracy. Democracy was for citizens, and the "Negro race," the court ruled, was "a separate class of persons," which the founders had "not regarded as a portion of the people or citizens of the Government" and had "no rights which a white man was bound to respect." This belief, that black people were not merely enslaved but were a slave race, became the root of the endemic racism that we still cannot purge from this nation to this day. If black people could not ever be citizens, if they were a caste apart from all other humans, then they did not require the rights bestowed by the Constitution, and the "we" in the "We the People" was not a lie.

• • •

On August 14, 1862, a mere five years after the nation's highest courts declared that no black person could be an American citizen, President Abraham Lincoln called a group of five esteemed free black men to the White House for a meeting. It was one of the few times that black people had ever been invited to the White House as guests. The Civil War had been raging for more than a year, and black abolitionists, who had been increasingly pressuring Lincoln to end slavery, must have felt a sense of great anticipation and pride.

The war was not going well for Lincoln. Britain was contemplating whether to intervene on the Confederacy's behalf, and Lincoln, unable to draw enough new white volunteers for the war, was forced to reconsider his opposition to allowing black Americans to fight for their own liberation. The president was weighing a proclamation that threatened to emancipate all enslaved people in the states that had seceded from the Union if the states did not end the rebellion. The proclamation would also allow the formerly enslaved to join the Union army and fight against their former "masters." But Lincoln worried about what the consequences of this radical step would be. Like many white Americans, he opposed slavery as a cruel system at odds with American ideals, but he also opposed black equality. He believed that free black people were a "troublesome presence" incompatible with a democracy intended only for white people. "Free them, and make them politically and socially our equals?" he had said four years earlier. "My own feelings will not admit of this; and if mine would, we well know that those of the great mass of white people will not."

That August day, as the men arrived at the White House, they were greeted by the towering Lincoln and a man named James Mitchell, who eight days before had been given the title of a newly created position called the commissioner of emigration. This was to be his first assignment. After exchanging a few niceties, Lincoln got right to it. He informed his guests that he had gotten Congress to appropriate funds to ship black people, once freed, to another country.

"Why should they leave this country? This is, perhaps, the first question for proper consideration," Lincoln told them. "You and we are different races . . . Your race suffer very greatly, many of them, by living among us, while ours suffer from your presence. In a word, we suffer on each side."

You can imagine the heavy silence in that room, as the weight of what the president said momentarily stole the breath of these five black men. It was 243 years to the month since the first of their ancestors had arrived on these shores, before Lincoln's family, long before most of the white people insisting that this was not their country. The Union had not entered the war to end slavery but to keep the South from splitting off, yet black men had signed up to fight. Enslaved people were fleeing their forced-labor camps, which we like to call plantations, trying to join the effort, serving as spies, sabotaging confederates, taking up arms for his cause as well as their own. And now Lincoln was blaming them for the war. "Although many men engaged on either side do not care for you one way or the other . . . without the institution of slavery and the colored race as a basis, the war could not have an existence," the president told them. "It is better for us both, therefore, to be separated."

As Lincoln closed the remarks, Edward Thomas, the delegation's chairman, informed the president, perhaps curtly, that they would consult on his proposition. "Take your full time," Lincoln said. "No hurry at all."

Nearly three years after that White House meeting, Gen. Robert E. Lee surrendered at Appomattox. By summer, the Civil War was over, and four million black Americans were suddenly free. Contrary to Lincoln's view, most were not inclined to leave, agreeing with the sentiment of a resolution against black colonization put forward at a convention of black leaders in New York some decades before: "This is our home, and this our country. Beneath its sod lie the bones of our fathers. . . . Here we were born, and here we will die."

That the formerly enslaved did not take up Lincoln's offer to abandon these lands is an astounding testament to their belief in this nation's founding ideals. As W. E. B. Du Bois wrote, "Few men ever worshiped Freedom with half such unquestioning faith as did the American Negro for two centuries." Black Americans had long called for universal equality and believed, as the abolitionist Martin Delany said, "that God has made of one blood all the nations that dwell on the face of the earth." Liberated by war, then, they did not seek vengeance on their oppressors as Lincoln and so many other white Americans feared. They did the opposite. During this nation's brief period of Reconstruction, from 1865 to 1877, formerly enslaved people zealously engaged with the democratic process. With federal troops tempering widespread white violence, black Southerners started branches of the Equal Rights League—one of the nation's first human rights organizations—to fight discrimination and organize voters; they headed in droves to the polls, where they placed other formerly enslaved people into seats that their enslavers had once held. The South, for the first time in the history of this country, began to resemble a democracy, with black Americans elected to local, state and federal offices. Some sixteen black men served in Congress—including Hiram Revels of Mississippi, who became the first black man elected to the Senate. (Demonstrating just how brief this period would be, Revels, along with Blanche Bruce, would go from being the first black man elected to the last for nearly a hundred years, until Edward Brooke of Massachusetts took office in 1967.) More than 600 black men served in Southern state legislatures and hundreds more in local positions.

These black officials joined with white Republicans, some of whom came down from the North, to write the most egalitarian state constitutions the South had ever seen. They helped pass more equitable tax legislation and laws that prohibited discrimination in public transportation, accommodation, and housing. Perhaps their biggest achievement was the establishment of that most democratic of American institutions: the public school. Public education effectively did not exist in the South before

Reconstruction. The white elite sent their children to private schools, while poor white children went without an education. But newly freed black people, who had been prohibited from learning to read and write during slavery, were desperate for an education. So black legislators successfully pushed for a universal, state-funded system of schools—not just for their own children but for white children, too. Black legislators also helped pass the first compulsory education laws in the region. Southern children, black and white, were now required to attend schools like their Northern counterparts. Just five years into Reconstruction, every Southern state had enshrined the right to a public education for all children into its constitution. In some states, like Louisiana and South Carolina, small numbers of black and white children, briefly, attended schools together.

Led by black activists and a Republican Party pushed left by the blatant recalcitrance of white Southerners, the years directly after slavery saw the greatest expansion of human and civil rights this nation would ever see. In 1865, Congress passed the Thirteenth Amendment, making the United States one of the last nations in the Americas to outlaw slavery. The following year, black Americans, exerting their new political power, pushed white legislators to pass the Civil Rights Act, the nation's first such law and one of the most expansive pieces of civil rights legislation Congress has ever passed. It codified black American citizenship for the first time, prohibited housing discrimination, and gave all Americans the right to buy and inherit property, make and enforce contracts, and seek redress from courts. In 1868, Congress ratified the Fourteenth Amendment, ensuring citizenship to any person born in the United States. Today, thanks to this amendment, every child born here to a European, Asian, African, Latin American, or Middle Eastern immigrant gains automatic citizenship. The Fourteenth Amendment also, for the first time, constitutionally guaranteed equal protection under the law. Ever since, nearly all other marginalized groups have used the

Fourteenth Amendment in their fights for equality (including the recent successful arguments before the Supreme Court on behalf of same-sex marriage). Finally, in 1870, Congress passed the Fifteenth Amendment, guaranteeing the most critical aspect of democracy and citizenship—the right to vote—to all men regardless of "race, color, or previous condition of servitude."

For this fleeting moment known as Reconstruction, the majority in Congress seemed to embrace the idea that out of the ashes of the Civil War, we could create the multiracial democracy that black Americans envisioned even if our founding fathers did not.

But it would not last.

Antiblack racism runs in the very DNA of this country, as does the belief, so well articulated by Lincoln, that black people are the obstacle to national unity. The many gains of Reconstruction were met with fierce white resistance throughout the South, including unthinkable violence against the formerly enslaved, wide-scale voter suppression, electoral fraud, and even, in some extreme cases, the overthrow of democratically elected biracial governments. Faced with this unrest, the federal government decided that black people were the cause of the problem and that for unity's sake, it would leave the white South to its own devices. In 1877, President Rutherford B. Hayes, in order to secure a compromise with Southern Democrats that would grant him the presidency in a contested election, agreed to pull federal troops from the South. With the troops gone, white Southerners quickly went about eradicating the gains of Reconstruction. The systemic white suppression of black life was so severe that this period between the 1880s and the 1920s and '30s became known as the Great Nadir, or the second slavery. Democracy would not return to the South for nearly a century.

White Southerners of all economic classes, on the other hand, thanks in significant part to the progressive policies and laws black people had championed, experienced substantial improvement in their lives even as they forced black people back into a quasi slavery. As Waters McIntosh, who had been enslaved in South Carolina, lamented, "It was the poor white man who was freed by the war, not the Negroes."

• • •

Georgia pines flew past the windows of the Greyhound bus carrying Isaac Woodard home to Winnsboro, S.C. After serving four years in the army in World War II, where Woodard had earned a battle star, he was given an honorable discharge earlier that day at Camp Gordon and was headed home to meet his wife. When the bus stopped at a small drugstore an hour outside Atlanta, Woodard got into a brief argument with the white driver after asking if he could use the restroom. About half an hour later, the driver stopped again and told Woodard to get off the bus. Crisp in his uniform, Woodard stepped from the stairs and saw the police waiting for him. Before he could speak, one of the officers struck him in his head with a billy club, beating him so badly that he fell unconscious. The blows to Woodard's head were so severe that when he woke in a jail cell the next day, he could not see. The beating occurred just four and a half hours after his military discharge. At twenty-six, Woodard would never see again.

There was nothing unusual about Woodard's horrific maiming. It was part of a wave of systemic violence deployed against black Americans after Reconstruction, in both the North and the South. As the egalitarian spirit of post–Civil War America evaporated under the desire for national reunification, black Americans, simply by existing, served as a problematic reminder of this nation's failings. White America dealt with this inconvenience by constructing a savagely enforced system of racial apartheid that excluded black people almost entirely from mainstream

American life—a system so grotesque that Nazi Germany would later take inspiration from it for its own racist policies.

Despite the guarantees of equality in the Fourteenth Amendment, the Supreme Court's landmark *Plessy v. Ferguson* decision in 1896 declared that the racial segregation of black Americans was constitutional. With the blessing of the nation's highest court and no federal will to vindicate black rights, starting in the late 1800s, Southern states passed a series of laws and codes meant to make slavery's racial caste system permanent by denying black people political power, social equality, and basic dignity. They passed literacy tests to keep black people from voting and created all-white primaries for elections. Black people were prohibited from serving on juries or testifying in court against a white person. South Carolina prohibited white and black textile workers from using the same doors. Oklahoma forced phone companies to segregate phone booths. Memphis had separate parking spaces for black and white drivers. Baltimore passed an ordinance outlawing black people from moving onto a block more than half white and white people from moving onto a block more than half black. Georgia made it illegal for black and white people to be buried next to one another in the same cemetery. Alabama barred black people from using public libraries that their own tax dollars were paying for. Black people were expected to jump off the sidewalk to let white people pass and call all white people by an honorific, though they received none no matter how old they were. In the North, white politicians implemented policies that segregated black people into slum neighborhoods and into inferior all-black schools, operated whites-only public pools, and held white and "colored" days at the country fair, and white businesses regularly denied black people service, placing "Whites Only" signs in their windows. States like California joined Southern states in barring black people from marrying white people, while local school boards in Illinois and New Jersey mandated segregated schools for black and white children.

This caste system was maintained through wanton racial terrorism. And black veterans like Woodard, especially those with the audacity to wear their uniform, had since the Civil War been the target of a particular violence. This intensified during the two world wars because white people understood that once black men had gone abroad and experienced life outside the suffocating racial oppression of America, they were unlikely to quietly return to their subjugation at home. As Senator James K. Vardaman of Mississippi said on the Senate floor during World War I, black servicemen returning to the South would "inevitably lead to disaster." Giving a black man "military airs" and sending him to defend the flag would bring him "to the conclusion that his political rights must be respected."

Many white Americans saw black men in the uniforms of America's armed services not as patriotic but as exhibiting a dangerous pride. Hundreds of black veterans were beaten, maimed, shot, and lynched. We like to call those who lived during World War II the Greatest Generation, but that allows us to ignore the fact that many of this generation fought for democracy abroad while brutally suppressing democracy for millions of American citizens. During the height of racial terror in this country, black Americans were not merely killed but castrated, burned alive, and dismembered with their body parts displayed in storefronts. This violence was meant to terrify and control black people, but perhaps just as important, it served as a psychological balm for white supremacy: You would not treat human beings this way. The extremity of the violence was a symptom of the psychological mechanism necessary to absolve white Americans of their country's original sin. To answer the question of how they could prize liberty abroad while simultaneously denying liberty to an entire race back home, white Americans resorted to the same racist ideology that Jefferson and the framers had used at the nation's founding.

This ideology—that black people belonged to an inferior, subhuman race—did not simply disappear once slavery ended. If the formerly enslaved and their descendants became educated, if we thrived in the jobs white people did, if we excelled in the sciences and arts, then the entire justification for how this nation allowed slavery would collapse. Free black people posed a danger to the country's idea of itself as exceptional; we held up the mirror in which the nation preferred not to peer. And so the inhumanity visited on black people by every generation of white America justified the inhumanity of the past.

Just as white Americans feared, World War II ignited what became black Americans' second sustained effort to make democracy real. As the editorial board of the black newspaper the *Pittsburgh Courier* wrote, "We wage a two-pronged attack against our enslavers at home and those abroad who will enslave us." Woodard's blinding is largely seen as one of the catalysts for the decades-long rebellion we have come to call the Civil Rights Movement. But it is useful to pause and remember that this was the second mass movement for black civil rights, the first being Reconstruction. As the centennial of slavery's end neared, black people were still seeking the rights they had fought for and won after the Civil War: the right to be treated equally by public institutions, which was guaranteed in 1866 with the Civil Rights Act; the right to be treated as full citizens before the law, which was guaranteed in 1868 by the Fourteenth Amendment; and the right to vote, which was guaranteed in 1870 by the Fifteenth Amendment. In response to black demands for these rights, white Americans strung them from trees, beat them and dumped their bodies in muddy rivers, assassinated them in their front yards, firebombed them on buses, mauled them with dogs, peeled back their skin with fire hoses, and murdered their children with explosives set off inside a church.

For the most part, black Americans fought back alone. Yet we never fought only for ourselves. The bloody freedom struggles of the Civil Rights Movement laid the foundation for every other modern rights struggle. This nation's white founders set up a decidedly undemocratic Constitution that excluded women, Native Americans, and black people and did not provide the vote or equality for most Americans. But the laws born out of black resistance guarantee the franchise for all and ban discrimination based not just on race but on gender, nationality, religion, and ability. It was the Civil Rights Movement that led to the passage of the Immigration and Nationality Act of 1965, which upended the racist immigration quota system intended to keep this country white. Because of black Americans, black and brown immigrants from across the globe are able to come to the United States and live in a country in which legal discrimination is no longer allowed. It is a truly American irony that some Asian Americans, among the groups able to immigrate to the United States because of the black civil rights struggle, are now suing universities to end programs designed to help the descendants of the enslaved.

No one cherishes freedom more than those who have not had it. And to this day, black Americans, more than any other group, embrace the democratic ideals of a common good. We are the most likely to support programs like universal health care and a higher minimum wage and to oppose programs that harm the most vulnerable. For instance, black Americans suffer the most from violent crime, yet we are the most opposed to capital punishment. Our unemployment rate is nearly twice that of white Americans, yet we are still the most likely of all groups to say this nation should take in refugees.

The truth is that as much democracy as this nation has today, it has been borne on the backs of black resistance. Our founding fathers may not have actually believed in the ideals they espoused, but black people did. As one scholar, Joe R. Feagin, put it, "Enslaved African-Americans have been among the foremost freedom-fighters this country has produced." For generations, we have believed in this country with a faith it did not deserve.

Black people have seen the worst of America, yet, somehow, we still believe in its best.

• • •

They say our people were born on the water.

When it occurred, no one can say for certain. Perhaps it was in the second week, or the third, but surely by the fourth, when they had not seen their land or any land for so many days that they lost count. It was after fear had turned to despair, and despair to resignation, and resignation to an abiding understanding. The teal eternity of the Atlantic Ocean had severed them so completely from what had once been their home that it was as if nothing had ever existed before, as if everything and everyone they cherished had simply vanished from the earth. They were no longer Mbundu or Akan or Fulani. These men and women from many different nations, all shackled together in the suffocating hull of the ship, they were one people now.

Just a few months earlier, they had families and farms and lives and dreams. They were free. They had names, of course, but their enslavers did not bother to record them. They had been made black by those people who believed that they were white, and where they were heading, black equaled "slave," and slavery in America required turning human beings into property by stripping them of every element that made them individuals. This process was called seasoning, in which people stolen from western and central Africa were forced, often through torture, to stop speaking their native tongues and practicing their native religions.

But as the sociologist Glenn Bracey wrote, "Out of the ashes of white denigration, we gave birth to ourselves." For as much as white people tried to pretend, black people were not chattel. And so the process of seasoning, instead of erasing identity, served an opposite purpose: In the void, we forged a new culture all our own.

Today, our very manner of speaking recalls the Creole languages that enslaved people innovated in order to communicate both with Africans speaking various dialects and the English-speaking people who enslaved them. Our style of dress, the extra flair, stems back to the desires of enslaved people—shorn of all individuality—to exert their own identity. Enslaved people would wear their hat in a jaunty manner or knot their head scarves intricately. Today's avant-garde nature of black hairstyles and fashion displays a vibrant reflection of enslaved people's determination to feel fully human through self-expression. The improvisational quality of black art and music comes from a culture that because of constant disruption could not cling to convention. Black naming practices, so often impugned by mainstream society, are themselves an act of resistance. Our last names belong to the white people who once owned us. That is why the insistence of many black Americans, particularly those most marginalized, to give our children names that we create, that are neither European nor from Africa, a place we have never been, is an act of self-determination. When the world listens to quintessential American music, it is our voice they hear. The sorrow songs we sang in the fields to soothe our physical pain and find hope in a freedom we did not expect to know until we died became American gospel. Amid the devastating violence and poverty of the Mississippi Delta, we birthed jazz and blues. And it was in the deeply impoverished and segregated neighborhoods where white Americans forced the descendants of the enslaved to live that teenagers too poor to buy instruments used old records to create a new music known as hip-hop.

Our speech and fashion and the drum of our music echoes Africa but is not African. Out of our unique isolation, both from our native cultures and from white America, we forged this nation's most significant original culture. In turn, "mainstream" society has coveted our style, our slang and our song, seeking to appropriate the one truly American culture as its own. As

Langston Hughes wrote in 1926, "They'll see how beautiful I am / And be ashamed— / I, too, am America."

For centuries, white Americans have been trying to solve the "Negro problem." They have dedicated thousands of pages to this endeavor. It is common, still, to point to rates of black poverty, out-of-wedlock births, crime, and college attendance, as if these conditions in a country built on a racial caste system are not utterly predictable. But crucially, you cannot view those statistics while ignoring another: that black people were enslaved here longer than we have been free.

At forty-three, I am part of the first generation of black Americans in the history of the United States to be born into a society in which black people had full rights of citizenship. Black people suffered under slavery for 250 years; we have been legally "free" for just 50. Yet in that briefest of spans, despite continuing to face rampant discrimination, and despite there never having been a genuine effort to redress the wrongs of slavery and the century of racial apartheid that followed, black Americans have made astounding progress, not only for ourselves but also for all Americans.

What if America understood, finally, in this 400th year, that we have never been the problem but the solution?

When I was a child—I must have been in fifth or sixth grade—a teacher gave our class an assignment intended to celebrate the diversity of the great American melting pot. She instructed each of us to write a short report on our ancestral land and then draw that nation's flag. As she turned to write the assignment on the board, the other black girl in class locked eyes with me. Slavery had erased any connection we had to an African country, and even if we tried to claim the whole continent, there was no "African" flag. It was hard enough being one of two black kids in the class, and this assignment would just be another reminder of the distance between the white kids and us. In the end, I walked over to the globe near my teacher's desk, picked a random African country and claimed it as my own.

meds means you're poisoning yourself. Taking meds is a concession to centuries of psychiatrization and abuse of mentally ill people, abuse that continues to this day.

Wait, that last one is actually somewhat true.

The movement to be more open about mental health, to confront, as people say, "the stigma," has had a profound impact on what it means to be mentally ill in America, especially for those of us with severe mental illnesses—commonly defined as mental illnesses that cause "serious functional impairment" that interferes with daily life, like some forms of bipolar disorder, schizophrenia, and major depression. People are much more open than they used to be. Social media has become a treasure trove of resources. For those with severe mental illness, this is a more fraught experience, one with much higher risks, one that makes them hesitant to be outspoken about their mental health conditions, though that, too, is beginning to shift due to works like Esmé Weijun Wang's *The Collected Schizophrenias.*

And so has the conversation about medications, in an effort to make people feel more comfortable about considering and using them. Advocates are eager to talk about how medication changed their lives, helped them get to therapy, helps them stay stable even in the face of adversity, has kept the monsters at bay. There's a strong emphasis on the good things about medication, and much masking of side effects—sometimes, even, a willful desire to suppress discussion about those side effects, perhaps for fear that it might scare people off or validate the worst myths about medication.

Sometimes the dose is the poison.

It started with thirst. Not the low-grade, constant thirst I had grown accustomed to after years of taking a medication that causes thirst. An intense, unslakable thirst, downing liters of water with no appreciable difference, stomach taut and swollen, but still thirsty, dreaming of water when I slept, waking up fumbling for

I wish, now, that I could go back to the younger me and tell her that her people's ancestry started here, on these lands, and to boldly, proudly, draw the stars and those stripes of the American flag.

We were told once, by virtue of our bondage, that we could never be American. But it was by virtue of our bondage that we became the most American of all.

ProPublica

FINALIST—PUBLIC INTEREST

In the early morning hours of June 17, 2017, the destroyer USS Fitzgerald *collided with a container ship in the Pacific Ocean twelve miles off the coast of Japan. "The collision of the vessels was the navy's worst accident at sea in four decades," writes the team of reporters—T. Christian Miller, Megan Rose, and Robert Faturechi—responsible for "Fight the Ship." "Seven sailors drowned. Scores were physically and psychologically wounded. Two months later, a second destroyer, the USS* John S. McCain, *broke that grim mark when it collided with another cargo vessel, leaving ten more sailors dead." Meticulously reported—and exciting to read—"Fight the Ship" was the first in a series of articles that not only detailed the experience of the crew of the* Fitzgerald *but probed the institutional failures that led to both collisions. The series won the writers a Pulitzer Prize. The nomination of "Fight the Ship" for a National Magazine Award was* ProPublica*'s thirteenth since 2011.*

T. Christian Miller,
Megan Rose, and
Robert Faturechi

Fight the Ship

A little after 1:30 a.m. on June 17, 2017, Alexander Vaughan tumbled from his bunk onto the floor of his sleeping quarters on board the navy destroyer USS *Fitzgerald*. The shock of cold, salty water snapped him awake. He struggled to his feet and felt a torrent rushing past his thighs.

Around him, sailors were screaming. "Water on deck. Water on deck!" Vaughan fumbled for his black plastic glasses and strained to see through the darkness of the windowless compartment.

Underneath the surface of the Pacific Ocean, twelve miles off the coast of Japan, the tidy world of Berthing 2 had come undone. Cramped bunk beds that sailors called coffin racks tilted at crazy angles. Beige metal footlockers bobbed through the water. Shoes, clothes, mattresses, even an exercise bicycle careered in the murk, blocking the narrow passageways of the sleeping compartment.

In the dim light of emergency lanterns, Vaughan glimpsed men leaping from their beds. Others fought through the flotsam to reach the exit ladder next to Vaughan's bunk on the port side of the ship. Tens of thousands of gallons of seawater were flooding into the compartment from a gash that had ripped through the *Fitzgerald*'s steel hull like it was wrapping paper.

As a petty officer first class, these were his sailors, and in those first foggy seconds Vaughan realized they were in danger of drowning.

At 6 feet, 1 inch and 230 pounds, Vaughan grabbed a nearby sailor by the T-shirt and hurled him toward the ladder that led to the deck above. He yanked another, then another.

Vaughan's leg had been fractured in three places. He did not even feel it.

"Get out, get out," he shouted as men surged toward him through the rising water.

Berthing 2, just below the waterline and barely bigger than a 1,200-square-foot apartment, was home to thirty-five sailors. They were enlisted men, most in their twenties and thirties, many new to the navy. They came from small towns like Palmyra, Virginia, and big cities like Houston. They were white, black, Latino, Asian. On the *Fitzgerald*, they worked as gunners' mates, sonar experts, cafeteria workers and administrative assistants.

Seaman Dakota Rigsby, nineteen, was newly engaged. Sonar Technician Rod Felderman, twenty-eight, was expecting the birth of his first child. Gary Rehm Jr., thirty-seven, a petty officer first class, was the oldest sailor in the compartment, a mentor to younger crew members.

As the water rose past their ankles, their waists, their chests, the men fought their way to the port side ladder and waited, shivering in the swirling debris, for their chance to escape.

Shouting over a crescendo of seawater, Vaughan and his bunkmate, Joshua Tapia, a weapons specialist, worked side by side. They stationed themselves at the bottom of the ladder, grabbing the sailors and pushing them, one by one, up the steps. At the top, the men shot out the small opening, as the rising water forced the remaining air from the compartment.

Suddenly, the ship lurched to the right, knocking sailors from their feet. Some slipped beneath the surface. Others disappeared into the darkness of a common bathroom, carried by the force of water rushing to fill every available space.

Vaughan and Tapia waited until they were alone at the bottom of the ladder. When the water reached their necks, they, too, climbed out the twenty-nine-inch-wide escape hatch. Safe, they peered back down the hole. In the ninety seconds since the crash, the water had almost reached the top of Berthing 2.

Now they faced a choice. Naval training demanded that they seal the escape hatch to prevent water from flooding the rest of the ship. But they knew that bolting it down would consign any sailors still alive to death.

Vaughan and Tapia hesitated. They agreed to wait a few seconds more for survivors. Tapia leaned down into the vanishing inches of air left in Berthing 2.

"Come to the sound of my voice," he shouted.

The *Fitzgerald* had been steaming on a secret mission to the South China Sea when it was smashed by a cargo ship more than three times its size.

The 30,000-ton MV ACX *Crystal* gouged an opening bigger than a semitruck in the starboard side of the destroyer. The force of the collision was so great that it sent the 8,261-ton warship spinning on a 360-degree rotation through the Pacific.

On the ship's bridge, a crewman activated two emergency lights high on the ship's mast, one on top of the other: The *Fitzgerald*, it signaled, was red over red—no longer under command.

The collision of the vessels was the navy's worst accident at sea in four decades. Seven sailors drowned. Scores were physically and psychologically wounded. Two months later, a second destroyer, the USS *John S. McCain*, broke that grim mark when it collided with another cargo vessel, leaving ten more sailors dead.

The successive incidents raised an unavoidable question: How could two $1.8 billion navy destroyers, protected by one of the most advanced defense systems on the planet, fail to detect oncoming cargo ships broadcasting their locations to a worldwide navigational network?

The failures of basic seamanship deeply embarrassed the navy. Both warships belonged to the vaunted Seventh Fleet—the most powerful armada in the world and one of the most important commands in the defense of the United States from nuclear attack.

ProPublica reconstructed the *Fitzgerald*'s journey, relying on more than 13,000 pages of confidential navy investigative records, public reports, and interviews with scores of *Fitzgerald* crew members, current and former senior navy officers, and maritime experts.

The review revealed neglect by navy leadership, serious mistakes by officers—and extraordinary acts of valor and endurance by the crew.

The *Fitzgerald*'s captain selected an untested team to steer the ship at night. He ordered the crew to speed through shipping lanes filled with cargo ships and fishing vessels to free up time to train his sailors the next day. At the time of the collision, he was asleep in his cabin.

The twenty-six-year-old officer of the deck, who was in charge of the destroyer at the time of the crash, had navigated the route only once before in daylight. In a panic, she ordered the *Fitzgerald* to turn directly into the path of the *Crystal*.

The *Fitzgerald*'s crew was exhausted and undertrained. The inexperience showed in a series of near misses in the weeks before the crash, when the destroyer maneuvered dangerously close to vessels on at least three occasions.

The warship's state of readiness was in question. The navy required destroyers to pass twenty-two certification tests to prove themselves seaworthy and battle-ready before sailing. The *Fitzgerald* had passed just seven of these tests. It was not even qualified to conduct its chief mission, anti–ballistic missile defense.

A sailor's mistake sparked a fire causing the electrical system to fail and a shipwide blackout a week before the mission resulting in the crash. The ship's e-mail system, for both classified and non-classified material, failed repeatedly. Officers used Gmail instead.

Its radars were in questionable shape, and it's not clear the crew knew how to operate them. One could not be made to automatically track nearby ships. To keep the screen updated, a sailor had to punch a button a thousand times an hour. The ship's primary navigation system was run by seventeen-year-old software.

The navy declined to directly answer *ProPublica*'s questions about its findings. Instead, a spokesman cited previous reports that the navy published during its own months-long review of the collisions.

The navy inquiries determined that there had been widespread problems with leaders regarding shortfalls in training, manning, and equipment in the Seventh Fleet. The navy fired admirals, captains, and commanders, punished sailors and criminally prosecuted officers for neglecting their duties.

Adm. John Richardson, head of the navy, called the two collisions "avoidable tragedies." The ships' commanders and their superiors, he said in a written statement to *ProPublica*, were responsible for the results.

"The tragedies of USS *Fitzgerald* and USS *John S. McCain* reminded us that all commanders, from the unit level to the fleet commander, must constantly assess and manage risks and opportunities in a very complex and dynamic environment," Richardson said. "But at the end of the day, our commanders make decisions and our sailors execute and there is an outcome—a result of that decision. The commander 'owns' that outcome."

Sidelined during years of land wars in Iraq and Afghanistan, the navy is now strategically central to containing North Korea's nuclear threat, China's expansionist aims, and a newly aggressive Russia.

Vice Admiral Joseph Aucoin was commander of the Seventh Fleet at the time of the collisions. A naval aviator who fought in the Balkans and Iraq, he made repeated pleas to his superiors for more men, more ships, more time to train. He was ignored, then fired.

More than eighteen months later, Aucoin believes that the navy has yet to disclose the full story of the disasters. Navy leaders, he said in his first extended interview, have not taken accountability for their role in undermining America's sea fighting ability.

"I just want the truth to come out," Aucoin said.

In the end, the *Fitzgerald*'s crew fought to keep the ship from sinking. They worked in the dark, without power, without steering, without communications.

A young officer scribbled algebraic equations in a notebook to figure out how to right the listing vessel. The crew bailed out the ship with buckets after pumps failed. As the *Fitzgerald* struggled to return to port, its navigational displays failed and backup batteries ran out. The ship's navigator used a handheld commercial GPS unit and paper charts to guide the ship home.

At the top of the flooded berthing compartment, just seconds after Tapia's shout, a hand thrust up through the scuttle opening. It was Jackson Schrimsher, a weapons specialist from Alabama. Vaughan reached down and pulled him up.

Schrimsher had gotten trapped in his top bunk by floating furniture that blocked the aisle. He climbed over to another bunk and jumped down. A wall of water rushed toward him, and a locker toppled onto him. Looking up, he saw the light coming from the open scuttle and fought his way toward it.

Schrimsher had recently become certified as a master helmsman, specially trained to maneuver the ship during complicated operations. With the *Fitzgerald* in distress, his skills were needed. He raced off for the ship's bridge, clad only in a drenched T-shirt and shorts heavy with seawater.

Vaughan and Tapia took one last look at each other. It was time to seal the hatch.

Chapter 1. The Commander's Quarters

"Fuck Your Boots, Captain, Grab My Hand."

At impact, the *Crystal*'s prow punched into another sleeping compartment, this one occupied by a single man: Cmdr. Bryce Benson, the forty-year-old captain of the *Fitzgerald*.

Benson's cabin lay high above the surface of the ocean, four decks above his sailors in Berthing 2. The *Crystal* had pierced the *Fitzgerald*'s hull right at the foot of Benson's bed. It crushed together the bedroom and office of his stateroom like a wad of tinfoil.

The collision jolted Benson awake. Metal ductwork had fallen on him. He was bleeding from the head. He tried to get up from his bed but could not. He was trapped, buried amid a tangle of steel and wires. He clutched the quilt his wife had sewn him, its blue and white squares forming the image of a warship.

The cabin was cold and dark. He felt air rush past him. With a shock, Benson realized he was staring at the Pacific. The tear in his cabin's wall had left Benson with a 140-degree view of dark water and dark sky. He could make out lights from the distant shore of Japan.

He suspected the ship had been hit. He could hear the shouts and groans of his sailors.

The captains of navy warships are uniquely accountable in the modern American military. They have "absolute responsibility" for their vessels and face absolute blame when something goes wrong—whether they are asleep or even on board. In the case of a collision, no matter how minor, the consequences are usually severe: The captain is relieved of command.

The outcome is common enough that captains joke with the young officers steering their ships. "In case anything goes wrong, call me so that I can see the end of my career."

Benson was determined not to be that captain. Just twenty hours earlier, he had set sail from the *Fitzgerald*'s home port in

Yokosuka, Japan, after receiving last-minute orders to head for the South China Sea. Benson had ordered all sailors to report to the *Fitzgerald* at six a.m. to get an early start so he could squeeze in some training.

The *Fitzgerald* didn't wrap up the long day of drills until eleven p.m. The ship was moving through a strait between Japan's Izu Peninsula and Oshima Island. It was roughly twenty miles wide and filled with scores of cargo vessels and fishing boats streaming into and out of Tokyo.

Exhausted, Benson made a change to the night orders to guide the sailors who would pilot the *Fitzgerald* during the dark early morning hours. Normally, Benson directed the officer of the deck to call him if the ship deviated from its planned course by more than 500 yards to avoid traffic. But this night, Benson doubled the number to 1,000 yards, giving the officer more room to maneuver without having to wake him.

At eleven-thirty p.m., Benson left the bridge to turn in for the night. Captains often insist on remaining on the bridge when maneuvering through traffic at night. Or they sleep in a special cabin on the bridge. They want to monitor their officers closely during less-than-ideal sailing conditions.

Benson judged he was suffering the effects of "fatigue and sleep deprivation." He needed to rest. He was concerned about the secret part of his mission. The *Fitzgerald* was going to sail through contested waters off China, which could result in confrontations with Chinese warships.

But Benson's decisions set up a risky situation: a relatively junior crew run ragged by a long day, loosened restrictions on the officers steering the vessel, and a captain not on the bridge.

Now, Benson realized that his worst nightmare had happened. His ship was in danger. And so was the crew. He was wet, chilled, and slipping into shock. Benson reached for the phone by his bed and stopped. His brain had failed him. He couldn't remember the four digits he'd called countless times to reach the bridge.

He fought through the confusion until the numbers came to him at last. He punched the keypad and hoped for an answer from above.

• • •

Benson and his sailors belonged to the Seventh Fleet, which won fame during the Second World War as "MacArthur's Navy," battling across the Pacific under the direction of the American general to retake the Philippines.

Its modern incarnation is based in Yokosuka—the navy's largest overseas installation. The historic base lies at the mouth of Tokyo Bay, near where Commodore Matthew C. Perry arrived with gunboats in 1853 to force the isolated island nation to trade with the United States. The Seventh Fleet encompasses about 20,000 sailors and some 70 ships and submarines. Its commander is responsible for an area with thirty-six countries and half the world's population.

The Seventh Fleet is one of the most important strategic commands in the military, and its sailors and ships fight an often shadowy battle against some of America's greatest geopolitical threats: China, North Korea, and Russia.

The fleet's eight destroyers are key to this fight. Tough, scrappy warships, they are designed to withstand enormous damage and return the same. In the Battle off Samar in the Philippines in 1944, one of history's greatest naval clashes, seven American destroyers, escorts, and aircraft carrier planes managed to fend off a flotilla of twenty-three Japanese warships, including four battleships.

Some Seventh Fleet destroyers, including the *Fitzgerald*, play an especially important role. They can track and shoot down ballistic missiles, making them almost unique in the nation's armed forces. No other missile defense can deploy as quickly or cover as wide an area. The system is far from perfect—it frequently misses targets during training exercises. But the half-dozen ballistic missile defense destroyers in the Seventh Fleet are the United States' first line of defense against a North Korean nuclear attack.

From his early days in the navy, Benson was determined to helm one of these frontline warships.

Benson dedicated himself to a career as a surface warfare officer. SWOs, as they are known, are the backbone of the navy's leadership—front-line warriors noted for their extraordinary commitment to success, but also for a competitive, sometimes backbiting culture. "SWOs eat their own" is a common navy refrain.

At every stage, he impressed his superior officers. Several of his commanders believed he would make admiral. "Make no mistake, THIS GUY IS GOOD," wrote one officer.

The first ship he captained was the USS *Guardian*, an aging minesweeper. It was made mostly of wood and was in constant need of repair. He learned to get material any way he could: scavenging equipment, pestering supply clerks and getting his machinists to make custom fittings. Under his watch, the Guardian received the highest rating in its class for combat readiness. "It is obvious he is an absolute ALL-STAR surface warrior," one superior wrote, "and the exact type of leader we need in COMMAND."

At five feet, ten inches and 160 pounds, Benson was not physically imposing and had a baby face that emphasized his youth. But he could turn fierce when confronted with a screw-up, fixing a backsliding sailor with a piercing stare, followed by a pointed and personal lesson.

His crew thought highly of him even though, or maybe because, he was tough. They liked how he'd walk the decks to stop and chat with sailors. He loved talking about football, especially his beloved Packers. He drilled his sailors on safety—including evacuation of the ship's sleeping quarters.

"He was about getting things done. He didn't accept a lot of excuses," Travius Caldwell, one of the ship's chief petty officers, said. "He leads hard."

• • •

On the *Fitzgerald*'s bridge, the jangle of the phone next to Benson's empty captain's chair pierced the chaos. Carlos Clark snatched up the receiver. It was Benson. His voice was shaky and uncertain. What had happened to his ship? He needed to get to the bridge, he said, but he couldn't. Clark, an enlisted sailor in charge of navigation, had never before heard his captain sound scared.

"I'm trapped," Benson told him.

Clark grabbed a sledgehammer, a couple of other sailors, and raced to the captain's room, two decks below. One of the men was Christopher Perez, the *Fitzgerald*'s senior chief petty officer for the ship's missile and gun systems. Decisive, sometimes headstrong, Perez served as a crucial link between the officers and the enlisted crew in weapons.

Outside Benson's cabin, the rescue party confronted the first obstacle: The captain's door, three-eighths-of-an-inch-thick metal, was locked shut. Chief Petty Officer Jared Ogilvie picked up the sledgehammer.

"Get the fuck back," he shouted.

Bald and broad-shouldered, Ogilvie cracked thirty to fifty blows at the door. Nothing. Next in line was Clark. Then came Ensign Joseph White—six feet, two inches, a former offensive lineman for the Bethune-Cookman Wildcats. He split open his hand trying to bash in the door. Two more chief petty officers took shots.

Benson's door bent only slightly.

From his bed, mangled steel just inches from this head, Benson could hear the banging. He was bleeding and soaked from a water pipe that had broken above him and could feel his body temperature dropping.

Trying to calm himself, the voice of his seventh-grade science teacher popped into his head: "Whenever you're in a sense of panic, just try to slow down because your brain is trying to sort through all the files and it's going too fast."

Clark rushed back to the bridge, where he kept a thirty-five-pound kettlebell for exercise. Swinging it high over his head, he smashed it against the door. Everyone ducked. The door cracked.

Perez stepped forward to finish the job. He grabbed White in a bear hug, and the two heaved their combined bulk against the door, pushing it back enough to reveal the captain's stateroom.

At first, the members of the rescue party thought they were looking at the back wall of Benson's cabin, at what appeared to be a light bulb hanging down and swinging wildly. Then, they realized that they were staring through a hole at the ocean. The light was the *Crystal*, hundreds of yards away, steaming away from the crash.

The cabin looked like a junkyard, the captain's desk pushed against the door, cold water flowing like a waterfall. The room had been compressed and shifted back twenty feet from its original position.

The men could not see Benson because of the dark and the detritus. But they could hear his pleas for help.

"We're coming for you," Ogilvie said. "Just keep talking, keep talking."

• • •

Benson had taken command of the *Fitzgerald* just a month earlier, on May 13, 2017, after a brief ceremony on deck during a stop at a navy port in Sasebo in southern Japan. He'd made a few remarks then issued his commander's philosophy to the crew: A simple acrostic—FITZ—meant to inspire the sailors: "Fighting, Integrity, Toughness, Zeal."

Benson knew intimately the precarious state of his ship and its sailors. He had served as the ship's second-in-command for a year and a half before taking charge from the outgoing captain, Cmdr. Robert Shu.

Sailors welcomed the change of command. Some felt that Shu had become too hands-off after three years in command. He "seemed indecisive, confused about what he wants," one lieutenant later told investigators. Benson "was a huge positive turn. He gave us focused, clear guidance." Naval investigators blamed Shu for creating a "culture of complacency" and "longstanding weaknesses" in training and tackling equipment problems that Benson would have to fix.

Benson also worried about the ship's physical state. The ship had recently spent eight months in Yokosuka's repair yards, where workers installed a new defensive system, overhauled its turbine shafts, and painted it a new coat of navy gray. But hundreds of repairs, major and minor, remained to be done.

Then there was the crew. In those eight months, nearly 40 percent of the *Fitzgerald*'s crew had turned over. The navy replaced them with younger, less-seasoned sailors and officers, leaving the *Fitzgerald* with the highest percentage of new crew members of any destroyer in the fleet. But naval commanders had skimped even further, cutting into the number of sailors Benson needed to keep the ship running smoothly. The *Fitzgerald* had around 270 people total—short of the 303 sailors called for by the navy.

Key positions were vacant, despite repeated requests from the *Fitzgerald* to navy higher-ups. The senior enlisted quartermaster position—charged with training inexperienced sailors to steer the ship—had gone unfilled for more than two years. The technician in charge of the ship's radar was on medical leave, with no replacement. The personnel shortages made it difficult to post watches on both the starboard and port sides of the ship, a once-common navy practice.

When the ship set sail in February 2017, it was supposed to be for a short training mission for its green crew. Instead, the navy never allowed the *Fitzgerald* to return to Yokosuka. North Korea was launching missiles on a regular basis. China was aggressively sending warships to pursue its territorial claims to disputed islands off its coast. Seventh Fleet commanders deployed the *Fitzgerald* like a pinch hitter, repeatedly assigning it new missions to complete.

Lt. Cmdr. Ritarsha Furqan, the ship's combat officer, worried that the constant pace was not providing enough time for necessary training and repairs.

"We'd find a part, find a body, make do, and get underway," Furqan later testified in a legal proceeding. "Sometimes it felt like it was unsafe or wrong."

In March, Furqan confronted Shu: "We are not ready," she told him. Shu, she testified, told her that he had already delivered that message to superiors. The missions would continue.

Benson's first test of leadership was improving the ship's state of readiness. In the months at sea after dry dock, the twenty-two-year-old destroyer deteriorated as its regular maintenance was repeatedly pushed back. Benson spent his first week in command as though he were again captain of an aging minesweeper, trying to tackle hundreds of repairs and begging technicians to fly over from the United States for help.

In the midst of the frenzied training and repairs, the ship's critical e-mail system collapsed. Neither classified nor unclassified material could be sent. Officers were forced to set up Gmail addresses to continue working.

By then, Benson was convinced that the shortage of sailors had become critical. Right before Benson assumed command, Shu had promised leaves to more than a dozen weary crew members. One sailor planned to return to Yokosuka to see his newborn for the first time. Another wanted to attend her mother's wedding. A third asked to go home to visit his mother, who was dying.

Benson called the sailors into his office, one by one. The *Fitzgerald* needed to be ready for war with North Korea. There were simply not enough crew members to replace them. He canceled all leaves.

"I need you. The ship needs you," Benson explained to each sailor individually.

Sailors started referring to the day as "Bloody Tuesday." Some sailors left Benson's rooms in tears. Another could barely bring herself to look at the captain for a week. One of the affected sailors was Perez. Benson told him that he could not afford to let him go.

"You're going to be on watch, and you might save my life," he told his senior chief. "You might save my life."

• • •

Perez and three other sailors barely paused to consider the dangers. Loose electrical cables dangled from the ceiling. Water spewed from a broken pipe.

Their biggest concern was the massive tear in the cabin wall. They thought Benson was in danger of falling into the ocean. The four held on to one another's belts as they crept forward in the dark, following the captain's voice.

Caldwell found Benson lying in his bunk. Showers of sparks from the cables fell like rain between them.

"Captain," Caldwell said. "Grab my hand."

"I can't get into my boots," Benson told him.

"Fuck your boots, captain," Caldwell said. "Grab my hand."

The two men locked arms as the black waters of the Pacific streamed past. The chain of men pulled back, maneuvering Benson out of his bunk and over his desk to the corridor in front of the cabin.

Benson was soaking wet, barefoot, and wearing only a long-sleeved T-shirt and exercise shorts. There was blood streaming down his face. He grabbed the ladder and began climbing.

Sixteen minutes after the collision, at 1:46 a.m., Benson staggered onto the bridge. Adrenaline, fear and anger shot through him. The ship was listing, wheeling in the dark uncontrolled. The electricity was out. The screens were off. Only emergency lanterns and moonlight illuminated the bridge.

Benson found the officer who had been in charge of the ship sobbing.

"Captain, I fucked up," she told him.

The bridge was in chaos. Both officers and enlisted crew were stunned. Flashlights and cell-phone lights danced in the dark, revealing blank, open faces. For sailors used to the constant thrum of a ship moving through water, it was eerily hushed.

Benson strode to his captain's chair. He needed to rescue the ship. But the instant he sat, he began to slide out. His forearms curled involuntarily toward his body, as though he were lifting an invisible barbell. His hands bent at the wrists and folded down and away from his body.

Ogilvie and White laid him on the floor of the bridge. Benson began to shiver uncontrollably. Ogilvie thought the captain was suffering from hypothermia. He told White to strip off his shirt and lay on Benson to warm him up.

White balked.

"Right goddamn now," Ogilvie said. It was the second time in twenty minutes that a lower ranking sailor had issued an expletive-laced order to a superior officer.

White lay chest to chest with Benson to keep him warm while Ogilvie slapped him or rubbed his sternum hard with his knuckles to keep Benson awake. They put boots on his feet.

The captain had suffered a traumatic brain injury. He drifted in and out of consciousness, his lip occasionally quivering before he started crying.

"My brain's not working the way it's supposed to work right now, I don't understand, I don't understand," he said at one point.

A senior officer told White to take Benson to the sea cabin, a small room with a bed just behind the bridge. "The crew can't see him like this," he said.

In the confines of the sea cabin, Benson would bark orders or ask about the ship's status. "What are the seas?" he'd ask before passing out again. He started calling his sailors by their first names—something he had never done before. At one point, he noticed a barefoot cafeteria worker named Freddy Peña. "Freddy," Benson said, "Get your boots on."

The young culinary specialist turned to the ranking officer standing nearby. Benson wasn't going anywhere. "Sir, can I wear Captain Benson's boots?"

It was an astonishing question in the strict hierarchy of a navy ship, in which the captain reigns supreme and officers live on top both figuratively and literally. When an enlisted cafeteria worker bends over the captain of the ship and asks to claim his boots, it is a sign that the rigid structure of life at sea was being undone by the demands of survival.

The officer looked at the cook. Could he have the captain's boots?

"Absolutely," the officer said.

The officer was the ship's second in command, Cmdr. Sean Babbitt. Tall, gaunt, he had joined the *Fitzgerald* only months before. He told Benson the ship was flooding. The *Fitzgerald* was now at war, the enemy the sea.

Benson realized he was no longer in command of himself, nor of his ship. He told Babbitt: "Sean, fight the ship."

Chapter 2. The Combat Room

"I Got a Ship"

Lt. Natalie Combs was already nearing exhaustion when she reported to the combat information center for her shift the night of the crash. Like many sailors on board, Combs had been up before sunrise.

Benson had appointed Combs as the tactical action officer for the watch. That made her responsible for the operation of the *Fitzgerald*'s combat information center—the warship's fighting heart.

The room stretches almost the width of the ship on the main deck and is filled with rows of long desks and dozens of screens. It looks like a combination lecture hall and sports bar—except that it is illuminated by pale blue light, thought to calm sailors charged with the launch of its deadly instruments. "The House of Blue Light," some in the navy called it.

All the ship's major weapons systems can be fired from the center—the missiles, torpedoes, the five-inch gun. The ship's multiple sensors pour in data. Radar screens can track planes, ships, and submarines from scores of miles away. Real-time information flows from an infrared camera and navigational, weather, and geographic equipment.

On the *Fitzgerald*, the combat room also contained a laptop displaying information from the Automatic Identification System. The AIS is a commercial system used worldwide to identify ships by their name, location, and navigational path. That made the laptop an important link in the array of equipment designed to alert the *Fitzgerald* to nearby dangers. The *Fitzgerald* didn't broadcast its position for security reasons. But the AIS allowed it to see civilian vessels.

The high-tech combat center, however, was like so much else about the *Fitzgerald*—less than it seemed.

As the ship sailed through the strait, an operations specialist named Matthew Stawecki sat in front of a radar known as the SPS-67, one of three radar systems on the *Fitzgerald*, and the primary radar in use in the combat room. He was charged with helping keep track of ship traffic around the destroyer. To track a ship, a radar operator must "hook" it—or direct an automated system to lock on the target and display its projected path.

The radar was supposed to automatically follow the hooked tracks on the screen. But *Fitzgerald* sailors had been unable to make the feature work.

To follow the hooked tracks, Stawecki had to repeatedly press a button that refreshed the display on his screen. The workaround made Stawecki look like he was sending a frantic message in Morse code. He would hit the button more than 1,000 times in an hour to keep the images of nearby ships updated. Just before the collision, Stawecki's screen showed five ships around the *Fitzgerald*, none of them close by, none of them threats, and none of them requiring reporting to the captain.

The SPS-67 had another problem: radars must be tuned to obtain the clearest images. On the *Fitzgerald*, technicians had covered a button to tune the radar with masking tape because it was broken. From his post, Stawecki could not tune the radar. So the only other thing he saw were false returns—so-called clutter that could result from the radar hitting waves, flocks of birds, or any other obstacle at sea. Stawecki would later testify that he saw no ships threatening the *Fitzgerald* in the crucial half-hour before the collision.

"There was a lot of clutter; I couldn't see a lot," said Stawecki, who had not rested during the day. He could remember tracking only a few contacts, all of them far away. "I can't remember exactly how far, but they were nowhere near us pretty much and, I believe, they were going the opposite direction."

• • •

The *Fitzgerald* belongs to the Arleigh Burke class of destroyers, named after the admiral who helped win the Second World War and led the navy during the Eisenhower years. It had beautiful lines—a steeply curving prow, four swept-back smokestacks, a foredeck with a powerful five-inch gun, and a flat aft deck for helicopter landings.

The *Fitzgerald* is about as long as the Washington Monument, and wider than a four-lane interstate highway, with a main mast soaring 152 feet high above the deck. The four gas turbine engines produce more than 100,000 horsepower, capable of driving it at speeds of greater than 30 knots. That speed—more than 34 miles per hour—placed the *Fitzgerald* among the fastest warships in the world.

Sleek, fast, strategically critical, the *Fitzgerald* could often seem closer to a wreck.

Due to their heavy use, destroyers in the Seventh Fleet were in constant need of repair. On the *Fitzgerald*, the list of maintenance jobs ran into the hundreds. Most of them were minor: a request for new coolant for a refrigeration unit, another for a certain type of washer.

But a dozen or so were considered more serious. They included problems with the ship's primary navigation system. It was the oldest such system among destroyers based in Japan. It was running on Windows 2000, even though other ships had been upgraded. It could not display information from the AIS.

The broken e-mail system had a "major impact" on the ship's day-to-day operations. Microsoft Outlook did not work. Nor could commanders communicate over a classified e-mail system. The ship's entire network was suffering. Officers could not access sailors' work profiles, order parts, or even keep track of new repair requests.

Technicians were constantly fixing the SPS-73, the other main navigational radar on the *Fitzgerald*. Sometimes, the radar would show the destroyer heading the wrong way. At other times, it simply locked up and would have to be shut down. The SPS-73's antenna was nearing the end of its life, and had been scheduled for replacement in April. But the maintenance had been delayed when the *Fitzgerald* was assigned to patrol North Korea.

A third radar, used for warfare, was slow to acquire targets, but technicians had installed a temporary fix that became permanent. "Problem known since 2012. Declared hopeless," read notes attached to the repair report.

Other equipment had been written off, too. The so-called Bright Bridge console was supposed to help the bridge crew by sharing information from the combat room. The console had been scavenged for spare parts, leaving the station unmanned.

When malfunctions occurred, it could take months to fix them. The *Fitzgerald* skipped or shortened four planned maintenance periods during the spring of 2017—due to the navy constantly issuing orders for new missions.

Almost two weeks before the collision, as the *Fitzgerald* approached its home port of Yokosuka, an engineer accidentally caused a small fire in one of the ship's switchboards. The *Fitzgerald* went dark, dead in the water.

The next day, the destroyer limped into Yokosuka harbor. For the sailors aboard, it was the first time home in four months. They did what they could not while on board: They hung out with family, took hot showers alone, and slammed down drinks at the Honch, the row of bars outside base. For Benson and his officers, it was another long week attacking the *Fitzgerald*'s long list of repairs and finding the right sailors to do the ship's many tasks.

Among its most serious shortcomings, the *Fitzgerald* lacked certification for providing reliable missile defense. In the best of circumstances, the *Fitzgerald* had a narrow window of time to take out a ballistic missile. It could target an outgoing missile only before it got too high in the atmosphere. But one officer fretted that a radar operator—reputed to be the best on the ship—was unable to locate and track missiles in the allotted time.

• • •

As the watch progressed into the dark early hours of June 17, Combs did not see much to worry her. All the screens in the combat room showed a quiet night on the seas. The big monitors displaying the ships surrounding the *Fitzgerald* showed none closer than 6,000 yards. An infrared camera operator saw maybe twenty to thirty vessels, including small fishing boats, but none a cause for worry. Combs, who had been through the area a number of times, judged the traffic a "three out of ten."

The number two on the midwatch was Lt. Irian Woodley, forty-two, the surface warfare coordinator. Woodley was what the navy called a mustang—an enlisted sailor who had risen to become a commissioned officer. An experienced sailor, Woodley evoked a mixed reaction. One senior officer thought he was one of the best watch standers on the ship; other sailors thought he was the worst.

Woodley shared Combs's opinion. He saw what his assistant, Stawecki, saw as he tapped away at his radar station: nothing near or dangerous.

"It appeared that we were pretty much in, you know, like in open water," he said.

Rainford A. Graham, an operations specialist on duty in the combat room, had also seen nothing on the radar. "You trust what's in the console," he said.

Graham's faith may have been misplaced. Even if the radars had been working properly, it's not clear the *Fitzgerald*'s sailors knew how to use them. One junior officer had never been trained on how to use the radars on the *Fitzgerald*, describing herself as "not highly confident" in their use. Technicians complained of being called to fix radar problems that were actually the result of operator errors. Radars are tricky instruments that need constant adjustments depending on weather and distance.

Aside from radar, however, the *Fitzgerald* had other systems in place to detect oncoming vessels. Among them was the simple act of talking.

One of Combs's most important responsibilities was communicating with her counterparts on the bridge. She was a backup set of eyes and ears, making sure that officers on the bridge knew about surrounding ship traffic detected in the combat room. Even the slowest shift was supposed to be punctuated with check-ins. "Why are we not seeing more ships?" is one question a tactical action officer might ask the bridge. Constant communication was needed to ensure that no dangers went overlooked.

Combs wasn't the best person for that task, in the eyes of some officers on board.

• • •

Combs had grown up in a navy family—her father was a retired admiral who had been one of the navy's first black senior officers. During the Second World War, her grandfather belonged to the Montford Point Marines, the Corps' first black service members.

After nine years in the navy, most of it in Japan, Combs joined the *Fitzgerald* just as it prepared to leave dry dock. Her primary job was as the operations officer, or ops, a notoriously busy position that made her responsible for a team of officers and sailors dedicated to intelligence, scheduling, and planning.

When she arrived, she had to figure out her new job on her own: "There was no turnover process," she said. "I was essentially just familiarizing myself with the ship as best as I could."

Benson and others had worked closely with Combs. Some officers considered her introverted, not the best characteristic for a tactical action officer responsible for communicating with the bridge.

In the thirty minutes before the crash from one to one-thirty a.m., Combs never once called the bridge to apprise its officers of the ship's surroundings—or even to question the odd lack of nearby ships in the crowded corridor. Nor did anybody from the bridge call down.

The long silence violated orders for constant communication between the two stations, even on a night that seemed slow.

"I did not see any contact that caused me alarm in regard to its distance for me," Combs said.

• • •

Although the *Fitzgerald* radars did not show them, more than two dozen ships surrounded the destroyer, all close enough to track. Three of them, large vessels off the starboard bow, posed a grave danger to the warship. They were closing in. Quickly.

But the ships didn't appear on the combat room's key radar, the SPS-67, because neither Combs nor Woodley nor anyone else realized that it had been set to a mode designed to scan the seas at a greater distance. With the SPS-67 button taped over, only specialized technicians could change the tuning from another part of the ship.

The lack of ships on the radar screen created such a false sense of security that Woodley felt comfortable asking Combs permission to leave his station for a bathroom break, which is rare for a shift in the combat room. When he returned at one-twenty a.m., he glanced at his screens. Nothing to concern him.

"I didn't get any radar, I didn't pick up anything on the Sixty-Seven," Woodley said.

Then, at 1:29 a.m., one minute before the collision, Woodley looked up at the laptop with the Automatic Identification System. He noticed a "pop-up"—a ship that he had not seen before. It appeared very close.

Woodley turned to Ashton Cato, a weapons specialist assigned to midwatch. Cato operated a camera with thermal imaging that could see miles away. On some nights, he would watch the crew on faraway ship decks lighting up cigarettes.

Woodley ordered Cato to point the camera in the direction of the approaching ship. As Cato moved the camera, the screen suddenly filled with the image of a fully loaded cargo ship, lit with white lights like a Christmas tree. It was headed straight at the *Fitzgerald*, a few hundred yards distant.

Cato only managed to get out a few words.

"I got a ship."

Chapter 3. The Bridge

"The Only Way for Things to Get Better Here Is for Us to Have a Serious Accident or Someone to Die."

Sarah Coppock, lieutenant junior grade, was the officer of the deck, responsible for the safety and navigation of the ship while Benson slept.

She'd started her day almost twenty-two hours before and had managed to rest for one hour before taking over on the bridge. She had navigated this route out of Tokyo only once, in daylight. Despite that, Benson, before going to bed, had ordered her to steam ahead at 20 knots.

The speed left Coppock nervous. Steering a massive warship through the ocean at night is an exercise in managed chaos. Imagine driving down a four-lane highway without guardrails, traffic stripes or dividers. It is pitch dark. Other vehicles, ranging in size from mopeds to tractor-trailers, zip around you. None of them have brakes that can stop quickly.

The bridge was the *Fitzgerald*'s navigation center. Perched high above the main deck toward the front of the ship, the officers and crew in the bridge held a 270-degree view of the ocean through a bank of thick windows.

The main steering console occupied the middle of the room, appearing like a cabinet with a small wheel sticking out of it to control the rudder and levers to control the ship's speed. Other blocky consoles featured radars, navigation screens and communication tools. There were only two seats in the room, one for the executive officer and a second for the captain—a leather chair, raised up on a small platform. Benson, and only Benson, could occupy the seat. The rest of the dozen or so officers and sailors that jammed into the cramped room literally stood watch, on their feet for four- or five-hour shifts.

The members of the team Coppock was leading that night were all certified for their posts. But they were tired and some were green.

Her number two, Lt. Raven Parker, twenty-six, the junior officer of the deck, had helped navigate through the area only once before, and that was in daylight. She, too, had grabbed only an hour of sleep since the start of the day.

Ensign Francis Womack, twenty-five, had worked nineteen hours without a break. He was serving as the conning officer. His job was to relay orders from Coppock to the enlisted sailors who operated the ship's controls at the helm.

Womack was almost as new as an officer can be. Before the *Fitzgerald*, he had been working at a restaurant and an industrial supply company. He told people that he was "not doing anything to make anyone proud." He'd joined the navy to fix that.

He set foot on the *Fitzgerald* in January, then returned to the United States for additional training. In all, he had spent only about a month's time at sea. He had only recently passed a test to stand watch. June 16 was the first night he had ever served as conn by himself.

"There's a lot of things that I didn't know," Womack would say later.

Benson, the captain, had spent hours putting the midwatch team together. He had drafted six lineups, his planning hampered by the ship's broken administrative network. He had tried to balance weaker officers with stronger ones. He regarded Coppock as one of the best officers that he had. She had impressed previous supervisors. One called her the best of his seventeen top officers. "PHENOMENAL LEADER," he wrote.

"I trusted her," Benson said.

Benson made clear in his orders what to do if the slightest thing went wrong: "CALL ME."

Trust is the currency of a navy ship. No high-tech weapons system or advanced technology can replace it. In order for a ship to run well, sailors must have faith in one another. Hence the navy belief that it's not the steel that makes the ship, it's the crew.

Coppock did not trust some of her team that night. She was especially worried about Woodley, who was responsible for watching the radars in the combat room. She didn't think he could be relied on to aggressively search for ships. Personality conflicts are the norm on a ship where crew members spend months in tight quarters. But they could impede the effectiveness of a watch team.

Still, Coppock, naturally self-assured, took the bridge undeterred. This was the Seventh Fleet. That's just how things were. Its sailors considered themselves the most driven in the navy. The action was constant, the missions important. They prided themselves on what navy investigators called a "can-do" attitude. If your ship sailed with too few sailors, or broken parts, it didn't matter. You made it work.

Coppock directed the *Fitzgerald* to head south down the coast of Japan, toward open ocean. She set the speed at 20 knots.

• • •

Earlier in the year, a rash of accidents and near misses had spooked the sailors of the Seventh Fleet. In January, the destroyer USS *Antietam* had run aground while in Yokosuka's harbor. Four months later, on May 9, the USS *Lake Champlain*, a guided-missile cruiser, collided with a South Korean fishing vessel in the Sea of Japan.

The *Lake Champlain* crash caused Babbitt, Benson's second-in-command, to issue a bulletin to the ship's officers. At six feet, five inches tall, with deep-set eyes, Babbitt was hard to ignore. He demanded vigilance from his sailors.

"CALL FOR HELP, USE THE HORSEPOWER TO MOVE, DO NOT COLLIDE," Babbitt wrote by hand in a note distributed to officers.

His worry almost instantly proved warranted. But his commands weren't followed.

On May 10, one night after the *Lake Champlain*'s mishap, a fishing vessel got close to the *Fitzgerald* while it was steaming off southern Japan. Coppock was serving as officer of the deck. Her conning officer was Eric Uhden. Like Woodley, he was an experienced sailor who served years at sea as an enlisted man before becoming an officer.

Uhden alerted Coppock to the potential danger. At first, she dismissed his concern. But a moment later, Uhden said that Coppock seemed to realize her miscalculation.

She ordered the *Fitzgerald* to dodge the fishing vessel by turning sharply left. The *Fitzgerald* missed the fishing boat by a couple hundred yards.

Uhden memorialized the incident in an understated note scribbled in his private journal: "Fishing vessel got close on watch." But nobody else knew about it. Coppock never told the captain, as she was supposed to do.

The next night, May 11, as the *Fitzgerald* steamed through the busy Tsushima Strait outside of Sasebo, another young lieutenant junior grade named Stephany Breau was serving as the officer of the deck. At around 11 p.m., Breau called the ship's then-captain for help. After he returned to his stateroom, Breau maneuvered safely through traffic for 45 minutes. Then she noticed a commercial fishing vessel sail out from behind another ship.

The *Fitzgerald*'s radar had not displayed the two ships.

"That ship is really close," Breau said to another officer. The fishing trawler was only 200 to 300 yards away, an extremely close distance for ships at sea.

Breau immediately ordered an emergency stop, directing all engines back full. The *Fitzgerald* sounded five short blasts from its whistle to warn the approaching vessel of an imminent crash.

Breau had executed a textbook response to avoid collision. Nonetheless, in a matter of three days, the USS *Lake Champlain* had crashed at sea and the *Fitzgerald* had back-to-back near misses. The close calls were significant events and should have been opportunities for critical examination.

On the *Fitzgerald*, that never happened. No senior officer ever heard about the first near miss. Only a handful of senior leaders were briefed on the second. Many junior officers, who might have benefited from a formal review, did not even know what had occurred.

Uhden confronted Babbitt with the ship's dysfunction.

"Sir, we have a serious problem on the ship," Uhden said he told the executive officer. "And the only way for things to get better here is for us to have a serious accident or someone to die."

Babbitt denied that such a conversation had occurred.

One more incident rattled the ship's officers. This time, Benson was to blame.

That spring, North Korea had stepped up missile tests. In an interview on *Fox Business News*, President Donald Trump promised to stop them. "We are sending an armada, very powerful," Trump said.

In May, the aircraft carriers the USS *Carl Vinson* and the USS *Ronald Reagan* steamed into the Sea of Japan, the first time two carriers had done so in decades. Benson got orders to join the armada. He would have to abandon the repairs he had planned to make and sail out with a crew that had never trained to sail with a carrier strike group, a complicated operation involving a dozen ships and thousands of sailors.

Benson could have taken the rare step of refusing the order, though he risked being fired by his superiors. But he believed his crew and his ship could do the job. On June 1, the *Fitzgerald* joined almost a dozen other warships to sail with the *Vinson* and *Reagan*.

The stirring image of steel and gun was just a show to warn Kim Jong-un, North Korea's leader. Normally, the ships in a carrier strike group do not cluster during operations—they are spread out over miles of sea. But even a moment intended as a display of navy might almost ended in embarrassment.

During maneuvers, Benson ordered the *Fitzgerald* to turn slightly to catch up with another ship in the armada. Uhden, who was the conning officer, thought they were getting too close. Benson leaned close and kicked Uhden in the back of the heel. "Make the turn," he told him. Coppock, also on the bridge, thought they might collide. She later told a friend that she had seen her career flash before her eyes, but could do nothing.

Benson had been giving the orders.

• • •

From the bridge, Coppock could see twelve miles across the ocean to distant lights glimmering in cities along Japan's coast. The moon had risen, casting a river of light across the Pacific. The temperature was around sixty-five degrees. The waves were cresting one to three feet.

Coppock glanced up at the SPS-73 radar screen in front of the darkened bridge. She noticed a cargo ship approaching the *Fitzgerald* from about twelve miles away. The radar indicated it would pass behind the *Fitzgerald*, about 1,500 yards to its stern. She began tracking the vessel but did not pay close attention to it.

Much like the radar in the combat room, the bridge radar was not providing a complete picture. In reality, there were three large cargo ships approaching the *Fitzgerald*, but the SPS-73 never showed more than two of them at the same time.

It remains unclear why the radar did not show an accurate picture of the ships at sea that night. One explanation is that the three ships were traveling close together. The cargo ship Coppock was tracking was west of the *Fitzgerald* but parallel to two other ships following roughly the same route. Closest to the *Fitzgerald* was a Chinese cargo vessel, the *Wan Hai 266*, slightly smaller than the *Crystal*. Next was the *Crystal*, about 1,000 yards past the *Wan Hai*. Farthest away was the 142,000-ton *Maersk Evora*, one of the beasts of the ocean at 1,200 feet in length. About two dozen smaller ships, many fishing boats, bobbed around them.

Another possibility is that Coppock may not have ensured that the radar on the bridge was properly adjusted to obtain a finer-grained picture. A postcrash reconstruction showed that Coppock lost sight of one of the ships due to clutter on the "improperly adjusted" SPS-73 screen.

Even without the radar, however, Coppock and the bridge team should have been able to see unaided the lights on the masts of the cargo ship she'd identified along with the two others running parallel to it. All three were headed toward the *Fitzgerald*—though at times, they would have obstructed one another from view.

A video taken just minutes before the accident, for example, clearly shows the *Maersk Evora* illuminated from 10,000 yards away. The *Crystal* also had navigation lights running, and it was less than a few thousands yards away at the same time.

But nobody, it turned out, was standing watch on the starboard side of the ship.

In years past, commanders traditionally posted lookouts on the port and starboard sides of the bridge. The lookouts had one job: search the sea for hazards. But navy cutbacks in personnel prompted Benson and other captains to combine the duties into a single job. "We just don't have enough bodies, qualified bodies, to have a port and starboard lookout," said Samuel Williams, a boatswain's mate first class.

Parker, Coppock's number two that night, was supposed to walk back and forth between the two sides during the watch, with the rest of the bridge team helping her keep an eye out.

But Parker had walked out onto a small metal deck located off the bridge on the port side of the *Fitzgerald* just after one a.m. She was there with Womack, trying to fit in some training by helping him develop his seaman's eye, the ability to estimate distance and bearing by sight. Parker had not received a promotion on a previous ship, after its commanding officer thought she had trouble assessing the risk posed by ships in the surrounding ocean.

Over the next fifteen to twenty minutes, the pair observed five or six ships. It may have been a good training exercise. But it was poor navigation practice. None of the ships on the *Fitzgerald*'s port side were a threat.

• • •

Coppock had grown up in Willard, Missouri, a town of 5,000 northwest of Springfield. During her sophomore year in high school, she flew to Hawaii with classmates from the Junior Reserve Officers' Training Corps.

There, she toured the floating memorial that sits above the wreck of the USS *Arizona*, sunk during Japan's attack on Pearl Harbor. Inside, Coppock stared at a white marble wall etched with the names of the 1,177 sailors who died that day.

Coppock knew she wanted to join the navy.

"I wanted to be part of something larger than myself," she said.

Coppock graduated from the University of Missouri on a navy scholarship. Her first ship was the USS *Ashland*, an amphibious landing craft.

Amphibious landing craft are ungainly vessels, built to ferry troops in hangar-like holds and launch helicopters from their broad decks. Their commanders were used to getting less attention than higher profile aircraft carriers and destroyers. Crews tended to be pugnacious and self-sufficient.

The ship's rough-and-tumble atmosphere added to the challenges facing Coppock. The navy can be a tough place for women: only about a fifth of navy sailors are female, and misogyny remains an occupational hazard.

But the five-foot-four-inch Coppock was used to giving what she got in the *Ashland*'s wardroom, where the ship's officers gathered to eat and talk. "You could sit there and scream at each other for hours and it was just to get stuff done. We really didn't care. It wasn't personal," she said. "We'd go out and drink afterwards."

It was a different story on the *Fitzgerald*.

Coppock stopped dining with her fellow officers in the *Fitzgerald*'s wardroom. By long navy tradition, attendance at such meals was considered necessary to forge the esprit de corps needed to run a ship. Not eating with them was akin to snubbing family.

Fellow *Fitzgerald* sailors noted her absence. To some, Coppock appeared disconnected. Other shipmates went so far as to call her "lazy" or "abrasive and unapproachable."

Coppock said she stayed away from the officers' mess because of criticism from fellow junior officers. She blamed their hostility on her singular focus on getting the job done. Mission came first, she said.

"They just kept telling me I was too aggressive, that I needed to . . . tone myself down," she said.

On one thing, however, both supporters and detractors agreed on: She was superb at her full-time job. Coppock was the *Fitzgerald*'s anti–submarine warfare officer. Sub hunting was a shadowy game of cat-and-mouse, played between navy destroyers and potential enemies from China, Russia, or North Korea, each sussing out the other's capabilities.

Coppock had displayed her skills in the weeks after Benson took command. She and her enlisted assistant, Alexander Vaughan, had stayed up almost forty-eight hours in the successful pursuit of a Chinese submarine off the coast of Japan. The achievement sealed Coppock's reputation as a hell of a sailor.

It also boosted her self-assurance. She considered herself one of the better officers on the ship.

Arleigh Burke, the admiral who lends his name to the model of ship that the *Fitzgerald* belonged to, once reflected on what made for the best kinds of officers.

"The difference between a good officer and a poor one," Burke said, "is about DATE \@ "M/d/yyyy" 8/19/2020 seconds."

• • •

Parker walked across the bridge to check the starboard side of the *Fitzgerald*. She glanced at a display to check the time. It was one-twenty a.m. As she stepped out onto the bridge wing, she saw lights shining from the bow of an approaching ship off in the distance, about six miles away. It was the *Crystal*. Parker alerted Coppock. Coppock told Parker not to worry—she was tracking the ship. She said it would pass 1,500 yards behind the *Fitzgerald*.

Parker had her doubts. "It doesn't look like it's going to cross us behind," she said. Parker stepped out to the bridge wing to check again. Suddenly, she noticed something strange. A second set of lights glided out from behind the first.

It was the first time that anyone on the *Fitzgerald* had realized that two ships were steaming toward the *Fitzgerald*'s starboard bow. The Chinese cargo ship was indeed going to pass behind the *Fitzgerald*. But the *Crystal*, which had slightly altered its course, was heading straight for the destroyer.

"We gotta slow down," Parker told Coppock.

No, Coppock told her again. "We can't slow down because it'll make the situation worse." Coppock worried that slowing down might bring her into the path of the ship that was supposed to pass behind them.

In such situations, Parker, the subordinate, is supposed to express concerns to a superior officer. The navy encourages what it calls a "questioning attitude" supported by "forceful backup." But Parker did not press her concerns with Coppock about the oncoming ship.

At one-twenty-five a.m., the *Fitzgerald* was 6,000 yards from the *Crystal*, 5,000 yards from the *Wan Hai 266* and on a collision course with the *Maersk Evora*, approaching from 14,000 yards away. There was still time for the highly maneuverable *Fitzgerald* to get out of the way.

But Coppock disobeyed Benson's standing orders. Rather than call Benson for help, she decided to continue on her own. Coppock didn't call down to the combat room to ask for help, either.

"I decided to try and handle it," she said.

At around one-thirty a.m., time had run out. Parker ran inside from the bridge wing, yelling, "They're coming right at us."

Coppock looked up and spotted the superstructure of the *Crystal* through the bridge windows. She stepped out on the starboard wing for a better look and realized she was in trouble. In navy terms, the *Fitzgerald* was in extremis—in grave danger of catastrophe.

To avoid the *Crystal*, Coppock decided to order a hard turn to the right, the standard action for an evasive maneuver under international navigation rules.

She shouted the command to Womack to pass on to the helmsman. But Womack did not immediately understand her order. After Womack hesitated, Coppock decided that she was not going to clear the *Crystal* by going toward the right. Such a turn would put her on a possible collision with the *Wan Hai 266*.

"Oh shit, I'm so fucked! I'm so fucked!" she screamed.

Coppock could have ordered the *Fitzgerald* into reverse; there was still time to stop. Arleigh Burke destroyers can come to a complete halt from 20 knots within 500 feet or so.

Instead, Coppock ordered a move that disregarded the very basics of her training. She commanded the helmsman to gun the destroyer's powerful engines to full speed and duck in front of the *Crystal* by heading left. "All ahead flank," she ordered. "Hard left rudder."

Helmsman-in-training Simona Nelson had taken the wheel of a destroyer at sea for the first time in her life twenty-five minutes earlier. Nelson froze, unsure of how to respond.

Petty Officer First Class Samuel Williams noticed Nelson struggling. He took control of the helm and did as Coppock ordered: he pushed the throttle to full and turned the rudder hard left. The ship's engines revved to full power.

The move put the *Fitzgerald* directly into the path of the oncoming *Crystal*.

Coppock did not sound the collision alarm to warn sailors of the impending risk.

"I just got so wrapped up in trying to do anything that I had to just drop the ball on everything else that I needed to do," she said.

Instead, she ran out to the starboard bridge wing. The *Crystal*'s blunt prow loomed above her, a wall of black steel angled sharply upward. To keep from pitching overboard, Coppock seized the alidade, a large metallic instrument used for taking bearings.

"Grab onto something," Womack shouted to his fellow sailors on the *Fitzgerald* bridge.

• • •

At 1:30:34 a.m. on June 17, 2017, at 34.52 degrees north latitude and 139.07 degrees east longitude, the ACX *Crystal* slammed into the USS *Fitzgerald*. The 30,000-ton *Crystal* was moving at 18 knots. The 8,261-ton *Fitzgerald* had accelerated to 22 knots.

The *Crystal*'s prow and its protruding lower bow seized the *Fitzgerald* like a pincer. The top dug into Benson's stateroom, 160 feet back from the *Fitzgerald*'s bow, shearing off the steel hull and crumpling his cabin. The bottom ripped across Berthing 2 and nearby compartments, leaving a hole thirteen feet by seventeen feet.

The *Crystal* swung 125 degrees to the right in two minutes. The impact knocked the cargo ship onto a collision course with the giant *Maersk Evora*. The captain of the *Crystal* took evasive action that unfolded slowly as the big ships carefully maneuvered around each other in the crowded seas. It would take an hour for the *Crystal* to return to the scene to offer aid. None of the *Crystal*'s twenty-member crew was seriously injured, but structural damage was significant. It would take thirty-five tons of steel to repair.

The *Fitzgerald* rolled sharply to port, snapping 20 degrees from right to left as it broke free of the *Crystal*. It settled out with a 7-degree list to starboard. Out of control, the destroyer spun 360 degrees through the water, completing the circle in five minutes.

When it came to rest, the *Fitzgerald* had lost power and communications.

The ship was dead in the water.

Chapter 4: Berthing 2

"Grandma's Prayers Are Still Working"

Petty Officer Second Class Rod Felderman had awakened in his top bunk at the moment of impact. He'd heard the shouts of water on deck. He pushed back his sleeping curtain. Dark, cold water was rising quickly around him. It had almost reached his rack.

Felderman stuck his legs out to jump down but felt a sailor below him and recoiled. However, he realized he had to get going. He put his legs in the rising water and lowered himself down.

He was instantly up to his neck. He fought his way to a ladder exiting the starboard side of the ship. He saw other men standing in line in front of him, their heads bobbing in the water. They were starting to panic.

"Go! Go!" one sailor shouted. "It is blocked," another sailor responded. Debris covered the door leading to the ladder and to safety.

Felderman was going to be submerged in seconds. He took a breath and went under. A battle lantern lit the quarters underwater, but the light was poor, and there was no clear path to escape. And now he was desperate for air.

He thrust himself upward. He burst out into a small pocket of air between two pipes. He found only inches of space between the water level and the top of the compartment.

He smashed his head into the opening so hard that he bruised his face, split his skin, and began bleeding.

"I was raving like a wild animal for air, pushing my face as high as I could," he remembered.

He sucked in what air he could and went under again.

The sleeping quarters on a warship can be surprisingly serene. Lights are on in the berthing from six to ten a.m. and from six to ten p.m. Otherwise it's dark, as sailors sleep in shifts.

The coffin lockers provide modest refuge, with only a curtain for privacy. The tallest sailors often try to get the top bunk, where they can stretch out more. The bottom racks were the least desirable, especially the ones near the busy ladder exits at each end of the berthing. Seasoned sailors preferred the middle bunks—shoulder height, easy to roll into. For some men, bottom rack or top, the rocking of the waves or the low, constant hum of an underway ship resulted in the deepest possible sleep.

Gabriel Cantu, a petty officer second class, had hit his rack at nine-thirty p.m. He had first watch the next day. Sonar Technician Kamari Eason had first watch, too, but didn't get to bed until midnight. Petty Officer 3rd Class John Mead managed to grab a shower before he turned in at eleven-thirty. Matthew King, a sonar technician first class, had just finished his watch shift. He had lain in his bunk—Berthing 2, port side, Rack 44—and watched a movie before falling asleep. Seaman Dakota Rigsby, one of the youngest in the compartment, had sacked out on a bench in the lounge—it was quieter than his bunk.

The *Crystal*'s lancing of the starboard wall of Berthing 2 shattered the calm.

One weapons specialist heard a sound like a bomb going off. Another sailor said he could hear what sounded like a huge waterfall and felt what seemed like a cold breeze blowing through the quarters. Denis Medved, a young seaman whose bunk lay closest to the hole, was blasted out of his bed to the other side of the berthing.

The sailors rescued one another. They grabbed shipmates from their beds. They hauled them through surging water, slipping, stumbling toward exits. They pushed one another to survive.

It was Khalil Legier's first night in Berthing 2, having moved earlier that day from another quarters. He rolled out of his bunk—bottom rack, port side, second row—and into the bottom rack across the aisle before standing up. Scott Childers was behind him but seemed frozen, unable to move. Legier grabbed Childers by the neck, and with his other hand grabbed the shirt of the sailor in front him. They started out for the exit as a threesome.

Seaman Brayden Harden broke for the ship's starboard side, straight into the maw of the flood. Someone grabbed him and hurled him toward the port side to the exit ladder there.

In another setting, the sudden inundation might have drowned everyone alive. But the sailors had been trained since their first days on the *Fitzgerald* to escape by putting on blindfolds and feeling their way to the exits.

What's more, the *Fitzgerald* sailors in Berthing 2 were close. They had spent four months at sea. They woke together. Showered together. Worked, ate, and relaxed together. And then returned at night to sleep in the same compartment together. Two men might spend twenty-four hours never more than three feet apart. They knew each other better than many brothers.

The trust explained the orderly line they formed at the ladder. As they clambered up, water in the compartment rose and forced air out of the berthing. Men flew out the small opening at the top like office messages through a pneumatic tube.

Twenty-seven men escaped up the port ladder in about ninety seconds.

• • •

The average temperature of the ocean off the coast of Japan in June is around seventy degrees. That temperature might be fine for a warm summer day. But it's dangerously cold for water.

Many people involuntarily open their mouths when they hit cold water, a reaction to the shock. If you manage to take a breath, you probably can't hold it long—panic makes the heart beat faster and the body use more oxygen than normal.

As water fills your mouth, it can flood the windpipe and the esophagus. Your body temperature drops. Your muscles weaken. Your lungs introduce water into your circulatory system, thinning your blood and causing abnormal chemical reactions.

Death usually comes from a heart attack or a reduced blood supply to the brain. Depending on psychological and physiological factors like your height and fitness, it can take seconds or several minutes.

The handful of men remaining in Berthing 2 were running out of time.

Mead, a burly weapons specialist from Scottsdale, Arizona, had been the last person to reach the line of men waiting to exit the port ladder. The water had reached his waist.

He looked to his right and saw water pouring into the compartment through a hole in the starboard side that reached from floor to ceiling. The weight of the incoming water threw the *Fitzgerald* off kilter.

Mead slipped on the tilting floor and felt something pull him backward. The floodwaters had forced open the door of the common bathroom, creating a vacuum that sucked in Mead and another man, Gary Rehm Jr., a weapons specialist from Virginia.

Mead fought his way out, but a pair of lockers blocked his path. As he struggled to get past, Mead felt a push and saw Rehm behind him.

As Mead half-walked, half-swam toward the open scuttle, he had to battle his way through debris.

Mead got wedged between a floating locker and the ceiling. The water was closing around him. He tried to take a final, deep breath but instead swallowed the salty, chemical-filled water. In his last seconds of consciousness, he grabbed an overhead pipe and propelled himself toward the escape hatch.

• • •

Tapia and Vaughan looked down into the scuttle one more time and noticed a ghostly shape moving through the water. The men reached down and hauled out Mead, the second, and last, sailor rescued by the two petty officers from Texas.

Tapia and Vaughan, joined by other sailors, tried to close the scuttle. But they'd waited too long. Water was flowing through. The men were now battling the force of the ocean. There was nothing they could do. They turned to Mead.

He was in bad shape. His eyes were bloodshot. He was coughing up water. Tapia and Vaughan grabbed Mead and headed to the mess room, the ship's main cafeteria and one of the biggest spaces on the *Fitzgerald*.

One sailor there asked a chief petty officer, "Are we abandoning ship, or are we fighting?"

"I don't know," answered the chief.

The mess room became a command post for the wounded—only a handful of sailors had suffered serious injuries, but many more appeared to be in shellshock, unable to function.

Vaughan took out a grease pencil and started writing on a table. Without electricity, he was trying to do a head count by memory.

After some confusion, it became clear that most of the sailors had escaped from Berthing 2.

But seven were missing.

Felderman found himself alone on the starboard side of the *Fitzgerald*. He was swimming through a dark swirl that didn't make any sense to him, even though he had trained blindfolded to be able to exit in the dark.

As he thrashed in the murk, his lungs and stomach hurt. He couldn't decide if he was dead or alive. "It felt like I could almost breathe underwater," he said. "Maybe I should just wait because this seems very unreal." He thought about his wife, Liz, and their soon-to-be-born daughter, Alice. Visions of them attending his memorial service played in his head.

"I tumbled like the mad swimming dog I was then toward a light," he remembered.

As he neared the starboard side escape hatch, he brushed against another sailor, floating near a water fountain. His head was above water, and Felderman thought he could hear him gasping for air.

Felderman began to lose energy. Somehow, he drifted up through the opening on the starboard side. He looked up and saw the door for Berthing 1—located one deck above Berthing 2.

"Grandma's prayers are still working," he thought.

A sailor found him outside the door. He walked Felderman to the personnel office for treatment. Felderman's face was bleeding, bruised, and swollen. Friends hurried to check on him. Felderman was a popular sailor. He loved *Star Wars* and could make a whistle that sounded like a sonar signal. He told them he was relieved to be alive.

But as he lay there, Felderman began to go into shock, shaking from the cold. He was having difficulty breathing and could only draw in short, shallow breaths. He was given an inhaler to help. Hospital corpsmen tried to start an IV and piled warm blankets over him. One sailor stayed with him, holding his head while he continued vomiting and helping him to urinate into a trash bag.

Felderman mistook the care for safety.

"We must not be sinking anymore," he recalled thinking.

• • •

The fate of the seven men in Berthing 2 turned into a test of command.

As dawn approached, Perez stormed up to Babbitt. He demanded permission to dive into the flooded compartment to rescue the men—or retrieve their bodies. They were his sailors and he was not giving up on them.

Babbitt refused. Such a rescue mission risked the lives of the rest of the crew and the ship by breaking flooding boundaries. Perez continued to argue. The heated exchange didn't end until the ship's highest-ranking enlisted man pulled Perez away to cool him down.

Perez did not give up. Ogilvie and Vaughan volunteered to make an attempt with him. The three petty officers went to a locker and retrieved diving fins and a mask. They made their way to the hatch leading to the starboard side of Berthing 1, which had not flooded to the top.

Peering down, the trio of sailors realized they were actually seeing down into Berthing 2. The 221-square-foot hole had exposed the *Fitzgerald* to open sea, allowing light from the sun rising at dawn to penetrate the hold.

"I think I see a shoe down there," Perez told Ogilvie, shining a flashlight.

"Okay, let's do it, man, let's go get this guy," Ogilvie said.

The two men played rock, paper, scissors. Perez won. He put on a diving mask, and Ogilvie and Vaughan lowered him into the water to retrieve the sailor. He returned empty-handed.

"I thought it was somebody," Perez told Ogilvie.

The men resigned themselves. The sailors were dead.

To prepare for possible retrieval of the bodies, several crewmen gathered in the chiefs' dining area. As a group, they decided: Whether the men appeared dead or alive, each would receive emergency treatment. The group would first strip them naked, dry them off, and then use the ship's automated external defibrillators. Then, they would do CPR by hand. If that didn't work, they would provide mouth-to-mouth.

It was desperate, even morbid. But the crew wanted to try something, anything, to relieve its helplessness and grief.

"Sitting and waiting for the bodies wasn't so bad at first, but the doc warned the group that some people would freak out and that the dead would spurt water when we did chest compressions," Alex Helbig, an ensign, later wrote. "I brought out a bucket for people to vomit in."

The plan was canceled when it was clear that nobody at that moment was going to retrieve the bodies.

Chapter 5. Fight the Ship

"I Realized That the Miracle Was You Guys, the Crew"

Lt. j.g. Stephany Breau had deftly handled the *Fitzgerald* during the near miss outside of Sasebo. Now she was called into action again. She was the ship's damage control assistant.

It was her job to fix the *Fitzgerald.*

Breau ran from her cabin through the darkness and in two minutes reached Damage Control Central—a special section in an engineering room designed to act as an emergency operations post.

She picked up a microphone for the shipwide intercom: "I assume all duties and responsibilities for damage control onboard USS *Fitzgerald,*" she announced. She sounded the alarm for general quarters, directing sailors to preassigned stations designated for emergencies.

Arleigh Burke–class destroyers are designed to be the most survivable ships in the navy. The *Fitzgerald* could defend against torpedoes, cruise missiles, and strafing. It had multiple backups for critical systems—three radar systems, four kinds of compasses, reinforced hulls, and stations throughout the ship that could be activated for navigation.

Now, that survivability was put to the test.

Fitzgerald crew members were missing. Five sailors were trapped in sonar compartments in the front of the ship. The seven from Berthing 2 could not be located.

The ship was flooding. By 2:45 a.m., the ship's forward compartments had flooded with some 85 tons of water. That figure would grow to 514 tons as the night progressed.

Its communications systems were collapsing. Breau's announcement was the last of the night from the ship's main intercom.

Without electricity, critical systems were on battery backups. Sailors used flashlights and cellphones to guide their way through the darkened ship. The space below decks grew sweltering without air conditioning.

The destroyer's propulsion system was damaged. A pump lubricating the starboard shaft failed, forcing its shutdown. The *Fitzgerald* was left with one propeller for power. It also could move no faster than about 5 knots, the speed of a person jogging. Any faster, and the amount of seawater rushing in would increase.

Breau attacked the greatest threat: water. Berthing 2 and Auxiliary Room 1, housing electrical equipment, had flooded. So, too, had a main passageway on the starboard side. Berthing 1 was inundated, too. All of its sailors managed to escape.

Breau had to worry about physics. The free surface effect describes a phenomenon when water partially fills a closed space. The weight of water shifting side to side in such a space can disrupt the ship's stability and threaten to capsize it.

She did algebra, scribbling calculations on the back of a notebook. She had to figure out the weight of water in the ship in case she needed to counterflood the *Fitzgerald*, a technique to deliberately flood other ship compartments to counterbalance areas already filled with water.

Perhaps the biggest worry was progressive flooding—water levels that continue to rise. The *Fitzgerald* had been set to condition Zebra: All necessary hatches and doors had been sealed tight. But still, water seeped through air ducts and open conduits between compartments. The levels kept rising.

Breau set up flooding boundaries, where sailors from the rapid response Flying Squad would hold the line against the inrushing sea. They set out with pumps to drain the hardest hit areas.

One piece of training that Benson did not have to postpone dealt with the safety of his sailors. From his first weeks on the ship, he had worked with Breau to drill sailors on condition Zebra and on getting out of sleeping quarters.

"These seamen knew exactly what they needed to do and how to do it," she said.

• • •

Up on the bridge, Babbitt was fighting to keep the ship afloat.

Sailors who had escaped drowning began to show up dressed only in T-shirts and underwear, covered in soapy firefighting foam from a pipe that had burst.

One was Jackson Schrimsher. He took over the steering controls but found that they were not responding. Babbitt ordered him to a backup navigation station in the back of the ship known in navy parlance as aft steering.

Babbitt jury-rigged a system to pass his orders. He would call Breau, who would then relay them back to Schrimsher via a special emergency intercom.

For the next fifteen hours, Schrimsher guided the ship from a small, windowless room. He had no relief: the ship's other master helmsman had drowned in Berthing 2. Schrimsher fought the list, the slowed propulsion, the shifting currents. Every three minutes he switched rudder positions to keep the *Fitzgerald* stable, tacking slowly back and forth. He made more than 300 course adjustments in all.

Babbitt was trying to save his sailors. The five crew members trapped in sonar were rescued early on. Womack appeared in a daze. Coppock was inconsolable, sobbing and berating herself.

Babbitt told her to go sit down.

• • •

At 4:37 a.m., just after sunrise, the first help arrived: Japanese Coast guard vessels and medical helicopters. The *Fitzgerald* immediately felt the loss of its sailors. Communication with the Japanese crew was difficult—one of those missing, Yeoman Third Class Shingo Douglass, was the only person on board fluent in Japanese.

Several chiefs strapped Benson to a stretcher, lowering him from the bridge to the flight deck located on the ship's tail. They passed Benson vertically from man to man down the steep ladders.

The flight deck on the rear of the ship was listing too hard for a helicopter landing. So a Japanese corpsman dropped down to the deck and hitched Benson's litter to a winch to bring him on board, followed by White, who had become Benson's caretaker.

Breau began to win the battle against the sea. Powerful pumps designed to quickly move huge amounts of water failed. Instead, Breau dispatched portable pumps, the kind available at many hardware stores, to the most seriously flooded compartments.

Exhaust from the gas-engine pumps reached dangerous levels in confined areas of the ship, creating an alarmingly thick haze. But they "saved our ship," Breau said.

One stubborn area remained: Water continued to flood into a lower deck compartment carrying equipment for the Tomahawk missile system. None of the pumps were powerful enough to carry the water out.

Breau's last trick was a bucket brigade. For ten hours, about two dozen sailors at a time snaked in a long, tight line from below ship up three ladder wells to the main deck. Sailors rotated in and out, relieving comrades fatigued by the nonstop passing of ten-pound buckets of water.

As pumps and generators and sailors worked to help, the water level began to stabilize.

At about 8:30 a.m., the first American rescuers arrived on scene, navy tugboats from Yokosuka. They lashed themselves to the *Fitzgerald* to correct the list and guide it forward. A few hours later, the USS *Dewey*, another Arleigh Burke–class destroyer, arrived to assist. Dewey sailors poured on board the *Fitzgerald*, bringing food, water, and fresh muscle.

It was then, at last, that Breau realized the *Fitzgerald* was going to make it back home.

Crew migrated to the main deck in search of relief and rest after what seemed an endless night. They lay down amid a tangle of twisting red fire hoses draining water from below.

They munched on slices of turkey and cans of tuna, handfuls of grapes and orange wedges, and drank bottles of water. Toilets were not working, so Babbitt ordered buckets put into two adjoining compartments.

Ogilvie sat down to smoke a cigar beneath a missile. Lighting up beneath hundreds of gallons of jet fuel broke all kinds of rules, not to mention common sense.

It just didn't seem to matter much at the moment.

• • •

The *Fitzgerald* came into view of Yokosuka harbor late in the afternoon on June 17. It was moving so slowly that it took several more hours to reach shore. All traffic headed into Tokyo Bay, one of the world's busiest harbors, stopped. It was an extraordinary sight: scores of massive cargo vessels slowly following a disabled American warship.

Just before seven p.m., the *Fitzgerald* finally tied up to Pier 12, the same place it had departed thirty-six hours before. Hundreds of people had gathered. Family and friends huddled under white tents. Sailors from all over the base arrived to help. The Red Cross and military charities stood by with food, water, and new clothes.

Navy divers had arrived in wetsuits and a rescue boat to retrieve the seven dead sailors. They stationed themselves by the *Fitzgerald*'s starboard side, which faced away from the pier to conceal the worst of the damage. They had trouble getting into the *Fitzgerald* at first. The hole on the starboard side was jagged. Inside, it was filled with debris. The water was oily and dark. It was not until 4:54 a.m. that they managed to swim into Berthing 2.

They found Seaman Dakota Rigsby first. He was floating in the starboard exit, his foot lodged between the exit ladder and the wall. It was unclear whether Rigsby had been trapped. He often slept on benches in the lounge area, where he could stretch out more than in his bunk.

Rigsby, nineteen, from Palmyra, Virginia, population 104, was the fourth generation in his family to serve. On the *Fitzgerald*, he worked in the cafeteria. He liked spicy foods, scary movies, and TV comedies. He guzzled energy drinks and consumed all things having to do with Pokémon and anime. He had recently become engaged and hoped to become a chief petty officer.

The divers placed Rigsby's body into a bag and swam toward the dive boat, stationed next to the *Fitzgerald*. They had stretched a tarp over the boat to shield the operation from the media, family members, and spectators. Rigsby's body was recovered at 5:23 a.m.

The same process was repeated six more times.

At 7:45 a.m., the divers brought up Douglass, of San Diego, California. His body was found floating in the starboard side lounge of Berthing 2.

Douglass, twenty-five, grew up in America and Japan, the son of a marine sergeant and a Japanese mother. The Seventh Fleet allowed him to live in both worlds. He was fluent in Japanese and had become a master helmsman.

At 8 a.m., Petty Officer First Class Carlos Victor Sibayan, twenty-three, was retrieved from Berthing 2. His body was also found in the lounge area.

Sibayan was born in Manila, Philippines, and grew up in Chula Vista, California. He had been raised navy: his father was a retired master chief who had lectured him on the importance of standing watch to ensure the safety of his ship, noted an obituary in the *Times* of San Diego.

At 8:15 a.m., the divers recovered Xavier Martin, twenty-four, of Halethorpe, Maryland. He was the third person found floating in the lounge.

The son of a veteran, Martin was one of Benson's favorites. He was an eager young sailor who had advanced quickly and impressed Benson with his initiative. Benson had made him a personal assistant.

As a personnel specialist, Martin was well known on board for his upbeat, cheerful attitude. He had a taste for sports cars and had purchased a bright yellow 1992 Mazda sports car in Japan, the steering wheel on the right side.

At 8:22 a.m., the divers raised Sonar Technician Third Class Ngoc "Tan" Truong Huynh, twenty-five, of Oakville, Connecticut. He was found beneath a television, though the divers assessed that he had not been trapped there.

Huynh had celebrated his twenty-fifth birthday one day before his death. A naturalized citizen who was born in Vietnam, he was the oldest of four siblings. He loved to watch soccer, and his favorite video games were Fallout and Lethal Weapon.

At 8:28 a.m., Noe Hernandez, 26, was found near the starboard lounge. He had a laceration on his head, its cause unknown.

Hernandez, a deeply faithful Roman Catholic, loved spending time with his wife, Dora, and three-year-old son. The family traveled extensively during downtime from their navy lives. He was a strong swimmer, worked out constantly, and was an avid outdoorsman.

At 8:35 a.m., the final body was brought to the surface. It was Gary Rehm, thirty-seven, of Hampton, Virginia. He was found inside the bathroom, its door closed—the last place he had been seen by Mead, who credited Rehm with saving his life.

Rehm was the oldest sailor in the berthing and considered one of the best watch standers on the ship. A married man, grandson of a World War II navy veteran, he was quiet, professional, reserved. He had served in Iraq and was nearing retirement from the navy.

• • •

Dora Hernandez was in the crowd when the *Fitzgerald* had at last arrived, desperate for news about her husband, Noe. The navy had not released any information. Rumors flew, but nobody officially knew who was alive or injured or dead.

For loved ones, the return of the *Fitzgerald* had been a macabre lottery. As sailors began to disembark, Dora watched several friends explode in joy at the sight of a loved one. "I was so happy for them," Hernandez said. "But it was hard."

Late that evening, after everyone had departed, Dora found herself left on the pier with a few friends. She decided to stay. For the rest of the night, she paced the concrete pier, back and forth along the 505-foot length of the *Fitzgerald*. In the morning, she brought fresh coffee to the sailors who stood watch. When told that navy divers had arrived to search the *Fitzgerald* and that the bodies would be taken to the hospital, Hernandez jumped into a car with a friend and raced off.

At the hospital, a navy officer delivered the news that the divers had retrieved Noe's body. Feeling numb, Dora had one request: could she see her husband one last time?

A navy doctor agreed on one condition. Dora could not touch her husband. The sailors were supposed to be examined by a coroner in the exact condition they were found.

She went into a hospital room. Her husband lay on a metal table in a body bag. It was unzipped to reveal his face and chest.

Dora and Noe had been high school sweethearts. They had grown up together in Weslaco, Texas, a suburban town that sprawled along the Rio Grande, the brown, serpentine river that formed the border between Texas and Mexico.

It looked to Dora like her husband was sleeping. She leaned close to him and prayed.

"I was torturing myself, sitting there. It was very surreal," she said. "Once I knew he was gone, there was nothing else I could do."

On June 20, the men were to be flown home. Navy leaders planned a small ceremony at the U.S. Air Force base near Yokosuka to send the men on a military transport plane to Dover Air Force Base outside of Washington, D.C.

Fitzgerald family and crew members begged to be allowed to attend the dignified send-off. The navy rounded up several buses to make the trip to the air base.

The crew gathered on the broad gray tarmac. The seven coffins sat on a makeshift bier in front of the transport plane. Hernandez was there with three-year-old Leon in a baby carrier strapped to her chest.

Adm. John Richardson, the head of the navy, had flown in from Washington. He delivered brief remarks.

When she heard Richardson, Hernandez decided she wanted to say something. He had not known the crew personally. But she had.

She stood nervously in front of the group, unused to being the center of attention. She looked out on the sailors of the *Fitzgerald*. Benson leaned against a cane. The sailors' faces were exhausted and worn. The disaster could have been so much worse. But they had worked together. They had saved each other.

"I was on the dock waiting for a miracle to happen, for my husband to come home," she told the crowd. "And then I realized that the miracle was you guys, the crew."

Epilogue

In the hours and weeks after the crash, the *Fitzgerald*'s crew members were besieged—by doctors, reporters, investigators. They gave firsthand accounts for formal inquiries. They spoke with therapists concerned about their mental health. They tried to reconnect with family and with one another.

They did not get much rest. Within weeks, the navy had begun to scatter crew members to other ships in the Seventh Fleet. Navy leaders needed their bodies to plug staffing shortfalls on other destroyers.

Some found it difficult to return to their old jobs. The trauma was too fresh. The navy supplied scores of additional psychologists, therapists, counselors, and chaplains. Many sailors were diagnosed with post–traumatic stress disorder, although the navy has never released a formal count.

Will Marquis, a petty officer first class who escaped Berthing 2, found himself unable to concentrate on even simple paperwork tasks. He was diagnosed with PTSD and is currently receiving treatment.

"A lot of people are having issues," Marquis said. "They didn't want to get help because they didn't know what it would do to their career or they figured they would get past it."

Felderman wrote a harrowing seven-page account of the ordeal. He illustrated it with haunting black and white drawings: bunkmates lining up for the inescapable starboard exit, sailors bobbing in seawater up to their necks, a body floating in the floodwaters. Felderman has returned home to the United States with his wife and daughter.

Some sailors were eager to get back to work. Vaughan limped around on his fractured thigh for several days until his own sailors told him to see a doctor. He did not go home for two months, crashing with friends on base.

"It definitely helped me to have people around," Vaughan said.

Vaughan, Tapia, Breau, Schrimsher, Stawecki, Ogilvie, Perez, Caldwell, and White were among the three dozen sailors given commendations for their actions in helping save crew members. Most remain in the navy and have moved on to different posts.

The navy's search for accountability made healing more difficult, especially after the collision of the *McCain* in August 2017. Suddenly, navy leaders had to explain to Congress how two American warships had crashed with two cargo vessels in the space of two months.

The navy's investigators concluded that sailors bore the primary blame for the collision. Benson, Coppock, and the bridge and combat information center watch teams had failed to use basic seamanship skills to escape an "avoidable" accident. They had been "excessively fatigued" and had not taken steps to rest. Coppock had ignored basic rules of the road and the captain's orders.

Shortfalls in training, the lack of personnel, and overconfident leadership were deemed contributing factors to the collision. Senior navy leadership fired several officers involved in the readiness of the Seventh Fleet. Aucoin, the Seventh Fleet commander, was relieved of command. Adm. Thomas Rowden, the navy's senior surface warfare officer, was forced to retire and stripped of a rank.

The navy explicitly ruled out problems with any of the ship's radars.

The investigation into the *Fitzgerald* sailors resulted in accusations of prosecutorial overreach and high-level interference. For instance, the navy charged Benson and other officers with negligent homicide—then abruptly withdrew the accusations without explanation last summer. Defense attorneys said navy officials were scapegoating low-ranking officers and sailors to conceal poor decisions made by senior navy leadership.

Coppock was charged with dereliction of duty and pleaded guilty. She remains in the navy and is expected to be a witness against Benson and Combs in their trials. Navy investigators have praised her candor and cooperation. She has a tattoo on her left wrist with seven shamrocks. It features the coordinates of the crash.

Combs has pleaded not guilty and continues to fight the dereliction of duty charge against her. Her trial is also scheduled for the spring. She remains in the navy.

Criminal charges against Woodley were dismissed, though he was referred for possible disciplinary action.

Babbitt was relieved of duty and given a formal letter of reprimand, effectively ending his chances for promotion. He has transferred to a new duty post in Europe.

Benson continues to struggle with what happened on the *Fitzgerald* and its aftermath.

After the crash, he was diagnosed with a traumatic brain injury and post–traumatic stress disorder. He remains in the navy and is currently receiving weekly treatment in Washington, D.C.

Talking about the accident is not easy for him. He has trouble remembering details. He is often seized by emotion. Sometimes he tears up. Sometimes he flashes the fierce, angry glare that he once reserved for errant sailors.

He was fired as commander of the *Fitzgerald*, a punishment he did not contest. He was the captain. The ship nearly sank. Seven sailors died. "It was my responsibility," he said.

But after the navy charged him with negligent homicide and other crimes, Benson fought back hard. He may have had problems as a captain. But he was not a criminal.

All but two charges against Benson have been dismissed. He faces one count of dereliction of duty and a second for mishandling the ship. Both are felony equivalents. A recent legal ruling has put the case in limbo and no trial date is set.

"A terrible thing happened. That's something I will live with the rest of my life, and dedicate my life to, honoring the men that I lost," he said. "But I don't see where I broke any laws."

The *Fitzgerald* was carried by an ocean-going transport vessel from Japan to a shipyard in Pascagoula, Mississippi. The estimated repair bill is $330 million.

A small crew remains with the ship. Every day, they pass by the crest of the *Fitzgerald*, a shield with four shamrocks above a blue cross.

It bears the ship's motto: "Protect Your People."

Paris Reiew

WINNER—ASME AWARD FOR FICTION

Jonathan Escoffery's "Under the Ackee Tree" was one of three short stories—the others were "Howl Palace," by Leigh Newman, and "Foxes," by Kimberly King Parsons—that won the Paris Review *the 2020 ASME Award for Fiction. "These remarkable stories," said the Ellie judges, "highlight* The Paris Review*'s mission of discovering and celebrating the best contemporary writers." Written in Jamaican patois, "Under the Ackee Tree" was described by the judges as "the poignant and haunting story of a family separated from their homeland and in danger of losing their culture." Born in Jamaica and raised in Miami, Escoffery received his undergraduate degree from Florida International University in 2010. He is the winner of the* Paris Review*'s Plimpton Prize for Fiction and a National Endowment for the Arts Literature (Prose) Fellowship. Founded in 1953, the* Paris Review *won National Magazine Awards for Jonas Bendiksen's photo-essay "Kibera," in 2007; John Jeremiah Sullivan's "Mr. Lytle: An Essay," in 2011; and General Excellence in 2013.*

Jonathan Escoffery

Under the Ackee Tree

If you're the only son of uptown Kingston parents, then you will have options. You can take Daddy's Datsun or Mummy's new '68 VW and fly past street urchins who sell bag juice and ackee at red lights down Hope Road to pick up Reyha or Sanya or Cherie.

If a Reyha you pick, you will carry she to the drive-in where you can stroke she hair while unoo watch Bond 'pon big screen. Reyha's family own the bread shop on Barbican Road where she work most afternoons, and you like sniff she hair since it always smell of coco bread or spice bun.

Is Cherie you like slow whine plenty nights down a New Kingston, whether Epiphany or Dizzy. She tease you, you see? Push up hard 'pon you in corners and grind she pelvis into yours before she laugh and push away.

A Sanya you like chat bad word with, so she you take a Hellshire to sit seaside and nyam escovitch snapper and chat bare fuckery till them tell unoo, You no see the sun gone and is time fi move you batty?

If you no careful, life go so carefree, till you daddy say, Time to get serious, boy, and stop all the play-play. Time to get job. Time to be a man.

If him say so, tell him say you wan' go a foreign fi art school and learn fashion design, and don' him see how your sketchbook full up with concepts and him can' see you stylee?

But if you say that, him will answer, Fashion? A my son a si' down an' sew panty an' frock? Wha' kind of little-gal fantasy that?

But, Daddy, man in Europe study fashion from time, you will tell him.

Me know, him will say. Batty man.

You'll ask him, How you can be so small mind? You'll puff up your chest and pace the veranda and wan' fling him furniture, because him can' beat you like him did beat you when you were a pickney.

Even he know him can' discipline you like before, so him say it calm: No bother with no foo-foo art school. If you can' be serious, you go work for me. And if you can' do that, you can leff me house.

And it don' feel then like you have too many options at all.

So you start oversee him construction jobs, though is little you know 'bout how man build house. Mostly, is make sure man show up on time and don' leave early. Mostly, is hunt worker down at bar after them disappear for lunch. When you run them down, the worker man malice you and call you rich man' boy, though your daddy' business not so big that him wealthy.

You don' like the job, but your father say, Since when man supposed to like job?

But him pay you and let you use him work vehicle and soon after you can afford apartment in Mandeville, and after that you feel large.

If you carry on like before with Reyha and Sanya and Cherie, is Sanya who will come beat down your door and cuss you while Cherie sneak out back. You'll make promise and beg you a beg for she hand in marriage one time. Is Sanya you love, like you love bread pudding and stew, which is more than you have loved before. You love that when she walk with she brass hand in yours, you can' tell where yours ends and hers begins. You love that where you see practical solution to the world' problem, Sanya sees only the way things should be; where you see a beggar boy in Coronation Market, Sanya sees infinite potential.

Most of all, is she smile you fall for. Sanya' teeth and dimples flawless and you hope she'll pass this to your pickney, and that them will inherit your light eyes, which your father passed down to you.

Sanya' tall. You tall to rass.

She quick-tongued, and you passed seven A levels. So your children will be bright.

You only hope them get she teeth.

If you marry she, you will have garden wedding, and you will design your suit and pay tailor to stitch it. You will send out invitation, and it will seem like the whole of Kingston will come celebrate unoo and see how you and Sanya styling. Later, in Mandeville, if you breed she, you'll make a boy, and it seem your every want must come to pass. You will thank Sanya for the boy, though you know it man give Y chromosome—you no ignorant gully boy. But you thank her still. And though it too early to know whether baby will have she teeth, him have your eyes, so blue them nearly violet, so you quietly grateful she no interfere with that. You will make the boy' middle name Christopher, after you, even when most people know you as Topper. You will make him first name Delano.

You'll drive Delano up and down mountainside when him bawl and can' sleep. And you don't speed like you did speed when it only your life JA' potholes threaten so, you drive the car slow-slow. Sanya will sing Delano Irish hymns she grandmother sang she when she was a pickney. And when neither she nor you can hold open your eyes, you will ask Jodie, your helper, to push him stroller 'round the block until him drop asleep.

If the night sounds shift from croaking lizard to machine gun ra-ta-ta-ta, you'll ask Jodie not to walk with Delano at night.

Your father will blame independence for the way things go, but you'll say, No, man, is the prime minister and all him socialist fuckery that cause the trouble.

Don' *you* voted Manley into office? him will ask you, like is you alone had the one vote.

Fool me once, you'll admit to him. But me never vote for him in '76.

Is rumor say that Manley buddy up with Castro, and what him thought, the Yankee them was going let a next island in them backyard turn communist? Rumor say it CIA flood the garrisons with cocaine and make JLP rudeboy war PNP badman with automatic rifle, when just yesterday them could've murder each other only with stone and rust blade.

If it just themselves the idiot boys slaughter, won't nobody care 'bout them buttoo war. Soon shots grow close, though, and is uptown woman them kill in crossfire and police say them can' chase the boy back in them slums because ghetto youth now outgun policeman. Then the military must get involved.

You daddy call, and you know from how him voice shake the war come show up at him doorstep. Gunman lick down them door and tie up you mummy and daddy, and thief off them money and jewelry and everything. Daddy them pistol-whip and you mummy . . . God knows how them feel her up so, even when she old to rass. But him tell you say it could have gone worse.

How it can go worse? you ask him. But not a month pass before them rape your neighbor and kill her husband in front of she.

The fucker them is all one man in your eyes. No, two man: Seaga' man and Manley' man. Though Uncle Sam' man also tryin' swing JA' elections.

From then you send off for U.S. visa and ask your daddy' brother fi sponsor unoo, since him been in the States for time. Things move fast: your visa come through and you ask your mummy and daddy whether them think you should really go, and them say, Boy, wha' wrong wi' you? You can' see the whole of we island turn into war zone? And, This what we gained independence for? Them say, Better g'wan save yourselves.

Jodie ask can you bring she to the States, but you can't afford to keep helper now. You tell she you mummy and daddy will take her, since them helper old and soon need help.

You think 'bout a New York, but is Miami you settle, because you visit your uncle Michael in Brooklyn one November, and if the fall can lick off your batty with cold tongue so, you no wan' know what winter go do.

Is Miami you have your second son. At hospital, when them hand you the boy' birth record to sign, under him birth year, 1980, in a section marked *Race of Father* them type *Negroid*. You tell the nurse, Me learn 'bout Negro, but what is *oid*? But she don' bother with you.

You name your second son Trelawny to remind yourself of home. It long enough after you reach that you miss JA bad-bad. You miss walk down a road and pick Julie mango off street side. When you try pick Miami street-side mango, lady come out she house with rifle and shoot your belly and backside with BB. In the back of your Cutler Ridge town house, you start try grow mango tree and ackee tree with any seeds you come by, but no amount of water or fertilizer will get them to sprout.

In spite of him name, Trelawny grow up strange. Foreign. You blame the nursery school teachers where you and Sanya leave him when you go work each morning, where you bring him from him turn six months old. You blame yourself since you can' afford to let Sanya stay home like when Delano did born. Still, when the boy start talk, you can' believe it: is a Yankee voice come out. You read and talk to him as much as you can, but the boy no wan' pick up nothing you say, not like him brother.

Him no say *mummy* for him first words, him say *mom*. Him have Sanya' dark eyes and none of she teeth or dimple. Him grow and soon it pain your ears to hear the boy say *water*, which him pronounce "wah-der."

You can' spend all day talking to the boy. You work twelve-hour shifts on used-car lot, sometimes selling car, most times selling nothing, until the day you take a man out for test drive and him stick him pistol in your gut and drive out all a Everglades and tell you say, Get out and walk, and if you turn around you're dead.

You walk and walk and wait to die, and when you hear him pull off, you walk some more. You no bother go back a work. Work fi wha'? So them can shot you? If you wanted bullet in your back you could've stayed a Kingston.

It four weeks before you admit to Sanya what happened and that you leave the job. In that time, when the house empty, you start sketch landscape from home off memory. You sketch Dunn's River Falls and Cockpit Country and Fern Gully, and it shaky at first, but then your steady hand return to you. You take a dozen sketches to the weekend flea market down the road and stand up all morning, but don' nobody wan' buy no colorless landscape. Them want garish flamingo watercolors like the lady at the next table selling. But you can't afford paint or canvas, or the time it take to put the two together. And when Sanya start ask where you find time to draw, and how it is your car sales drop from little to zero, you have to tell she the truth.

Sanya look at you cross and say, You think me wouldn't rather stay home and doodle?

You know she right, but she didn't have to put it so.

You call your daddy and say you wan' expand him business into the States. But him say, The business barely holding on since Manley piss off the IMF and make price of everything skyrocket. You say, But, Daddy, don't Seaga is prime minister now? But all him can say is, Chuh. Still him send you small loan through money wire.

You start basic. You go round and gather up man all a flee JA crime wave and see what all them can do. Is roof you can repair? Unoo know plumbing system? You can fix AC? You use you father' loan to put out advertisement and soon you start broker deals, send man out on job and collect small fee off it. It don' pick up straight away, and Sanya make more from she secretary job than you. She bright, so soon she them make office manager, even when no man wan' woman manage them. Still, your combined income less than what you alone made in Jamaica and it seem you never can catch up back. But if you scrimp and scrounge and keep in luck' favor, you family can just keep afloat.

• • •

If years slip by, Delano will grow athletic and is he the neighborhood boys will wan' quarterback when them play American football in the street, and him afi quarterback for both teams, or else the boys cry, It no fair. Him start smile with him mummy' mouth, and you can see how the young girls already crush after him. It seem him can do most anything. Him ask for guitar and lesson, and him pick it up fast-fast. The boy sing out in him bedroom "Where Did You Sleep Last Night" and "Purple Rain," and play along as he sing. Then him play "Pass the Dutchie" and you know him never learn that from him teacher.

Trelawny no wan' bother with sports or music. Him take book and you find him hiding in closet with flashlight. When you ask him a question, him twist up him mouth and stare on you blank with him big black eyes. If you say, Answer me nuh, boy, him look 'pon him brother, and if Delano repeat your question, Trelawny finally answer, like him need him brother to translate.

Every day is a next thing. Him start draw on him bedroom walls, and no matter how you threaten him with belt, him can' stop. Him get As in class but can' figure out how to tie him shoe, so him sneakers must have Velcro. You tell Sanya, Something wrong with the boy, but she tell you, Be patient. At him school open house, Trelawny' teacher say she wan' put him in t'ing called Gifted. You say, Wha' that, special ed? She say is for advanced children so him don't get bored, but you tell her, Teach him to tie him shoe, then we can talk.

Then him start shit him pants, even when he long past potty training.

If you take him for doctor visit, the pediatrician will come out the examination and say Trelawny have anxiety. What him have to be anxious about? Him no pay bills. Doctor say, Just give him time.

Then Hurricane Gilbert come mash up Jamaica, and you can think 'bout nothing but how the people back home devastated. You can' get through to your parents, and the news say hundreds dead across the Caribbean. You call everyone you can think of in Jamaica to see whether them can check on your mummy and daddy, but don' nobody phone work. The feeling you get is that everybody' dead. And you never should have left them behind.

You sit Delano and Trelawny down for breakfast the next morning and try teach them them culture to make sure it survive. The tropical market on Colonial start carry canned ackee and green banana and salt cod, so you cook the boys ackee and saltfish and try explain why it Jamaica' national dish. You see this here, you say. The ackee grow in a pod and it must open on it own or else the ackee poison you. You point to the picture on the can, so them can see how it grow, and it remind you that you never eat ackee out of no can before. You tell them, Enslaved Jamaicans used it to kill off slave driver and free themselves to the mountains. But you don't know if them legends true.

Delano say, I remember Jodie used to cook it for us.

Trelawny say, It looks like scrambled eggs.

You think me would stand up a two hour and cook the thing if it only taste like scrambled eggs?

It better than eggs, Delano say, but when Trelawny taste it, him spit it out and say, Eew. How him can say *eew*?

Then your father call and say everything okay. Mostly it man who live in zinc house and homeless who live in the gullies that dead. Man and them children. Him say it just as well, since the people in the garrisons so ignorant, them don' bother get prenatal care, then wonder why them baby come out malnourished or deformed. You say, Daddy, when you ever set foot in a tenement yard to know poor people business? And him suck him teeth like him done with you.

Him say, Send what you can, so you go buy canned food and baby formula and get the boys to help gather up them old clothes to send. You can' help hoping it only bad-mind people the storm kill off—the ones who wrecked the island with them violence—so JA can return to how it was in your youth. But you know it never go so. It always innocent randomness choose to kill.

Work pick up, because now it seem you know everybody that gone and flee Jamaica. If not gunman, is Gilbert send them here. South Dade start fill up with Yardies, and if you hang out where them hang out, you get job, since them no wan' bother with the Spanish man who them can' understand or the white man who can' understand them, even when all three speak a English.

But Sanya no wan' see you hang out. She wan' see you home.

She start malice you and say, If a work you go work, is how you smell like overproof? Is how you come home two in the morning? She don' understand it through socialize you get job. It seem like one long fight you're locked in.

Then Jodie call one day and you say, Jodie, if you go call long distance me know someone de go dead.

But you never guess she would've say is both. You know is gunman finally kill off you mummy and daddy, and you never should have left them there, but Jodie say it car accident kill them.

You call Uncle Michael in New York and tell him say is time fi go home. You both fly back straightaway to arrange funeral and when you go to collect them body, the policeman on duty have your daddy lay out on the gravel, baking in the rhatid heat.

Your uncle say to the copper, How you can have him on the ground like dog? And him say, Please, please treat him with dignity. All from him breasts to him belly a tremble with rage.

The copper say, Morgue full up. There's no place else me can put the t'ing.

Uncle Michael cry, T'ing? T'ing? And him start bawl. Is then you know the man turn soft in a New York.

You tell the copper, Hear me nuh, boy. Take out a next corpse and bring my father inside until the undertaker reach. You can cuss and talk 'bout what him muma fi do and say duppy de go haunt him for disrespect the dead so, but you know it the twenty dollars U.S. that make the man do what you say.

Him and him partner lift your father inside and dump out a next corpse on the roadside with the others.

Only a Kingston have more dead than morgue, you tell your uncle. You tell him, You forget how things work down here? You say, That no Daddy, you know? Daddy gone.

But all him can do is cry.

At funeral, crowds come from so far as Negril, which take longer to reach from than Miami and maybe even New York. Even Reyha come to the repast and squeeze your hand when she think Sanya no look, and you resist sniff she hair to see whether she still smell of spice bun because Sanya always a look.

Is not till after funeral—after weeks sorting your parents' affairs and after schoolboy show up at your daddy' door and hand you him grade sheet and say your daddy promised to pay him tuition if him do well, and you tell him your daddy dead, and the boy start cry, like is he fate dealt the harshest lick, so you write out check to the academy, and after you slip under the white rum one mournful evening and let Jodie crawl 'pon your lap and start ride your cocky while unoo bawl 'bout how your mummy and daddy gone, and after you return a Miami—that Sanya say, Things must change now.

How you can say so, you ask her, when me parents dead a three week?

She say, Me no wan' dead before you decide to come home at night.

But you no ready fi hear that. You rather sleep 'pon sofa. You rather things were the way they were in Mandeville, when you could take care of she and Delano, and she no worry so much 'bout where man supposed to be. You wish for some way to go back, but if a Kingston you stayed, your parents still would've dead. If a Kingston you stayed, you could've dead long time.

And you don' wan' admit you start get used to American convenience, too much to go back. But you know Sanya' right, something must change.

Then Hurricane Andrew hit and everything change.

House roof tear off and you all must cram up in apartment in Fort Lauderdale. And for a month or so, it seems you and Sanya must come together and make up. But with everyone house blow down, and fema start hand out check, is more work than all the years you've been here combined. You start recruit man from Miramar where must have more Yardman than all South Dade' neighborhood combined. And you're on the road from dawn till deep night getting man working. Sanya stop complain because she know people need them house fix. And she know is like gold rush how the jobs come in. And even she get a next promotion at work, so in all the destruction unoo find your silver lining.

It nearly a year before your house can fix because you're so busy a make money, you only can fix your house part time. One day, you're back down a Miami and it late and you decide to stop by the Fence where all the Yardies start reconvene, even when the house next door still have blue tarp for roof. You sip 'pon your white rum when you feel tug from behind and you turn and see Cherie, still look the same like she travel through time. She hug you up and say how she sorry to learn 'bout your mummy and daddy. She tell you how she move up here when she house get destroy in Gilbert. You say, Boy, seem like storm knock we back into each other' arms. But you no mean nothing by it.

If she hear song she say is she favorite, she'll take your hand and pull you to the dance floor. She start grind she pelvis into yours and you feel you're a young man again. But after three or four dance your legs start to ache and you know it time to put an end to the reunion. You know there's no returning to youth. You kiss Cherie' cheek and when you think she going beg you fi stay, she give small wave and start dance with a next man.

The drive back long, and when you reach, Sanya is up, waiting on the couch, like she have a sixth sense for Cherie alone. Wha' you a go do? she start yell. Wha' you go do? And is phone she have in she lap. Is just dance, you start say, when you're sure is a *suss suss* business get back to she, but she say, Jodie call. She say, She call and the boy have your eyes.

If Sanya throw the phone you won't bother block it. The handset clip your forehead and leave gash that later scar because you never get stitch. You deserve the scar and much worse. Especially since the vexation mark Sanya with white streak through she hair that show up overnight.

You sleep with she the whole time? Sanya want to know. And you knew she would think that, if she ever find out, even when you never look 'pon the girl Jodie before the funeral. And you can see it in Sanya' eyes that suspicion and hurt start flood all she memories. Now everything sour, down to the root.

And you beg her. You tell her is Jodie take advantage of you in your weakened state. And of course you never touch the girl when Sanya was pregnant with Delano, even in the time you and Sanya stop having sex.

Sanya smile when she say, I believe you. And you go in to hold her and she box your face, even as blood leak from your forehead into your eyes. I believe you will regret this for the rest of your life, she say. And you know she mean it with that demented smile. And you hate yourself for taking away part of she and replacing it with disfiguration. And more than that, you hate that she is right.

• • •

If you go see the boy, it will be late summer. Jodie' family called and called to tell you say you must come see your baby, but them never let you talk to Jodie and so you wan' ask if there's a baby fi true, or if this a kidnap scheme. But you no wan' put that idea in them head.

Still, you fly down a Kingston alone, since your shame won't let you bring witness. You hire car and drive to a shantytown buried in the mountains, halfway to Spanish Town. She cousin call the last time to say the baby sick, and is him give you directions, since where she live now don't have phone, and when you pull off highway and start drive down dirt path and see shacks made of lean-to zinc, you can see don' nobody here have phone. The shantytown walled in, like this a housing scheme, and you wonder whether it have name like Tel Aviv or Jungle or anything that signal man like you should not be here. Man who maybe should be here guarding the entrance and him tell you, you better park and walk in.

You made sure to leave home everything valuable, because you hear stories that things so bad now in JA that man hand get chop off with cutlass because thief want him wristwatch and don't bother asking. The cash you brought over you hide in your sock.

You approach the guard and him say, White man, you 'ave business 'ere?

You almost laugh, but say, Is me you think is white man? And him say, You the whitest man me ever see, and him no say it with humor.

You say you're there to see Jodie and the man wrap him arm around you and show big teeth and say, Cousin! You know him not the same man you spoke with on the phone, because this man say a whole heap of words now, and you can' understand half of it, because you never hear a bush patwah like that. You wonder whether everyone in this shantytown is Jodie' cousin.

Him start walking you inside and telling you how beautiful the baby you make is, but all you can think 'bout is how it good your mummy and daddy never lived to see this. More than that, you think 'bout how you break Sanya' heart. And about how she make you choose between Delano and Trelawny to take back to the house you finally rebuild and how she say she will never set foot inside that house again. You told her you don' wan' take either son from she and she say, You think I go let you walk away from your responsibilities? Like that your plan the whole time. She say, You will take Delano, because me don' trust you with Trelawny. And you can' deny you felt small bit of relief.

Jodie cousin walk you past a group of barefoot pickney kick soda bottle back and forth between them and woman who all a carry bucket of water on them head, and when you peek in the gaps in them lean-up tin walls, and see is all one room and no plumbing or bathroom, you wan' shout, But how people can live so?

You know then that you must take Jodie and the baby back with you, because no boy of yours can grow up in such circumstance—if the baby truly yours.

The man who say him Jodie' cousin walk you into a rusted hovel and there you find Jodie sit down on a blanket on the dirt and hold a baby in she arms, and when she see you, she look up and smile. But the smile demented, like how Sanya smile the night she find out, and you never realize till now is a second woman you mutilate.

You kneel down next to she and when she hand you the baby, is two things you see: Him have your eyes, fi true, so him must be yours. And that the baby dead from time. Jodie cousin stand up at the entryway and menace you with him big teeth and say, You just miss him. You hand the baby to Jodie and untuck the bundle of cash you hiding in your sock and leave it in Jodie' lap. Then you go back to the car and drive straight to the airport, certain them could no drag you back to this godforsaken island again.

• • •

If you're a man who utterly failed his child, you can either lie down to join him in death, or you can do more for those remaining. If the latter you choose, the first thing you can do is call your wife and beg she to take you back. You can leave message on she answering machine and explain there's no more reason you must be apart, and if it embarrass she feel, no one up a stateside has to know. At least, no one has to talk about it.

But if you do this, man will show up at your door early one morning, and when you answer him, Yes, I'm Topper, him will smile and hand you a manila envelope and say, You've been served.

It Trelawny you start worry after, because even when Delano don't do too well in school, him is a boy who will make something out of nothing. The day him graduate, Delano start him own landscape business and have man your age working under him. But when you pick up Trelawny from Sanya' new house in West Miami, the boy can' hold nobody eye when him talk. And him barely talk, like him 'fraid of his own voice. Him dress up in baggy clothes and hoodie, like him hiding, even when it summer.

You stop bring him down to your house, because the first time you see how it hurt him to watch him brother and you living where him once had a proper family. It loss him feel, but you wonder whether it also envy of him brother. You take Trelawny out to eat instead, every few weeks.

And every few weeks him seem to change who him trying to be. First, is only tegareg rap music beat out his headphones. Then it booguyaga dancehall. When you ask how it only ghetto music him listen to, him say him wan' connect with him people. You say, Boy, them buttoo singer not your people. You think your grandfather would let them type of man on him veranda?

But Trelawny say him don' remember him grandfather too well.

If you buy two acres of land in Palmetto Bay and start make plans to build new house, you'll try involving the boy. You sketch design of what the house could be, and it good to feel your hand drawing over paper after so long. You try show Trelawny your mock-up and where him room might be when he visit, but him no bother pay much attention and stare out restaurant window instead. You know him resent you for the divorce, and you wonder what ideas him mother put in him head. You almost tell him it Sanya split up your family and make you choose Delano over him, but you don't want to have to explain the reasons why.

When the construction soon start, you ask Trelawny if him wan' help, the way Delano helped rebuild the Cutler Ridge town house, but him say, How much does that pay?

You tell him you're trying to teach him something, but him say, I already learned Lincoln freed the slaves. Him add, Maybe Delano should have paid more attention in school.

The boy think him smart, you see?

Back home, you ask Delano why him brother must be so cantankerous.

Delano say, We all have to be what we have to be.

You ask, Who told you that? And when him shrug you say, Unoo go soon learn, if you wan' make it in this world, you best be better than that.

• • •

One day, while you and Trelawny out at lunch, Delano page you and say him have surprise, and you're to meet him at the construction site in Palmetto Bay. When the two of you reach, you see is full-grown ackee tree Delano have him crew transplant in the backyard. Him say man in Coconut Grove paid them to chop it down, but him save it and bring it here instead. Them had to get tractor and trailer and permit to transport the thing, and if you have any luck at all, the tree should survive and start bear fruit in a year or so. Your eye start water and you see how it not everything lost after all; you see your legacy can grow, even in a foreign soil.

You thank Delano with handshake, and out the corner of your eye, you see Trelawny look bewildered, like him don't get the significance, like him don' understand why him brother would bother.

• • •

When he finally take himself away to university, you hope Trelawny will meet people like him, people who find them worth in books. Sensitive people. Him think him is hard, since him put off college for several years to work warehouse job. But when you suggest that him throw out him wardrobe and buy proper clothes when he arrives in the North, suggest that he's old enough to stop wear clown clothes, Trelawny look like him wan' cry. How him can upset so easy? Miami too rough, too much like home for the boy. You don't see how him can survive here, where man always try test you, and always try get over. So you're glad when him leave for someplace he can find his true self.

But when him graduate, Trelawny move back.

You ask him, What you go do now? But him only shrug and stick him hands in him pockets and say him go figure it out. But you no see him figure nothing. Only him hide in the room you give him in your new house. Only him sit down 'pon him computer and do God knows. Seem like university only make the boy less fit for work.

This is how it's done now, Trelawny tell you. You apply online. No one wants me showing up in their lobby, reeking of desperation, him say. No one will hire me if they suspect I need a job.

But what kind of backward thinking that? You tell Trelawny to check his brother for work, but him say, You think I got my B.A. so I could start mowing lawns?

It just as well because Delano' tree service struggling through 2009 recession. And now Delano have wife and pickney of his own, so him can' carry his brother. And your business grind to a halt, so it better you just retire from now.

Anyway, you can' tell Trelawny nothing. Him think them teach him everything up North and the whole of Miami is ignorant. When him reach back, you tell him that with all the job loss him better stay away from certain neighborhood, and the boy say, There's no such thing as a bad neighborhood, and it's systemic racism and white-collar greed cause the crime—like him knowing the source can stop bullet; like him will sit down with robber and explain to him 'bout subprime mortgage and school-to-prison pipeline.

Even if things tight, you'll decide to hold retirement party, since you reach the age where all your friends start die off, and you wan' show people the house while there's still people left to show. Plus you start feel you no have too many ifs ahead, only bleak certainties.

Your house finally finish the way you want, with in-ground pool and bar and more fruit trees flanking your ackee tree, lining the backyard perimeter. It the house you always dream 'bout and a part of you sad Sanya will never see it, since she still hate your guts after all these years.

She called before Trelawny graduate and told you how she was moving back to Kingston. You said, Sanya, you crazy?

But she say, Just look after the boy, nuh.

And the boy Trelawny back not a two week and him say him going invite up him friend from JA—girl he meet when him spend him summer break in Kingston.

You think, Careful she not after you for green card, but it not nice to say those things. Instead, you ask the boy where him did apply today, and him admit him no apply for job today at all. Instead, him say him applied for a grant to go live in Jamaica for a year and do research.

You must wan' study how to get your brains blown out, you tell him.

Him say next him go apply for Jamaican passport.

You say, Boy, is a death wish you and your mother share?

But the boy just turn back to him laptop like you not there speaking.

The night of the party, you make Trelawny help set up tiki torch poolside and get the yard trim up nice, and you get caterer to set up buffet in the backyard, and have them serve a jerk pork and 'bout three sets of curry. You put out old table, so man don't brukup your good dining table with them dominoes. You drape lights from the roof of the pool deck and turn pool light on, so everything glow, even when you know none of your friends wan' take off them shirt and frock to get in no pool at night.

The ackee tree bearing fruit now and some of the ackee pods start open, so you buy salt cod to pair with it for breakfast the next morning. The invite list long and even Uncle Michael fly down from New York and you can' believe how him get mawga and him tell you him can't believe how you get old.

Delano come with Shelly-Anne and them two boys, and when Shelly ask whether you wan' hold the baby, you say no, because both him boys get your father' eyes and you think 'bout Jodie' baby and feel haunted.

Delano get him band to set up on the patio and play roots music and them bring all the young people, and all your old crowd from the Fence come through. Even Cherie show up eventually, but she don't want nothing to do with you, besides be friends.

Trelawny' girlfriend Zoë show up, too, and you can' believe how the girl gorgeous, like girl you would've date in your day. And Trelawny stand up straight and tall like you never see him stand up. And him finally wearing clothes that fit properly. Still, you don' want to admit you wonder what she can see in him. But maybe she see something you can't.

The party go on late and man start in on the white rum and maybe you take down too much, because Trelawny start look 'pon you sideways. But the boy always look at you sideways, so you don' know. In the kitchen, you start talk politics back home with Zoë, but Trelawny keep interrupt. Trelawny say Manley had the right idea, wanting to spread wealth to the poor people.

You tell him, Boy, is Manley mash up the country. Equal parts he and your CIA.

Then we should have stayed to defend it, the boy tell you, like he was there.

If we stayed, you wouldn't be alive, you tell him, I can promise you that.

Then how come Zoë is here? he asks you. And him laugh. Her family stayed. They turned out fine. More than fine.

Zoë nod, but you can tell she' uncomfortable.

You don' wan' say it, but ask her, Is how much bar your windows have? How much guard dog in your yard? You can walk down your street and feel safe?

She say, Me have car, me no need to walk nowhere, and she laugh, too.

You tell Trelawny, Pickney who grow up in a hellhole can't know the difference.

Zoë start say, It have its problems, but—

Trelawny cut she off and say, I was just there and it's better than this.

Better than what? you wan' know.

This . . . second-class citizenship, him say. And you don't know what rubbish the boy talking now.

What them teach you at school? you ask. Only self-pity?

Him say, You and Mom never should have left.

And that really make you vexed, so you say, Look here. Don' tell me 'bout my business when you never lived through it. Talk 'bout Yankee business. No bother talk to me 'bout Jamaica. Don't care what them showed you on vacation. You spend three week in JA and you think that make you more than tourist?

Him shrug and look 'round with him eyes low, like him embarrass, but you go on: Boy soft like you never could have make it. Boy who can' take get him hands dirty. Your brother maybe, but you wouldn't last a day. Soft boy like you would've dead long time. So just be grateful we left. Even if our leaving what make you turn out so . . . And you know you must stop talk, but you add the word you been thinking ever since him reach back a Miami, and long before him left . . . defective.

And you know from everyone face you take it too far. Trelawny won't even look at you, but him head nod slow-slow. Uncle Michael looking at you disappointed and Shelly start carry she pickney away. You think him might need air, so you say, Trelawny, do me a favor, go take down some ackee for me, nuh, so I can make it for breakfast. And him nod still and you can' be sure he even hear, but then him stand up and walk out back. Make sure it the open ackee only, you yell after him, because you can' tell if the boy remember anything you taught him from him was a child.

You try smile with Zoë, but she look to the front door like she wondering how she can get home. You start get up and Uncle Michael say, You don't have to give the boy such a hard time, you know. But him them already turn soft, so you no bother with the old man.

You go out to the patio and wonder why everyone is turned around in them chairs, peering off into the dark, but then you hear it: loud grunt and dull thud. And you see Trelawny' silhouette under the ackee tree, all with ax in him hands. And him talking to himself now. And him swinging the ax.

And you start after him, but Delano grab your wrist and shake him head and hold you back. And is then you know it serious. And you think how Sanya' right, you regret everything. And you wonder if it's you must be defective since you ruin everyone.

And you know the boy ruin, because is same words him repeating like warped 45:

I'll chop down your tree.
I'll chop down your tree.
I'll chop down your fucking tree.

Permissions

"Jerry's Dirt," by Jacob Baynham, originally published in the *Georgia Review*. Copyright © 2019 by Jacob Baynham. Reprinted by permission of Jacob Baynham.

"Can We Build a Better Women's Prison?" by Keri Blakinger, originally published in the *Washington Post Magazine*. Copyright © 2019 by the Washington Post Magazine. All rights reserved. Reprinted by permission.

"Tactile Art," by John Lee Clark, originally published in *Poetry*. Copyright © 2019 by John Lee Clark. Reprinted by permission of John Lee Clark.

"False Witness," by Pamela Colloff, originally published in the *New York Times Magazine*. Copyright © 2019 by the New York Times Company. All rights reserved. Used under license.

"Under the Ackee Tree," by Jonathan Escoffery, originally published in the *Paris Review*. Copyright © 2019 by the Paris Review. All rights reserved. Reprinted by permission.

"Epidemic of Fear," by Erika Fry, originally published in *Fortune*. Copyright © 2019 Fortune Media IP Corporation. Used with permission.

"Our Founding Ideals of Liberty and Equality Were False When They Were Written. Black Americans Fought to Make Them True." by Nikole Hannah-Jones, originally published in the *New York Times*. Copyright © 2019 the New York Times Company. All rights reserved. Used under license.

"We've Normalized Prison," by Piper Kerman, originally published in the *Washington Post Magazine*. Copyright © 2019 by the Washington Post Magazine. All rights reserved. Reprinted by permission.

"Las Marthas," by Jordan Kisner, originally published in *The Believer*. Copyright © 2019 by Jordan Kisner. Reprinted by permission of Jordan Kisner.

"Fight the Ship," by T. Christian Miller, Megan Rose, and Robert Faturechi, originally published in *ProPublica*. Copyright © 2019 by ProPublica. All rights reserved. Reprinted by permission.

"Nothing Sacred," by Ligaya Mishan, originally published in *T: The New York Times Style Magazine*. Copyright © 2019 by the New York Times Company. All rights reserved. Used by permission.

"An Assault on the Tongue," by Ligaya Mishan, originally published in *T: The New York Times Style Magazine*. Copyright © 2019 by the New York Times Company. All rights reserved. Used by permission.

"Interlopers," by Ligaya Mishan, originally published in *T: The New York Times Style Magazine*. Copyright © 2019 by the New York Times Company. All rights reserved. Used by permission.

"Unlike Any Other," by Nick Paumgarten, originally published in the *New Yorker*. Copyright © 2019 by Nick Paumgarten. Reprinted by permission of Nick Paumgarten.

"India: Intimations of an Ending," by Arundhati Roy, originally published in *The Nation*. Copyright © 2019 by Arundhati Roy. Reprinted by permission of Arundhati Roy.

"When Disability Is a Toxic Legacy," by s.e. smith, originally published in *Catapult*. Copyright © 2019 by Catapult. All rights reserved. Reprinted by permission.

"The Ugly Beautiful and Other Failings of Disability Representation," by s.e. smith, originally published in *Catapult*. Copyright © 2019 by Catapult. All rights reserved. Reprinted by permission.

"What We Don't Talk About When We Talk About Mental Health and Medication," by s.e. smith, originally published in *Catapult*. Copyright © 2019 by Catapult. All rights reserved. Reprinted by permission.

"Kanye West's Sunday Service Is Full of Longing and Self-Promotion," by Jia Tolentino, originally published in the *New Yorker*. Copyright © 2019 by Jia Tolentino. Reprinted by permission of Jia Tolentino.

"Love, Death, and Begging for Celebrities to Kill You," by Jia Tolentino, originally published in the *New Yorker*. Copyright © 2019 by Jia Tolentino. Reprinted by permission of Jia Tolentino.

"E. Jean Carroll's Accusation Against Donald Trump, and the Raising, and Lowering, of the Bar," by Jia Tolentino, originally published in the *New Yorker*. Copyright © 2019 by Jia Tolentino. Reprinted by permission of Jia Tolentino.

"The Schoolteacher and the Genocide," by Sarah Topol, originally published in the *New York Times Magazine*. Copyright © 2019 by Sarah Topol. Used by permission of the Wylie Agency LLC.

"Elizabeth Warren's Classroom Strategy," by Rebecca Traister, originally published in *The Cut*. Copyright © 2019 by Vox Media, Inc. All rights reserved. Reprinted by permission.

Contributors

Jacob Baynham is a freelance journalist and essayist. He has written about criminal justice for the *Christian Science Monitor* and about parenting for *Outside*, as well as reporting internationally for *Newsweek*, the *San Francisco Chronicle*, *Slate*, and other publications. He lives in Missoula, Montana, with his wife, Hilly McGahan, and their two boys.

Keri Blakinger is a reporter for the Marshall Project and a former criminal justice reporter for the *Houston Chronicle.*

John Lee Clark is the author of a collection of essays about his experiences as a DeafBlind writer called *Where I Stand: On the Signing Community and My DeafBlind Experience* (Handtype Press, 2014). He travels widely teaching Protactile, an emerging tactile language.

Pamela Colloff is a senior reporter for *ProPublica* and a staff writer for the *New York Times Magazine.* She has been nominated for seven National Magazine Awards and won for Feature Writing in 2013 and Reporting in 2020. In 2014 the Nieman Foundation for Journalism at Harvard University awarded her the Louis Lyons Award for Conscience and Integrity in Journalism.

Jonathan Escoffery's writing has appeared or is forthcoming in *AGNI*, *Creative Nonfiction*, *Electric Literature*, the *Paris Review*, *Pleiades*, *ZYZZYVA*, and elsewhere. His most recent honors include the 2020 Plimpton Prize for Fiction, a 2020 National Endowment for the Arts fellowship, and a 2020 Helene Wurlitzer Foundation of New Mexico grant. He has received awards and distinctions from the Best American Short Stories series, Aspen Words, Bread Loaf Writers' Conference, Kimbilio Fiction,

Passages North, *Prairie Schooner*, and elsewhere. Escoffery earned his MFA from the University of Minnesota and attends the University of Southern California's Ph.D. in Creative Writing and Literature Program.

Robert Faturechi is a Pulitzer Prize–winning investigative reporter for *ProPublica*. He was previously a reporter at the *Los Angeles Times*. His stories have resulted in congressional hearings, new legislation, federal indictments, resignations, and major reforms.

Erika Fry is a senior writer at *Fortune*, where she writes features and investigative pieces on healthcare and international business. Before joining *Fortune* in 2012, Erika worked as a writer and associate editor at *Columbia Journalism Review* and was an investigative reporter with the *Bangkok Post* from 2006 to 2010. A native of Cedar Rapids, Iowa, Fry graduated from Dartmouth College and received an MA in political journalism from the Columbia University Graduate School of Journalism.

Nikole Hannah-Jones is a domestic correspondent for the *New York Times Magazine* focusing on racial injustice. In 2020 she won the Pulitzer Prize for commentary for her essay in "The 1619 Project," "Our Democracy's Founding Ideals Were False When They Were Written. Black Americans Have Fought to Make Them True," which traces the central role black Americans have played in the nation, including its vast material success and democracy itself. Hannah-Jones has written on federal failures to enforce the Fair Housing Act, the resegregation of American schools, and policing in America. Her extensive reporting in both print and radio on the ways segregation in housing and schools is maintained through official action and policy has earned the National Magazine Award, a Peabody Award, and a Polk Award. "The 1619

Project" won a News Leaders Association Award and received a special honor from the George Polk Awards. Nikole was also a finalist for a Scripps-Howard Award in Opinion and won a National Magazine Award. Hannah-Jones earned her bachelor's in history and African American studies from the University of Notre Dame and her master's in journalism and mass communication from the University of North Carolina at Chapel Hill. She is a cofounder of the Ida B. Wells Society for Investigative Reporting, housed at UNC Chapel Hill. She lives in Brooklyn with her husband and very sassy daughter.

Piper Kerman is the author of the memoir *Orange Is the New Black: My Year in a Women's Prison.*

Jordan Kisner is the author of the essay collection *Thin Places,* which was published by Farrar, Straus & Giroux in March 2020. She writes for *The Atlantic, The Believer, n + 1, The Guardian,* the *New York Times Magazine,* the *Paris Review,* and many others.

T. Christian Miller is a senior editor for *ProPublica.* He is a two-time winner of the Pulitzer Prize. Previously, he worked for the *Los Angeles Times* and the *Tampa Bay Times.* He is married, with three children.

Ligaya Mishan writes for the *New York Times* and *T: The New York Times Style Magazine.* Her essays have been selected for the *Best American Magazine Writing* and the *Best American Food Writing* anthologies, and her criticism has appeared in the *New York Review of Books* and the *New Yorker.* This year she was a finalist for a National Magazine Award and a James Beard Journalism Award. The daughter of a Filipino mother and a British father, she grew up in Honolulu.

Nick Paumgarten is a staff writer at the *New Yorker.*

Megan Rose, awarded the 2020 Pulitzer Prize for National Reporting with two colleagues, investigates criminal justice and the military for *ProPublica.* She has reported from two war zones, and her work has resulted in high-level staff changes, congressional inquiries, and several wrongfully convicted men clearing their records.

Arundhati Roy is the author of two novels, *The God of Small Things* and *The Ministry of Utmost Happiness.* Her collected nonfiction, *My Seditious Heart*, was published in 2018. Her new book, *Azadi: Freedom. Fascism. Fiction.*, will be published in the fall. Her work has been translated into more than fifty languages. She lives in New Delhi.

s.e. smith is a Northern California–based writer who has appeared in *Bitch*, *Catapult*, *Esquire*, *The Guardian*, and *Rolling Stone* and numerous other fine publications.

Jia Tolentino is a staff writer at the *New Yorker.* Her first book, the essay collection *Trick Mirror: Reflections in Self-Delusion*, was published last year.

Sarah A. Topol is a writer at large for the *New York Times Magazine.* For over a decade, Topol has reported from more than two dozen countries in the Middle East, the former Soviet Union, and Africa. She won the 2012 Kurt Schork Award in International Journalism for her coverage of the civil war in Libya for *GQ.* Her story for the *New York Times Magazine* about Nigerian boys' being abducted and forced to fight for Boko Haram received a citation from the Overseas Press Club for best international reporting on human rights. It was also a finalist for the 2018 Dart Awards for Excellence in Coverage of Trauma.

Rebecca Traister is writer at large at *New York*. She writes a regular column for *The Cut*, as well as features and columns for the print magazine, covering women in politics, media, and culture. Traister was previously a senior editor at the *New Republic* and before that spent ten years at *Salon*. She is a contributor to *Elle* and has also written for *Glamour*, *Marie Claire*, *The Nation*, the *New York Times Magazine*, the *Washington Post*, and other publications. She was inducted into the American Academy of Arts and Sciences in 2018 and was awarded the 2018 National Magazine Award in Columns and Commentary for her writing on the #metoo reckoning and sexual harassment and the 2016 Hillman Prize for Opinion and Analysis Journalism. She has won several Front Page Awards from the Newswomen's Club of New York, as well as the 2012 Mirror Award for Best Commentary, Digital Media, from Syracuse University's Newhouse School. She is the author of *Good and Mad* (Simon & Schuster, 2018), a *New York Times* best-seller, which was also selected as a *Washington Post* and *People* ten best books of 2018, as well as *All the Single Ladies* (Simon & Schuster, 2016), a *New York Times* best-seller and Notable Book of 2016, which was also named one of the best books of 2016 by the *Boston Globe*, *Entertainment Weekly*, *Library Journal*, and NPR. Her first book, *Big Girls Don't Cry* (Free Press, 2011), about women in the 2008 election, was a *New York Times* Notable Book of 2010 and the winner of the Ernesta Drinker Ballard Book Prize. Traister lives in New York City.